ISLAM AND THE LIBERAL STATE

ISLAM AND THE LIBERAL STATE

National Identity and
the Future of Muslim Britain

Stephen H. Jones

I.B. TAURIS
LONDON • NEW YORK • OXFORD • NEW DELHI • SYDNEY

I.B. TAURIS
Bloomsbury Publishing Plc
50 Bedford Square, London, WC1B 3DP, UK
1385 Broadway, New York, NY 10018, USA
29 Earlsfort Terrace, Dublin 2, Ireland

BLOOMSBURY, I.B. TAURIS and the I.B. Tauris logo are trademarks of
Bloomsbury Publishing Plc

First published in Great Britain 2021
This paperback edition published in 2022

Cover design: Adriana Brioso
Cover image © Shaz Begg

A catalogue record for this book is available from the British Library.

A catalog record for this book is available from the Library of Congress.

ISBN: HB: 978-1-8386-0585-8
PB: 978-0-7556-3526-9
ePDF: 978-1-8386-0588-9
eBook: 978-1-8386-0587-2

Typeset by Newgen KnowledgeWorks Pvt. Ltd., Chennai, India

To find out more about our authors and books visit www.bloomsbury.com
and sign up for our newsletters.

CONTENTS

PREFACE AND ACKNOWLEDGEMENTS

When I was a postgraduate student, I took a short course in academic writing with a teacher who liked to begin classes by remarking that writing always involves making the claim that you have something to say worth reading. This was his way of trying to convince my peers and me that we should regard writing as a craft and as something to take time and care over. What it suggested to me, though, was that writing for a public audience involves a certain amount of arrogance. We live in a time when attention is a prized commodity and vast sums of money can be made by convincing people to spend 30 seconds reading a listicle about cats or the current whereabouts of 1990s film stars. Writing a book means asking for at least two days' worth of many total strangers' concentrated attention: no one, surely, could decide to do this without first convincing themselves they have something vitally important to say and that they are the best person – perhaps the *only* person – who can say it.

For anyone who doesn't have an ego the size of Texas, this means that anxiety is always present during the writing process, like background noise. In my case, this has been amplified because of the nature of this book's subject matter and my relation to it. A person picking this book up might well wonder why I – a person who is not Muslim – feel able to opine on, among other things, Islam's relationship to 'Britishness'. Or then again, perhaps they won't: if there is one thing Anglophone public discourse is not short of right now it is people who are not Muslim telling people who are how their religion needs to change. Nor is it short of writers who boldly claim to have a unique and vital insight into Muslims' lives or Islam's nature; just look at the many recently published books with some variation of the title 'Islam Unveiled'. Many of these books teach their readers little more than how to be more rigorously prejudiced,[1] and so a large part of my nervousness in writing this book is that I will end up being allocated to a club that I have absolutely no interest in becoming a member of.

The other reason for my nervousness is that I am getting involved in deliberations about theology and Muslim identity, despite not having skin in these games myself. Andrew March, a non-Muslim scholar of Islam who has given extended consideration to these questions, writes that 'believers may be particularly resistant to arguments posed by outsiders – who are, after all, persons who publicly reject the truth-claims of the religion in question'.[2] While I do not regard myself simply as an 'outsider' to British Muslim life, I have certainly faced this (understandable) resistance at times. When I have spoken in Islamic institutions, for example, one of the objections occasionally made about my comments concerning religion and nationhood is that Islam not only transcends but also *refuses* national borders: the Prophet was not sent to divide people into tribes but as a 'mercy to humankind'.

I have no objection to this contention (quite the contrary, in fact). The best response I have is to say that this is a work of social science, albeit one that wears its political opinions on its sleeve. Whatever people's aspirations to universality, everyone speaks religion with an accent.[3] The task I have set myself here is to trace how British Islam's accent has changed over the years and to explain why that matters. Ultimately, my hope is that all will be able to learn from it, whatever their personal beliefs.

It is impossible to carry out a task like this without incurring many debts. I have benefitted from a huge amount of support and encouragement during the long period carrying out research and constructing my arguments and can list only a few names here. Raheel Mohammed and Iram Janjua provided invaluable guidance in the early days of my research, while Victor Jeleniewski Seidler was a generous mentor, along with many other friends and colleagues at Goldsmiths, University of London. Philip Lewis and Maleiha Malik were careful critics of my early writing and have shaped and supported my subsequent research. Much of my thinking on the subject of British Muslims, citizenship and governance emerged out of a period working at the Centre for the Study of Ethnicity and Citizenship at the University of Bristol in the early 2010s. I am indebted especially to my colleagues Therese O'Toole, Daniel Nilsson DeHanas, Nasar Meer and Tariq Modood. I was able to test out the arguments made in this book in lectures at the Centre for the Study of Islam in the UK, Cardiff University, and the Department of Theology and Religion, University of Birmingham, and I would like to thank Sophie Gilliat-Ray, Michael Munnik, Haifaa Jawad and Jørgen Nielsen for their invitations. I was fortunate to be appointed general secretary of the Muslims in Britain Research Network between 2017 and 2020, and I am grateful to my colleagues Alison Scott-Baumann, Sadek Hamid, Mobeen Butt, Ayesha Khan and Yahya Birt for their pointers and words of support. Rajnaara Akhtar, Timothy Peace, Haroon Sidat, Glen Moran, Jan Dobbernack and Daniel Nilsson DeHanas, along with anonymous reviewers, provided detailed and perceptive critical comments on all or part of the manuscript. The book is significantly better because of their expertise and insight – although, of course, I take sole responsibility for any errors. I want to thank Alex Wright, Sophie Rudland and Yasmin Garcha at IB Tauris for supporting the project and Fern Elsdon-Baker for ensuring I had the space to complete it. Finally, and most importantly, thanks to my parents for their constant support and to Beck, Alice and Felix for being a refuge – especially from the madness of academic life – as well as for putting up with my inability to formulate sentences after a day's writing. Love to you all.

ABBREVIATIONS

AOBM	Association of British Muslims
BIS	Department for Business Innovation and Skills
BMSD	British Muslims for Secular Democracy
BRAIS	British Association of Islamic Studies
BSBT	Building a Stronger Britain Together
CCE	Commission for Countering Extremism
CLG	Department for Communities and Local Government
COIM	Council of Imams and Mosques
COM	Council of Mosques for the UK and Ireland
FOSIS	Federation of Student Islamic Societies
HEA	Higher Education Academy
HEFCE	Higher Education Funding Council for England
ILCD	Institute for Leadership and Community Development
IMPACT	Initiative for Muslim Progression and Advancement of Community Tolerance
IPSO	Independent Press Standards Organisation
ISB	Islamic Society of Britain
KP	Khyber Pakhtunkhwa (province)
LBC	Leading Britain's Conversation (radio station)
LGBT	Lesbian Gay Bisexual Transgender (umbrella term)
MAB	Muslim Association of Britain
MCB	Muslim Council of Britain
MEND	Muslim Engagement and Development
MET	Muslim Educational Trust
MHCLG	Ministry of Housing, Communities and Local Government
MIHE	Markfield Institute for Higher Education
MINAB	Mosques and Imams National Advisory Board
NCTL	National College of Teaching and Learning
NMWAG	National Muslim Women's Advisory Group
NQF	National Qualifications Framework
Ofsted	Office for Standards in Education
OIC	Organisation of the Islamic Conference
ONS	Office of National Statistics
PET	Preventing Extremism Together working groups
QAA	Quality Assurance Agency
RMW	Radical Middle Way
SNP	Scottish National Party
SOAS	School of Oriental and African Studies
STREET	Strategy to Reach, Empower, Educate and Transform

TERFOR   Task Force on Tackling Radicalisation and Extremism
UKACIA   UK Action Committee on Islamic Affairs
UKIM   UK Islamic Mission
UMO   Union of Muslim Organisations of the UK and Ireland
WICS   World Islamic Call Society
YMO   Young Muslims Organisation
YMUK   Young Muslims UK

TRANSLITERATION

For transliteration of Arabic words, I have attempted to follow a simple system based on that of the *International Journal of Middle East Studies* as closely as possible. The system uses the following conventions:

- No diacritical marks are used.
- The letter *'ayn* is indicated by ' and *hamza* is indicated by ', but only when it comes in the middle of the word.
- The plurals of Arabic words are written with an *s*, except the plural of *'alim*, which is given as *'ulama*.
- Doubled vowels in the middle of words are indicated by *-iyya* or *-uwwa*.
- Diphthongs are indicated by *-aw* or *-ay*.
- Al- is prefixed the first time an Arabic name is used, but omitted later.

This does not eliminate all confusion, as some Arabic terms are spelled in various ways by Muslims in the UK. An Islamic seminary may be described as a *darul uloom*, a *darul ulum*, a *dar ul-ulum* or (the style I use in the thesis) a *dar al-ulum*. When quoting essays that use Arabic words I have amended transliterations on occasion to keep the style consistent throughout. Of course, errors or inconsistencies in transliteration are my responsibility alone.

Quotations from the Qur'an are taken from M. A. S. Abdel Haleem's new translation, published by Oxford University Press.

GLOSSARY OF NON-ENGLISH TERMS

All terms below are Arabic unless otherwise indicated:

Agunah **(Hebrew)** A Jewish woman who is 'chained' to her marriage after being refused a divorce by her husband (plural, *agunot*)

'Alim[ah] An Islamic religious scholar, literally a 'person with knowledge'; in Arabic the letter *taa' marbuuta* (here rendered as '*ah*') is added to words to indicate the feminine, in this case a female scholar

Angrezi Shariat **(Urdu)** 'English Sharia'

Aql 'Reason' or 'rationality'

Aya A verse of the Qur'an, literally a 'sign'

Ayatollah Literally meaning 'sign of God', this term is best known as the formal title of senior religious leaders in Shia Islam, although it has a broader meaning

Beth din **(Hebrew)** Jewish religious 'court' (plural, *battei din*)

Bid'ah Usually translated as 'innovation' or 'accretion', this refers to heretical ideas and practices introduced into the Islamic tradition

Biraderi **(Urdu)** A 'brotherhood' or patrilineal kinship network

Dalil Evidence, scriptural justification

Dar al-ulum In the UK, an Islamic (especially Deobandi) seminary, literally a 'house of knowledge'

Dar ul-qaza **(Urdu)** Informal religious courts in British India

Da'wah Witness, testimony or preaching in Islam

Dayan **(Hebrew)** A religious (specifically, Jewish) judge

Faqih An Islamic jurist

Faskh An annulment of an Islamic marriage

Fatiha The name of the first *sura* of the Qur'an ('the Opening'), consists of seven verses (*ayas*) that are recited as part of the Islamic ritual prayer (*salat*)

Fatwa An Islamic legal opinion

Fiqh Islamic jurisprudence

Furu' Literally, the 'branches' of Islamic law that are derived from its 'roots' (*usul*)

Get **(Hebrew)** A Jewish divorce

Ghar **(Urdu)** Extended family networks, literally 'house'

Hadith A narration or saying attributed to the Prophet Muhammed, collected across several volumes (plural, *ahadith*)

Halaqah A gathering (literally, a 'circle') for storytelling and the study and discussion of Islamic scripture and tradition

Haram An act that is prohibited in Islamic law

Hukm A term referring to arbitration or judgement by God, as well as temporal rule or power

Ibadat Islamic legal term referring to worship and ritual, often contrasted with *mu'amalat* (public affairs)

Ijaza A certification that allows its holder to transmit a certain form of Islamic knowledge

Ijma' Consensus (of jurists/Islamic scholars, the Companions of the Prophet or the Muslim community as a whole), traditionally viewed as the third source of authority in Islamic law, after the Qur'an and *Sunnah*

Ijtihad The practice of using independent reasoning to reach legal judgements

Iman Trust in God and the other five articles of faith in Islam

Irtidad Renouncing Islam, apostasy

Isnad The (human) chain of transmission that authenticates a particular *hadith*

Izzat (**Urdu**) Honour

Jihad Literally meaning to 'strive' or to 'struggle', a term that covers all personal struggles for a just cause, ranging from armed conflict to overcoming individual vices (*jihad al-nafs*)

Khul' A form of Islamic divorce in which divorce is granted by the husband at the wife's request

Kufr Rejecting or 'covering up' the truth of Islam; infidelity, unbelief

Madhhab A school of Islamic law

Madrasah An Islamic school or college, although in the UK the term is typically limited to describing an Islamic supplementary school

Mahr A gift given by a groom to a bride as part of an Islamic marriage (*nikah*)

Manhaj Method or practice, especially in Salafi Islam

Manqulat Formalised techniques of exegesis, textual interpretation

Ma'qulat The rational sciences of philosophy, grammar and logic

Maqasid The objectives or goals of Islamic law (*maqasid al-Shari'a*)

Masjid A mosque or house of prayer

Maslaha An Islamic legal concept referring to the public good or the public interest

Mawlid The birthday of the Prophet Muhammad (see also *milad*)

Milad The birthday of the Prophet Muhammad (Milad un Nabi, see also *mawlid*)

Mu'amalat Islamic legal term referring to public affairs, contrasted with *ibadat* (worship)

Muwahhidun 'The monotheists', a term that is used to describe Salafis/Wahhabis (as well as historical Muslim sects)

Naql Transmission, rote learning

Nasheed An Islamic devotional song

Nikah An Islamic marriage contract

Nizam-u-kufr An heretical or unreligious social system

Nushuz Disobedience, especially within marriage

Pir An honorific term used within Sufi orders to signify a spiritual guide

Purdah (**Persian**) The practice of female seclusion, literally meaning 'curtain'

Riddah Rebellion or apostasy, can refer to renunciation of Islam or to political revolt (and specifically the wars following the death of Muhammad)

Rihla A spiritual/educational retreat, or travelling to seek knowledge

Sahih Authentic or sound, used in particular to refer to *hadith*

Salaf The 'predecessors', usually interpreted to mean the first three generations of Muslims

Salat Islamic ritual prayer consisting of a repeated sequence of actions and words, traditionally performed five times each day

Shahada The Islamic declaration of faith ('There is no God but God and Muhammed is his messenger')

Shari'a A term referring to the overarching normative framework prescribed by God (see Chapter 4)

Shura   A Quranic term referring to 'consultation', can refer today to various forms of committee structure, frameworks of governance and deliberative processes

Sunnah   The example of the Prophet Muhammad, considered the second source of Islamic authority after the Qur'an

Sura   The books of the Qur'an

Tafriq   A form of Islamic divorce

Tafsir   A commentary on the Qur'an, or the discipline of Quranic exegesis

Tajwid   Recitation of the Qur'an and the formal study of the rules for, and methods of, recitation

Talaq   A form of Islamic divorce instigated by the husband

Talaq al-tafwid   The delegation of the right to initiate an Islamic divorce to the wife

Taqlid   To follow or imitate an Islamic authority or guide

Taqwa   Consciousness of God

Tawhid   A term referring to the indivisibility and oneness of God

'Ulama   Islamic scholars, literally 'People of knowledge'

Umma   The community of Muslims

'Urf   Local custom, especially a local custom that can be incorporated into Islamic legal practice in a given setting

Usul   The sources of Islamic law, literally the 'roots'

Wali   'Guardian' or 'friend', can refer to a custodian (especially a male relative of a Muslim woman) or an Islamic saint

Zat (Urdu)   Status or caste

Chapter 1

INTRODUCTION: ISLAM, LIBERALISM AND THE NATION STATE

British Islam in a 'post-liberal age'

This book is concerned with three subjects: Islam, national identity and the liberal state. Over the pages that follow, I offer a qualified defence of liberal approaches to minority inclusion and consider how Western governments might facilitate the incorporation of Muslim populations and institutions. In doing so, I contest the popular view that liberal and Islamic traditions are incompatible; indeed, I propose that, if done right, the incorporation of Muslim minorities might facilitate democratic renewal. I also dispute the idea that national identification inevitably results in coercive measures against cultural minorities and the stifling of political dissent. These arguments then come together in an overarching narrative about the emergence of a distinctive British Islam.

I probably do not need to state that in making these related arguments I begin on the back foot. Exemplified by the decision of the British electorate to exit the European Union and the election of Donald Trump as president of the United States in 2016, liberal democratic structures and procedural norms have been weakened by the recent successes of populist politicians who appear to see parliaments and judiciaries as an inconvenience. The term 'liberal' has become little more than an insult not just for these politicians but for many of their leftist opponents, who characterize liberalism as fatally compromised by economic elites. Chauvinistic varieties of national identity appear to be in the ascendant and, accordingly, conditions for migrants and religious minorities look set to get worse in the UK as well as in many other parts of the world. To argue for a religiously inclusive, liberal national identity in such circumstances can feel at times analogous to arguing for monastic culture during the reign of Henry VIII. Writing about 'British Islam' – already a term freighted with political baggage – involves a particular risk. The UK's referendum on membership of the EU had the effect of driving Scotland and England further apart and jeopardized a fragile settlement in Northern Ireland. As I write, it is far from certain what British identity will look like, or even if Britain will exist as a polity, in five or ten years' time.

The situation for Muslim minorities seems most perilous of all. Anxieties about the threat of terrorism and loss of cultural identity colour almost all popular

debates that touch, even tangentially, on the subject of Muslims and Islam, from
state education (*Islamist plot … to replace teachers … with radicals*)[1] to foster care
(*Christian child forced into Muslim foster care*)[2] to regulations for animal slaughter
(*Animals dying in pain because of Muslim ignorance*).[3] Baseless and distorted
headlines about Muslims – the three I just quoted are all good examples[4] – have
appeared intermittently on newspaper front pages for two decades, and negative
attitudes towards Muslims have accordingly risen steadily,[5] with anti-Muslim views
now being common even among individuals who display tolerant attitudes towards
other ethnic and religious minorities.[6] Against this backdrop, the proposition that
British Muslims might facilitate democratic renewal feels not ambitious so much
as entirely out of touch with the painful reality.

While there may be many legitimate criticisms one could make of this book,
however, being divorced from reality is not one of them. To the contrary, one of
the aims of this book is to give the debate about British Islam a dose of empirical
medicine. For reasons that I shall explore in just a moment, public debate about
Islam and British nationhood has been polemical and typically ignorant of recent
research into the development of the Islamic tradition in the UK. This book
seeks to remedy this ignorance. In what follows, I do make the case for a *vision*
of a British Islam. In pursuing this, the book draws on liberal political theory
and enters into discussions about the state's role in marking out the appropriate
place of religious discourse and in shaping the character of religious communities
and traditions. Alongside this normative argument, however, I also make a claim
about the current state of Islamic Britain that is based upon my own and others'
sociological research. What I argue over the course of the book is that, over a
period of decades and across a range of institutional domains, Islam in Britain
has *reoriented itself*, reshaping itself around British public and institutional
norms. My specific focus is on three domains: education, law and government.
What I seek to show is that slowly, and largely unnoticed by academics and the
media, Islamic institutions operating in these three domains have adapted to, and
in some cases intermeshed with, established infrastructures and that this process
of adaptation has facilitated transitions within the various Islamic traditions
that have set down roots in the UK since the 1950s. When I suggest that British
Muslims might contribute to the flourishing of democratic life in the UK, then,
I am not tasking this overburdened minority with changing the direction of British
politics or reconciling its contradictions. Rather, I am looking to draw lessons, and
inspiration, from Muslims' agency as well as from localized interactions that have,
in most cases, occurred under the radar.

What does it mean to write about 'British Islam'?

In order to develop this argument about the emergence of a distinctive British
Islam, I need first to do a little groundwork. This is because 'British Islam' is a
phrase that is invoked regularly but often without being given serious thought.
Not only this, it is generally invoked in such a way that it has acquired strong

political overtones, most of which I want to contest. Public debate in the UK has become rather fixated on the question of how 'Islam' and 'Britishness' fit together. In the six-month period between March and September 2017, 1,093 newspaper articles were published in Britain that referred to the phrase 'British Muslims'. In the same period, the number of articles referring to 'British Christians' was just 23. The phrase 'British Islam', although less popular, follows the same pattern: 113 references compared with 13 for 'British Christianity'.[7] What this suggests is that the British public talk about the faith and national identity of Muslims somewhere between ten and fifty times more often than they talk about faith and identity of Christians, the UK's dominant religious population most of whose members belong to the country's national churches.

This fixation is long-standing – during the same period in 2006 'British Muslims' appeared in 1,445 articles – and it has made talking about British Islam difficult. One of its effects has been to transform Muslim identity from a neglected social characteristic that had to fight for recognition[8] into something that is next to impossible to downplay. Today, 'Muslim-ness' is routinely seen as the most noteworthy part of a Muslim individual's identity, even when that person makes no effort to emphasize it themselves. 'Islam', likewise, is offered as the explanation for all Muslims' actions, especially when those actions are violent or criminal. An abusive husband who is Muslim is described as perpetrating 'honour-based violence', for example, while a white non-Muslim is described simply as 'evil' – if the media write about him at all.[9] In such circumstances, Muslims find themselves constantly battling to express their identities on their own terms rather than being fixed by the Medusa-like gaze of the media.[10]

This, moreover, is not the biggest problem. Islam was thrust into the spotlight in direct response to the attacks on New York in September 2001 and on London in July 2005. In 1999, just 73 newspaper articles mentioned 'British Muslims' between March and September. This increased to 303 in 2003, before ballooning into four figures over the following three years. It only takes a small amount of reading between the lines to see that 'British' and 'Muslim' were brought together in response to the threat of militant Islamist extremism and that this bringing together involved strengthened national identity being posited as the best way of keeping British Muslims at a safe distance from the violent Islamist movements that have emerged on the world stage. British political leaders have, in fact, explicitly argued this in recent years, and it is their statements, more than anything else, that have shaped the popular connotations of the phrase 'British Islam'. In 2007, for example, Ruth Kelly, then Labour secretary of state for communities and local government (CLG), published an article in the left-wing magazine *New Statesman* entitled 'Time for a British version of Islam…'.[11] Her article would have been striking at any time, given that politicians typically don't seek to dictate the character of religious communities. What made it even more so was that it was timed to coincide exactly with the release of *Preventing Violent Extremism: Winning Hearts and Minds*,[12] a CLG report that signalled the dramatic expansion of 'Prevent', the UK government's policy programme concerned with reducing the appeal of violent extremism. (Further details of this programme can be found in Chapters 3 and 5.)

This pattern of promoting 'Britishness' can be encountered across the political spectrum. Former UK prime minister David Cameron (2010–16) and his successor, Theresa May (2016–19), both repeatedly stressed the need for Muslims in the UK to accept a collection of imprecisely specified 'British values'.[13] And again, this emphasis on Britishness has taken concrete form in counter-extremism policy, with the Conservatives' iteration of Prevent[14] placing burdens on a range of publicly funded institutions to give 'due regard' to the risk of extremism, defined in terms of opposition to 'fundamental British values'. Most recently, the Casey Review – a government-initiated report ostensibly concerned with the generic subject of opportunity and integration but focused predominantly on the position and place of Muslims in British society – ushered into public discourse the idea of obliging new migrants and those holding public office to take an 'Oath of Integration with British Values and Society'.[15]

Across these examples, it is possible to discern some commonalities that give an indication of why the public conversation about British Islam has become so fractious. In both media and political discourse, the interest in British Islam seems to be purely *strategic*. Arguments in favour of reshaping Islam along national lines are justified primarily, or even entirely, as a means to the end of thwarting extremism. Muslims' troubles – whether to do with discrimination, social isolation, economic deprivation or religious transmission – would almost certainly not merit a mention were it not for militant Islamism. Furthermore, British Muslim communities, and the varieties of Islam they practice, emerge as *deficient*. Kelly's and other similar demands strongly imply that Islam, because of either prejudice directed towards it or (more commonly) Muslims' supposed reluctance to 'integrate', stands apart in the UK – *in* Britain but not *of* it. These demands are then made in a context in which Muslim religiosity is routinely seen as a threat to national coherence. In media coverage of Muslims, nation and religion are often depicted as in a zero-sum game: competitors for loyalty rather than categories that operate on different, but related, planes (which is how British Muslims themselves appear to see the two).[16] Data showing that Muslims in the UK[17] display stronger identification with Britishness than the wider British public[18] are bypassed in favour of sensationalist 'Muslim first, British second' scare stories.[19] In such a situation, calls by politicians for 'more Britishness' easily come across, intentionally or not, as demands for 'less Muslim-ness'.

'British Islam', then, has come to be regarded by many, with some justification, as a phrase whose effective function is to discipline a minority whose religion will never be allowed to fully fit in. It implies a separation between Muslims and the wider public, as well as within a British Muslim population that is divided into 'good' and 'bad' citizens principally, if not solely, on the basis of support for counterterror laws and policies.[20] Against the backdrop of the 'War on Terror' and its continued fallout, a vast body of scholarship has been produced examining the 'securitization' of Muslim identities – which is to say, the process of counterterror measures mixing with cultural norms to produce social regimes within which Muslims are viewed primarily as a potential security threat.[21] Barring a few exceptions,[22] in this literature the discourse of nationhood is conceptualized as a tool that political and media elites use to place (arguably impossible) demands on Muslims and exclude those who fail to meet them. 'British Islam' emerges as a device that distils conflicts shaped by myriad political, social and historical developments into one problem: that of Muslim 'inwardness'. It places Britain's burdens squarely on its Muslim citizens' shoulders.

I am in broad agreement with this analysis of the way the UK government understands British Islam. Indeed, I find official references to 'British Islam' frustrating for the additional reason that they narrow our historical understanding. Calls for a British Islam, when made by Kelly and others, imply that Islam is something that has come to Britain and now needs to respond and adapt to British ways. This position entirely ignores the multiple historical connections between Islam and the UK, especially in the colonial period. Such has been the global impact of the British Empire that there are, in truth, few Islamic traditions in Britain that exist independently of British interference overseas. Wahhabi Islam, which predominates in Saudi Arabia and is regularly associated with extremism, attained prominence in part due to British efforts to secure exclusive oil mining concessions in the early twentieth century.[23] The context for the emergence of the Salafi movement in Egypt was set by the British occupation of Cairo in 1882.[24] The two most influential Islamic traditions in Britain – the Deobandi and Barelvi movements – were both formed as a response to British rule in India.[25] British Islam can be, in Jonathan Birt's words,[26] conceptualized as the 'postcolonial fruit' of 'Britain's long and intimate relationship with the Indian subcontinent', but this much richer understanding is made impossible by the forgetful narrative that is presently promoted by the British state.

Despite these shared frustrations, however, this criticism is not all that there is to be said on the subject. One of the things that the overwhelming majority of advocates and critics of the promotion of a 'British Islam' share is obliviousness to how the concept has been treated by British Muslims. Discussions about this phrase can be found as far back as the late nineteenth century among the UK's small missionary and convert communities, and it was a 'hot topic' in the British Muslim public sphere in the 1990s.[27] On this and many other subjects, Muslims in Britain have actually remained some distance ahead of the political debate about them. One thing in particular that usually gets left out is *religious change*, and specifically the changing orientations of British Islamic traditions and institutions. To incorporate religious change into our understanding of British Islam is, I want to propose, to see this debate in a new way.

To illustrate, consider for another moment the point above about the history of the British Empire. It is hard to dispute this without descending into historical revisionism, but even though it is correct – and important – one can still ask questions about whether the Middle Eastern and South Asian Islamic movements found in Britain have started to differ from their contexts of origin. If such differences can be identified – and one of my goals is to show that they can – then it contains lessons both for politicians calling for a British Islam *and* for critics who see such calls as a means of disciplining and excluding Muslim communities. If a 'British Islam' is already appearing, then political narratives about Islam's failure to adapt to the UK's cultural norms start from the wrong point and so risk proposing solutions that are ineffectual or harmful. At the same time, the notion that 'British Islam' represents little more than a discursive device whose function is to place pressure on Muslim communities also emerges as flawed, for this neglects British Islam's recent history – and British Muslims' agency in making it. It forgets that the idea of a British Islam does not *belong* to political elites but, first and foremost, to the people who make up Muslim Britain.

Writing Islam as a social scientist

Within academia, this neglect of religious change is not just found in scholarship focused on counterterror policies, although state-led, security-focused research funding programmes have ensured that it is especially pronounced in that context.[28] Rather, it is woven into academic languages and norms across the social and political sciences, including my own discipline of sociology. Certainly, there has been an explosion of sociological scholarship on Muslims in Europe since the turn of the millennium, building on an already substantial corpus. Within this corpus, however, Muslims' identities have attracted more attention than themes such as religious interpretation and authority. Studies highlighting religious change within British Islamic institutions do exist, and I will draw upon them throughout this book, but they have generally remained on the margins of academic scholarship, having an impact mainly within religious studies rather than the (sadly) more influential social and political sciences.

Of course, given the overemphasis on 'Muslim-ness' in the Anglophone press some caution about discussing religious traditions and ideas is understandable. When Muslims are always viewed *as Muslim* above all, and when political violence is regularly attributed to this or that verse in the Qur'an, there is considerable value pointing out when Islam *doesn't* matter to people and where it *isn't* influential in action: for example, instances where Muslims feel the need to speak out as Muslims not for religious reasons but because they feel they have been misrepresented.[29] A degree of scepticism can be particularly helpful when examining writing that takes institutional and organized Islam as its main point of focus, as this book does. As I will discuss in Chapter 5, academic researchers, and even more so government representatives, have an occasional habit of taking leaders of Muslim institutions as exemplary and letting them stand for all Muslims in Britain, despite these people generally being more conservative in outlook. Contrasting and competing traditions – from effervescent South Asian cultural and aesthetic formations,[30] to British Asian popular counterculture,[31] to South Asian secular and communist political movements,[32] to 'everyday' forms of Islam[33] – not only are neglected through this move but also have their identities and options enclosed. For politicians, use of 'community leaders' can be a way of avoiding the hard work of democratic inclusion; for academics, it can be a way of avoiding the hard work of nuanced representation.

There is, however, a point at which such cautiousness about talking Islam moves from healthy wariness of overstating the social significance of religious identity to something more troubling and rooted either in illiteracy or in secular biases against religious forms of knowledge. By this, I do not mean avowed *dislike* of religion, although there are occasional cases of that. Rather, my main concern is the more common tendency among social scientists for questions about religious interpretation and change to be bypassed by researchers badly equipped to answer or discomfited by them, or simply squeezed out by an academic culture that considers such matters unimportant. This can affect even topics that are of direct interest to the British Muslim population. Sociological writing on urban ethnic diversity, for example, typically takes as its focus those parts of the UK and Europe where Muslims are concentrated. Often, however, such writing dissolves religious vocabularies into secularized accounts of multicultural conviviality.[34] The focus is placed on informal varieties of cultural production and everyday interactions across ethnic and faith lines, with religious interpretation, change and authority generally being left out of the picture.[35] In academic scholarship on the theme of Islamophobia, too, there has been a recent tendency to focus on the (of course, important) subject of how Muslim identity is racialized and a concomitant shift towards conceptualizing Islamophobia as a form of racism.[36] This has been a positive change in many respects, with anti-Muslim prejudice gaining greater (although still limited) recognition and past tensions between anti-racist and Islamic activists diminishing (see Chapter 5). At the same time, however, injustices linked to the misperception of Muslims' beliefs and the misrepresentation of Muslim institutions have been badly neglected.[37]

A particularly good example of the difficulty scholars have responding to the prominence of Islam can be found in the spirited defence of multiculturalism authored by Anthony Giddens.[38] Giddens's defence is instructive because, in common with much social scientific academic writing, it responds to allegations about Islam's supposed negative influence on Western societies simply by taking the focus away from the Islamic tradition. He defends it by arguing, effectively, that it doesn't really matter and that there is nothing distinctive about it. In his account, Giddens takes the various claims that are made about Muslims one by one. He observes that, contrary to popular perceptions, Britain is becoming more mixed in ethnic terms, not segregated, so claims about Muslim self-segregation do not stand up to scrutiny. He argues that the majority of violent events witnessed in recent years in which 'Islam' appears to have played a significant role have had larger structural causes: most can be explained by international geopolitical struggles or social dislocation engendered by the process of settling in a new country across generations. He contends that the majority of Muslims in the UK feel little or no contradiction between their faith and their national identity, in part because, he says, 'many Muslims … are not very religious at all'. Of the Islamic tradition itself he says little apart from making the curt observations that fundamentalism should be restrained and that all of the Abrahamic religions have their share of religiously conservative members.

I do not wish to dispute these individual points and will elaborate on and provide supporting evidence for those that are contested in the next chapter. What interests me here, though, is how they work to dodge the central question.

Consider another opinion that is regularly repeated in newspaper columns in the UK: that while the majority of British Muslims (as members of various ethno-religious communities) are good citizens, Islam (the moral tradition) fits into liberal democracies at best awkwardly. This is a criticism to which Giddens, like many social scientists, has very little to say. Indeed, he leaves his readers with the suspicion that Muslims are likely to fit in within British society only if they remain loosely connected to the Islamic tradition – meaning, of course, that the more committed a person is, the more likely he or she is to be alienated or disruptive. As far as Islam *is* influential, in other words, it could still be a problem. This is not a good impression to leave in Britain, not just because of the prevalent hostility towards Islam but because it can be clearly demonstrated that, in Clive Field's words, British Muslims are a 'remarkably religious' population that will grow in the near future.[39] The Islamic tradition is likely to become more socially significant in the UK, but Giddens doesn't face this possibility head-on, meaning that he fails to directly challenge the people threatened by it.

In saying this, I am not trying to make adversaries of authors I admire and from whom it is possible to learn a lot. Rather, I am pointing to a *structural neglect* of Islamic (and other religious) vocabularies. Academic scholarship in the social and political sciences follows a set of secular norms that, although valuable, can lead to certain types of argument and vocabulary becoming prominent while others become alien. The predominance of certain (progressive) moral and (positivist, Marxist or Nietzschean) philosophical perspectives means that seriously engaging with the Islamic tradition involves work crossing intellectual bridges and engaging with concepts and moral principles that, sometimes, one disagrees with. Often, this is work that social and political scientists won't do (or aren't equipped to do: the isolation of the sociology of religion from the wider social sciences means that, even where there may be the will, there is not the ability to discuss religious belief).[40] Unlike in the wider Western world, gut hostility towards Islam and Muslims is rare in academic life, but this means that Islam, newly visible in Western liberal states, becomes like an unfamiliar person at a dinner party: the well-meaning guests all want to be polite but don't always know how to engage it in a conversation. One of the strange consequences of this is that, within academia, books discussing how the West has *imagined* Islam as nightmarish can become set texts, with some becoming globally famous,[41] while those that attempt a conversation with the tradition gather dust. In other words, even in discussions *about* Islam the focus, ultimately, remains on Western traditions of thought, meaning any inclusion of the Islamic tradition is generally limited.

Islam in no man's land

This inability to talk about the dynamics of religious knowledge within the academy reflects and indeed reinforces a harmful pattern of religiously illiterate political debate outside of it, although in the wider world the tone is lower and the consequences greater. It is an understatement to say that public knowledge of Islam in the Anglophone world is not especially good. So poor is the public conversation about the tradition that it is not an exaggeration to say that most people – even many who see themselves as well disposed to Muslims – have a distorted view of it. I imagine that most of the readers of this book will understand (or at least, will recognize) the terms *Shari'a*, *jihad* and *fatwa*, but far fewer will be able to say the same about *fatiha*, *taqwa*, *tawhid*, *iman* and *shahada*. Within the Islamic tradition, the terms in the second of these two lists are far more fundamental than those in the first; trying to understand Islam without these terms is like trying to understand Christianity without concepts like 'the Lord's prayer', 'salvation', 'the Trinity' or 'grace'. Anyone who recognizes the former list and not the latter, then, sees only a few elements without recognizing a wider landscape. Indeed, their understanding of even these elements will be severely limited due to it being cut away from the rich tapestry of legal, moral and philosophical concepts and narratives that supply them with meaning.

This selective literacy makes it next to impossible to talk in a constructive or meaningful way about Islam across the thousands of articles published on the subject of Islam in Britain. It also makes it harder to develop responses to misleading and prejudicial claims. To illustrate, consider a short example. In early 2016, the then secretary of state for justice, Michael Gove, started to apply considerable pressure to Muslim chaplaincy services. This move was seemingly justified on the basis that most Muslim chaplains are Deobandis, a tradition often characterized as maintaining 'anti-British' attitudes and thus at odds, in Gove's view, with the government's stated commitment to promote 'British values'.[42] As we will see in Chapter 3, there is a degree of truth to this portrayal: opposition to 'Britishness' has long been an aspect of Deobandi Islam due to its colonial origins. Gove's efforts, however, ignored the profound changes the tradition has gone through in the UK and, to a lesser degree, abroad. Fortunately, his efforts were abruptly halted when the EU referendum resulted in him being consigned to the backbenches. While the controversy was ongoing, however, the silence from those concerned with racism and discrimination was notable. No criticism was made outside of the Muslim press, despite the serious potential consequences for Muslim chaplains' livelihoods. Secular publications did not seem able to recognize the misrepresentation, so could not criticize it.

Public discussion of Islamic law offers a still clearer illustration of the problem. It has been abundantly clear since 2008 – when the then Archbishop of Canterbury, Rowan Williams, spoke positively about incorporating Islamic law in England – that simply to take on the question of Islamic law's place in the UK's legal systems is to invite accusations of, in the words of one tabloid response, 'handing victory to Al-Qaeda'.[43] The conservative wing of the British press consistently presents '*Shari'a*' as a fixed, comprehensive code of law: a system that, applied properly, supplies a state's constitutional foundations and sets down positive commands and punishments for transgressions. Groups such as Al-Qaeda and ISIS thus emerge in the British public sphere merely as the groups *most committed* to the implementation of Islamic law, with other Muslims being less invested but understanding Islamic law in broadly the same way. In the liberal press, it is sometimes recognized that mainstream

Islamic organizations in the UK seek to apply Islamic law only to family matters such as marriage, divorce and, in some cases, inheritance and custody of children. Some even go as far as to highlight how the tabloids wrongly take the most extreme advocates of 'Shari'a law' to be mainstream in the Islamic tradition. However, any recognition that the term *Shari'a* has multiple meanings – including sometimes referring simply to 'appropriate conduct' – or that the Islamic legal tradition has always been multivocal and in a state of flux is left to specialist publications.

This leaves Muslims in no man's land between, on the one hand, the caricatures of the tabloid right and, on the other, secular and liberal voices who do worry about the rise of Islamophobia but who aren't able to say much about what that actually looks like.[44] As I shall show in Chapter 5, the institutions that offer some kind of service – mostly, a divorce service – guided by a conception of Islamic law do raise genuine questions about Muslims' rights and access to justice. Working through these questions requires, I will suggest, not just consideration of how secular jurisdictions might deal with such institutions but also consideration of how Islamic legal practices in the UK have shifted through time and how they might change in the future. Even in the best circumstances, addressing these questions is difficult, but if public spheres in the West cannot engage with the idea that Islamic law is an evolving and discursive tradition then it will be impossible. The work of thinking through what it means to follow 'God's path' in the UK will remain a question Muslims face alone.

Locating Islam in Britain

This book is, then, my attempt to put questions of religious interpretation, institutionalization, authority and change back into a debate about British Islam that has so far kept them to the periphery. It emerges out of a desire to make sense of this phrase – or rather, a conviction that this phrase has a meaning beyond that given by politicians and media commentators. My conviction has developed over many years working in the field of British Muslim studies, during which time I have witnessed a consistent pattern of social and religious change. I endeavour to describe this pattern in the chapters that follow but should say from the outset that there are several relevant themes that I do not cover. I do not talk, for example, about the emergent sphere of British Muslim arts, where mostly younger British Muslims have created spaces for expression that respond directly, and critically, to traditional British Islamic institutions *and* to experiences of discrimination and misrepresentation in wider UK society.[45] In this sphere, as in my case study contexts, British-born Muslims are beginning to find a voice, albeit a limited one, in mainstream organizations. I do not talk, either, of efforts to rediscover British Muslim heritage through exhibitions about Muslim involvement in the World Wars, the history of buildings such as Shah Jahan mosque in Woking or specific personalities such as Abdullah Quilliam, the Liverpool-based early convert to Islam.[46] There are numerous other subjects I can only name here: journalism, music, finance, fashion, television.

Why, then, focus on the three domains of education, law and Muslim–state relations? In part, my reasons are practical. Some Islamic educational centres double up as '*Shari'a* councils' and many employ individuals who are involved in consultations with local and national government. This has made carrying out the empirical research for this book feasible. This, however, is not all there is to it. In this book, I seek to understand the transmission and transmutation of Islamic traditions in the UK. One might therefore characterize it as a 'sociology of Islam' more than it is a 'sociology of Muslims', in the sense that it focuses on Islamic languages and knowledge more than the identities and experiences of those who class themselves as, or who are perceived as, Muslim.[47] Education, law and Muslim–state relations are all sites where Islamic knowledge is created, transmitted and transformed into social practices and public arguments. This makes them ideal sites for understanding religious change in Islamic Britain. Analysing the Muslim arts scene, say, means taking on a slightly different set of questions. Of course, much that goes under the heading of 'Muslim arts' involves a religious message or is motivated by religious sentiment – but not always. Some Muslim art is more interested in recording the history of Muslims as people or with responding to misrepresentation. There is also a vigorous debate about the extent to which Muslim artists can escape labels: that is, whether Muslims can make art without it being (seen as) 'Muslim art'. These kinds of questions are less relevant in institutions whose function is the production of Islamic knowledge or articulation of Islamic arguments. They become central in this book only when I turn to Muslims' political representation in Chapter 5.

The other reason behind my choices is that each of these cases raises profound questions about the liberal state and relates to debates in liberal political theory. In the case of Chapter 3, the question is the state's proper role in the formation of people and the transmission of knowledge, especially religious knowledge. In Chapter 4, it is the appropriate interaction between civil jurisdictions and customary legal orders. In Chapter 5, it is the role of religious traditions and organizations in political movements and influencing public policies and decision-making. Each chapter, then, provides the opportunity to think in a theoretical but not wholly abstract way about Islam and liberalism. Indeed, each of these three chapters, as well as forming into a narrative about change in British Islamic institutions, makes a distinctive argument that should stand on its own terms for a particular interpretation of liberal politics and its relation to religious institutions and justifications. I need to say a little, consequently, about how I position myself within the liberal tradition in this book.

Islam, liberalism and multiculturalism

Liberalism and the social sciences have an uneasy relationship, and sociologists are frequently among the fiercest critics of liberal politics. The liberal tradition is often characterized (sometimes caricatured) as individualist, while sociologists are interested in how people are bound together by social structures. Liberalism emphasizes the moral significance of personal reflection and decision-making,[48] while the social sciences emphasize how the judgements we make are shaped by unacknowledged background influences. Perhaps the twentieth century's most influential liberal philosopher, John Rawls – someone who I will draw upon at various points – began his best-known book, *A Theory of Justice*, by asking his readers to imagine what society they would create if they had no awareness of their place within it: that is, of their class, status, ethnicity, gender or religion.[49] Such requests are enough to bring many sociologists out in cold sweats. Yet although these tensions are deep, and I won't pretend to be able to resolve them here, I want to argue there is still value in reading sociological and liberal traditions together. What the liberal tradition contains is a set of resources for thinking about how to engage with other people's conceptions of the good and the vocabularies in terms of which those conceptions are understood. A common definition of liberalism is a system of politics in which the goal of a state is to give equal consideration to each person's conception of the good life.[50] A question animating my arguments here, then, is: What does it mean to give due consideration to those whose understanding of the good life is worked out using terms supplied by a religious tradition? I want to argue that it requires precisely the kind of *attentiveness*[51] to religious vocabularies that is lacking in academic and wider public life. In the social sciences, the norm is for Muslims' beliefs to be treated in a hands-off way or to be subsumed by an overarching social theory. This, as Maleiha Malik has remarked, leads to a 'hollow' form of respect that pays no mind to the reasons why a moral tradition is actually valued.[52] At its best, sociology is, as Les Back has put it, 'a listener's art',[53] and one of the ways in which it can work productively within the liberal tradition is by attending to and making liberal states aware of the dynamics of religious traditions.

As well as being concerned with equality and respect, liberals have a long-standing interest in the subject of *deliberation* – that is, in the ways in which we articulate our understanding of the good as part of an effort to change laws and social practices. This focus has allowed for some degree of crossover between the two traditions.[54] Deliberation, after all, is a social practice that occurs in concrete settings that are subject to all kinds of power relations. One of the best recent examples of a sociological treatment of deliberative processes is John R. Bowen's study of Islamic law in Britain, which the author describes as offering an 'anthropology of public reasoning'.[55] This book, while taking a more top-down approach quite different to Bowen's ethnographic work, can be described in similar terms. It uses two principal sources of primary empirical data – interviews with individuals working for, or with, Muslim institutions and analysis of public events arranged by such institutions – and combines these with overviews of the research literature on the three cases I cover. This allows me to explore the interests of, and the challenges faced by, Muslim institutions, as well as the way Muslims in these institutions have engaged with public bodies and spheres, including both spaces where Muslims predominate and those in which they form an (often badly misunderstood) minority.

Of course, these two paragraphs paint the liberal tradition in a positive light and mask some of the entrenched disputes within and about it. The tradition is commonly, and justifiably, characterized as dominated by a variety of rationalism that is hostile to religious vocabularies and that seeks to freeze religious people out of public life.[56] Postcolonial theorists have highlighted how the tradition, in the past and up to the present day, includes individuals who view Islam, in particular, as exemplifying everything that liberals are against – intolerance, patriarchy, ideological inflexibility and so on.[57] Indeed, one of the tensions with which this book wrestles is that, while it affirms certain liberal principles and points to successful outcomes resulting from liberal norms of governance, it is located in a context where recently a self-styled 'muscular' liberalism has been mobilized *against* Muslim minorities.[58] This is a difficult conflict to resolve, but I endeavour to resolve it in two ways. The first is to try to *reclaim* liberalism from political leaders who preach liberal values while moulding state apparatuses into more coercive (and therefore illiberal) forms. Recent UK governments have weakened *habeas corpus* rights, made citizenship more conditional, delegitimized dissent and become more willing to intervene in religious knowledge production.[59] As we will see in Chapter 5, this has extended to the active promotion of a 'liberal Islam', which, rather than weakening extremist movements as intended, has done little more than engender damaging divisions between Muslim organizations while facilitating, if not promoting, anti-Muslim prejudice. Opposing these measures does not mean opposing the liberal tradition; these interventionist tactics have little or no justification in contemporary liberal thought. Rather, it recognizes that the UK and other Western states increasingly use liberalism as an identity label, in much the same way that white nationalists in the United States use Christianity in their opposition to stricter controls on owning automatic weapons.[60]

This is not to let the liberal tradition off the hook, however. There is a solid basis to the claim that liberalism's underlying ethos engenders a disconnect between religious identities and public life and that this makes it easy to turn the tradition against Muslim minorities. The second way I try to resolve the tension, then, is by picking an argument *with* liberalism. In this book I take a position within the liberal tradition, advocating what is known as a 'political' liberalism that sees legitimacy as grounded in an 'overlapping consensus' of philosophies rather than a 'comprehensive' liberalism that understands the role of the state as being to support and promote a conception of human flourishing which emphasizes the inherent value of individual autonomy.[61] The most influential varieties of political liberalism, notably Rawls's own,[62] include a norm of 'public reason' that proposes we should 'bracket' our ultimate beliefs when entering into deliberations about how society should be ordered. This norm is often caricatured by liberalism's opponents, and while I try to sidestep such mistakes myself I nevertheless argue that de-coupling public issues from comprehensive philosophies works to stultify public conversation and hinder the inclusion and flourishing of religious minorities. I argue for a variety of liberalism that involves a more 'moderate' form of secularism[63] and that – as the reader will see – draws almost as much from socialist, communitarian and post-structuralist critics of liberalism as it does from political liberals.

This openness to religious discourses is one reason why this book offers a more positive account of multicultural politics than readers might expect. 'Liberalism' and 'multiculturalism' are generally represented as opposed philosophies, and with some justification. Many of those who have started to speak more loudly in favour of 'muscular liberalism' in recent years, such as Cameron, have done so as part of an argument against 'the doctrine of state multiculturalism'.[64] Within the field of political theory, advocates of multicultural politics have often charged liberals with paying insufficient attention to the consequences of the stigmatization of minority groups.[65] I do not deny that there are meaningful differences between those who march beneath these two banners. Nevertheless, much of this conflict is exaggerated or even fabricated. Critics of multiculturalism, such as Cameron, charge the tradition with encouraging 'different cultures to live separate lives'. When one looks at the policies on the ground that pass as 'multicultural' today, however, they are unrecognizable from this portrayal. In the UK, the term 'multiculturalism' was popularized against a backdrop of campaigns for equal treatment by minority ethnic groups that originated from former British colonies, and almost all theoretical articulations of multicultural politics have internalized the theme of equality. Multicultural policies have usually been locally negotiated and marked by a mixture of welcoming rhetoric, commitment to even-handedness and willingness to engage with distinctive concerns, including (most controversially) those of ethnic and religious minority organizations. Crucially, they have also been increasingly oriented towards the incorporation of ethno-religious minorities into British national and local civic traditions. *Pace* Cameron and others, multiculturalism in the UK has not sought simply to preserve 'minority' cultural practices in opposition to a 'mainstream' national culture but, rather, has generally sought to utilize political ritual to unify the country's many ethno-cultural traditions.[66]

What this means is that multicultural political practice includes much that liberals *and* nation-conscious conservatives can support – *if* they are able to move beyond abstractions and political posturing. Of course, in the case of Cameron and other centre-right politicians it is hard to escape the conclusion that posturing is the whole point, with opposition to 'multiculturalism' functioning as a signal to voters who are uncomfortable with the UK's ethnic diversification. Such conclusions are hard to avoid because, as Tariq Modood has highlighted, political leaders across Western Europe who have been vocal in their criticisms of 'multiculturalism' have also, for reasons of political expediency, often partnered with and even created minority representative organizations.[67] (That is to say, they have maintained the aspects of multiculturalism that are most contentious.) This does not, however, alter the fact that, whether one is talking about theory or practice, the gap between liberalism, multiculturalism and integrationism is not as big as it is made out to be. Indeed, in one sense this book can be read as a thoroughgoing affirmation of multicultural political practice. I narrate in this book a process of change within British Islamic institutions which involves adaptation to, and integration with, public infrastructures. This process of adaptation has, as we will see, been facilitated by multicultural incorporation at different levels and across different domains. When bridges have been built by the state and Muslim groups this has moderated anti-liberal perspectives. In other words, I aim to show how multiculturalism in Britain has had a *demonstrable* acculturating effect.

The structure of this book

As I mentioned at the start of this chapter, this book is oriented around three case studies. In order to set the context for these case studies and to provide readers who are not familiar with the subject of Islam in Britain with an introduction to the area, Chapter 2 provides an overview of the origins, settlement patterns and demographic growth of Britain's Muslim population. Chapters 3, 4 and 5 then deal, respectively, with Islamic educational institutions, institutions concerned with Islamic law, and Muslim representative and lobbying organizations. (The change of terminology here is not, I should note, accidental: the first two cases are concerned with the transmission and institutionalization of Islamic principles, while the third is typically concerned with speaking on behalf of Muslims.) In Chapter 3, I examine the ways Islamic educational institutions have built bridges with wider British society, within and beyond the higher education sector, and place this in the context of debates about how the state shapes its citizens. In Chapter 4, I look at how Islamic legal institutions (or as I more accurately term them, Islamic dispute resolution institutions) have adapted to take into account English legal procedures and consider how secular norms, specifically norms of 'public reason', might facilitate or hinder changes to these institutions. In Chapter 5, I consider the maturation and pluralization of Muslims' engagement with the state and argue against those who describe Muslims' relationships with the state as being characterized only by state discipline of the British Muslim population. The final chapter, Chapter 6, then reviews these changes as a whole, sets out a vision for British Islam and considers the wider question of what religious traditions add to liberal democracies.

Before proceeding, I need to say a few words about the research on which this book is based. This started in 2006 when I was a PhD student with a period working for a London-based Muslim educational charity, Maslaha, before the research proper began in 2007. The research continued after my PhD was completed, with the last interview being carried out in 2018. During this period I have been involved in several projects that have involved research on Muslim organizations – in particular, a project on religious literacy in higher education,[68] a large-scale research project on Muslim participation in local and national governance in Britain[69] and a project examining faith-based campaigns relating to the financial sector.[70] All of these projects are distinct from the present study and I refer to them here as such, but they nevertheless altered my thinking considerably on the questions this book addresses and offered opportunities to build networks and make return visits to institutions I had previously investigated. For example, I visited one institution I speak about in Chapter 3, the Markfield Institute for Higher Education, first as a PhD student in 2007 and then a further five times between 2007 and 2015, interviewing five staff in total across different research projects and independently. This interaction came about because the Markfield Institute, like many similar organizations, has important functions as an educational centre and the home for several representatives of interfaith and policy organizations that have been involved in local and national governance. It has also – as we shall see in Chapter 3 – been through a process of religious change. This study does have limitations. My research has generally focused on English South Asian movements, on Sunni Islam and on comparatively outward-looking organizations and individuals. This is a weakness of research in the field of British Muslim studies as a whole to some extent, although fortunately in recent years important accounts have emerged of more insular organizations and less researched (especially Middle Eastern Shia) populations and communities. I use these to broaden my focus and strengthen my thesis.

The argument that this book advances was developed a posteriori; my views about the idea of a British Islam were not the same in 2007, when Kelly published her article, as they are now. What has become apparent to me is that Islamic institutions of different kinds are all modifying in similar, broadly positive ways in response to comparable demographic and social pressures. Such changes have been happening to some degree independently of the short-term – and in many contexts counterproductive – political strategies employed by governments to address counterterrorism and integration (two policy domains that often merge, in spite of a recognized need for them to be kept distinct). Whatever reservations one may have about the ever-present danger of chauvinism within narratives about the nation state, this transition deserves a name. If one is trying to name sociocultural adaptations that distinguish Islamic institutions in the UK from those in other states, including the states in which British Islamic traditions were first formed, then what better term is there? If something looks and sounds like a distinctively British Islam, why not refer to it as such rather than just accepting at face value the narrative that British political leaders offer?

Chapter 2

THE SHIFTING FOUNDATIONS OF ISLAMIC BRITAIN

The growing social significance of Islam in Britain

Following the attacks of 11 September 2001 on New York, a new body of conservative opinion emerged in the West that depicted Europe as, in the words of Matt Carr, 'a doomed continent, on the brink of cultural extinction in the face of a relentless and co-ordinated campaign of Islamicisation'.[1] Although this narrative goes back at least to the Iranian Revolution, the new millennium saw it moving out from fringe neoconservative and far-right groups to become mainstream. 'A youthful Muslim society to the south and east of the Mediterranean is poised to colonize – the term is not too strong – a senescent Europe', wrote the influential conservative historian Niall Ferguson in the *New York Times* in 2004.[2] This claim has been repeated as though a leitmotif in European and American public discourse, the most recent case being Douglas Murray's widely praised and best-selling 2018 book *The Strange Death of Europe*, in which he speaks of a 'continent and culture caught in the act of suicide'.[3]

This Spenglerian view of Europe's long-term future has not gone unchallenged over the last two decades. Indeed, while it has proven hard to limit the argument's popularity, researchers of Muslim Europe have found it easy to knock away several of the struts propping it up. The predictions of Muslim population growth on which it is based are typically fantastical. One testament to this – and to the argument's unfortunate influence – is the fact that European publics tend to estimate that their country's Muslim population is two or even three times its actual size.[4] It overemphasizes the influence of religious knowledge, elevating this at the expense of economic and political factors.[5] Perhaps most importantly, it also involves, as scholars of Islam such as Karen Armstrong and Sophie Gilliat-Ray have shown, a carefully maintained level of ignorance about the influence of Muslim cultures on Europeans ranging from Fibonacci to Roger Bacon.[6] The books that comprise the 'Eurabia' literature – a term adopted from the revisionist historian Bat Ye'or (aka Giselle Litmann) – portray Islam as a foreign pollutant within European culture, despite the fact that the page numbers of all these books are written in Arabic numerals.

Yet, although it may be simple to undermine, this narrative has kept European Muslims, and scholars of Muslim Europe, on the defensive. It has led to an understandable tendency to emphasize continuity over change, with Islam's probable future impact being downplayed. At worst, it can even give the unintentional appearance that, despite disagreeing about the *extent* of demographic change, both sides agree that a substantial demographic shift, and an associated growth in Islam's public presence and influence, would present a problem for European states. To put this another way, the Eurabia literature has *distracted* scholars. Toni Morrison famously observed that 'the function of racism ... is distraction': 'Somebody says you have no language and you spend twenty years proving that you do. Somebody says your head isn't shaped properly so you have scientists working on the fact that it is.' Racist discourse 'keeps you from doing your work': racism prevents its victims from considering the questions that are vital to their flourishing.[7] The Eurabia thesis – which bears more than a little resemblance to classic racist prophecies about 'rivers of blood' – has had precisely this effect, preventing a conversation in which one can ask imaginative and far-reaching questions about European Islam's future.

It is inarguable that the Muslim population of the UK – and Western Europe – has increased exponentially over the last seventy years. In 1951 there were 21,000 Muslims living in Britain,[8] which represented 0.05 per cent of the population. In 2011 that figure was 2.8 million, or 4.4 per cent.[9] Estimates of the current population range from 3.4 million (5.2 per cent)[10] to 4.1 million (6.3 per cent),[11] and, as we will see below, it is certain that this will continue to grow even if the UK continues to pursue increasingly restrictive immigration policies. (Incidentally, in 2016 the British public put the Muslim population at 15 per cent and projected an increase to 22 per cent by 2020.) While this will never amount to 'colonization', it does mean Islam will become one of the significant moral traditions that make up British liberal democracy, playing a more important role in shaping what the UK is and what it stands for. Put another way, in the 1950s Islam was not part of the constellation of moral traditions that comprised liberal democracy in the UK. Now it is, and it will become more so.

What questions does this raise? Is it possible to talk about this as a significant and meaningful change without resorting to scaremongering? Across this book, I want to argue that we can and should, but first we will need a more realistic description of the coming-to-prominence of the UK's Muslim population. In this chapter, therefore, I provide an overview of the growth and current character of Muslim Britain, as well as of the religious institutions that have been established with the aim of serving it. By providing this (extremely brief, and therefore inevitably flawed) outline of the British Muslim population, I will be able to do two things: first, allow those who are not familiar with the topic to understand some of the important contrasts within the British Muslim population; and second, to give a flavour of the changes that have started to take place within British Islam, and why those changes matter. Conflation of distinct currents of Islamic thought and ignorance of profound changes within the British Muslim population is embarrassingly common in the UK, even among those who should know better, and has caused not just confusion but very real damage to communities and organizations. This chapter's aim is to clear the ground and make it possible to talk about British Islam sensibly.

My primary – but by no means exclusive – interest in this chapter is in changes that have occurred *across generations*. There are many interesting things one can say about the contrasts between British-born Muslims and their overseas-born parents or grandparents, relating to income, family size, working life, marriage arrangements and geographical distribution. While I will touch on all these themes, I will pay particular attention to changes in *patterns of belief*, for these provide the backdrop for the institutional transformations that I will endeavour to describe over the next three chapters. My aim, ultimately, is to take us to the point where this split between an overseas-born 'first' generation and its British-born 'second' or 'third' generation begins to break down.

From the first 'renegades' to postcolonial communities

Prior to the mid-nineteenth century, Muslims existed in Britain only as tiny eccentric sects, viewed by the majority population as deviants, heretics and renegades.[12] In fact, the terms 'renegade' and 'renege' entered into the English language from Spanish in the 1580s to describe Christian sailors who had converted to Islam. The prospects for such individuals were generally bleak: Sir Walter Raleigh recorded that 'Renegadoes, that turn Turke, are impaled.'[13] Many of the earliest British Muslims, fearing such severe consequences, no doubt kept their beliefs hidden well from public view.

From the 1850s onwards, the development of coal-fired steamships began to open up new opportunities for men from the British colonies. The owners of these new ships struggled to attract British-born individuals into what was extremely physically demanding work. Many relied on itinerant labourers from the British-controlled areas of South Asia and the Middle East, which led directly to the establishment of communities of *lascars* – as sailors from the Indian subcontinent and Arabic-speaking world were known – in port towns such as Cardiff, Liverpool and South Shields, as well as the docklands of London. These communities did not have to hide their identity in the way their predecessors did – by the 1930s some religious figures had begun to negotiate successfully with local civic leaders[14] – but their life was still difficult. Many Muslim *lascars* were brought to the UK to ease labour shortages during the First World War, playing an invaluable role when the country was under huge economic strain, but after the war they were treated appallingly. The return of demobilized soldiers and the sharp economic downturn led to increasing hostility towards 'coloured' workers, and the passing of the Alien Restriction (Amendment) Bill in 1919 and the Aliens Order in 1920 severely restricted the ability of non-white British residents to get paid work.[15] Many Muslim men were driven into desperate poverty, to which the white majority responded by arguing that their squalor was a consequence not of unfair treatment but of their lack of proper 'Christian' morals.

Alongside these small settler groups, in the nineteenth century relatively affluent Muslims – some originally from South Asia, others native-born converts – established small but highly active communities that helped Islam in

Britain develop a public face. In Woking, a South Asian barrister transformed the UK's first purpose-built *masjid* – the ornate and extremely exclusive Shah Jahan Mosque – into a successful mission.[16] A similar enterprise was set up in Liverpool by the influential convert Abdullah Quilliam (who has, interestingly, recently become something of a figurehead for Muslims seeking new directions in British Islam: see Chapter 5). Many of these mission groups were sympathetic to Islamic modernism. Recognizing that Islam would never have mass appeal unless it was presented to British people in a form they would recognize, they wrote in English, drew parallels with Christianity and challenged traditional Islamic teachings regarding the seclusion of women (*purdah*) and punishments for 'apostasy' (*riddah* or *irtidad*).[17] In his public speeches, Quilliam skilfully contrasted the Prophet Muhammad's supposed 'fanaticism' with that of venerated English radicals such as William Wilberforce.[18] Members of the Pan-Islamic Society in London also distilled the major *hadith* collections into short books with the aim of correcting misconceptions about the Islamic tradition.[19]

Yet, as the statistics above indicate, these modernist and labouring groups were both small compared to the communities that formed following the Second World War. During the 1950s and 1960s large numbers of Muslims came to the UK from what were mostly by that time former colonies,[20] drawn by a demand for labour that promised wages greater than, for example, the £30 per annum that was standard in 1960s Pakistan.[21] This migration tended to take the form of a 'chain', with initial 'pioneer' migrants from South Asia being joined first by their immediate family and then often members of extended kinship networks. These migrants originated from specific areas – such as the Mirpur District in Azad Kashmir, Pakistan, or Sylhet in Bangladesh – and tended to identify in localized as much as national terms, in part because of carefully maintained transnational social relationships. From the 1970s onwards, this body of predominantly South Asian Muslim migrants then began to diversify, driven by a combination of the 1973 oil crisis and political unrest in various Middle Eastern and African states.[22] Such 'push factors' shaped Muslim migration prior to the 1970s; the construction of the Mangla Dam near Mirpur in 1960, for example, forced many Mirpuri Muslims to make the journey to Britain. In the 1970s, however, such factors became more significant. The division of Cyprus in 1974 resulted in Turkish Cypriot Muslims settling in large numbers,[23] while Arabs from Syria, Iraq, Jordan and Egypt – especially affluent businesspeople and dissidents – sought to escape political instability. Despite this diversification, however, South Asian Muslims remained dominant, in large part because the implementation of 'Africanization' and nationalization policies in East Africa led to Asian elites living in states such as Kenya, Tanzania and Uganda being expelled. Large numbers of predominantly Gujarati Indians – mostly Hindus, but also many Muslims – settled in places such as Leicester, where they used their English and entrepreneurial skills to profoundly reshape that city's business and political landscape.[24]

By sheer weight of numbers, these South Asian migrants have come to define the character of Islam in Britain, with the modernist revivalism of Quilliam and others pushed to the margins. Censuses between 1951 and 2001 did not include a religion question. (Its reintroduction actually makes for an interesting story of Muslim campaigning, which I touch upon in Chapter 5.) Demographers have estimated, however, by applying 2001 religion data to the ethnic composition of previous censuses, that somewhere between nine hundred thousand to one million Muslims were living in Britain in 1991,[25] with South Asians comprising around 80 per cent of the British Muslim population at that point.[26]

Postcolonial community formation

South Asian traditions may have become dominant in Islamic Britain, but for South Asian and other Muslim migrants Islam was, initially at least, a background feature. Overwhelmingly, Muslim migration to the UK was not driven by 'religious' reasons – unless one counts those fleeing religious persecution – but by material need. Those who migrated to fill labour shortages usually saw Britain as only a temporary home and so felt little need to set down roots.[27] As we will see in Chapter 5, migrants from the Indian subcontinent were typically perceived in ethnic ('Asian') rather than religious ('Muslim') terms. South Asians' public struggles were mostly against racist harassment and lack of acceptance in organizations such as labour unions rather than for religious recognition.[28] Muslim belief was often less about personal piety and more about participation in communal life,[29] with the mosque being a refuge from a world that offered little esteem. For older migrants especially, religious buildings were places where the social status that they were used to in their country of birth could be maintained.[30] For all but a few personalities, *da'wah* was low on the agenda.

Gradually, though, religious transmission did become a concern and spurred localized campaigning. As the first generation of Muslim migrants' dreams of returning to their native country began to fade, they began to construct institutions and communities that would enable them to practice their faith as best they could and help them preserve their traditions for future generations. They made efforts to import their particular understanding of Islam into Britain – often literally, with imams being brought to the UK from overseas – and from the 1960s through into the 1970s and 1980s these forms of Islam became established. Mosques, and later *madrasah*s, were set up that reflected the particular linguistic and doctrinal character of their founders.[31] As Humayun Ansari has observed, Muslims who had initially grouped together formed into distinct groups:

> Previously ethnically mixed Muslim communities increasingly fragmented according to village-kinship, tribal, ethnic and sectarian affiliation. Indians, Yemenis and Turkish Cypriots who had lived together in boarding houses during and after the Second World War, sharing more or less the same religious facilities, gradually separated to form ethnic settlements that then established their own distinct institutions. Mosques and religious schools also reflected this process of segmentation, and imported religious functionaries reminded Muslims of their traditional values and reinforced conformity to embedded

practices. These Muslim communities, close-knit and relatively self-contained though often internally divided, became, as Fred Halliday has put it, 'urban villages' interacting with the broader society surrounding them in a selective fashion.[32] They were able to generate and sustain institutional infrastructures that embodied and perpetuated specific religious and cultural norms. What emerged at the end of the 1970s was a patchwork of communities, each impressing its particular national, ethnic, linguistic and doctrinal character on the organisations it had created.[33]

Needless to say, because the branches of the British Muslim family tree reach into almost every corner of the world it is impossible to describe all the varieties of Islam that emerged in the UK following the post-Second World War period of migration. There is, however, value in outlining some dominant traditions. Finding the right vocabulary to describe these can be taxing; often categories that English speakers consider to be dichotomous – such as 'traditionalist' and 'reformist' – can be applied equally to South Asian Islamic movements. This is, in part, a consequence of these movements' position in relation to British colonialism and the language of 'modernity' and 'progress' in which Western colonial endeavours were clothed. Here, I want to concentrate on what one might term *society-oriented* traditions, which tend to be less politicized, before discussing *state-oriented* revivalist movements – as well as some traditions that trace their roots to other parts of the world – later in the chapter. I want to introduce two specifically: the Deobandi and Barelvi traditions.

Barelvi Islam

The Barelvi and Deobandi traditions developed in mid-nineteenth-century India. Both were profoundly shaped – if not created – by the gradual incursion of the British into Indian institutional and intellectual life, in particular by the imposition of direct British control following the brutal suppression of the 1857 rebellion. Direct control had the effect of sharpening the previously blurred boundaries between Hindus and Muslims and of relegating religious authorities' influence to family law and religious education.[34] Accordingly, these movements focused on moral and cultural renewal.[35] In terms of numbers of followers, the former is the largest in Britain, followed by the latter. Barelvis follow a form of Sufi-inspired devotional Islam which was consolidated in Bareilly in northern India, after which the tradition is named. Bareilly was host to the tradition's founder, Maulana Ahmed Riza Khan (1856–1921), and remains the site of its best-known educational centre.[36] The Barelvi tradition is marked by devotional love of Muhammad: the Prophet is believed to predate creation and considered an emanation of God's light (a doctrine known as '*Noor-i Muhammad*').[37] This veneration is reflected in the Barelvis' preferred name for their tradition, the *Ahl al-Sunnat wa-al-Jama'at*, meaning 'people of the Prophetic path'. Mystical experience and intercession between layperson and God by minor saints (*wali*, usually translated as 'friend of God') and charismatic spiritual teachers (*pirs*) are both seen as acceptable, a tendency that goes against Deobandi orthodoxy as well as puritanical traditions such as Salafi-Wahhabism. In Britain, Barelvi groups are aligned with the Chishti, Naqshbandi and Qadiri Sufi orders. Cities such as Bradford have significant Barelvi communities, with eleven of the thirty mosques based there in the late 1980s being linked to the tradition.[38] Birmingham, too, has numerous Pakistani Barelvis, while nearby Nuneaton hosts the first – and thus far only – Sufi shrine in Western Europe, that of Pir Abdul Wahab Siddiqi (1942–1994).[39] In the UK, Barelvi mosques are often the most visible, being larger and centrally located.[40] Barelvi Islam is, however, a custom-laden folk tradition embedded among rural communities,[41] and so, in general, it is less institutionally developed in the UK than Deobandi Islam.

Deobandi Islam

The Deobandi movement is historically based on the teachings of the Dar al-Ulum Deoband in India, which was founded in the 1860s by a group of religious scholars (*'ulama*) who were committed to preserving Islamic scholarship and traditions at a time when the influence of the British placed these under threat. The founders' primary aim was to create centres for the study of Islam that would be independent of British and other aristocratic sources of patronage.[42] The movement is 'reformist' in the sense that it challenged South Asian Sufi customs and revised educational traditions. It is, though, also scripturalist, heavily emphasizing the authority of the Hanafi school of law,[43] the importance of 'imitating' a scholarly authority (*taqlid*) and the necessity of linking Islamic principles to scriptural proofs (*dalil*) found in the Qur'an and collections of *hadith*. This scripturalist orientation has led to it marginalizing previously influential South Asian traditions of philosophy, logic and literature and to the movement being regarded – especially by Barelvi and modernist opponents – as literalistic and puritanical.[44] This reputation is not altogether undeserved, yet in contrast to Islamist movements such as Jamaat-i-Islami, the Deobandi movement has tended to emphasize the importance of individual moral reform rather than reform of society or the state. Although it has shaped politics in Afghanistan and Pakistan (where it has fomented sectarian conflicts and influenced the Taliban: see Chapter 3), many strands are apolitical or even anti-political.[45] In the UK, this anti-political trend has become predominant,[46] partly due to the offshoot proselytizing movement Tablighi Jama'at, which has its European headquarters in Dewsbury in Yorkshire.[47] The Deobandi tradition is particularly strong in areas with large numbers of East African Asians, notably Leicester, as well as places such as Bolton and Blackburn. In contrast to the folk-oriented Barelvi tradition, the Deobandi movement, with its self-conscious focus on institutionalization, has been successful in establishing a sizeable network of *dar al-ulums* in locations across the UK, with a main centre near Bury, Greater Manchester.

Unsurprisingly given their theological differences, the Deobandi and Barelvi traditions have often conflicted in South Asia,[48] with each anathematizing the other in the early twentieth century.[49] Disputes between the two have occurred in the UK too, focusing on matters such as the legitimacy of celebrating the Prophet's birthday (*mawlid* or *milad*), which many Deobandi scholars have decried as a heretical 'innovation' (*bid'ah*).[50] Such contests can take the form of struggles over mosques[51] or in the creation of rival umbrella organizations (see Chapter 5). For example, the Mosques and Imams National Advisory Board (MINAB), an umbrella body established in 2006 with help from the Labour government, has been accused of excluding Deobandis from its Board.[52] These differences are usually manageable; in recent years especially the two traditions have learned to rub along in places like Bradford, where the leadership of the Bradford Council of Mosques alternates annually between Deobandi and Barelvi.[53] Even so, occasional low-level disputes still flare up.

Even if these traditions have existed in tension, however, they have also shared a trajectory in Britain, having gone through the same process of community formation. Both Deobandis and Barelvis – and indeed Muslims belonging to less well-represented traditions – created networks reaching across state lines that offered an alternative source of status and support to the British state and UK employment and education sectors. These established with the aim of facilitating religious and cultural transmission to those born in the UK with little experience of South Asia. Such networks existed separately from – and, as we will see in Chapter 5, in some tension with – politicized forms of ethnic minority activism, which drew on socialist traditions and focused on racial discrimination. Even if political strategizing was not a pre-eminent concern, though, as interest in the transmission and institutionalization of Islam grew localized political negotiation started to take place relating to state education[54] and planning permissions for religious and community infrastructure.[55]

Ethno-religious community: A safety net or spider's web?

Exploring this process of religious institutionalization reveals some hugely impressive stories of community mobilization. Early 'pioneer' religious leaders managed to raise hundreds of thousands of pounds to develop Islamic institutions, inspiring people whose financial and cultural capital was extremely limited. One such figure, Pir Maroof Hussain Shah (1936–), established bases in Sheffield and Oldham in the 1960s and led a network of Barelvi institutions in Bradford at the same time as earning a modest living working in textile mills.[56] Another, Yusuf Motala (1946–2019), facilitated the creation of the network of Deobandi educational institutions that forms the focus of Chapter 3. This mobilization was all the more impressive for being carried out in the face of fierce prejudices. In schools at the time, it was not unknown for Islam to be taught in terms of the 'fanaticism of the infidel'.[57] Councils, spurred on by local newspapers, often found spurious reasons to block mosque planning applications.[58] At the best of times, it is difficult to navigate planning law in the UK, which is full of arcane regulations. (Gaining planning consent is simpler if a building does not change purpose, for example, which is why many mosques occupy desacralized churches or disused synagogues, as in the case of the famous Brick Lane Mosque in East London.) Successfully navigating such a system when its intricacies are used vexatiously against you takes particular perseverance. It is a testament to first-generation migrants' resolve that they weathered such problems to establish places of worship that also provided wider social support.

At the same time, it is hard to deny that these community networks, in which religious, ethnic and cultural identification were all tied into one another, could act as a spider's web as well as a safety net. The first Muslim migrants, having successfully created their own infrastructures, often defended them possessively, meaning that young people and women became involved in intense micro-political contests over public recreational spaces.[59] Mosques have been guarded with particular care, often remaining completely inaccessible to women especially;[60] in 2009, a survey of 500 mosques indicated that just 46 per cent had any women's prayer facilities.[61] Beyond these institutions, community networks have played a similarly ambivalent role. Anthropologists and sociologists such as Pnina Werbner and Parveen Akhtar have skilfully mapped the way in which honour, patronage and a sense of moral community all work to hold ethno-religious communities together, impacting on public and private life.[62] Arranged marriage partners have often been chosen from within a specific community or extended kinship network, particularly within Bangladeshi and Pakistani families with strong rural ties.[63] We will see in Chapter 4 how, as overseas marriages have increased, sometimes intolerable pressures have been put upon younger Muslims, especially girls and young women. In the domain of local politics, too, South Asian kinship networks – or *biraderi*s, as they are termed in Urdu – have impacted on party loyalties. In the later decades of the twentieth century, such social bonds were sometimes utilized to create what Philip Lewis has termed 'ethnic vote banks' in places such as Bradford, Birmingham and Leicester, with the Labour Party typically being the beneficiary of such mobilizations.[64]

Parallel lives? Residential segregation and deprivation

In discussions about the challenges associated with British Muslim community formation, the subject that attracts the most public attention is what is commonly termed 'self-segregation', although that phrase is far too loaded to be of any real use. Residential clustering is a complex matter deserving extended consideration, not least because this will help us move out of the late twentieth century and towards the present day.

Most scholars of migration processes readily accept the reality of geographical clustering of British Muslim populations, as well as most other ethno-religious minorities. The historian Humayun Ansari, in his rigorous and highly sympathetic history of Muslims in Britain, observed that between 1981 and 1991 ethnic minority concentration of Pakistanis and Bangladeshis increased to the extent that some areas evolved into, as he put it, 'ghetto-like communities'.[65] The reasons behind these changes are, however, not all widely recognized, especially in popular

debates where residential clustering is usually regarded as a function of minorities'
unwillingness to become part of the mainstream. Certainly, the desire to live
among those of a similar ethnic and religious background plays a significant
role, as does the movement of white British people away from areas of Muslim
residential concentration (so-called 'white flight'). The availability of cheap
housing has played a major role as well, though: poor migrants tend to cluster
where they are able to afford property.[66] So, too, has racial discrimination – and
not just discrimination by white British against South Asian migrants, but also
Hindus and Muslims discriminating against one another.[67]

More than anything else, though, it is *age structure* that has determined changes
in ethno-religious residential concentration in the UK, especially more recently.
Because British Muslim (and especially Bangladeshi and Pakistani) populations
have a younger median age than the white British majority, they have what
demographers call 'age momentum'.[68] A greater proportion of the population is
at an earlier stage in life, meaning that more are yet to have children. This leads
to population growth even without additional factors such as migration or
larger family size. Contrary to what tends to be assumed in discussions about
ethic minority communities living 'parallel lives' – to use Ted Cantle's influential
phrase[69] – Muslim minorities in the UK have moved out from inner-city areas
as they have socially integrated and become more affluent. The effect of age
momentum has meant, however, that this has not always been large enough to
reduce residential concentration. So while there may be some truth to comments
about 'segregation' in certain places, the extent to which this is a matter of *choice*
by ethno-religious minorities is questionable.

Furthermore, there is a danger of this debate becoming stuck in the past. The
ethno-religious composition of Britain is not the same today as it was in 2001, with
shifts since the turn of the millennium prompting calls for a new way of viewing
ethno-religious diversity. Policymakers and journalists in Britain have become
used to describing ethnic minorities as discrete 'communities', generally from
former British colonies: Indians, Pakistanis, African-Caribbeans and so on. Even
the UK census is oriented around these familiar categories. In a hugely influential
article published in 2006, however, the sociologist Steven Vertovec showed how
this way of thinking is fast becoming outdated.[70] Rather than consisting mainly
of citizens of former colonies, migrants to the UK now identify with a vast range
of ethnicities: Turks, Iraqis, Syrians, Kurds and Somalis, among many others.
This shift is easily illustrated by comparing the 2001 and 2011 censuses.[71] The
South Asian and African-Caribbean populations of England and Wales increased
during this decade, albeit modestly in the latter's case (4 per cent). Other migrant
groups, however (which are lumped together into generic census categories),
grew exponentially. The 'African' population increased 100 per cent to 989,628
while 'Other Asian' increased 238 per cent to 835,720. Vertovec coined the term
'superdiversity' to describe this shift, and while this term is unfortunate in some
ways – it lends itself to celebratory accounts of ethnic plurality, and because of this
tends to obscure the brutal, racist reality of modern migration policies[72] – it does
describe an important social transition.

Table 2.1 Change in the ethnic composition of the Muslim population of England and Wales between 2001 and 2011 censuses

Census Year	2001		2011	
	No.	**Percentage**	**No.**	**Percentage**
White	179,409	11.6	210,620	7.8
Mixed	64,958	4.2	102,582	3.8
South Asian or Asian British	1,048,612	67.8	1,628,048	60.2
Other Asian	89,704	5.8	194,485	7.2
Black or black British	106,717	6.9	272,015	10.1
Chinese and Other ethnic groups	57,225	3.7	298,316	11.0
All Muslims	1,546,625	100	2,706,066	100

This, of course, has affected the composition of the British Muslim population (or better, populations). Between 2001 and 2011 the South Asian population decreased relative to African, Arab and other migrant groups (see Table 2.1). In the 2011 census of England and Wales,[73] 60.2 per cent of Muslims identified as South Asian heritage (38 per cent Pakistani, 15 per cent Bangladeshi and 7 per cent Indian) compared with 67.8 in 2001; 7.7 per cent were black-African, 6.6 per cent were Arab and 7.8 per cent were white.[74] Population growth has meant that residential concentration has increased in some parts of the UK, but, in general, outmigration has led to an overall decrease in Muslim residential clustering since 2001.[75] Undifferentiated statistics on the geographical concentration of British Muslims also, furthermore, mask increasing ethnic diversification. For instance, in the Spinney Hills ward of Leicester – the city's 'Muslim area' since the 1970s – Muslim residential concentration stayed almost static between the 2001 and 2011 censuses, at around 70 per cent Muslim.[76] Yet this figure masks an important transition from South Asian to Somali Muslims: the latter now make up 10 per cent of the population of some areas. Leicester's Somalis attend separate religious institutions and have somewhat uneasy relations with the South Asian Muslim populations.[77]

Relatively little is known about these smaller and less established populations of British Somalis, Kurds, Malaysians, Lebanese, Yemenis, Syrians and Turkish Cypriots, although we do know of some differences. For example, while established Muslim populations from South Asia have, over time, increasingly emphasized their religious – at the expense of ethnic – identities, Kurdish Muslims buck this trend, largely because of their distinctive status as a stateless ethnic group involved in struggles for autonomy and recognition in Iraq, Turkey and Syria. Although Kurds in Britain are highly religious by conventional measures of belief and practice, they identify in ethnic, more than religious, terms.[78] Each Muslim population group, then, needs to be treated on its own terms, but doing this is very difficult in practice. The 39.8 per cent of British Muslims that do not trace their heritage to South Asia are, as the list above suggests, extraordinarily ethnically diverse, making it impossible to describe all groups. This problem is compounded by the fact that there is a comparative lack of in-depth research into most of these communities.[79] This is a problem sociologists have started to recognize, however, and I want to use some recent research to introduce Britain's Shia communities, which have, as we will see in Chapter 3, made a significant contribution to British Islamic educational institutions in particular.

The 'Shia mile of London'

In all the countries of the Indian subcontinent, Shia Muslims are a (frequently embattled) minority.[80] Largely because of this, while demographers think there are more South Asian than Arab Shias in Britain,[81] the former attract less attention. The most prominent British Shia organizations derive from Middle Eastern movements and religious communities, especially those based in Iran and Iraq where Shia Muslims are in the majority and where major centres of religious authority are located. Census data fail to distinguish between Shia and Sunni, so it is impossible to give figures on what exactly the British Shia population looks like and where it is located. Almost all scholars agree, however, that the centre of British Shia life is Brent in north-west London.[82] Brent is among the most ethnically diverse areas of the UK, with only the London borough of Newham outranking it in ethnic diversity indices. Its Arab population is relatively small, with estimates putting the figure at 15,600, compared with 59,400 Indians and 54,400 white British.[83] Despite this, Brent is the hub for several contrasting Shia traditions, most linked with equivalents in Iraq.

The Iraqi population of Brent initially emerged in the 1970s and 1980s following the Arab nationalist Ba'athist Revolution of 1968 and, later, the coming-to-power of Saddam Hussein in 1979. Throughout the 1990s and 2000s, large numbers of Iraqi Shias arrived in Brent after fleeing the brutal suppression of the 1991 uprising against the Ba'athist regime and the 2003 war that led to the deposition of Hussein by the UK and the United States. Today, a constellation of lobbying, community and educational institutions are situated in the borough. The Al-Khoei Foundation acts as the quasi-official representative of mainstream Twelver Shi-ism; the Al-Hussaini Association follows a form of Shia Islam associated with southern Iraqi folklore; and the Rasool Al-Adham community centre acts as the centre of Brent's Shiraziyyin, a working-class movement aligned with a network of clerical families opposed to pre-eminent ayatollahs in both Iran and Iraq. According to the journalist Innes Bowen, the appeal of Islamism among the British Iraqi Shia population is limited, primarily because this population looks to the Najaf-based Ayatollah Ali al-Sistani for leadership rather than Ali Khamenei, the Supreme Leader of Iran.[84] Nevertheless, Brent is also host to Dar al-Islam, a Shia community centre that is sympathetic to the Iranian leadership and acts as the London base of the Hizb Al-Da'wa, the main Shia Islamist party in Iraq.[85] Political differences between these groups are fierce and are often expressed in ritual performance. The Shiraziyyin, for example, continue to practice self-flagellation during Ashura, the day on which Shia Muslims mark the martyrdom of Husayn, the son of Ali. (The term 'Shia' is abbreviated from '*Shiat Ali*', or 'partisans of Ali'.) This is done in defiance of *fatwas* opposing the practice by Iran's religious authorities, making it an expression of religious difference *and* opposition to the Iranian regime. It is one means by which Brent's urban environment has been, in Emanuelle Degli Esposti's words, 'sectarianised'.[86]

Economic development and disadvantage

The fact that such a broad array of traditions exists within just one comparatively small pocket of British Islam should make it clear that Muslims are not a group that fits easily into a single box. There is, however, one thing that can be said, to varying degrees, about almost all Muslim communities: they are deeply disadvantaged economically. One can, in fact, cite a long list of statistics about British Muslims' relatively high levels of deprivation and exclusion: 50 per cent of the British Muslim population lives in poverty, which is more than any other religious group and 32 percentage points higher than the UK population as a whole;[87] 46 per cent of the Muslim population of England lives in the most deprived 10 per cent of local authority districts. Just 15 per cent of Muslims own their home, compared with 31 per cent overall; 5.1 per cent of Muslims live in homeless shelters or temporary accommodation, compared with 2.2 per cent overall.[88] The proportion of long-term unemployed among working-age Muslim men is 10.3 per cent, compared with 4.3 per cent for non-Muslims. (For women, the difference is enormous: 38.6 per cent compared with 5.9 per cent, although this is heavily influenced by religio-cultural factors that I will discuss below.)[89] Muslims also suffer the greatest levels of disadvantage in the workplace of any minority group in the UK, especially in elite professions, with religious discrimination compounding the 'ethnic penalties' that all non-white groups face.[90]

Against this backdrop, it becomes easy to understand why, despite their undoubtedly much higher levels of religious commitment, *economic* issues top the list of Muslims' concerns not just in Britain but across Western Europe, ahead of extremism and religious decline.[91] Since settling, many Muslims' lives in Britain – especially after the country's manufacturing decline – have been marked by material struggles and struggles for equal opportunity. Muslim voters have, since their arrival, voted for left-liberal parties rather than social conservatives whose positions on issues such as marriage and the family have generally been closer to Muslims' views. In the 2010 general election, for example, 65.7 per cent of Muslims voted Labour and 17.4 per cent voted Liberal Democrat, while only 12.9 per cent voted Conservative.[92] This is, of course, partly due to the latter's history of hard-line stances on immigration and reluctance to support anti-discrimination legislation, as well as Labour's exploitation of patrilineal kinship networks. But it is also a reflection of numerous Muslim migrants' self-identification as, in the words of a Muslim Labour councillor I interviewed in 2011, 'labourers, fundamentally'.[93]

Without taking this disadvantage into account it is impossible to fully understand not only politics and patterns of residential concentration but also the nature of Muslims' religious expression. Few analyses of Muslims in the UK show any interest in how economic marginalization influences religiosity. When comparisons are made between Muslim populations in the UK and the United States, for example – even by thoughtful journalists and academics such as Sunny Hundal or José Casanova – the democratic cultures of the two nation states are typically posited as the primary reason for variations in religious expression.[94] The United States is more comfortable with hybrid identities and public religion, the argument goes. Therefore, despite anti-Muslim hostility being as bad – and maybe worse – in the United States than it is in Europe, the former country is better placed to 'integrate' Muslim migrants and isolate advocates for groups like ISIS. The differences identified between these two states and their Muslim populations are genuine: to take an example I discuss below, American Muslims seem less likely than their British co-religionists to express a preference for a state based on Islamic law.[95] What such analyses tend to bypass, however, is that America's Muslims are almost as likely as its non-Muslims to have a degree or household income of over $100,000.[96] Questions about integration need to be understood in this light: when religious minorities turn inwards – like Muslim migrants to the UK for whom the mosque was a place of refuge – this is often a matter of mutual dependence as much as it is religious commitment or communal loyalty.

Generational tensions and young religiosities

The claim that British Muslims are economically disadvantaged has purchase, then, but so too does the generalization that things are changing between generations. These changes between those who moved to the UK in the mid- to late decades of the twentieth century and those born in Britain, furthermore, do not impact just economic positioning but a whole host of social factors. Changes in family structure, for example, have been observed among South Asian Muslims as far back as 1997, with Pakistani and Bangladeshi families becoming smaller and arranged marriages less common.[97] Various social norms persist against this backdrop of social change: as we shall see in Chapter 4, among British Pakistani Muslims negotiating a marriage overseas remains a common option, complicating the very notion of 'first-generation' and 'second-generation' Muslims. Generally, however, such persistent norms exist in a context of vast shifts in economic, political and religious participation that have had huge impacts upon Muslims' lives, both positive and negative.

Let me take the unemployment rate among Muslim women, which I touched upon earlier, as a starting point. British Muslim women's high level of unemployment is a widely remarked upon phenomenon. The percentage not working is considerably higher for Muslim women than it is for other predominantly South Asian religions as well as for the general population. The figure of 38.6 per cent British Muslim women who have never worked or who are long-term unemployed from the 2011 census compares with a figure of 14.6 per cent for British Hindu women and 13.7 per cent for British Sikhs. There are a number of reasons for this, and many have little to do with religion. Bangladeshi and Pakistani Muslims typically originate from smaller rural communities of unskilled labourers, while many British Hindus, as we saw earlier, originate from an East African elite. Part of the variation, then, is ethnic: British Indian Muslims – both men and women – tend to perform better in the employment market than their Bangladeshi and Pakistani co-religionists, although not as well as their Hindu co-ethnics.[98] Alongside this, Muslim women have high levels of participation in informal labour (unpaid roles in family-run businesses, say),[99] and discrimination in workplaces affects Muslim women especially badly.[100] Religion is, of course, part of this story, but its precise role is not simple. Among British Muslim women, there is no clear link between strength of religious belief or frequency of practice and economic activity. Rather, what affects such activity is *family structure*, which is the product of a complex mix of ethno-religious social norms – the norm that Muslim women should not mix freely with men or that the man should be sole breadwinner – as well as class and education.[101]

What happens, then, when that structure is disrupted? What has become increasingly clear recently is that Muslim women born and raised within the British context are progressing into employment and indeed salariat positions.[102] Among the population of the UK as a whole, women's long-term unemployment rate decreases with age: the younger you are, the more likely you are to be out of work. At the time of the 2011 census, 6.8 per cent of women aged 16–24 in England and Wales were long-term unemployed, while among those aged 50–64 the same figure was 3.6 per cent. For Muslim women, however, this pattern is reversed: 17.7 per cent of those aged 16–24 were unemployed in 2011 compared with 54.6 per cent of those aged 50–64 (see Figure 2.1). These figures also do not take into account discrimination and deprivation; once these factors are controlled for, the difference in unemployment rates between Muslim and non-Muslim young women undoubtedly diminishes still further. One of the most striking illustrations of how changing family structure impacts upon economic outcomes for Muslim women can be found in Labour Force Survey data. These show that among women who are married, have children and no degree the difference in economic activity between white British Christians and Muslims is an enormous 55 per cent. Among women who are single, degree educated and have no children, though, the difference reduces sharply, to just 6 per cent (see Figure 2.2).[103]

These are, of course, positive changes, but they have thrown up numerous problems for families. As old norms struggle to keep up with new socio-economic realities, relationships can become almost impossible to negotiate, especially for women. As Olivier Roy has observed, the tensions between child and parent over marriage partners that I mentioned briefly above are a *product* of detraditionalization and generational change, with conflicts emerging as young people challenge social conventions.[104] There is also a growing cohort of professional British-born Muslim women who are single or divorced and finding it extremely difficult to find a partner – a situation the sociologist Fauzia Ahmad has dubbed the 'British Muslim relationship crisis'.[105] For the increasing number of high-achieving Muslim women, not only in the UK but in many Western contexts,[106] parental, family and social networks that once would have been relied

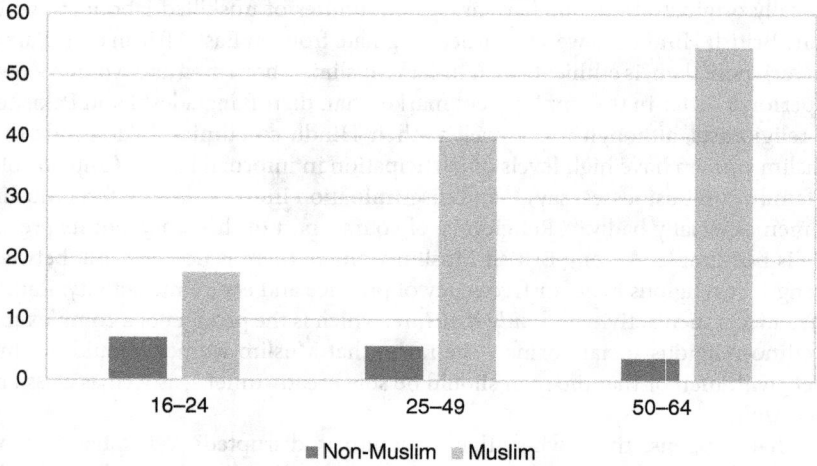

Figure 2.1 Percentage of women who are unemployed or who have never worked by age and religion (2011 census).

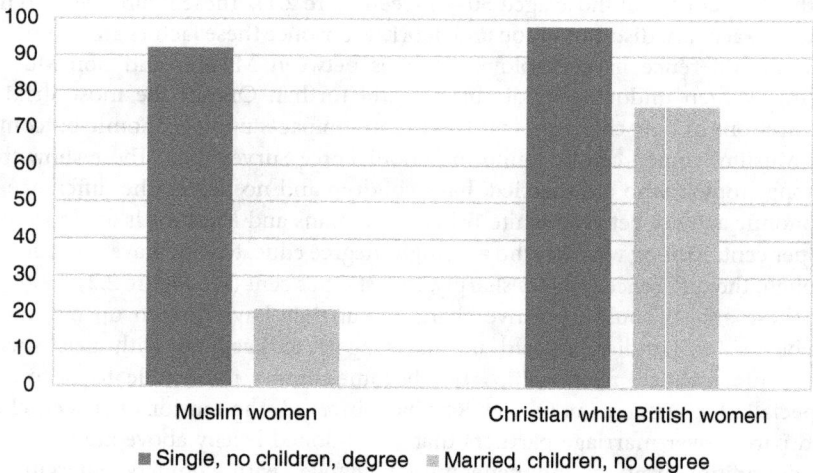

Figure 2.2 Percentage of women who are economically active by family/education status and religion (Labour Force Survey 2002–13).

upon as a resource for finding a marriage partner are failing. Where such networks are used, the 'match' can be unsuitable and marriage breakdown is increasingly the consequence (see Chapter 4). At the same time, many Muslim women still feel unable or unwilling to engage in 'dating culture' or to marry outside their faith or ethnic group. They can be perceived as 'no longer marriageable' once they have completed higher education and established a career foothold.[107] One response to these problems is the commercialization of marriage: professionally run Muslim marriage events and dating sites are rapidly increasing in size and number.[108] Even these services offer an imperfect solution, however. Commercial marriage services remain taboo, for some people at least. There is also a striking imbalance, particularly at events for those over 40. Men, Ahmad finds, generally find it easier to marry beyond kinship networks (frequently overseas) and their age is regarded as less of a barrier. Women therefore almost always outnumber men at Muslim marriage events; one example from Ahmad's research had 170 women to just 63 men. Remaking traditional frameworks in a 'post-traditional' context is then, for some at least, a difficult and painful process.

Religious interpretation is another area in which big differences between older and younger generations often emerge, and staying with the case of marriage allows us to illustrate what these look like. Reading ethnographic and interview research on young Muslims and marriage in Britain, one comes across countless examples of younger Muslims making criticisms of their parents supposedly getting 'religion and culture mixed up' or confusing 'the traditions of their little village with [Islam]'.[109] These narratives cut against the dominant portrayal of arranged marriage, which tends to depict conflicts between parents and children about the choice of a partner (especially extreme cases involving actual or threatened violence) as involving young people who are more 'Western' and 'modern' and older relatives who are more 'Islamic' and 'traditional'. Instead, what these accounts reveal is young Muslims drawing upon Islamic knowledge to contest inherited traditions, with the ultimate aim of allowing them greater control over their lives. Gradually, such contestations have moved British Muslim families away from a fixed notion of 'arranged' marriage and towards, in Ahmad's terminology, 'assisted marriage' and 'halal relationships'.[110]

Such differences within families can be seen as illustrative of a much broader shift in knowledge acquisition within Islamic Britain and indeed elsewhere. For younger Muslims, alternative sources of religious knowledge - accessed directly, usually in the medium of Arabic or English - have facilitated a reformulation of Islamic belief and identity.[111] While it is rare, at least outside of Salafi revivalist groups, for young Muslims to openly reject South Asian religious traditions such as Barelvi and Deobandi Islam, what is clear is the sense of disenfranchisement felt by the many young Muslims who claim British Islamic institutions do not serve their needs.[112] Within Islamic activist networks where - as we will see in Chapter 5 - younger Muslims have had more say, it is common to hear calls for Muslim self-education in order to challenge the religious leaderships that represent British Islam. The following comment, made by the activist Fatima Zohra during debate about women and Islam at a London-based university in 2008, is a helpful example:

> We need the confidence, and I believe that this comes through self-education. We are self-educated about our rights not just as Muslim women but as human beings, our rights in this country, our rights on this planet, then that enable us to go to the imam and say, 'Hold on'.[113]

Needless to say, these social changes are not unique to Muslims. Many synagogues and churches in the UK struggle to speak in a language that is appealing to young people. Research into British Sikhs has also found that fewer young people are actively attending Sikh temples (*gurdwaras*) and are instead seeking religious knowledge from other sources, online in particular.[114] Muslims are, however, the largest religious population in Britain that is predominantly composed of migrants and their (grand)children. They also originate from an extraordinary range of national contexts – a much wider range than any other religious tradition found in the UK. This means the challenge of religious transmission is particularly pronounced. Institutionalized Islamic traditions that are intertwined with particular ethnic cultures today sit awkwardly alongside the individualized styles of belief favoured by younger people. These styles of belief tend to be self-conscious and informed directly by scripture rather than being transmitted through culturally embedded rituals. They may disavow, downplay or even actively oppose ethno-cultural identification, preferring instead conscious affiliation with an 'unblemished' variety of Islam. Often, they focus on international politics and not local matters like the communal traditions that were established in the UK in the 1960s–80s.

With many young Muslims' religiosity being vocal and seemingly self-assured, observers often assume that the detraditionalization of Islam amounts to an Islamic 'revival' or 'resurgence'. Whether this assumption is correct is, however, far from clear. Among social scientists, one can find supporters both of this idea and of the opposite thesis that conventional patterns of secularization and acculturation apply.[115] In truth, both and neither sides of this debate are correct. Surveys of British Muslims clearly show – against the idea that young Muslims resolutely refuse to accommodate British cultural norms – that religious practice among young Muslims is lower than their parents, and inter-religious mixing is higher.[116] In that respect, Muslims seem to be secularizing in the same manner as the rest of the UK (and, importantly, living less segregated lives). This extends to young Muslims holding more liberal views about rights and citizenship. In polls, young Muslims tend to be more accepting than their parents of gay marriage, legal abortion, free mixing of genders and equality between sexes. Just under three-quarters support legal recognition of some kind for same-sex unions, for instance.[117] This is often ignored, however, because younger Muslims are also, despite their lower levels of religious *practice*, significantly more likely to emphasize religious *identity* than older Muslims. This extends to a larger percentage of young Muslims advocating '*Shari'a* law' than older Muslims, as well as supporting the idea of a 'global Caliphate'. Support among young Muslims for such ideas approaches 40 per cent in some surveys, suggesting that ideals popularized by Islamist movements have significant appeal.[118]

Making sense of this confusing and contradictory mix is not easy. Some scholars, like Justin Gest and Clive Field, are sympathetic to the idea that Britain's young Muslims are split between an increasingly liberal population and a small group who are alienated by, and opposed to, British society.[119] There is no doubt an element of truth to this, but it is perhaps not all of it. There are numerous qualitative indications that British-born and -raised Muslims do not just fall neatly into a 'liberal' majority and a 'radical' minority. As we will see in Chapter 5, Islamic youth networks, some with Islamist leanings, have appealed to young Muslims partly because they have been more accommodating of women than traditional community institutions, as well as more participatory and internet savvy.[120] Within these movements, and elsewhere in Islamic Britain, revivalism, literalism, liberalization and individualization can overlap, even coexist in one person. Like the rest of the UK population, young Muslims' political positions are often confused, inventive and sometimes incoherent. (Surveys, too, are not the reliable representational instrument they are often treated as: subtly different question framings can generate wildly different images of society, and questions about support for Islamic law are, as we will see in Chapter 4, often deeply flawed.) Yet, amid this confusion, it is just about possible to make out the image of a population that has been pushed by a range of factors – from endless negative media coverage of Muslims and Islam to far-reaching social and demographic changes – towards an assertive religious identity, even as it liberalizes in other respects.

Islamism and Muslim extremism

This is not to dismiss public worries about politically extreme Islamic movements and their appeal to young British Muslims, but it is to suggest that appearances can be deceptive and that the topic of extremism needs to be approached with caution. Many analyses of political extremism in the UK not only offer a clumsy portrait of the beliefs and characteristics of the British Muslim population but also shed very little light on the parties and movements that are described (sometimes with justification, sometimes not) as 'extremist', 'fundamentalist' or 'Islamist'. I want, then, to explore the last of these three terms now, which has been applied to a vast range of Islamic movements: Wahhabism, Salafism, Jamaat-i-Islami, the Muslim Brotherhood, Hizb ut-Tahrir, Ennahda, Al-Qaeda and ISIS, among many others. I will say a little about these movements and then about their influence in the UK and how they fit into the story of intergenerational transitions in Muslim Britain.

Perhaps the most important thing to say about the movements and organizations listed above is that they differ substantially both in their aims and in the means they regard as legitimate. They range from murderous militia groups (ISIS) to non-violent anti-democratic movements (the UK

arm of Hizb ut-Tahrir) to religio-political parties committed to change
via democratic means (Ennahda). Some even contain factions that are not
politicized: Salafism in the UK and elsewhere is, as Anabel Inge has shown,
host to conflicting pietistic and militant factions, with piety movements now
dominant in Britain.[121] Precisely because of this variety, using catch-all terms
like 'Islamist' involves a considerable risk of creating more confusion than it
clears. Many scholars, myself included, have reservations about the term and
some refuse to use it altogether. The main reason for this is that it is easily
inflated to cover *any* form of political activism or theorizing justified using an
Islamic vocabulary.[122] When interpreted like this, the term can be applied to
almost all Muslim civil society organizations, which has the effect of tainting
Muslim activism as inherently anti-democratic. We will see in Chapter 5 how
deep this problem is, but the term does still have some utility if it is defined
appropriately. Specifically, it remains a useful way of describing varieties of
politicized Islamic revivalism that emerged in the early to the mid-twentieth
century, growing out of globally significant geopolitical shifts and changes in
the nature of Islamic authority.[123] Islamism is a phenomenon made possible by
European colonialism and the crude division of much of the Arabic-speaking
world following the First World War and the collapse of the Ottoman Empire.[124]
Modernization and technological change, which eroded formal techniques of
knowledge transmission and authorization, have been crucial to its emergence,
creating the conditions for the growth of a range of related organizations that,
while often seeing themselves as part of a global 'Islamic movement', focused
their energies on the capture of state apparatuses.

Salafiyya

Of the movements above, Salafism stands out in its relationship to Islamism.
Certain Salafi groups – especially so-called 'Salafi-jihadi' groups like Al-Qaeda –
certainly fit with this understanding of Islamism, but in discussions of Islamic
activism in Britain these two terms are, for good reason, frequently treated as
separate (even competing) categories.[125] To make sense of the complex relationship
between Islamism and Salafism, I want to look briefly at the history of Salafi ideas
and the myriad ways they influenced Islamist, modernist and pietistic movements.
Salafism was initially popularized by Egyptian reformist and modernist thinkers
during the nineteenth and early twentieth centuries. In Egypt, Islamic reformist
thought developed as British influence in the country grew, with the British
occupation in 1882 marking a turning point. Early Egyptian reformists, like
Rafaʾa al-Tahtawi (1801–1873),[126] engaged with Western intellectual traditions in
a comparatively relaxed way because the European powers, in Albert Hourani's
words, 'had not yet become so great as to constitute the central problem of political
life.'[127] Later reformist thinkers, however, such as Muhammad ʿAbduh (1849–1905)
and Rashid Rida (1865–1935),[128] were forced to reckon with the brute fact of
colonial power alongside their engagement with European intellectual traditions
and technologies. (ʿAbduh, for example, was involved in the ʿUrabi revolt that

led to British occupation.)[129] Because of this, 'Abduh, Rida and many of their contemporaries were deeply ambivalent about the West. They were impressed by European sciences and were concerned that some Islamic traditions had hindered the development of the Islamic world, yet also portrayed Europe as a place of widespread hypocrisy and profligacy.

Wary of European power and dissatisfied with classical Islamic juristic frameworks, 'Abduh and Rida advocated thoroughgoing reformulation of Islamic intellectual traditions. While they drew from classical legal concepts and schools, placing emphasis on the importance of *maslaha* (public interest) in particular, they adopted an approach now familiar across Islamist movements, ignoring classical precedents when required and opposing the 'imitation' (*taqlid*) of scholarly authorities. 'The nations of the West will suffer from the troubles of their civilisation and its political decadence to such an extent that they will be forced to seek an outlet,' 'Abduh wrote. 'That outlet will be found only in Islam – the Islam of the Qur'an and the *Sunna* and not that of the theologians and jurists.'[130] 'Abduh, accordingly, helped to establish a reform movement called *Salafiyya*, the name of which referred to the 'predecessors' (*salaf*): the people living at the time of Muhammad and the two generations that followed him.[131] Echoing Protestants' use of the Bible in opposition to Catholic tradition and authority, this movement opened up the task of interpreting Islamic sources, and these interpretations went down several paths, largely reflecting ambivalences in 'Abduh's thinking.[132] On the one hand, intellectuals such as Ahmed Lutfi al-Sayyid (1872–1963) further liberalized 'Abduh's thought, eventually transforming it into an Egyptian nationalism in which Islam was less prominent.[133] On the other hand, Salafis shaped more directly by calls for Islamic reform and revival began to retreat into the past. 'Abduh was a modernist in many respects, but his ideas were extended by some of his supporters to emphasize the normative significance of the first generations of Muslims at the expense of historical contextualization and developments in practices and belief. 'Abduh inspired Islamic thinkers who idealized a lost age, reinterpreting it as a time of Islamic perfection and developing it into a model for a hoped-for Islamized society of the future.

The Muslim Brotherhood and Jamaat-i-Islami

Two individuals influenced by this latter line of thinking were Hassan al-Banna (1906–1949), who founded the Muslim Brotherhood (*al-Ikhwan al-Muslimun*) in Egypt, and Abu al-A'la Mawdudi (1903–1979), who established Jamaat-i-Islami ('Party of Islam') in what was then British India.[134] The impact of these two individuals has been immense, stretching far beyond their countries of birth. They endeavoured to rework the Islamic tradition into a social and political force, one geared towards resisting British colonialism in particular. There are significant differences between the two figures and the movements they inspired. Banna, for example, placed greater emphasis on bottom-up community organizing and moral reform, and the Muslim Brotherhood has, partly as a consequence, retained mass appeal across the decades.[135] Both, however, as Andrew March has recently shown, wove together a narrative of divine and popular sovereignty: Muslims were imagined as a single cohesive *umma* and Islam as a complete and total system oriented around the Qur'an.[136] They built movements committed to pan-Islamic ideals and, in their early years, paramilitary or Leninist methods, with Mawdudi in particular placing emphasis on a 'vanguard' that could implement 'the Islamization of society from above'. Over time, however, pragmatic considerations led to both movements becoming active in governments and elections across the Middle East and South Asia, with revolutionary tactics slowly giving way to a more gradualist approach.[137] Jamaat-i-Islami served General Zia-ul-Haq's military government in Pakistan in the 1970s and 1980s. After being severely repressed in the mid-twentieth century, the Muslim Brotherhood in Egypt briefly took power via democratic elections following the Arab Spring.

Within Sunni Muslim contexts, at least, it is these two organizations that stand out as the exemplars of 'Islamism' because of the scope of their intellectual and political impact. The Muslim Brotherhood has branches throughout the Middle East and spawned militant offshoots, notably Hamas, while Mawdudi's import as a thinker is undoubted. The reach of the two groups has meant that, although they have interacted and intersected with the Salafi movement, they stand independently of it. Jamaat-i-Islami and the Muslim Brotherhood are sometimes described as having, in Gilliat-Ray's words, 'departed somewhat from the original *salafiyya* vision by virtue of their often dominant political orientation'.[138] This is partly why 'Salafi' and 'Islamist' have come to be treated as separate, with the former referring to a scriptural method and the latter to a political orientation. Of course, the fact that both the Muslim Brotherhood and Jamaat-i-Islami have shifted between revolutionary, participatory and democratic politics contributes significantly to the confusion surrounding the term 'Islamist', with that confusion increasing markedly as one begins to factor in offshoot movements like the Muslim Brotherhood-inspired Tunisian party Ennahda, whose 'post-Islamist' orientation is loosely consistent with liberal political norms. Twentieth-century Islamist thinkers inspired brutal violence but at the same time – March argues – sowed the seeds for Islamic justifications for democratic politics. One thus has to be wary of assuming anything about what their followers believe.

Salafi-Wahhabism

There is another important twist in the tale of Salafi Islam and its relationship with Islamic politics, however. Today, the term 'Salafi' has been almost entirely emptied of modernist and reformist connotations in large part because in the twentieth century it came to be applied to an older revivalist movement: Wahhabism. The Wahhabi movement emerged in Arabia in the eighteenth century as a challenger to the theologies of the declining Ottoman Empire. The movement's intellectual figurehead and eponym, Muhammad ibn 'Abd-al-Wahhab (1703–1792), maintained that Ottoman Islam had become impure and that for the tradition to be restored it would have to be purged of the innovations (*bid'a*) that had crept into the religion, including mysticism, intercession and Greek rationalism. It was, and remains, a rigid, anti-intellectual movement that is disdainful of non-Muslims and indeed many Muslim traditions, notably all Shia branches of Islam. It became, however, hugely influential as Wahhabis formed an alliance first with the Al-Sa'ud family in 1744 (which wanted to defeat other contenders to rule Arabia) and then with the British government in 1915 (which wanted a strong power in the peninsula that would grant exclusive oil-mining concessions). Wahhabism remains influential today as the form of Islam given recognition in the Kingdom of Saudi Arabia.[139]

This has led to problems of perception. The Arabian Peninsula is where Muhammad lived; practising Muslims turn towards it in prayer five times a day. For that reason, it is easy to regard Saudi Arabia as the core of Islam, comparable to what Vatican City is for Catholics. In truth, until recently the region was – although obviously significant for Muslims – on the intellectual margins, in no way comparable to places such as Cairo or Istanbul. This is not immediately clear to non-specialists, however, so when grotesque reports emerge in the Western media of women being tried for adultery after being repeatedly raped, or of girls being left to burn to death in fires rather than being allowed out in public unveiled – both of which have occurred in Saudi Arabia in part due to the influence of Wahhabi ideas[140] – the immediate response among many is to see that as authorized by the highest Islamic authority. In reality, the Saudis' management of Mecca and Medina has caused enormous controversy. The marriage of puritan zeal and oil money in the kingdom has led to the destruction of historical sites including the homes of Muhammad's first wife, Khadijah, and his father in law and successor, Abu Bakr.[141] These demolitions are permitted by Saudi *'ulama* because of Wahhabism's official opposition to devotional shrines, which are believed to go against the idea that there should be no privileged mediators between humans and God. Instead, the skyline of Mecca has become dominated by shopping precincts and hotels such as the gargantuan Royal Clock Tower Hotel.

In the twentieth century, Wahhabism had a huge intellectual influence overseas too. For much of its history, Saudi Arabia has been viewed with suspicion by many Muslim-majority states. The country's long-standing alliance with Western powers and dependence on Islamic authority meant that during the Cold War the kingdom contrasted sharply with Arab nationalist states in which religious leaderships had been sidelined or co-opted.[142] Egypt under Nasser – which was aligned with the USSR and which brought religious authority, notably the venerated Al-Azhar University, under state control – was implacably opposed to the Saudis and even attempted to challenge their rule.[143] These political differences were compounded by the Wahhabis' rejection of various strands of Islam and their uncaring attitude to sites of Islamic significance. Wahhabism therefore needed to establish its credentials and win international support, and *Salafiyya* ideology provided a means of doing this. There are points of affinity between Wahhabi ideas and the *Salafiyya* movement. Rida, in particular, was sympathetic to the Wahhabis' preferred Hanbali *madhhab* and in later life welcomed the Saudi–Wahhabi conquest of the Hejaz.[144] These affinities were, however, cemented by a global campaign of Saudi proselytism, to the point where Salafism and Wahhabism became, in the words of the scholar of Islam Khaled Abou el Fadl, 'practically indistinguishable'.[145] Supported by Saudi oil money, Wahhabis, along with exiled Muslim Brotherhood supporters, set up institutions such as the Islamic University of Medina (1961), the Muslim World League (1962) and the Organisation of the Islamic Conference (1969) as a counterweight to Nasser's socialism. It has been estimated that Saudi spending on religious causes abroad was between two and three billion dollars a year from 1975 onwards, spent on publishing houses, mosques and Islamic schools, many located in the West.[146]

Islamism in the UK

It is beyond doubt that these efforts have had an enormous impact on Islamic knowledge production, although determining the extent and nature of it is hard. The predominantly pietistic Salafi organizations that exist in the UK look mainly to Saudi *'ulama* for guidance,[147] while militant Salafi-jihadi movements like Al-Qaeda and ISIS, although disowned by the Saudi elite, emerged out of a combination of Muslim Brotherhood and Wahhabi influences.[148] (Salafi Muslims themselves, I should note, typically reject the term 'Wahhabi' on the basis that they do not venerate 'Abd-al-Wahhab. As well as the term Salafi, they prefer *al-Muwahhidun*, or 'the Montheists'.)[149] Beyond self-identifying Salafi groups, mass investment in the dissemination of Salafi-Wahhabi teaching through publishing and the internet has also contributed towards a diffuse 'salafization' process, which has impacted upon a variety of Islamic traditions in the UK and elsewhere. Much Saudi support for religious institutions is, as Yahya Birt has observed, 'pretty benign' or even positive.[150] Saudi funding has supported some of the most prestigious Islamic study centres in the UK and the United States, from Edinburgh to Harvard, and some Saudi-funded UK institutions have moved in a liberal direction (as we shall see in later chapters). Even so, one can build a reasonable case that Salafi-Wahhabi funding has helped popularize radical views about, inter alia, the primacy of 'Islamic' over secular laws. I have myself heard complaints from British Muslim scholars of a 'recession' in some Islamic institutions from a 'relatively hospitable openness' to a 'closure of the Muslim mind'.[151]

The influence in the UK of some of the other revivalist movements listed above has been far more direct. As we will see in Chapter 5, from the 1960s through to the 1990s a varied, if at times deeply unpleasant, landscape of Islamic activist movements emerged in Britain, following competing trends associated with different forms of Islamic revivalism.[152] This happened in large part on college and university campuses, where Muslims in their teens and early twenties had become frustrated with Deobandi and Barelvi traditions and were thus beginning to disengage from the varieties of Islam practiced at home. Salafism was represented via the organization JIMAS (*Jam'iat Ihyaa Minhaaj Al-Sunnah*, or the 'Association to Revive the Way of the Messenger'), which was set up in 1984. Hizb ut-Tahrir ('Party of Liberation'), a transnational revivalist movement founded in Palestine in 1952 with the goal of establishing a global Caliphate, also gained a foothold. A UK branch was set up in 1986 and it quickly gained a reputation for combative opposition to democratic politics and giving a platform to antisemitic conspiracy theories. Hizb ut-Tahrir's most hard-line members, such as the notorious Omar Bakri Muhammad, then formed the splinter group Al-Muhajiroun, which, after its proscription in 2005, morphed into the successor organizations 'Al-Ghuraba', the 'Saved Sect'[153] and, most recently, 'Islam4UK'.[154]

Jamaat-i-Islami has had a particularly notable impact on British Muslim activist networks on account of its roots in South Asia. Some of the organization's most senior figures have been based in the UK,[155] and the disputed role of its leadership in the conflict that led to the separation of West and East Pakistan (now Bangladesh) in 1971 remains a point of fierce dispute, especially among British Bangladeshis. A number of the organizations that emerged on the Muslim activist scene in the later decades of the twentieth century were shaped by Jamaat-i-Islami in some way. In 1963, a group of students and young professionals set up the heavily Jamaati-influenced UK Islamic Mission (UKIM), with a youth wing, the Islamic Youth Movement, established in the 1970s. A Bengali-led offshoot organization, Dawat-ul-Islam, was set up in 1978, with an associated youth group, the Young Muslims Organisation (YMO). In 1984, the Islamic Youth Movement morphed into Young Muslims UK (YMUK), a group which maintained a national following throughout the 1980s and 1990s. These splits and shifts were generally the result of differences in personality, ethnicity and political loyalty. The creation of Young Muslims UK, for example, reflected growing unease with the UK Islamic Mission's unswerving loyalty to the founder of Jamaat-i-Islami, Mawdudi, as well as its atmosphere of puritanism and elitism.[156] Young Muslims UK allowed more open space for the discussion of questions directly relevant to British Muslim youth. Nevertheless, all these organizations retained the overarching goal of transforming Britain into a 'truly Islamic' society and state.

The fate of these organizations forms a supporting strut to the argument that I want to build over the coming chapters, notably Chapter 5. What is germane to this chapter, however, is their appeal within the UK context. Many Islamist movements, notably Jamaat-i-Islami, have attracted support primarily from devout middle classes based in urban regions, rather than rural areas.[157] This has left them better placed to attract literate, politically conscious young Muslims than the Deobandi and, especially, Barelvi traditions. In Britain, as we saw earlier, Jamaat-i-Islami-inspired groups have been more comfortable using English as the main medium of communication and have met in dedicated annual camps and groups often far removed from mosque life. They thus offered an escape, of sorts, from the parochial concerns of traditional religion. Their narratives of decline and Islamic revival attracted individuals who felt uprooted and treated as dangerous interlopers. Many former members and affiliates of groups such as Hizb, JIMAS and Young Muslims UK have acknowledged that the 'purity' of the revivalist message offered an appealing contrast to the impenetrable traditions of mosque and home.[158] Hassan Saleemi, for example, a former Islamist who recently worked for the Islam Channel, was drawn as a young man to Hizb ut-Tahrir after being caught between a rock (the stifling culture of his local mosque) and a hard place (the xenophobic context of 1980s England):

By the age of eighteen – with the unearthing of Public Enemy, who were talking about 'fight the power', imperialism and slavery – I was unhappy with Pakistani Asian culture, I was unhappy with British culture and I was not happy with the sectarianism in my local mosque. I felt alienated from Muslims and I had some grounding in colonialism. I had a history GCSE and was doing a history A-Level as well, so I knew a bit about colonialism … and … Bosnia …. And [then] there was a tall white guy outside my mosque talking about Bosnia and Kashmir, and giving out leaflets – and the fact that he was white struck me. I attended the talk, and you could say that the rest is history.[159]

Even if Islamist revivalism has often stressed the need to return to a 'pure' form of Islam, what this quote highlights – with its references to 1980s US hip-hop acts – is how syncretic Islamic activism in the West has been in practice. Indeed, Islamist revivalism, while looking to the past, has always been a thoroughly 'modern' phenomenon. Islamist extremism conflicts with the conservative tendencies of classical Sunni legal thinkers, most of whom were implacably opposed to revolutionary politics.[160] It has therefore often turned to the militant left for ideas – the idea of the vanguard in particular.[161] In addition, what becomes clear when one examines British Muslim activist movements is that, no matter how abrasive and uncompromising they may have been, they were almost always influenced by the very Western trends that groups such as Hizb ut-Tahrir loved to hate. Male members of JIMAS, for instance, became conspicuous in the 1990s for combining Saudi-style headgear with army fatigues and boots: not exactly a diligent replication of the Prophet and his Companions![162] As Olivier Roy has observed, what starts out as a search for religious 'purity' often ends in that most 'Western' of tendencies: self-definition through careful attention to style.[163] This is perhaps part of the explanation behind the curious mix of opinions young British Muslims have, which we observed earlier. While some British Muslims have become involved in sloganeering about a global Islamic renewal, few have managed to elude Europe's hyper-commercial, individualistic social norms completely.

Beyond myth-busting: Or, British Islam in middle age?

At the start of this chapter, I referred to a collection of texts typically referred to as the 'Eurabia literature'. This literature is typified by – indeed, bases its arguments on – two linked assumptions. The first is that 'Islam' and 'the West' represent two distinct, internally coherent and incompatible cultural formations. The second is that the former of these formations is resistant to change: that Islam and the civilizations influenced by it are marked by unchanging cultural norms. The 2001 attacks on the World Trade Centre in New York can, on this reading, be regarded as the results of those formations colliding, like two tectonic plates. Indeed, pretty much every wrong committed by a Muslim – from domestic abuse to civil unrest – can be viewed as caused ultimately by a profound pressure generated as Islam becomes more significant in Europe, a medieval peg gradually being driven into a modern, secular hole.

Armed with the information laid out in this chapter, taking apart these assumptions is a simple task. Let's take one example to illustrate, authored not by a far-right prophet of Europe's doom but by the British government. Under the Liberal Democrat–Conservative coalition government of 2010–15, a new strategy to address extremism was developed by the then UK home secretary and future prime minister, Theresa May.[164] Initially developed in 2011, this was expanded in 2015 to include proposals to bar 'non-violent extremists' from broadcast media and university campuses and to review '*Shari'a* councils' in the UK ostensibly to assess their impact on rights and cohesion. I will leave it to later chapters to analyse different components of this strategy in more detail, but what is worth dwelling on now is the way it conflated different facets of British Islam. The presence of 'non-violent extremists' on university campuses is a problem[165] associated with the Islamist revivalisms that have tended to appeal to younger Muslims. By contrast, British '*Shari'a* councils' are, as we will see in Chapter 4, part of the communal infrastructures established by the first generation of Muslim migrants. The leaders of these institutions have absolutely nothing to do with – indeed, are deeply hostile to – Al-Muhajiroun and other provocateurs who advocate for the total application of '*Shari'a*' in the UK. That the UK's political leaders happily amalgamated these opposed strands of Islam into a single whole is a testament to how widespread the stereotyped view of Islam as a monolith is and how often people view extremism as grounded in a commitment to Islamic traditions rather than as a modern phenomenon.

What we have covered here, however, is not sufficient to correct another simplistic stereotype. Emphasizing this generational division often lends itself to a portrayal of Muslim Britain as a setting within which a committed and well-established constellation of Islamist institutions is able to operate with impunity, taking advantage of a dilapidated and inward-looking communal infrastructure to win over an alienated younger demographic. Sociologists sometimes reinforce this by embedding a strong distinction between older and younger generations into their research methods, with survey analysis – as we have seen – concentrating on the differences between those aged from 18 to 30 and those over 30.[166] A vast literature has been dedicated to profiling the figure of the 'young British Muslim': five UK-focused books have been published with some variation on this title since 2007.[167] When done well, this research is entirely justified, especially as there is clearly significant elements of truth to the narrative of a break between younger and older generations. Increasingly, though, this narrative looks tired. It emerged in the early 2000s out of the shadows cast by September 11 and disturbances involving predominantly Muslim young people in Bradford, Burnley and Oldham in 2001. The people who took part in those disturbances are now, however, around 40 – and therein lies the problem. We may now be past the point where half of Muslims in the UK were born in the UK. (In 2011, the figure was 47.2 per cent.)[168] The attention given to young people masks the fact that significant numbers of Muslims who were born in Britain are now established in their careers and some are beginning to move into senior or leadership roles – some in Muslim civil society and activist organizations, others in 'regular' professions such as universities, schools, hospitals, banks and legal partnerships. Aside from a few exceptional publications,[169] most discussions of UK Muslims do not recognize this, instead working from the template of older, foreign-born Muslims and UK-born youth.

This means, in turn, that the *impacts* of these demographic changes have seldom been accounted for. There is a stereotype of Muslim representative organizations as dilapidated entities led by older, invariably male individuals born overseas, for example. But does this stereotype still hold true? What changes are we seeing, as British Islam moves into middle age? Are the Islamic educational institutions established to transmit South Asian traditions of Islam still doing so, untouched by emerging religious leaderships? Have the Islamist networks that emerged and flourished across the British Muslim activist scene across the 1980s and 1990s remained consistent in their far-reaching political goals? These are the questions to which I now want to turn. Exploring them will reveal an important story about how operating in liberal democratic structures has impacted on Islamic institutions, and this in turn will allow us to consider where Islam sits within liberalism and how liberal states should respond.

Chapter 3

ISLAMIC EDUCATION: SCHOOLING FOR *NAQL*-HEADS?

A lesson in alienation?

Over its history, the Islamic tradition, much like its Jewish and Christian siblings, has witnessed various debates about the importance of reason relative to the authority of scripture and tradition. Probably the most famous of these were the contests that took place during the time of the Abbasid Dynasty (CE 750–1258) over what ancient Greek philosophy could teach Muslims about morality, politics and God. The intellectual heavyweights of the medieval Islamic world, Ibn Sina (aka, Avicenna, d. 1037), Al-Ghazali (aka Algazel, d. 1111) and Ibn Rushd (aka, Averroes, d. 1198), differed fiercely on the status of the Greek thinkers, with each of these individuals seeing his predecessor's position as incoherent and even heretical (*kufr*).[1] In Islamic law, too, there have been long-standing debates about the importance of independent reasoning (*ijtihad*) in determining legal principles relative to the accepted sources of scriptural authority, the Qur'an and *Sunnah* (Prophetic example), and scholarly consensus (*ijma'*).[2] It is often claimed – sometimes as part of an argument about Islam's supposed resistance to modernity[3] – that around the ninth century CE Islamic jurists (*faqihs*) came to a consensus that all essential questions about Islamic law had been settled and that it was thus time to 'close the gates of *ijtihad*' (*insidad bab al-ijtihad*). Whether such a closure ever took place is up for debate, however;[4] and even if it did, the gates have since been broken open again by modernist and Salafi movements, as well as the proliferation of new media and communication technologies that allow everyone unlimited access to 'Sheikh Google'.[5]

Islamic education – the subject of this chapter – has featured comparable discussions, with Islam in South Asia offering a helpful illustration. Islamic education in the Indian subcontinent traditionally follows a curriculum established by a dynasty of scholars based at Farangi Mahall, an institution founded in Lucknow in 1695 and influenced heavily by Persian sources.[6] This curriculum is divided into two branches: *manqulat*, which refers to the formalized techniques of exegesis that are included within the traditional Islamic sciences; and *ma'qulat*, which refers to rational sciences such as philosophy, grammar and logic. These terms are, respectively, cognates of *naql*, to 'transmit', and *aql*, 'reason' or 'rationality'. Originally, Farangi Mahall's teaching prized *ma'qulat* as a basic grounding for anyone considering the study of religious texts, but this has often been threatened. The capture of Delhi by Nadir Shah in 1739, around the time the scholars of Farangi Mahall were formalizing their teachings, prompted some of South Asia's most esteemed religious scholars to argue for the reassertion of teaching methods based on rote learning. This meant sidelining *ma'qulat*, which was seen not as necessary grounding for study but, rather, as a source of confusion and deviation from Islam's revealed truths.[7]

Although this example is distant, geographically and temporally, from present-day Britain, it is nevertheless highly relevant to recent debates about British Islam. In the UK, journalists and politicians have popularized a narrative that claims British Muslims are being badly served by Islamic educational institutions and, in turn, the religious leaders trained in them: people who are supposedly capable of transmitting texts (often in a foreign tongue) but unable to equip students with the interpretive tools necessary to connect with public life in the UK and address its problems.[8] This, they claim, encourages young Muslims' alienation from British society, leaving them unable to access jobs and consequently vulnerable to religious extremists. UK-based centres of Islamic higher learning – known, depending on denomination, as *hawzas*, *jamias* or *dar al-ulum*s – are portrayed as isolated from British culture and doing little more than churning out what the American Islamic scholar Hamza Yusuf calls 'naql-heads': people who know the texts but cannot use their minds to engage with contemporary social questions.[9] Rarely are these critiques knowledgeable enough about Islamic history to talk in terms of the concepts above, but they actually involve a claim about teaching in institutions most of whose history can be traced directly to the scholars of Farangi Mahall.

This narrative of rigid teaching and alienated students is what I intend to analyse and evaluate in this chapter. In it, I introduce a range of Islamic educational institutions that can be found in the UK, providing detail about their background and sectarian influences. I focus primarily on institutions offering education at further and higher levels – typically in some kind of combination with traditional Islamic education – rather than schools catering for under 16s. I will look at what these institutions offer, the challenges they face and what is being done to address these challenges, including internal reforms and the foundation of distinctive centres. In keeping with the overarching thesis of this book, what I want to show is that there has been a gradual change in Islamic higher learning. I will try to give the reader a sense of a reorientation that has been going on in Islamic education in recent years (or better, decades). This includes a range of disparate examples, from institutions that have moved slowly away from their original countercultural ethos to the emergence of a distinctive class of 'Muslim chaplains' that has no parallel in the Middle East or the Indian subcontinent. There is a similar tendency, I argue, across these examples towards in-depth engagement with British society and institutions.

As with the other domains that I focus upon in this book, the British government has been a significant actor in the sphere of Islamic education, although its actions have not always been helpful. The UK government has funded several research projects investigating the state of Islamic higher learning in the UK (sources on which I rely extensively in this chapter, I should note). It has set up several practical initiatives, including training courses for imams and the prioritization of Islamic studies in English higher education. There has also been growing discussion about the possibility of linking *dar al-ulum*s with publicly funded universities and colleges in the UK. In this chapter, while I dispute the idea that these manoeuvres by UK governments are the *main* source of the changes I describe, I outline these policy developments and how they have pushed British Islamic education in particular directions.

In doing this, I touch upon what the political theorist Kwame Anthony Appiah terms *soul making*.[10] As the state has taken a more direct role in influencing knowledge production within Islamic institutions, it has raised complex questions about how governments should shape their citizens' religious identities. Liberals tend to think people ought to be left alone to work out what they believe and that state involvement in religious or non-religious instruction cannot therefore be justified. This argument has, however, repeatedly been challenged in practice by the presence of state funding for religious institutions and in theory by those who emphasize that we cannot *fully* be the authors of our own beliefs, just as we speak and write in languages we didn't make up.[11] Here, I cautiously defend the idea of state engagement with religious educational centres. There have been a series of important transitions within Islamic education, and, I suggest, these transitions are something that the state should support. As we will see, I am fundamentally opposed to governments trying to craft a 'liberal Islam' through state-led transformation of Muslim institutions, for a whole variety of reasons. Nevertheless, I do want to argue in favour of the state providing the *tools* that allow people to build more reflective forms of religious faith. This, I argue, implies a challenge not just to inflexible forms of secularism but also to the dominant ethic of marketization in English education (especially higher education) policy.

The emergence of Islamic education in Britain

As we saw in the last chapter, while proselytism was not a priority for Muslim migrants to the UK, transmission of traditions to offspring certainly was. In keeping with this, one of the earliest points of focus for localized Muslim political activism was education policy; the Muslim Educational Trust (MET), set up in 1966, was among the first national-level Muslim lobbying organizations.[12] Small Islamic study circles and supplementary schools – known in the UK as *madrasahs*, although this word has a broader meaning elsewhere – were soon set up once Muslims settled in sufficient numbers. Larger centres offering formalized pre- and post-16 education in the traditional Islamic sciences emerged shortly after, with one of the functions of these institutions being to train religious scholars, or *'ulama* (literally, 'those with knowledge'; singular, *'alim/'alimah*). Estimates of the number of such institutions vary. One 2010 survey carried out by Alison Scott-Bauman and

Mohamed Mukadam suggested that thirty-eight Islamic educational institutions are in operation in the UK providing faith leadership training alongside general secondary level, and in some cases further, education.[13] They also identified fifteen institutions that offer theological and faith leadership training just at further and higher levels.[14] Their list is not exhaustive, however, and the precise number is hard to determine.[15] Across the centres they name that were set up to offer leadership training, just one – Darul Uloom al-Arabiya al-Islamiya, the pre-eminent Deobandi centre of learning in the UK – was established in the 1970s. Four more were set up in the 1980s before the 1990s saw rapid expansion, with at least twenty new centres being set up to provide religious training. Since 2000, growth has continued but at a reduced rate, with fourteen institutions established until 2010.

Among these institutions, almost all the Islamic traditions that have a significant presence in Britain are represented. Barelvis in Britain have established a number of schools and one or two centres for higher level training of male and female 'ulama, such as Hijaz College in Nuneaton and Jamia Al-Karam based in Eaton, Nottinghamshire. Barelvis also make up a substantial portion of the student body of two other educational centres, The Muslim College in Ealing, London, and Cambridge Muslim College in Cambridge, both of which I will discuss later in the chapter. Shia Muslims, although in the minority in Britain, are catered for by institutions such as The Islamic College, founded in 1998 in Willesden, London; the liberal Al-Mahdi Institute, founded in Selly Oak, Birmingham, in 1993; and the Institute of Ismaili Studies, a well-established Isma'ili (as the name suggests) Shia institution that was set up in 1977. British Shia institutions, as we will see, have had particular success in gaining accreditation and forming alliances with secular institutions. Politicized movements such as the Muslim Brotherhood and Jamaat-i-Islami have also had an impact on the institutional landscape of Britain, although the extent of these movements' influence in recent times is disputed (again, something I will discuss later).

It is the Deobandi tradition, however, that has had the most success in establishing Islamic educational institutions in the UK. In an older 2003 survey of Islamic educational institutions – this time listing religious affiliation – sixteen of twenty-three were identified as Deobandi.[16] The figure has grown since to at least around twenty-two Deobandi *dar al-ulum*s,[17] some formally aligned with Darul Uloom al-Arabiya al-Islamiya, others independent. Although more Muslims in Britain are raised in the Barelvi than the Deobandi tradition, those who pioneered the institutionalization of Barelvi Islam in Britain tended to place greater emphasis on the preservation of community languages than the development of religious leaderships and institutions to train them. In part, this reflects differences between the traditions themselves. Barelvi Islam is oriented around customary folk traditions of devotional Sufi ritual. Deobandi Islam, by contrast, developed with the central purpose of defending and preserving authentic religious belief and practice, and the establishment of self-sustaining seminaries has long been seen as vital to this mission. Accordingly, it has been estimated that around 80 per cent of the roughly 140 students graduating from 'alim courses in Britain each year are schooled in Deobandi institutions. Students looking to study in Barelvi-influenced institutions are more likely to travel abroad.[18]

Given the breadth of the network, Deobandi institutions would seem the obvious main point of focus for a chapter on private Islamic educational institutions in the UK. I want now, then, to build on the previous chapter and say a little more about the development of this tradition.

Ideological roots: *The Deobandi* dar al-ulums *of South Asia*

We saw in Chapter 2 that the Deobandi tradition formed directly in response to British rule in India, with the new movement arising, in Ron Geaves's words, 'out of long-term concerns with the consequences of the loss of Muslim power and a more short-term reaction to the failure of the 1857 uprising'.[19] With Western education increasingly becoming the established route to positions of influence in British India, and Muslim law's purview being restricted to the family sphere, Deobandis felt a need to shore up the Islamic tradition to prevent it dwindling into insignificance. The early Deobandi leaders thus sought to erect symbolic and institutional bulwarks against external interference, meaning the movement acquired an insular and oppositional ethos.[20] The Deobandi tradition was a product of processes of modernization. Even in its early days, the movement was 'modern' in the sense that it utilized mass education and communication technologies as a means of religious formation and community building. Its disavowal of intercession by saints and emphasis on individual self-reliance also implied a form of 'disenchantment', in the classic Weberian sense.[21] Yet, despite adopting some of the bureaucratic methods used by the British, the movement defined itself in opposition to the British and whatever they stood for. Of course, Britain's representatives in India felt that their nation epitomized modernity and progress, so Deobandi institutions accordingly developed certain anti-modern tendencies. One of the tradition's most important early personalities, Ashraf 'Ali Thanawi (d. 1943) – the author of the hugely influential manual on women's conduct, *Bahishti Zewar* (*Heavenly Ornaments*) – placed 'modern' emphasis on reform of the self but nevertheless argued that 'to like and appreciate the customs of the infidels' was inherently sinful.[22] Deobandi *'ulama* stood opposed to many Indian and Pakistani modernists, such as the renowned science education advocate and supporter of British rule Sir Syed Ahmed Khan (d. 1898)[23] and Fazlur Rahman (d. 1988), who directed the Pakistani government-backed Central Institute of Islamic Research in Karachi in the 1960s.[24] Although some varieties of Deobandi Islam remain heavily influenced by Sufi traditions, the movement's oppositional ethos extended to fierce arguments against South Asian shrine culture (whence much of the movement's antipathy towards Barelvi Islam).

The tradition has impacted on the politics of the Indian subcontinent in a variety of ways, with religious leaders lending their support to noble as well as unsavoury causes. Prior to Partition, some Deobandis agitated for the end of British rule, with numerous senior figures being arrested during the First World

War for supporting the Ottomans.[25] Hard-line Deobandi *'ulama* were also central to the successful demand for the constitutional declaration of Pakistan as an Islamic state.[26] Since independence, Deobandis have pushed for several legal measures against religious minorities. Deobandi institutions in Pakistan were involved in successful campaigns for a constitutional amendment defining the country's Ahmadis as non-Muslims and for legislation preventing this minority group from using Islamic symbols in religious practice.[27] Some Deobandi *dar al-ulums*, such as the Jami'at al-Ulum al-Islamiyya in Karachi, have been heavily involved in anti-Shia lobbying too, including similar (though so far unsuccessful) calls for state excommunication. Most concerning for British and American authorities, some Deobandi institutions, especially those based in the Khyber Pakhtunkhwa province (KP, formerly the North-West Frontier Province), have also acted as sources of refuge for fighters in the Taliban's military operations in Afghanistan, both against the Soviet Union in the 1980s and against the United States today.[28]

Despite this, it is unhelpful to describe Deobandi Islam as an 'Islamist' movement. In India, the Deobandis have coexisted more amicably, readily accepting the notion of a 'composite nationalism'.[29] Even in Pakistan, sectarian activism has been limited to certain personalities and institutions. Most importantly, in contrast to Islamist movements Deobandi Islam has, from its founding onwards, focused primarily on personal moral reform rather than concentrating its energies on the state – an emphasis that is especially prominent in the offshoot missionary movement, Tablighi Jamaat. Consequently, while there is antipathy towards 'the West' across many Deobandi institutions, 'the West' tends to be seen, as Jonathan Birt and Philip Lewis observe, 'as a source of corruption to Muslim individuals rather than a supranational entity to be resisted through collective political action'.[30] For many Deobandis, the central aim is not to take political control but simply to maintain a constant faith and Islamic lifestyle even in difficult contexts. This is especially the case in Britain, where the largest Deobandi *dar al-ulum*s have significant ties with the Mazahirul Uloom of Saharanpur (est. 1867) in Uttar Pradesh, North India, which is marked by pietist and anti-political tendencies. Politicized varieties of Deobandi Islam have had an impact in the UK, with pockets of support for the Taliban and militant Kashmiri groups emerging during the 1990s, but this has been limited.[31]

In 2008 Geaves, after some extraordinarily elaborate negotiations with senior Deobandi *'ulama*,[32] was permitted access to Indian seminaries for research purposes, giving a fascinating insight into what the Deobandis' strategy of oppositional isolation means in practical terms today. He spoke to fifty-seven religious leaders in twenty-seven institutions in Gujarat, uncovering, among other things, how some Deobandi educators are also significant players in diasporic networks, visiting South Africa, Canada and, unsurprisingly, Britain. What stood out in his research was the way his interviewees talked about *culture*. Many of the *'ulama* characterized the primary purpose of Deobandi education as being to promote 'Muslim culture' and prevent 'Westernization'. When Geaves asked the interviewees what exactly this meant, the responses were revealing:

Muslim culture was described to us primarily in terms of appearance, that is, the significance of the beard and even prescriptions on how high above the ankle trouser legs should end. Western dress was described as 'the cloth of the transgressor', so that even the clothing of the West was associated with 'sin' ....
Many of the books written by Deobandi *'ulama* and sold in Deobandi bookshops deal with 'Islamic ways' and include rules that should be observed when setting off on a journey, the regulations that should be followed when having sex, how to use a mobile phone correctly, and the rewards offered in paradise for those who use a toothpick or maintain the correct style of beard.[33]

What is striking about this list of rules is how far it is – with its self-conscious attention to clothing style and commentary on mobile phone use – from what we might think of as pre-modern tradition. Indeed, this very emphasis on 'culture' involves a concession of sorts to Western modernity. The mapping of 'races' and 'cultures' was, of course, a central feature of Western colonialism, but this mapping had the unintentional effect of facilitating what Marshall Sahlins[34] calls 'cultural self-consciousness': the notion that one belongs to a 'culture' that is distinctive and that has value. 'Among the most successful Western cultural imports,' Appiah comments, 'has been the concept of culture itself.'[35] Deobandi leaders worry about the dominance of 'Western culture', but in proposing 'Muslim culture' as its antithesis they ultimately follow postcolonial trends, borrowing concepts from their perceived adversary.

The fact that the Deobandi tradition has adopted certain 'modern' ideas does not make it any simpler to transplant its educational institutions into Britain, however. Deobandi *dar al-ulum*s vary greatly in their outlooks, but the desire to preserve a tradition and protect it from external influence – especially 'Western' interference – is widely felt. Even sympathetic researchers such as Geaves recognize the significant challenges of incorporating the tradition in British cultural and institutional life. One of the most fundamental of these relates to the curriculum taught within Deobandi *dar al-ulum*s. Within the Indian subcontinent, the dominant curriculum used in Islamic education is descended directly from the Farangi Mahall scholars mentioned at the start of this chapter and is known as *Dars-i Nizami*. *Dars-i Nizami* is named after Mulla Nizam al-Din Muhammad (d. 1748), a Lucknow scholar who supposedly played a role in the formalization of Farangi Mahall teachings.[36] In its early forms, it incorporated a rich set of teachings encompassing the study of logic and philosophy alongside traditional Islamic sciences such as *tafsir*, *hadith* and *fiqh*. It placed emphasis on the historical contextualization of religious texts, so the transmission of traditions could be done in a rounded way. In the context of the late Mughal Empire, this relatively fluid body of teachings was well-regarded and extremely useful to Indian Muslim elites who sought prestigious official positions.

Both Barelvi and Deobandi movements adopted the *Dars-i Nizami* and indeed still use it. The curriculum has, however, changed over time. By the late nineteenth century the last Mughal rulers had been deposed and the demand for Farangi Mahall education had collapsed as a result. Among the revivalist traditions that maintained *Dars-i Nizami*, Barelvi Islam followed an older, Persianate tradition – something still reflected in the teachings of Hijaz College.[37] In Deobandi contexts, however, *ma'qulat* was thinned down and the study of religious texts became more fundamental. As the *Dars-i Nizami* became fully standardized as the basis for Deobandi education – a process that, again, is thought to have been prompted by the roll-out of British educational models in India[38] – historical contextualization also fell by the wayside, leaving an etiolated form of the Lucknow syllabus taught to aspiring Deobandi *'ulama*.

Accordingly, research into UK-based Deobandi educational institutions conducted in the early 2000s portrayed their version of the *Dars-i Nizami* as focused on text, with teaching covering Quranic Arabic, the translation of *hadith* from Arabic to Urdu and Qur'an recitation (*tajwid*). Hanafi *fiqh*, which predominates in South Asia, forms part of the syllabus, as well as a limited selection of historical commentaries on the Qur'an and Islamic belief, most dated between CE 1150 and CE 1500. This devotional curriculum, according to these accounts, then runs on 'parallel tracks' to the obligatory study of core secular National Curriculum subjects such as English and Maths.[39] Of the teaching style employed, Birt and Lewis write that 'teaching is one way – with opportunity for questions to clarify rather than challenge the contents of these revered texts. The aim is the mastery of key texts rather than the systematic and critical exploration of subjects.'[40] 'What is striking,' concurred Sophie Gilliat-Ray in a 2006 article, 'is the absence of subjects that might help graduates engage with British Muslim youth and the society in which they are based.' There is a 'radical difference' between these institutions and most centres of further and higher education.[41]

This body of research painted a very similar portrait of the institutional culture of Deobandi *dar al-ulum*s. In the early 2000s, even well-established academic researchers were treated with suspicion by Deobandi institutions.[42] From the insights they were able to glean, they painted a picture of places where life is rigidly structured: teaching starts early and finishes late, TV and radio are off limits, genders are kept separate and conduct is strictly regulated.[43] Within wider British Muslim communities, private Islamic educational institutions developed a reputation to match. British Muslim independent schools – both Deobandi and Barelvi – are often characterized as disciplinary institutions that can 'save' Muslim children who are at risk of going off the rails. Hassan Rabbani – now a Barelvi *'alim* – was sent from Pollokshields in Glasgow to Jamia Al-Karam's (now closed) boarding school aged 11 because his father, he says, did not want him to become 'like the rest of the Asians, involved in drugs and crime.'[44] Similarly, Abdur-Rahman ibn Yusuf Mangera, a Deobandi *'alim* schooled at Darul Uloom al-Arabiya al-Islamiya, laments that Deobandi *dar al-ulum*s are seen by the British Muslim population as a place for 'the reject or the troublemaker.'[45]

These accounts feed into wider concerns about what Safia Shahid,[46] a Scottish *'alimah* taught in Syria and now principal of the Women's Muslim College, calls a 'crisis of Islamic leadership' in the UK. In contrast to Anglican clergy, imams in the UK are often subordinate to mosque committees, many of whom source faith leaders from overseas. Surveys have indicated that around 8.1 per cent of imams were born in the UK, with less than a quarter having lived in Britain for more than ten years.[47] Such statistics are usually cited in the context of discussions about religious extremists and younger Muslims and women being alienated from places of worship,[48] but they also inform conversations about the low status and financial reward available to imams in British mosques. Overseas sourcing contributes to an oversupply of *'ulama*, which has led to serious concern about the employment prospects – or lack of – of those graduating from *Dars-i Nizami* courses.[49] This is compounded by what Rabbani describes as a 'colonial mind-set' among Muslims that regards *dar al-ulum* education – in Britain and elsewhere – for the 'less educated' compared to more prestigious Westernized institutions. There seems, then, to be a two-sided problem where, as Shahid comments, 'British Muslims do not recognise the *'ulama*' and, in turn, the *'ulama* do not recognize the society that exists around them. Or, as Gilliat-Ray put it in a 2005 article, British Deobandi institutions exist in a social world 'fearful of cultural annihilation' and marked by a 'blanket suspicion of virtually *all* outsiders'.[50]

The state and the building of British Islamic education

These verdicts would likely have gone almost unnoticed had they been made in the 1980s or 1990s. After all, the number of graduates from Deobandi institutions represents only a fraction of the number of students at just one major UK university. At best, they might have been a minor point of concern for local councils or bodies such as Ofsted and QAA tasked with ensuring standards in further and higher education. Today, however, the political context is very different. Deobandi institutions sit at the heart of now widespread concerns about Muslim community networks and Islamic institutions leaving young Muslims badly equipped to flourish in British society and vulnerable to charismatic extremists. In unsympathetic accounts, Deobandi *dar al-ulum*s are depicted as inadvertently helping young Muslims gradually move along a 'conveyor belt' to violent extremism. They might be apolitical, but, according to these accounts, their opposition to 'British values' enables a 'swamp' to fester in which extremism flourishes.[51] In still more uncompromising narratives, which appear recurrently in the conservative tabloid press, Deobandi institutions are described as directly involved in promoting militant extremism.[52]

The connection that these narratives have with the truth is generally tenuous. As we have seen, whatever might be said about the 'anti-British' perspectives of Deobandi elites, the movement in Britain is interested primarily in personal moral reform rather than Islamic states. Indeed, its reluctance to engage with questions of political change is arguably one of the reasons why it has struggled to appeal to young Muslims.[53] The debate about whether rigidly conservative norms and generic opposition to 'Britishness' can set disaffected individuals on a path towards violence is more complicated (we shall look at it in Chapter 5), but we can say that the evidence is unclear at best.[54] Overwhelmingly, Islamist militants tend to be relatively religiously uninformed and marginal to institutions, while immersion in youth culture and a history of criminal activity are common.[55] To date, no graduate of a British Deobandi *dar al-ulum* has been convicted of involvement in acts of terrorism.

What is of interest to me here, though, is less the truth of such narratives but their influence, which has been substantial. Politicians and public figures from across the political spectrum have been prompted to take interest in the transmission of Islam, with both *dar al-ulum* courses and informal supplementary classes coming under scrutiny. In his 2015 speech to the Conservative Party conference, for example, then prime minister David Cameron spoke of '*madrasahs*' in which children have 'their heads filled with poison and their hearts filled with hate'.[56] Statements such as the following, from Paul Goodman, the former Conservative shadow minister for communities and local government (who left politics for journalism in 2010), have been common:

> The consensus about how to combat violent extremism can be summed up in three words: reform the mosques. British mosques and *madrasahs* – the argument runs – are dominated by elderly men from abroad who don't speak English and have limited means of communication with the younger generation. This leaves young British Muslims vulnerable to exploitative English-speaking al-Qaeda operatives. The solution to this seems obvious: open up the mosques. Bring in young, English-speaking people to run them. Sweep away the old-fashioned assumptions, and empower Muslim women. Above all, monitor the *masjids* and *madrasahs*. Inspect them, regulate them, control them and subject them to the blizzard of best practice and quality standards guidance that's done so much for local government.[57]

The startling thing about this statement is how little distinction Goodman makes between local government – which is regulated and controlled as part of the state – and religious institutions. What is clear from his rhetoric is that this is a subject that raises profound questions (to be discussed later) about balancing the state's duty to equip citizens with the skills needed to understand and navigate British society with the need to treat religious institutions as independent moral voices. This is all the more the case because this passage offers a reasonably accurate description of recent public policy in this area, especially under New Labour, whose decisions Goodman is responding to. Islamic educational institutions in the UK have not just featured in speeches but have been impacted by a powerful and elaborate policy machinery aimed at their integration into British society. Since 2007 most, though not all, of this has been subsumed within the 'Prevent' programme and justified in terms of thwarting violent extremism. Prevent has been through several iterations and its form has shifted across New Labour, coalition and Conservative governments (I say more about this in Chapter 5). For now, what is important to note is that between 2007 and 2010, under New Labour, Prevent was extremely well-funded – one analysis puts total Prevent funding between 2008 and 2011 at £186 million[58] – and covered several departments of government.[59] During this period it was delivered through a model of partnership between the state and Muslim community organizations and appeared, at certain moments at least, to have the ambition of substantially remaking Muslim community infrastructure and even reorienting British Muslims' perspectives on society and politics.[60]

In keeping with these general aims, numerous steps were taken by government that directly affected institutions that produce and transmit Islamic knowledge. Some of these were set up as part of the Prevent programme, while others remained formally independent but were in keeping with Prevent's aims. In 2007, for example, a faith leaders' training initiative aimed primarily at Muslim leaders was set up by government, the official aim of which was, in Ruth Kelly's words, to 'help them get a better grasp of the leadership and communication skills they need to engage with the community'.[61] The then minister of state for higher education, Bill Rammell, also commissioned Ataullah Siddiqui of the Markfield Institute for Higher Education (MIHE) to report on the condition of Islamic studies in England, both in British universities and privately funded *dar al-ulums*.[62] The influence of this report can be debated: Siddiqui himself has said that most of his recommendations were ignored.[63] Its publication was, however, followed by Islamic studies being recognized by the Higher Education Funding Council for England (HEFCE) as a 'strategically important subject' in 2008 – a label that is generally only applied to science and engineering subjects rather than the comparatively neglected humanities disciplines.[64] This development led to the funding of the Islamic Studies Network by the Higher Education Academy (HEA) in 2009, which morphed into the British Association of Islamic Studies (BRAIS), now a major subject association, in 2011.[65]

Further moves followed that sought to build bridges between Islamic educational institutions and the mainstream higher education sector. The Department for Communities and Local Government (CLG) funded a project based at the University of Cambridge called 'Contextualising Islam in Britain' whose main aim was to allow Muslim religious leaders and activists from different traditions to come together to discuss what it means to faithfully live as a Muslim in modern Britain.[66] CLG also commissioned research assessing the training and development of Muslim faith leaders whose recommendations included better accreditation of private Islamic institutions within the standard National Qualifications Framework (NQF: now the Qualifications and Credit Framework).[67] This was complemented by work funded through academic research councils that has been broadly supportive of removing barriers between *dar al-ulums* and mainstream university Islamic studies departments, as well as recognizing qualifications gained in *dar al-ulums*.[68] Even Conservative governments, which have been deeply reluctant to fund community capacity building work (see Chapter 5), have continued these efforts, with CLG's successor, the Ministry of Housing, Communities and Local Government (MHCLG), supporting work to help Islamic institutions achieve accreditation in 2019. Through these various projects, a degree of structural pressure has been generated whose broad aim is to bring *dar al-ulums* and similar institutions into more sustained and deeper contact with public and publicly funded institutions.

These all represent what I will call 'soft' measures to influence the transmission of Islam. In the UK – as indeed in much of Western Europe – such measures have typically been established alongside 'hard' regulatory or disciplinary mechanisms. In Britain under New Labour, these included conditions being imposed on religious professionals seeking permission to work in Europe, as well as increased powers to deport those who are deemed to have generated, in the words of Charles Clarke, former home secretary, 'fear, distrust or division' in society.[69] More recently, the Conservative government elected in 2015 outlined proposals to require *madrasahs* and comparable religious supplementary schools to register with the state and be open to inspection[70] and even to create a national register of vetted faith leaders.[71] At the time of writing, these proposals have not moved beyond speeches and stalled plans, but they retain support at the highest levels of government. Most *dar al-ulums*, as they offer secondary and further education, are already registered and inspected by Ofsted, but in this setting, too, Conservative policies have had a substantial impact. In particular, Conservative-led iterations of Prevent have placed a statutory duty on both state-funded and independent schools to 'actively promote fundamental British values', defined in terms of 'democracy, the rule of law, individual liberty, and mutual respect and tolerance of those with different faiths and beliefs'.[72] Deobandi *dar al-ulums*, then, with their history of antipathy towards British rulers, are now required by law to show their active support for 'Britishness'.

Alternative approaches and 'post-Dars-i Nizami' education

I shall say more about the strengths and weaknesses of these efforts, and the impact that they have had, in subsequent sections of this chapter. It would be remiss of me to do so, however, without first mentioning that these have not been the only sources of pressure on Islamic education in Britain. As I observed in Chapter 1, much academic writing on Muslim organizations and Prevent in the UK tells a story only of state discipline and Muslim community resistance, with the policies of the UK government towards British Muslims being characterized as a set of strategies and policy mechanisms designed to contain dissent, 'securitize' Muslim communities and 'domesticate' Islam.[73] Of course, from what we have seen already – by no means the whole story of Prevent and the security apparatus in which it is embedded – it is easy to see why this story is persuasive. Policy changes and proposals have consistently had the effect of making Muslims into, as Derek McGhee has put it, 'conditional citizens' for whom standard rights frameworks can be suspended when the state deems it to be necessary.[74] Even the support offered to Islamic educational institutions, because it has emerged against this backdrop, comes across as designed to reform Muslims' conduct rather than enable the flourishing of Muslim communities.

This focus on the state, however, can give the misleading impression that probing questions about Islamic education's orientation towards British society are recent and have been asked only by politicians and journalists. The reality is that

Muslim voices have been contributing to this debate for much longer than there has been any policy interest in the subject.[75] One such voice is that of Maulana Shahid Raza, a senior imam in Leicester and former director of the Mosques and Imams National Advisory Board (MINAB):

> There are many institutions – in the Midlands, in the North – and when you go there you see that some of the British-born children are being educated over there …. [In some of] these institutions, geographically they are here but ideologically they are somewhere else – they are in Saudi Arabia, or in Pakistan, or somewhere else…. They will be influenced by institutions created maybe one-hundred years ago in the Subcontinent or in the Middle East [that] have been imported, without any amendment, to our children. They get knowledge, but that does not make these young Muslims suitably qualified to lead the community in this country…. When you go to a Sunni *dar al-'ulum* they are only teaching Sunni theology, they are not teaching Shia theology at all, or if it is being taught it is completely refuted.[76]

The Muslim College

Raza made this point in an interview in 2009, and he has been making similar comments since at least 1991.[77] He is part of a conversation that has been ongoing among British Muslims for so long that not only has the issue become widely recognized, but there have been several attempts at developing institutional responses, the majority independent of any government intervention. One of the oldest examples is The Muslim College, which was established in 1987 by the late Zaki Badawi (d. 2006), with Raza joining him shortly after its foundation to serve as its deputy director. In his lifetime, Badawi arguably did more than anyone else to establish Islamic institutions in Britain and set out arguments in their favour.[78] Although he certainly had fierce Muslim critics, he remains the closest British Islam has ever had to a nationally recognized figure of religious authority akin to figures such as Jonathan Sacks, the former chief rabbi of the United Hebrew Congregations of the Commonwealth. His vision for The Muslim College was, in his own words, to 'formulate the future of Islam in the homeland'.[79] To that end, the institution, which is based in a small premises in a residential area of Ealing, East London, offers an MA and BA in Islamic studies following a modular structure similar to other British higher educational institutions alongside short courses, including an introduction to Islam for those newer to the tradition. It has sought to move away from a faith-based and scriptural model of teaching to an approach that is historically contextualized and covers a range of Muslim traditions. As Shahid Raza puts it: 'Here we teach Sunni and Shia theology, Hanafi, Maliki, Shafi'i and Hanbali schools of law,[80] and we teach Salafis and Wahhabis and Sufis all together…. We do not try to evangelise anybody. We just give them the historical facts.'[81] Various steps have also been taken to build associations and accreditation arrangements with mainstream British universities, such as the School of Oriental and African Studies (SOAS), University of London, and the

Open University. These efforts, however, have not so far developed into anything long-standing (for reasons I explore below).

The Muslim College is an illustration not only of novel approaches in Islamic education but also of the challenges that Islamic educational institutions can encounter. A centre that seeks to provide students with a traditional Islamic education *and* an understanding of British religious and cultural life ideally requires teachers who can speak with authority on both subjects, but such people have been hard to find in practice. In The Muslim College's case, despite the aim of building an authentically British Islamic system of higher education, the search for new senior staff has often been concentrated not on the UK but on Libya or the Al-Azhar in Egypt, one of the oldest and most significant centres of Sunni religious learning and the place where Badawi was taught.[82] This is not lost on some competing Islamic educational centres I have visited, where The Muslim College was judged to provide an 'Azhari' perspective rather than teaching that is 'culturally British'. Although of Egyptian heritage, Badawi's efforts to unite Muslims during his lifetime also tended to generate support among Barelvis, with Deobandis remaining distant.[83] This is illustrated by the fact that Raza is himself the head imam at the Barelvi Leicester Central Mosque. Alongside this, ensuring a stable income has been difficult. Religious training does not usually lead to a high-earning career, so class sizes tend to be small even when fees are kept low. To make ends meet, therefore, many institutions have to win support from overseas, which in turn raises questions about independence. Funding for The Muslim College has come from the World Islamic Call Society (WICS), a body based in Libya, which has allowed fees for students to be reduced or even waived. Under Gaddafi, WICS was associated with the Libyan government, which prompted understandable queries about the College's autonomy. Badawi always insisted that this funding did not involve any interference with the institution's outlook or curriculum design.[84] There is no reason to doubt this, but it is notable that the current principal, Mohamed Benotman – who now leads the College with little apparent input from Raza – was appointed directly by WICS and moved to Ealing from a lecturing post at Sirte University. The Libyan organization, then, seems to act as more than simply an arm's-length benefactor to the College.[85]

The Markfield Institute of Higher Education

The only other Sunni institution of similar age that offers a comparable curriculum is the Markfield Institute of Higher Education (MIHE) in Leicestershire. This institution's history, however, is very different. MIHE emerged out of the Islamic Foundation, which was established in 1973 in Leicester, moving to its present home in the village of Markfield in the 1990s. When it was set up, the Foundation's central functions were training, education and publishing – although its activities have since grown beyond these initial points of focus to include support for new Muslims, policy analysis and a range of other things besides. It is active in governance networks locally and nationally in the UK, while being influenced by associates and movements overseas. MIHE was founded in 2000 and, although it is legally distinct from the Islamic Foundation for administrative purposes, it retains close links.

What makes these two institutions interesting is that when the Islamic Foundation was set up, its leadership was loyal to Jamaat-i-Islami and to a wider Islamist effort to mobilize a global Islamic movement. Although it remained formally independent, two of the organization's former directors, Khurram Murad and Khurshid Ahmad, have held leadership roles in Jamaat-i-Islami in Pakistan, with the latter acting as deputy *Amir* in the 1990s.[86] The Islamic Foundation's published output in this period included numerous political works by Abul Ala Mawdudi, Jamaat-i-Islami's founder, and it was involved in a major project translating and publishing Mawdudi's commentary (*tafsir*) of the Qur'an in English. In the first three decades of its existence, the influence of Jamaat-i-Islami could be seen in much of the Islamic Foundation's *da'wah* (proselytizing) activities, which had the overarching aim of what Séan McLoughlin terms 'counter-cultural Islamisation'.[87] In 1988, for example, the Islamic Foundation was one of the early drivers of the campaign against *The Satanic Verses*. It collaborated with associates in Chennai and supporters in Saudi Arabia to photocopy and distribute offending passages of Rushdie's book to mosques and other Muslim organizations throughout Britain, as well as the British embassies of the member states of the Organisation of the Islamic Conference (OIC).[88]

The Islamic Foundation's move away from countercultural Islamist activism represents one of the most striking cases of adaptation within this book. While its senior leaders have often pursued ends consistent with the general outlook of Jamaat-i-Islami, the Islamic Foundation has long been host to a variety of personalities and schools of thought. Since its very early days, the organization has been deeply involved in interfaith work and much of its involvement in local governance has been channelled through Leicester's strong and politically connected interfaith networks.[89] One of the organization's former leaders, the late Faiyazuddin Ahmad, was a founder member of Leicester Council of Faiths in 1986, while another former employee, Sughra Ahmed (who we will meet again in Chapter 5), sat on the Bishop of Leicester's Faith Leaders Forum until 2013. Ataullah Siddiqui, too – whose is of Indian heritage and has no biographical associations with Jamaat-i-Islami – has been prominent in Leicester's interfaith organizations for over twenty-five years. The Markfield site has also occasionally hosted competing activist networks and schools of thought, such as the 'Traditional Islam' network. This network takes the medieval theologian and philosopher al-Ghazali as its main inspiration, emphasizes convivial engagement and is opposed to Salafi and Islamist thinking (see Chapter 5), but it held its 1999 Rihla programme at the Foundation.[90]

As time has passed, the diversity of perspectives has grown and the organization's ethos has slowly shifted in response. Its published output and wider work began to change towards the end of the 1980s, and during the 1990s and 2000s the organization slowly de-emphasized its original goal of countercultural Islamization. The make-up of the staff and leadership altered, such that, as Gilliat-Ray remarks, 'with the appointment of each new Director General, the significance and influence of the Jama'at-i-Islami in Pakistan has gradually begun to recede'.[91] Today, as Peter Mandaville concurs, 'the vast majority of the staff, teachers, and intellectual output of [the Islamic Foundation and MIHE] have departed from [Jamaat-i-Islami] influence'.[92] The Foundation has not rejected its own past. There has been no purge of the old leadership, with Khurshid Ahmad, although now past retirement age, retaining a senior visiting position within the organization. Indeed, there are indications that the transformation of the organization has been the result of not just staff churn but also the conscious decision-making of the established leadership.[93]

None of these changes have affected the way that the organization has been portrayed by the national media. The Islamic Foundation and MIHE have been regular targets for journalists and politicians keen to make headlines by uncovering alleged associations between the state and Islamist groups. In 2005, for example, the Islamic Foundation was ruthlessly criticized as an 'outpost of militant Islamist ideology' in a BBC *Panorama* documentary.[94] Similarly, when Ataullah Siddiqui was asked by Bill Ramell to report on the study of Islam, Michael Gove, then shadow housing spokesman, raised questions in Parliament seeking clarification over Siddiqui's relationship with Jamaat-i-Islami.[95] This needlessly makes MIHE's life difficult and blinds public debate to an instructive case of institutional change. It is hard to say exactly what prompted the Islamic Foundation's transition towards more open-ended perspectives. McLoughlin has suggested that the shift might be linked to a move away from reliance on Saudi funds and towards independent financing through Kube Books – the Foundation's publishing arm – and MIHE, both of which are run on a commercial basis.[96] The organizations' deepening civil society links have almost certainly played a part, however. Interfaith networking has enabled the Foundations staff to contribute to everything from Parliament-led consultations on Prevent[97] to the Labour government-sponsored National Muslim Women's Advisory Group (NMWAG),[98] and as they have done so the nature of the organization has shifted. This cuts directly against the arguments of the present Conservative government, which has continually reaffirmed the position that groups affiliated with Islamist movements and parties should be shunned by the state. For the Conservatives, speaking to any Islamist organization, peaceful or not, gives credence to and ultimately strengthens anti-liberal views.[99] The case of the Islamic Foundation and MIHE, though, suggests this argument fails.

MIHE started with a sole programme in Islamic studies, mainly populated by students from overseas. In 2003 it began supplementing this course with higher level modules in Islamic finance and Muslim community studies (now Muslim education). Most recently, the Institute has started to offer dedicated chaplaincy courses, whose significance I discuss further below. Today, it tries to act as a 'bridge' between traditional *Dars-i Nizami* qualifications and UK society, offering those with religious qualifications accreditation the opportunity to complete a BA in two years rather than three. Teaching is co-educational, with a specific emphasis placed on transcending the divide between academic Islamic studies and the traditional Islamic sciences. As Siddiqui explains:

[We want to encourage people] to reflect critically about how those traditions [Islamic sciences and Islamic studies] have over the years helped or hindered what new things you need to do. So those things, history, traditions, contemporary *fiqh*, *usul al-fiqh*,[100] all those things need to be opened and looked into in an open critical way in classes .... Subjects students haven't studied in *madrasah* they will study here. That includes Islamic history and, in a different way, Prophetic traditions, but also philosophy, inter-faith relations, Christianity and religious studies – all those things they haven't done, we could do that and they will have a much wider perspective.[101]

Cambridge Muslim College

MIHE's conscious effort to bridge the divide between traditional *Dars-i Nizami* curricula and the accreditation frameworks used in the mainstream education sector is similar to that of a third case: the Cambridge Muslim College. Established in 2009, the Cambridge Muslim College is based on the original vision of Abdal-Hakim Murad (aka Tim Winter), a convert to Islam who works as a lecturer in Islamic studies at the University of Cambridge while also being a renowned religious authority (with occasional appearances on the BBC Radio 4 programme *Thought for the Day*). Murad is informally aligned with the Traditional Islam network and is among its most skilled spokespersons. He is self-consciously traditionalistic – even anti-modern – in outlook, though his deep familiarity with British cultural norms and its Christian heritage has meant that he is able to connect with Muslim youth with greater success than many *'ulama* from overseas. His wide-ranging writings, which are littered with references to everyone from Thomas Carlyle to Thomas Aquinas, consistently stress the importance of roots. Drawing on the language of the 'roots' (*usul*) and 'branches' (*furu'*) of Islamic law, he describes the Islamic tradition as a tree tended over many centuries that allows Muslims to remain connected to the past. This is part of a polemic against what he calls the 'false Salafism', but it also allows him to make an argument for an acculturated form of British Islam. He has a strong desire to give Muslims, he says, 'a sense of how they can authentically belong, geographically, to things that are sacred and profound'.[102] This even extends to editing a music collection entitled *Muslim songs of the British Isles*.[103] 'The British Isles have for several hundred years been the home of individuals whose religious and moral temper is very close to that of Islam,' he writes. Britain's 'moderate, undemonstrative style of piety, still waters running deep; its insistence on modesty and a certain reserve, and its insistence on common sense and on pragmatism, combine to furnish the most natural and easy religious option for our people'.[104]

The Cambridge Muslim College was founded as the institutional expression of this argument. As well as offering short-term research positions, the institution provides a BA in Islamic studies and diploma in Contextual Islamic Studies and Leadership. Even more so than the Markfield Institute, its courses are designed to cater for those who have already undertaken *'alim* studies but who do not necessarily have the pastoral skills to address challenges facing British Muslims or familiarity with the wider social context of the UK. Social sciences, the British state, Islam in Britain and the 'world religions' are all covered during the diploma. Notably, the College has sought to promote Muslim women's religious leadership by adopting a quota system to maintain balance between genders: each year, at least one-third of the incoming cohort of students must be women. According to the College's former academic director, Atif Imtiaz, expanding on this requirement has proven difficult.[105] Mukadam and Scott Bauman's analysis suggests that twenty-two of the thirty-eight secondary-level Islamic educational institutions in Britain are for boys only (although the overwhelming majority of higher level institutions are co-educational).[106] This leaves the College with a limited pool of female students graduating from courses that offer the full *Dars-i Nizami* curriculum.

Despite such challenges, there have lately been promising developments. Recently established Islamic educational institutions have often had to rely on what Ibrahim Lawson, a senior staff member of the comparable Ebrahim College in Tower Hamlets (established 2003), calls 'peer accreditation', which involves Cambridge, Ebrahim and others collaborating and recognizing each other's work, and this being used as a way of validating institutions' activities.[107] The close connections between Murad and the mainstream university sector mean that it has long been able to burnish such credentials with high-profile visiting academic experts.[108] In 2017, however, the Cambridge Muslim College built on these sources of authority by gaining formal accreditation from the Open University for its BA in Islamic studies, going somewhat against recent trends (see below).[109] The College also appears to have had some success in crossing traditions. Despite Murad being aligned with the Traditional Islam network and heavily influenced by Sufi traditions, the Cambridge Muslim College has been, at least according to one scholarly account, successful at recruiting graduates from Deobandi institutions.[110]

Women's Muslim College

The fourth case I want to introduce – Safia Shahid's Women's Muslim College – helps to both bring this overview up to date and consider in more depth the background to the challenges the Cambridge Muslim College has faced recruiting female students. In contrast to the Roman Catholic Church, the Islamic tradition has tended not to place de jure restrictions on training women for religious leadership (even if leading prayers is an almost exclusively male role). Yet, as Kecia Ali observes, while 'there are no restrictions on female participation in scholarly endeavors in theory – and a number of exceptional women, past and present, have been recognized as religious authorities – there are significant practical obstacles to female education in madrasa settings'.[111] In the UK, not only is there greater provision for men's education but the religious training at women's institutions is typically more limited.[112] In consequence, Muslim women's theological education has often been delivered via small study circles (*halaqahs*) that are held predominantly in private and domestic settings.

Over the past two decades, however, women-led efforts to democratize Muslim communities[113] have increased opportunities for Muslim women's Islamic education in institutional contexts. As Ustadha Iffet Rafeeq, an Islamic scholar educated in the Barelvi Jamia Al-Karam, Eaton, remarks in an account by the anthropologist Giulia Liberatore: 'before it was really about intimate, private circles … the wives of Shaykhs or young scholars holding meetings in homes or prayer rooms. But over the last five or six years some of us have started to go public.'[114] Only in the very recent past has this gradual change found institutional form, with the Women's Muslim College being founded in 2017 by Shaykh Muhammad al-Yaqoubi, a member of the Shadhili Sufi order, with Shahid as its principal. Shahid represents, in Liberatore's terms, a member of the 'middle generation' of British Islamic scholars who are British-born but with seminary qualifications from overseas – specifically, Damascus – rather than from a UK-based institution. The relationship between her and Yaqoubi is illustrative of the relationship between male and female scholarly authority. As Liberatore points out, women scholars' 'legitimacy is tied in complex ways to that of male scholars': 'Studying in a renowned seminary (like Al-Karam) or receiving an *ijaza* under a famous male scholar (e.g., Shaykh al-Yaqoubi) is important for the women's futures, as they benefit from the support of the scholars as referees and promoters of their work.'[115] It seems possible, however, that in the near future bodies like the Women's Muslim College will begin to disrupt this dependence on male authority.

The Women's Muslim College's curriculum offering is similar to the courses offered by the other three institutions covered here, with the organization offering certificates, a diploma and a four-year programme in the 'Islamic Sciences in a Modern Context'. What separates it from these others is its operational structure. Rather than being based in one location, the institution offers courses in Birmingham, Leicester and Hounslow, London. Its short certificates in areas such as *fiqh* and *tajwid* (recitation of the Qur'an), as well as its four-year course, are available in distance learning formats, too. This geographically diffuse mode of operation is likely a reflection of the institution's recent foundation, as well as, perhaps, of the distinctive development of women's scholarship.

Educational initiatives outside the classroom

This way of doing business aligns the Women's Muslim College with programmes set up independently of formal educational organizations. These can take the form of speaker tours, workshops or short, sometimes web-based classes.[116] A good example of an initiative of this kind is Maslaha, an organization with its base in Tower Hamlets in East London. Maslaha – whose name is taken from the Islamic legal term for the 'public interest' or 'common good' – came into being in 2007 largely due to the work of Rushanara Ali, who went on to be elected as member of Parliament for Bethnal Green and Bow in May 2010. It was established as a response to what Ali and founding director of the organization, Raheel Mohammed, felt to be, in the words of the former, the 'lack of available intellectually grounded knowledge of Islam' in the UK.[117] Alongside interests in healthcare provision and cultural history and exchange, Maslaha aims to disseminate knowledge about the principles of Islam. To do this, the organization works with academics and

Islamic scholars whose opinions it makes available on issues ranging from the permissibility of getting a mortgage to whether a Muslim woman can refuse a proposal of marriage against the wishes of her parents. Mohammed's hope is that by transmitting this knowledge to those who may know little of it from their upbringing or from the national curriculum, Maslaha might be able to encourage different ways of thinking. As he put it to me in conversation, 'If I can get just one young person to come away thinking a little differently, with a little less frustration, then I'll be happy.'

A similar organization is the Radical Middle Way (RMW), an initiative that grew out of the magazine *Q-News*.[118] *Q-News* was a Muslim magazine established in the early 1990s by Fuad Nahdi (d. 2020), a journalist and activist who grew up in Kenya but who did more than arguably anyone else to develop a confident and articulate British Islamic voice. The magazine covered lifestyle and social issues alongside religious affairs. Although discontinued in 2006, in its heyday in the late 1990s it maintained a readership of around 60,000 people, comprising mainly second- and third-generation British-born Muslims as well as non-Muslim religious educators and policymakers. Justly viewed[119] as an innovative publication, in part because of the role women like Shagufta Yaqub and Fareena Alam played as editors, the magazine did not affiliate with any Islamic tradition but bore the imprint of the Traditional Islam that also influences the Cambridge Muslim College. It was, accordingly, respectful of Islamic tradition but tended to treat Muslim representative organizations with a degree of scepticism. The same can be said of RMW, whose name is a reference to the second *Sura* of the Qur'an (2: 143) in which Muslims are described as a 'balanced community' or a 'community of the middle way' (*umma wasat*). RMW styles itself as giving a voice to classical Islamic traditions, which in practical terms means hosting pre-eminent *'ulama* – some from the UK, others from abroad – whose writings would not otherwise find their way into the hands of young Muslims in Britain.[120] It has given a platform to Islamic scholars from Yemen, Germany, America and Egypt, and in the period between 2007 and 2009 it attracted sizeable audiences – sometimes upwards of a thousand – to events in Bradford, Birmingham and around London. This includes conscious attempts to promote Muslim women's scholarship, most notably through its 2009 'Shaykha Unplugged' tour, in partnership with the British Muslim women's charity An-Nisa and renowned German *'alimah* Halima Krausen.[121]

These two organizations are similar in their age and aims, but it is what separates them that makes them particularly valuable as case studies for understanding Muslim institutions: namely, their funding sources. From the outset, Maslaha has eschewed direct government support in favour of charitable endowments and donations from a wide range of bodies (including NHS trusts and other public bodies). Despite being launched during the period when Prevent funding for community organizations was most plentiful, Mohammed spurned these sources due to concerns about its impact on his organization's credibility, autonomy and long-term financial viability. In contrast, RMW was set up with government funding – £350,000 was given to the organization in 2009 alone by the CLG[122] – making it deeply entangled in state-led efforts to reorient Islamic knowledge production in Britain. The organization faced, in the words of Abdul-Rehman Malik, formerly one of RMW's senior staff, 'a big trade-off in terms of fighting for credibility and fighting for the money to operate'.[123] It has also encountered problems due to the capriciousness of government policy agendas. As we will see in Chapter 5, after New Labour left office in 2010 Prevent shifted away from its strategy of delivering policy via community organizations, and the generous grants on which the RMW relied swiftly dried up. Consequently, while Maslaha – with its deeply held belief in the idea of Muslim self-organization – has maintained its operations, RMW now only maintains a presence on Facebook.[124] Following a long period of chronic ill health, Nahdi passed away in 2020 after contracting coronavirus, and without a similar personality to steer the organization its future looks uncertain.

Islamic education in the UK higher education sector

These contrasting fortunes, and the challenges bodies like The Muslim College have encountered sourcing funds, provide a salutary reminder that material contexts matter. Islamic educational institutions need to raise the money to operate, and whether they can do so depends in large part on education policies, many of which are neglected in discussions about this subject. For the most part, debate about Islamic education's place in the UK is conducted as though the main question is how to navigate between liberal and faith-oriented educational models – that is to say, between teaching students about Islam and teaching them how best to be Muslim. This question is, of course, crucial, but these are no longer the only or even the dominant educational frameworks operating in Britain. UK higher education has been a site of continuous reform since the start of the twentieth century, but since the 1970s these reforms have been in a specific direction: away from the traditional liberal and Christian principles on which the UK's higher education institutions were originally founded and towards a market-mimicking system in which degrees are seen primarily as a way of generating income.[125] In England and Wales (though not Scotland), student maintenance grants have slowly been replaced by increasingly large course fees, in most cases financed by loans from the state. Various forms of competition have also been introduced into the sector: deregulation of student number limits has forced universities to fight for applicants and the money that follows them. This shift towards a *neoliberal* educational model has radically reshaped the environment within which private higher education institutions operate and has had both positive and negative impacts on Islamic education.

One of the most profound impacts of the marketization of higher education has been the prioritization of subjects that suggest a clear career path in which earnings are high. When degrees are viewed as a personal financial investment on which one should seek a material return subjects such as religious studies and theology, which have no clear vocational application (or which suggest a career in which earnings are relatively limited), are devalued. Over many years, religion has been marginalized in the academy by anti-clerical forces and growing disciplinary specialization,[126] but this new market-oriented model has accelerated this marginalization by making humanities subjects less appealing.[127] What this means for Islamic educational institutions is unclear, as we will see in a moment, but it is possible to point to a fundamental policy contradiction that this situation creates. One arm of government in the UK has, as we have seen, encouraged associations between Islamic and mainstream education sectors. The overarching thrust of higher education policy, with its constant focus on economic benefit rather than social and public mission, undermines this, however.

To add to this difficulty, universities have, under Conservative and Conservative-led governments since 2010, been hard hit by increasingly stringent immigration restrictions. International students have been for many years a significant source of income for higher education institutions, both private and publicly funded. For Islamic institutions with ties to South Asian or Middle Eastern religious communities this is particularly the case, with many attracting Muslims from abroad to study subjects such as Islamic finance. One large institution contacted as part of my research acknowledged that almost all of its efforts to recruit and generate income were focused overseas. This industry in foreign students is, however, currently threatened. Overseas students are now more limited in their ability to work in the UK after graduating, making the UK a less appealing place to study.[128] For most private institutions the situation is even worse: individuals at these institutions usually cannot work part-time even while they are studying.[129] This is a major frustration for the leaders of private Islamic educational institutions; Ataullah Siddiqui describes the policy as involving a profound 'double standard' that does significant damage to MIHE's ability to compete with the wider sector.[130] The same hard line also contributes to difficulties developing accreditation agreements between Islamic institutions and universities. In the past, course validation offered a way for universities to accrue income, but recent scandals centring on the accreditation of bogus colleges – most notably at the University of Wales in 2011[131] – have made universities more anxious about offering their stamp of approval. Some have ceased external accreditation completely, either for business reasons or because the reputational risk is perceived as too great. One Islamic institution I visited has been forced to change accrediting institutions twice in a decade, while others have struggled to obtain accreditation at all. This is an especially significant issue for those institutions that want to build bridges between *dar al-ulum* education and the wider university system. Their aim is to help students undertaking *'alim* qualifications to progress onto other courses through Recognition of Prior Learning and then go on into work. Without validation, bridging that gap is much more difficult.

At the same time, Islamic educational institutions could stand to benefit from some aspects of recent higher education policy, although it is too soon to be entirely sure of this. The drive by successive Labour and Conservative governments towards the creation of a market-mimicking sector has resulted in steps being taken towards levelling the playing field between privately and publicly funded providers of higher education, to the point where the line between the two categories is now very blurry.[132] The clearest evidence of this is the extension of government-backed loans from Student Finance England to students studying at privately funded institutions. Although these loans, of up to £6,000, are only available to full-time students studying certain designated courses at privately funded providers, the field would only need to be levelled a little further before Islamic educational institutions could begin to feel the benefit.

Indeed, even the increasingly narrow focus on employment outcomes could have upsides for private Islamic higher education institutions. Faith-based and theological education has declined substantially in British universities. Until the mid-nineteenth century higher education in England was for Anglicans only and theology was the 'queen of the sciences', embedded into all areas of study.[133] Now, however, theology and religion is the subject of choice for only 0.4 per cent of students.[134] As religion has become marginalized in publicly funded universities in Britain, though, a gap has opened up in the market and there is limited evidence that privately funded providers are filling it. Among the estimated 150,000 students studying at private higher education providers, as many as 12.1 per cent study religion and theology.[135] It is hard to draw firm conclusions from this, but it seems that as religion has been squeezed out of publicly funded institutions, private institutions – most Christian, but some Islamic – have responded.

The increase in university fees for students in England – which were elevated to a maximum of £9000 per year in 2010 – has also encouraged some individuals to found competing institutions with a social justice ethic. One example of this is the Institute for Leadership and Community Development (ILCD) in Washwood Heath, Birmingham, which was established in 2014. ILCD was set up to cater for those who do not feel able to attend a publicly funded university following the fee rise. From the outside, ILCD does not appear to be a 'religious' institution; the name certainly gives nothing away. The purpose of the institution is, however, to combine traditional Islamic education with courses in management and community development. Secular courses are taught, but the institution has an Islamic ethos and library. In common with other recently established Islamic educational organizations, ILCD sees itself as different from traditional *dar al-ulum*s that do not, in the view of its director, Iqtidar Karamat Cheema, equip their students for roles in British society. Its aim is to draw in students by offering them a more grounded and useful education at a lower cost – although whether this business model will work remains to be seen.[136]

Even leaving security and counterterrorism policies to one side, then, it is clear that Islamic educational institutions operate in a ruthlessly competitive and bafflingly complex policy environment. Policymakers have consistently preached deregulation in education but practised something different, creating a convoluted regulatory system of which it is easy to fall foul.[137] (One example of this: during the course of my research one institution I contacted described itself in emails, though not on its website, as an 'Islamic University', seemingly in contravention of the Companies Act 2006, which requires colleges using 'university' in their description to gain approval from the government ministry with responsibility for universities.)[138] More than ever before, government ministers are relaxed about higher education institutions 'failing'; little serious thought is given to the long-term stability of private institutions especially. Any innovations in Islamic education are made, then, in a climate of risk and profound uncertainty.

Evaluating the state's role in producing Islamic knowledge

Against this backdrop of competing – and in some cases contradictory – pressures, what is the likely future for Islamic education in Britain, and what future should we seek for it? Can a case be made for linking the traditional Islamic sciences taught in *dar al-ulum*s with Islamic studies departments in secular institutions, and if there is, what is the basis for this? The last element of this question is important because it is entirely possible to agree that some of the steps taken by the British state – reviewing and enhancing Islamic studies provision in UK universities, for example – are commendable but have been undermined by being justified mainly or solely in reference to instrumental concerns about violent extremism that are, at best, only partly relevant. Then finally, if one *can* build a case for more government involvement in the production of Islamic knowledge, how does one bring it about in a marketized education sector? What might a call for greater institutional interpenetration mean for how we think about higher education's future structure and purpose?

Evaluating 'hard' measures

Earlier in this chapter, I made a distinction between 'hard' and 'soft' measures that have been implemented or proposed by government to influence Islamic education. To make headway, I would like now to define these more formally. By 'hard' measures, I mean steps taken to directly influence what is taught in Islamic educational institutions – as well as teaching methods – via regulation, monitoring and the enforcement of curriculum standards. There are multiple examples of this, and many are entirely uncontroversial. For example, all institutions offering secondary level education are regulated by Ofsted, so private Islamic schools are required to give pupils 'experience in linguistic, mathematical, scientific, technological, human and social, physical and aesthetic and creative education' in accordance with the Education Act 1996.[139] More recent reforms, however, have caused significant controversy. We have already seen how Goodman and others have charged Islamic institutions in Britain with failing to provide students with the skills to engage with British society, thereby putting students' welfare and that of the British polity at risk. He – and many of his politician and journalist colleagues – now thinks the state should step in to compel these institutions to do what they, allegedly, can't or won't. Thus we have seen proposals to 'vet' religious leaders and enhance Ofsted's remit to cover supplementary religious instruction, as well as the implementation of the duty to promote 'British values' in schools. This, in turn, has triggered a response from the leaders of Islamic institutions who fear their ability to transmit moral traditions on their own terms is being threatened. In 2015, around five hundred mosques and thirteen thousand people signed up to a 'Keep Our Mosques Independent' campaign, which objected that the British government was unduly encroaching on British Muslims' right to instruct their children in their religion.[140]

The two sides to this argument are reflected in a long-running debate in liberal political theory about the limits of civic education. On one side are figures, such as Stephen L. Carter, who prioritize protecting the ability of religious institutions to transmit moral teachings on their own terms – even when those teachings are isolationist or anti-political – on the basis that independent communities of belief 'serve as the sources of moral understanding without which any majoritarian system can descend into simple tyranny'.[141] On the other are liberals, such as Amy Gutmann, who insist on utilizing state education to achieve the comprehensive inculcation of 'democratic virtue' – which means, inter alia, giving people the capacity to engage meaningfully in public deliberations.[142] Across this debate, there are profound disagreements on more subjects than I am able to list here, but what is striking is that there are certain basics on which all parties agree. Carter, for example, prizes the ability of parents to educate children as they want but recognizes that religious groups should not get to set the terms of public education. (As a US citizen, his position on this is, unsurprisingly, stricter than UK policy is.) Likewise, Gutmann argues for a strong civic ethos in state-funded schools but says little of religious instruction outside of school. No theorist, to the best of my knowledge, seriously suggests that governments should have the right to regulate children's supplementary religious education.

This makes it easy to dismiss the most invasive measures proposed by Conservative governments, such as setting up a government register of religious leaders or inspecting informal religious lessons. Of course, no one would claim that private, informal classes should be completely free from legal interference when there are serious concerns about the safeguarding of children. (As John Rawls rightly puts it: 'If the so-called private sphere is alleged to be a space exempt from justice, then there is no such thing.')[143] Rather, the point that Carter and others make is that state regulation of religion needs to be carefully circumscribed because states can, and often do, set down rules that respond not to genuine problems but to the majority's prejudices – in this case, the questionable notion that Islamic education 'teaches people to hate'. Muslim and other organizations' resistance to introducing inspections of supplementary religious education is, then, unquestionably justified.

The case of teaching 'British values' in schools is more complex. There would appear to be little wrong with mandatory teaching about democracy, the rule of law, liberty and mutual tolerance. Certainly, extending such teaching to private schools – which in England can opt out of the National Curriculum – is a significant step but one that is ultimately defensible. It seems to be consistent with the views of not only figures such as Guttman, who are happy for the state to prevent communities from using private education to stifle 'rational deliberation', but also the more limited political liberalism of Rawls, Martha Nussbaum and

Stephen Macedo.[144] For these, the authority to compel people to act and think in certain ways is only legitimate if it is justified by the end of securing the coherence of democratic institutions, and not for individuals' own benefit. This means talk of contestable ideals about human perfection and of 'virtues' tends to be avoided in favour of emphasis on the simple capacity to understand and navigate one's political and social context. In other words, for political liberals, Christians should be taught about what it is that Jewish, humanist, Sikh and Hindu people do and believe, but states ought not to seek to influence Christian beliefs and identities. This position is far more modest than that taken by Gutmann and 'perfectionist' liberals,[145] but it certainly doesn't rule out teaching the values listed above: people need to know the concepts on which their polity is founded, even if they may disagree with them.

The problem with the 'British values' agenda, however, is not so much the principles that are listed but the fact that these are embedded within a wider framework whose overarching function is the identification of extremists. Rather than being justified in limited civic terms, it claims a 'political copyright' – to use Les Back's apt phrase[146] – on certain concepts and uses these as a litmus test: in current policy, to question these concepts is to risk being classed as a threat. Instead of facilitating overlapping consensus across worldviews, then, the values are co-opted by an exclusivist narrative of national identity and loyalty. In practice, schools and other public bodies have found ways to recast Prevent and the teaching of 'British values' so that it takes on a more inclusive form;[147] indeed, we will see that such teaching has been successfully incorporated in private *dar al-ulums*. This does not, though, make the duty itself helpful. Rather than facilitating the embedding of shared values in national culture, the 'British values' duty reduces a list of constitutional essentials to an unthinking shibboleth, transforming them into identity labels and reducing their actual force in law and policy. As evidence of this, one only needs to consider how, in the UK, the perceived threat of terrorism has been used to justify contradictory policy developments. On the one hand, under this duty 'the rule of law' is formally classified as a value whose acceptance marks out the integrated British citizen from the extremist. On the other, there has been an exponential growth in cases of British citizens – almost all Muslim – being stripped of their citizenship without trial or charge, with the only public justification sometimes being that they 'displayed bad character'.[148] The official messaging of Prevent has long been that critical thinking is crucial to challenging the 'single narrative' of extremists,[149] but it is impossible to support both these changes and keep one's critical faculties intact.

Evaluating 'soft' measures

I would like now to broaden the focus. This chapter has been predominantly focused on further and higher education, and in these contexts 'hard' measures are less relevant due to government having less say in the content of curricula. The Prevent duty does apply to universities and colleges but has considerably less impact on teaching. Let's turn, then, to 'soft' measures. By 'soft' measures, I mean steps taken by government to influence Islamic education by influencing the wider context within which institutions operate, especially via facilitating opportunities and encouraging connections. Hard measures relate to what Isaiah Berlin called 'negative liberty': coercion and its absence. By contrast, soft measures relate to 'positive liberty': the possibilities available.[150] Like hard measures, soft measures involve shaping individual and institutional identities. Their influence is less direct, though, and so theories of legitimate coercive authority are less relevant. More relevant are theories of *personal formation*, or what Kwame Anthony Appiah calls 'soul making'.[151]

Liberalism, especially political liberalism, has tended to emphasize self-authorship and so has often been criticized for having an unrealistic understanding of how people's 'souls' are made. For example, I referred above to the liberal notion that states should teach about what it is different people believe but should not seek to influence people's fundamental beliefs. However, just by making people aware of traditions and political principles does not the state subtly shape people's views on life and, through this, their identities? That, certainly, has been the argument of some religious traditionalists. In the *Wisconsin v. Yoder* (1971) and *Mozert v. Hawkins* (1983) court cases in the United States, Amish and Protestant fundamentalists, respectively, objected that even-handed exposure to alternative worldviews undermined the 'simplicity' and 'other-worldliness' of theirs.[152] This objection, at first glance, seems to undermine political liberalism's guiding principle that one should seek to secure a stable polity but not influence individuals' beliefs. It is an argument that simplifies liberal theories, however. All but the crudest varieties of liberalism recognize that political decisions will influence people's identities and that we are formed through dialogue. Rather, to cut a lengthy debate crudely short, liberals tend to argue that the state should act, so to speak, at one remove. The state should not tell you what to write in your life's story, but it will have a role in providing you with the tools and concepts you use. It will not tell you which road to travel on, but it will provide the roads.[153]

I want to argue that successfully addressing questions about Islamic education's place in the UK means paying greater attention to soft measures that sit at one remove, and less to the hard measures that have been the focus of political debate. That is to say, when thinking about Islamic educational institutions, policymakers should think not (only) of telling them what to teach but also of the opportunities they have. Sariya Cheruvallil-Contractor and Alison Scott-Baumann describe such opportunities in terms of the creation of 'bridges' and 'permeable membranes' between different intellectual spheres: for example, providing greater opportunities for institutional collaborations, opening pathways for scholars and students to move between different types of institution and facilitating forums in which institutions of different types can exchange ideas and insights.[154] We have already encountered cases of this. The British Association of Islamic Studies – which was set up with a grant of £1 million from government but which is now independent and self-funding[155] – is a good example, especially as it has included on its governing committee individuals based both in secular universities and in private Islamic colleges. Other examples can be found at institutions I have not yet discussed. The University of Warwick, for example, in 2018 established a Postgraduate Award in Islamic Education, the explicit aim of which is to 'bridge the gap between Islamic seminaries and modern tertiary education'.[156] To the best of my knowledge, this is the first and so far only case of a large university taking steps initially pioneered by the likes of MIHE.

Some of the most valuable cases of institutional collaboration emerge out of Shia contexts. In 2018, the Al-Mahdi Institute and the Department of Theology and Religion at the University of Birmingham set up an agreement that allows students taking the former's *hawza* course to pursue an MA in Islamic Studies.[157] Likewise the Islamic College – an institution located on the 'Shia mile of London' in Brent – has had aspects of its teaching validated by Middlesex University since at least 2010, and this has extended into a long-standing alliance covering two BA courses, four MA courses and shorter certificates. Many of these courses are non-sectarian and do not emphasize the distinctive nature of Shiism;[158] indeed, my own interactions with staff at these institutions suggest they are happy to recruit students from across a range of Islamic traditions. Even so, the Islamic College's BA Honours in Hawza Studies has been validated. These varieties of collaboration between religious and secular teaching, and between privately and publicly funded institutions, offer a better path forward, I propose, than trying to dictate what Islamic institutions teach – in part because, as we will see, such measures follow a general trend in British Islamic education.[159]

One reason such measures are preferable to 'harder' alternatives is the different way they stand in relation to principles of equality. While sensationalist proposals by David Cameron and others about extending the regulation of *madrasahs* have been well received by the political right, they run into the problem that they cannot be implemented in practice without either singling out Islam or similarly affecting Christian, Jewish, Sikh and other religious institutions. (Christian leaders were, in fact, crucial to thwarting the Conservatives' planned expansion of Ofsted inspections.)[160] In the case of 'soft' measures, though, the demand is not to single Islam out but to treat it as other religious traditions are already treated. Not only in the UK but across Western Europe there are countless 'bridges' and 'permeable membranes' between universities and Christian institutions of various denominations.[161] Many secular institutions, such as the University of Birmingham, have historical and contemporary associations with independent theological foundations.[162] Numerous faith-oriented institutes, such as the William Temple Foundation, are associated with, or based within, universities. Among the more recently validated 'post-1992' universities there are also fifteen institutions where churches are involved in governance. Proposing the expansion of links between Islamic and secular domains, then, doesn't involve anything that is not already firmly established in the case of Christianity.

Basing my argument simply on the principle of equality is, though, not sufficient. After all, secularists do not view the existence of state-funded Christian schools as justification for the creation of state-funded Muslim or Hindu schools, and I am sure the same would apply here. A more fundamental argument is that building such bridges can facilitate more reflective and informed varieties of religious belief – something that is worthwhile for reasons of social cohesion and because religious traditions can be sources of wisdom and philosophical insight even for those who do not have a religious faith. In his recent writing, the sociologist Olivier Roy speaks of a trend towards what he calls 'holy ignorance' – that is, the growth of assertive, often anti-intellectual forms of belief.[163] Today, he argues, religious belief is increasingly not grounded in philosophy or theology but a scriptural reading of the sacred texts and an immediate understanding of truth through individual faith. The underlying causes of this shift are many and varied, but they can generally be captured in Roy's term 'deculturation'. By this, Roy means a process by which religion is no longer woven into the collective fabric of life and no longer influences administrative, educational or legal institutions, but is instead a matter of personal affirmation and identity. It is a trend facilitated by industrialization, globalization and free market capitalism, and it can even be thought of as the by-product of secularization. In Roy's analysis, contemporary religious revivalisms, including Islamist revivalisms, do not constitute evidence against secularization but can be seen as a by-product of religion being marginalized within contemporary societies.[164] Recent policy transitions in UK higher education fit neatly into his analysis: with economic justifications dominating higher education policy in the UK, the study of religion is being driven outside of academia, and as a result, it becomes far harder for religious ideas to interact with other knowledge traditions in the humanities or the sciences.[165]

In academia and in wider public life, many commentators point to extreme, intolerant or anti-intellectual varieties of religion – and of Islam especially – as part of a justification for a stance of disengagement. Many *soi-disant* spokespersons for secularism in the UK routinely and fiercely chastise any politician who shares a platform with a religious – especially Muslim – leader known to have advocated objectionable views on sexual morality, gender relations or religious freedom. This argument can also be found in the most recent iterations of Prevent, where government has, supposedly in order to thwart extremism, attempted to stop public bodies from interacting with people it considers 'non-violent extremists'.[166] What Roy's analysis implies, however, is that this strategy of dissociation is, in the long run, counterproductive. A religious organization whose leadership and members never come into contact with a university biology department, for example, is not going to have any reason or support to think in an informed way about questions relating to creation and biological evolution. By the same token, as we saw with the case of the Islamic Foundation, engagement by public organizations can facilitate positive change.[167]

Nothing that I am supporting here contradicts the principles of liberal education. These forms of collaboration have two central aims. The first of these is enhancing individual career opportunities. Scott-Baumann and Cheruvallil-Contractor note – bluntly but with justification – that the lack of recognition for courses in private Islamic educational institutions means that 'the male seminary graduate usually becomes a taxi driver and the female seminary graduate usually becomes a housewife'.[168] Extending accreditation agreements and Recognition of Prior Learning has the potential to help *dar al-ulum*-educated students to gain acceptance and to make use of their skills in wider British society. The second is exposing people to different knowledge traditions. One of the traditional aspirations of liberal education is to expand people's horizons and make people aware of the varied forms of life around them.[169] The fact that ethnic and religious minority students, despite entering universities in high numbers and with good grades, consistently struggle to progress in UK higher education is, however, a testament to how *narrow* liberal educational institutions can be, especially at elite level.[170] Certainly, partnering with institutions whose worldview is genuinely distinctive creates challenges, but it also raises the prospect of exposing students (and staff) to knowledge traditions that have not been 'domesticated' by academic institutionalization. As long as partnerships can be developed on a voluntaristic basis, they can, then, be justified in liberal terms.

The difficulty, however, is that these are not the terms in which education policies *are* today justified. The support offered by the British government for bridge-building between institutions has emerged out of a policy discourse interested mainly in limiting the threat of extremism. Beyond this, education is treated as an investment in 'human capital' within a 'knowledge economy'. Connections between institutions can usually only be justified if they provide one partner with a revenue stream, and even these remain unstable due to ever more invasive immigration policies. Calls for an education sector that recognizes the social benefits of education – including of maintaining varied traditions of knowledge – appear therefore ever more radical.

The contours of a new British Islamic education

We do not need to end, however, on this pessimistic note. Instead, let's return to the Islamic education sector to look at recent developments and how the sector is working as a whole. Above, we saw how 'bridging institutions' have attempted to remedy the perceived deficiencies in Islamic education, making religious qualifications gained in *dar al-ulum*s more relevant to the UK context. These, however, typically had different sectarian affiliations to the dominant Deobandi institutions. Indeed, in the past Deobandi Islam has been hostile towards the devotional, Sufi-influenced varieties of Islam that the founders of bridging institutions have, in the majority of cases, espoused. Indeed, Deobandi Islam appears, with its conscious attempts to build up bulwarks against 'Western' intellectual interference, to have an ethos not far removed from the Christians in the *Mozert v. Hawkins* case. It is reasonable to ask, therefore, whether the 'soft' approach proposed above is realistic. Will it not be the case that, while the more progressive institutions may seek links with UK universities, the more isolationist Islamic traditions that concern politicians will remain on the margins? Might we not expect Deobandi institutions to reject outright any attempts by government or by publicly funded institutions to build bridges with them?

Happily, the evidence suggests the answer to these questions is no. Although sectarian divisions and suspicion of public bodies can be found in some areas, reform within the Islamic education sector appears to have taken place across the full range of traditions and institutional contexts. One striking illustration of this is the emergence of the professional role of the *Muslim chaplain*. Chaplaincy is, of course, a Christian concept, the word stemming from the term 'chapel'. As Gilliat-Ray has observed, the 'traditional role of chaplain is unique to the Christian church', with other traditions lacking a 'formalised tradition of "pastoral care" linked to clergy'.[171] Since the late twentieth century, however, across the West the professional role of chaplain has largely ceased to be about reinforcing Christian culture and become a service focused upon coordination, counselling and crisis management. It has broadened out to incorporate a multitude of religious traditions (and indeed non-religious traditions: humanist chaplains are increasingly common). In the UK as elsewhere[172] there has been, accordingly, a proliferation of Muslim chaplains in recent decades, with these being found in prisons, hospitals and the military as well as in universities and other educational settings. In Britain, this responds to increases in both demand and supply: while public institutions have had to address the needs of a more religiously diverse public, British *'ulama* have had to find professional roles.[173] In total, there are now over two hundred Muslim chaplains and, in contrast to British imams, around half of these are British-born.[174] Particularly striking is that around half are also from a Deobandi background, making chaplaincy one sphere where *dar al-ulum* education has found a practical application.

Furthermore, Gilliat-Ray and her colleagues have clearly demonstrated that chaplaincy services have profoundly altered the nature of religious leadership within British Islam.[175] Chaplains' location within both religious and secular worlds enables them – indeed, requires them – to develop the ability to move smoothly between the sometimes insular worlds of seminary and mosque and secular and religiously diverse contexts. Whatever the specific theological background of Muslim chaplains, they must offer teaching and support that transcends sectarian boundaries. Importantly, too, the demand for Muslim *women's* chaplaincy, specifically, has contributed to the development of sites like Safia Shahid's Muslim Women's College for training women leaders. A wide range of British Islamic traditions have shown themselves to be entirely comfortable recognizing this new role. As Siddiqui – whose institution, MIHE, now runs a dedicated MA in Muslim chaplaincy which incorporates a work experience placement – comments, 'We adopted the word chaplaincy in part because it is a legal term, [but] it is now very much part of the fabric of Muslim society.'[176]

What the example of Muslim chaplaincy suggests is that there is more to British Deobandi Islam than one can find in most scholarly and virtually all popular accounts of the tradition. So finally, let's return to look again at the case of Deobandi *dar al-ulum*s directly. The public perception of British Deobandi institutions is largely based upon research conducted in the mid-2000s, but these accounts are now not the only ones available, with new research being published in the 2010s by Geaves and Gilliat-Ray, as well as former *dar al-ulum* students such as Haroon Sidat.[177] Geaves, for example, following his visit to Indian Deobandi institutions, went on to carry out similar research in England supported by the

Islamic Studies Network in 2011.[178] Using relationships that he built up with senior *'ulama* during his interactions with Indian institutions,[179] he carefully negotiated entry and, although he did not refute past research into Deobandi institutions, did manage to paint a more detailed portrait.

What Geaves found were places where pupils were highly motivated and self-aware and where IT facilities bore comparison to those in most English secondary schools. Importantly, learning, rather than being one-way, 'ranged considerably from the didactic to interactive' depending on teacher and subject. The language of instruction varied as well. While there was 'more memorisation than expected from children in state schools', some classes involved discussion of social issues.[180] In classes on inheritance laws, for example, students were encouraged to author *fatwa*s which, once cleared by the teachers, were made public to the Muslim populations of Blackburn and Bury, where Geaves's research was focused. Certainly, the status of the *Dars-i Nizami* as sacred was a prevailing theme across the institutions he studied, but teachers and students were interested in where the qualifications might lead and keen in particular for pupils to use their qualifications to go on to higher study elsewhere.

This raises an interesting question: Does the picture Geaves presented reflect recent changes in the institutions, or has the lack of research access led to the institutions being misrepresented? It is hard to say for sure, but what seems most likely is both explanations are partly true. The teaching quality seems to have been underestimated somewhat. However, accounts that have emerged subsequently suggest a potentially significant shift is underway. Geaves found that some *dar al-ulum*s were interested in partnerships with local colleges and securing recognition for the *Dars-i Nizami* curriculum, but their efforts had not got very far. Since then, that interest has expanded and, in places, come to fruition. Jamiatul-Ilm Wal-Huda in Blackburn now delivers courses in partnership with Preston College. Middlesex University offers 240 'credits' (short of a full BA) for a programme running at a seminary in the north of England. Cardiff University has been approached by no less than three Deobandi *dar al-ulum*s in the last ten years to explore the possibilities for validation of curricula.[181]

One of the most vivid illustrations of this shift is that Gilliat-Ray – whose accounts of frustrated efforts to access Deobandi institutions in the mid-2000s did much to reinforce the image of them as insular – managed to negotiate a 'Memorandum of Understanding' with a Deobandi *dar al-ulum* in southern England in 2017 to conduct research. Rather than being down to luck, she concludes that this change in her fortunes reflects the fact that student need 'has pushed the *dar al-ulum* sector towards more outward-facing engagement, attention to issues of graduate employability, and aspirations for academic excellence among their students'. There is emerging evidence of

> a shift from what [Manuel] Castells[182] would term 'resistance identity' – shaped by perceptions of external hostility and rejection of dominant secular-liberal values – to 'project identity' that seeks to redefine the social position of Muslims,

not through withdrawal to the 'trenches', but through proactive engagement with civil society.[183]

The change that is afoot even extends, in some Deobandi institutions, to adopting the bureaucratic language of 'assessment criteria' and 'module outcomes' that are commonplace in UK universities.[184] The largest British *dar al-ulum*s have responded to past criticisms of teaching methods, even drawing 'British values'-related praise from Ofsted for using art to represent similarities between British and Islamic culture.[185] As Abdur-Rahman Mangera, the religious leader and former *dar al-ulum* student we met earlier, puts it:

> In a lot of these *madrasahs*, seminaries as well, there is massive change going on right now. Massive change. There is one seminary where they are working on a new curriculum, there is a board that is being created with muftis to develop a new curriculum and I see a better future, *inshallah*.[186]

None of this is to claim there isn't a long way still to travel or that the road ahead is smooth. Many Islamic institutions follow different interpersonal norms to conventional further and higher education institutions, not only being single sex but uneasy about adolescent males travelling alone into gender-mixed environments. This is likely to limit the extent of interaction. Nevertheless, there is a general trend across the Islamic education sector, with many different institutions moving broadly in the same direction. Twenty years ago, Britain was host to a collection of Islamic educational institutions that were interested in stabilizing the Islamic tradition in an unfamiliar environment or, in the Islamic Foundation's case, agitating for utopian goals derived from Islamist movements. What we have now is a diverse landscape of new and old educational institutions, some more conventional than others, that are much more outward looking and committed to the society in which they are based. They have professional goals and new roles are opening up, changing the nature of Muslim leadership in the UK. And underpinning all this, as Gilliat-Ray observes, is the fact that *dar al-ulum*s have now 'produced a generation of British-born Islamic scholars and imams':[187] people far from the stereotype of the unthinking '*naql*-head'.

Chapter 4

WHAT IS THE FUTURE FOR MUSLIM PERSONAL LAW IN BRITAIN?

Imposed meanings

When reading Anglophone accounts of Islam, I am often reminded of the philosopher Michel Foucault's contention that language is not a way of representing the world but rather 'a violence we do to things' or 'a practice which we impose upon them'.[1] Most people who write about Islam – both media pundits and academics – see themselves as *describing* the tradition, but too often we *impose a set of meanings* on it. Usually these impositions take the form of subtle resonances, but sometimes they are easy to point out. For most English speakers, *jihad* has become synonymous with terrorism, while *fatwa* has come to mean a death warrant. An *ayatollah* is a theocratic tyrant rather than a 'sign of God' (the term's literal and traditional meaning: the verses of the Qur'an and sights of nature are each 'signs of God'). Even *The Guardian*, a liberal newspaper that generally goes out of its way to avoid offending identity groups, defined *nasheed*s in 2014 as '*jihadi* songs', which is a bit like describing Gregorian chanting as 'Crusader music'.[2] In the West, the issue is not (simply) that people are ignorant of Islam but that people *know* these concepts: these impositions form part of our taken-for-granted common sense.[3] The West has created a version of Islam for itself, a distinct religion that uses the same language but with meanings far removed from Muslims' own historical and contemporary understandings.

The term '*Shari'a*' is perhaps the best example of such an imposition. In the West, people think of this term as describing a legal system that stipulates permissible and illegal behaviour, sets out standards of proof and determines appropriate punishments, including execution and beating for sometimes trivial wrongdoings. This conception in turn encourages the (sometimes well-meaning) view that Islam is potentially compatible with liberal democracy on the condition that 'the *Shari'a*' is jettisoned. This conception of Islamic law and its relation to liberal democratic norms is not just simplistic, however, but makes the hoped-for reconciliation much harder to achieve. The reason for this is that the word *Shari'a* does not describe a set of rules or even a 'law' per se. Literally, the term – which is used only once in the Qur'an (45: 18) – refers to a 'path'. Traditionally, as Khaled Abou El Fadl, a Kuwaiti American scholar of Islam, puts it, the word is 'a symbol of society's collective efforts to work out what God wants from human beings'.[4] One way to render it in English, then, would be 'God's path': something that signifies authenticity and legitimacy as well as an everyday reference to 'good conduct'. This term then contrasts with *fiqh* (usually translated as 'jurisprudence'), the tradition of formal normative reasoning. In the Islamic tradition, a jurist's (or *faqih*'s) goal is to discern the *Shari'a* in much the same way that a philosopher of aesthetics endeavours to work out the nature of beauty.

Clearly, this is not to deny that terrible actions have been legitimized by making a claim upon the *Shari'a*. It is one of a long list of high ideals – including 'progress', 'justice', 'security' and indeed 'liberalism' – that have been used to justify appalling acts. The *fiqh* tradition was formalized around the ninth century CE,[5] and it was through this process that the specified rules today associated with '*Shari'a* law' emerged. While the medieval *fiqh* tradition was deeply illiberal by contemporary standards, it was always multivocal and usually remained at one remove from secular powers. Only with the emergence of the Islamist ideal of the 'Islamic state' – which itself was a reaction to the creation of states in Muslim-majority contexts against a backdrop of colonialism – did the concept of *Shari'a* as a top-down, totalizing legal system take hold, usually with disastrous consequences.[6] With the term '*Shari'a*' retaining its overarching meaning as the path ordained for humans by God, however, it is easy to see why, despite these consequences, Muslims are rarely willing to disown the concept entirely.

This insight makes it easier to see why the survey questions about *Shari'a* discussed in Chapter 2 are hard to interpret. If we understand *Shari'a* not as a programme of law but as a symbol of what God wishes for humans, asking Muslims whether they would 'prefer to live under sharia law rather than British law [*sic*]'[7] becomes confusing or even meaningless – something that does not compare alternatives. How, one might ask, would this answer, by the Belgian scholar of Islam, Yahya Michot, fit the question above?

> Ibn Qayyim al-Jawziyya [a revered Islamic scholar, d. 1350] says: 'When the signs of justice appear and its face is radiant, by whatever means it may be, there you find the *Shari'a* of God and his religion.' So when you have, for example in this country, people saying, 'Oh, Muslims want to implement the *Shari'a* as part of English law', a good answer to this could be: 'Yes, but when there is justice in English law there already is the *Shari'a*.'[8]

These problems plague debates about the theme of this chapter: the question of whether or not the UK's jurisdictions should 'recognize' Islamic law. This is a subject media commentators all appear to have an opinion on, but most draw on the image of *Shari'a* as a comprehensive and fixed system of law. This means that a particular perspective invariably dominates: that, as one conservative commentator put it in 2008, 'you can't just have a bit of sharia – it's all or nothing'.[9] This view not only misreads the concept of *Shari'a* itself but ignores the multiplicity of ways that the *fiqh* tradition interacts with legal practices in over fifty states worldwide. A person speaking about 'Islamic law' might have in mind the suffocating system applied in Saudi Arabia or the personal laws accommodated in varying ways across the Indian subcontinent. They might be thinking of a utopian Islamist vision of an Islamic state not yet realized or informal marriages contracted in North Africa.[10] They might simply have in mind greater recognition of Muslim religious rites within the UK's legal systems.

In this chapter, my focus will be on institutions that offer some kind of service – mostly in the area of marriage and divorce – guided by a conception of Islamic law. My objective, though, is to broaden the discussion not just of these institutions but of the concept of Islamic law itself and its relation to the state. My concern about Anglophone debates on this theme is in part simply that misperceptions – as well as outright prejudice – are commonplace. As well as addressing these, however, I want to encourage readers to see Islamic law not just as a set of principles, which European states may or may not accommodate depending on their willingness to formally recognize the Islamic religion, but as a living tradition of moral argumentation that encompasses a range of normative perspectives. Islamic law is as much a *language* as a code, and I want to suggest it needs to be treated in this way by governments.

For that reason, this chapter will place Islamic law against a backdrop of debates about the concept of 'public reason'. After making basic points about how to discuss Islamic law in the UK, I begin with an introduction of how and why 'Shari'a councils' emerged, before going on to discuss the dilemmas they address and create. Then, rather than just moving on to consider the issue of state recognition, I first examine debates over whether or not citizens, when they seek to convince others to support or oppose a law, should feel free to articulate 'comprehensive' reasons – that is to say, justifications that are explicitly based on contested religious or metaphysical notions. The reason I do this is that when one examines debates among lay Muslims and Islamic scholars about Islamic law and its place one comes across varied interpretations of Islamic law and how it relates to civil law, which may involve calls for changes in civil practice or suggest that current practice is 'Islamic'. This raises questions not only about possible *recognition* of Islamic practices but also about a deeper and more fundamental *negotiation* of the Islamic tradition and secular norms in Britain.

Islamic law in Britain: What do we know? What can we say?

I should say at the outset that this chapter's subject is the most challenging of those covered in this book – for a range of reasons, of which the public understanding of *Shari'a* in the UK is only one. It touches upon highly technical questions about overlapping, and at times conflicting, cultural traditions and legal jurisdictions. In debates about Muslim marriage and divorce in Britain, a wealth of classical Islamic legal concepts are deployed along with examples from a wide range of Muslim-majority jurisdictions, as well as legal precedents and real-world cases from the UK. One comes across painful cases of domestic breakdown – some of which involve criminal as well as civil law. This pain and complexity is amplified by Muslim Britain's (dis)engagement with Britain's (especially England's) legal system, which has a significant impact on Muslims' access to justice and rights. For this reason, it is not always easy to be positive, especially given the hostile context in which debates about Islamic law take place. Nevertheless, even in this context the thesis I am advancing over the course of this book remains valid. That is, it is possible to map real and meaningful transitions in this sphere of British Islam, in spite of the very real problems.

Part of the reason this subject is challenging is that it is hard to make generalizable claims about how Islamic law operates in the UK. One problem is that there is limited reliable empirical research. As with the case of the private Islamic educational institutions discussed in the previous chapter, access to those institutions in the UK that attempt to resolve family disputes by reference to Islamic law has often been hard to negotiate. Samia Bano, whose research into this subject is among the most detailed available, writes that accessing sites to conduct her research 'proved difficult, lengthy and problematic'.[11] This means that some forms of research are more common than others. Most research in this area, including the first-hand research I have carried out myself, has been based on interviews with, and the public pronouncements of, the leaders of such institutions, who are not necessarily impartial observers. Documentary research analysing the case files of *Shari'a* councils is rarer; in situ research that observes the institutions at work is even less common; and research that interviews service users one-on-one (and that can begin to provide an idea of *why* British Muslims are making use of these institutions) is most limited of all. Generalizations therefore have to be made very cautiously, if made at all.

At the same time, investigations by journalists, and even studies by academic researchers, have sometimes sought to fill the vacuum in our understanding opportunistically and unethically. In these cases, authors claim to have gained 'unique' or 'unparalleled' access – a claim that in practice can amount to one or two interviews, a day's observation or even just browsing a list of *fatwas* on the internet.[12] In 2016, for example, the Dutch academic Machteld Zee published a study that was supposedly 'based on the most detailed and informed analysis of the workings of British sharia courts ever undertaken' and that concluded such 'courts' are 'locking women into "marital captivity"' and doing nothing to officially report domestic violence'.[13] Her account, as we shall see, was not wholly baseless but was so one-sided as to present an irresponsibly distorted picture. The claim to unparalleled access – she attended fifteen hours of hearings at two institutions, supplemented by interviews – was also straightforwardly false. First-hand, rigorous empirical studies of Islamic law in England have been carried out not only by Zee and Bano but also by John R. Bowen, Rajnaara C. Akhtar, Elham Manea, Julie Billaud and Nurin Shah-Kazemi, whose groundbreaking study, *Untying the Knot*, was every bit as detailed as Zee's and was published in 2001.[14] Religious 'courts' were also the subject of a multisite academic research project by Gillian Douglas et al. in 2011.[15] The accounts I have collected myself in this chapter, then, are one addition to a considerable body of empirical research. It is, of course, responsible to be mindful of and acknowledge gaps in research. The social and cultural processes within families and wider kinship networks that shape when, and why, British Muslims use *Shari'a* councils *are* poorly understood; men's experiences are especially neglected. Here one has to be aware too, though, of gaps being overstated in order to advance a political agenda.

So on the basis of this research, what can we say? The first thing to note is that Britain's *Shari'a* councils do not constitute a system, and certainly not a standardized one. Even without extending beyond Sunni Islam in the UK (my focus here) it is possible to identify widely varying practices, with some institutions accepting practices that others do not. This is one of the reasons why it is sensible to disregard anyone making bold claims about 'Islamic law in the UK'. Most of the research so far conducted concerns a very limited number of the more well-established institutions. Three or four appear in multiple studies while smaller, less formal operations have been neglected. Even between these established examples, there are cases of both good and bad practices. For example, while most institutions will do their best to ensure that civil legal processes run in parallel with Islamic ones, there are also examples of bad experiences and indications of practices that put abused individuals at risk.

Estimates of the number of these institutions vary markedly, with some authors putting the number as high as eighty-five.[16] Definitive figures are, however, almost impossible to ascertain. One of the reasons for this is that it is not clear what counts as an institution and what does not. In the UK, Islamic law generally falls between what Prakash Shah describes as 'first-order' and 'second-order' spheres of dispute resolution: the former refers to family, friends and wider kinship and community networks, and the latter to formal legal redress.[17] An imam in a mosque, for example, may offer informal advice to a couple experiencing marital difficulty that is guided by his understanding of the *Shari'a*. By doing this, is he offering advice as a friend and peer, or offering a legal service in a 'parallel jurisdiction'? Should this mosque be listed among the eighty-five? Doing this would seem odd: many religious leaderships and church volunteers offer congregants informal guidance when they are going through difficult times, including divorces, and this is not regarded as a quasi-legal activity. (Christian and Jewish groups within Britain offer more formal divorce services too, which engender considerably less consternation.)[18] If these activities aren't counted, the number of *Shari'a* councils in the UK could shrink considerably: in Bowen's interviews with the leaders of such institutions, most interviewees estimated the number to be between twelve and fifteen (although in some cases these take the form of a network of institutions rather than being located on a single premises).[19]

This brings us to the next point to consider: what should we refer to them as? Should they be described as 'courts', as they routinely are in the popular press? A case can be made both for and against. On the one hand, even the more established institutions prefer to describe themselves as 'councils' or, in the case of some that offer dispute resolution services that go beyond matrimonial matters, 'tribunals'. Often, this is done in recognition of these institutions' lack of legal authority in the UK and is a reflection of their self-perception as mediation and reconciliation services as well as bodies that adjudicate on matrimonial disputes and provide Islamic divorce certificates.[20] The term 'court' can also be confusing to those unfamiliar with British Islam, suggesting as it does an adversarial contest in an open forum rather than the humdrum settings in which meetings often take place. First-hand accounts of hearings in *Shari'a* councils tend to describe meetings between a few people in a simple premises: a small back office in a mosque or converted shop. On the other hand, though, there is a degree of power and authority in the judgements such institutions take, even if they are not recognized in English or Scottish civil law. Research into *Shari'a* councils has highlighted how some take care to produce documents that imply authority and formality.[21] If these institutions are not 'courts', some do try to maintain an authoritative tenor, for example, by advertising themselves with an austere image of an American judge's gavel. This can even extend to the way in which offices are set up. Conversations with clients may take place on a raised dais, the aim of this being to imbue proceedings with a sense of solemnity.[22] Ultimately, however, while some (certainly not all) institutions might try to convey formal authority, they currently do not have it, and most are open about this. Using terms like 'courts' or even 'legal institutions' risks obscuring this. In this chapter, then, as well as using self-descriptors, I reluctantly opt for accuracy over brevity and refer to them as 'Islamic dispute resolution institutions'.

Finally, how popular are they? What kind of place do they have within Muslim populations? Are they widely used by Muslims, or are they a sideshow? Undoubtedly, this is the most difficult question to answer and the best I can offer are a few hints using mismatched statistics on separation and divorce. (For reasons I explain below, the provision of religious divorces has always been the principal activity of Islamic dispute resolution institutions in Britain.) The institution of which we arguably know most, the Islamic Sharia Council at Birmingham Central Mosque, deals with around 150 cases per year, almost all involving a couple seeking to divorce or end a cohabiting relationship.[23] This is, of course, only one of a number of institutions operating across the UK, and there are others that deal with a similar number of cases. The Leyton-based Islamic Sharia Council, another relatively large and well-known example, dealt with around 150 cases a year in the first decade of its existence and has continued to operate successfully since then.[24] Given these figures, the total number of cases dealt with by Islamic dispute resolution institutions in the UK could be in the region of 750 to 1,000 annually. This is still a tiny number when set against the divorce industry in Britain as a whole. There are approximately 135,000 divorces per year in the UK, and this does not include cohabiting couples that separate.[25] Such aggregate numbers, however, tell us little. What we really need in order to assess the popularity of Islamic dispute resolution institutions is the overall number of Muslim divorces and separations, but making an accurate estimate of this is next to impossible. Divorce figures in the UK are not broken down by religion, so sociologists tend to use lone parenthood as a proxy. This suggests that separation is marginally more common in Muslim households: in 2011, 13.4 per cent of Muslim households were single-parent families, compared with an average in England and Wales of 10.6 per cent. (Notably, this is a recent development: between the mid-1990s and 2001 the percentage of lone-parent families of South Asian heritage doubled, possibly due to young people being better supported to divorce and remarry.)[26] This is still of limited help, however, because Muslim couples are (as we will see) much less likely to register their marriages than the wider population. The proportion of British Muslims – 5.2 per cent of the UK population (see Chapter 2) – would suggest a figure of around seven thousand Muslim civil divorces annually, but actual figures could be very different to this due to cohabitation being more common in Muslim communities. Even if the total number of married and cohabiting Muslim couples who separate is much higher than this – in the low tens of thousands, say – it still seems safe to say that Islamic dispute resolution institutions are involved in a significant minority of Muslim separations.

Why did Islamic dispute resolution institutions emerge?

Islamic dispute resolution institutions in the UK occupy an unusual position within British Islam. They are generally, like most mosques in Britain, run by an older generation of British Muslims. Indeed, most emerged under the guidance of mosque leaders, with many being established because imams were finding that far too much of their time was being taken up with attempting to resolve marital disputes.[27] Largely because of this, the largest councils – which were established in the early to mid-1980s – can be seen as part of the process of community formation outlined in Chapter 2. However, dispute resolution institutions differ from mosques and *dar al-ulum*s in important respects. Mosques, as we have seen, often cater for a particular ethnic community and reinforce ethnic ties, with Punjabi, Gujarati, Urdu or Somali being commonly used in sermons alongside Arabic and English. Newer Muslim migrant communities, such as Somalis, often break away from religious institutions established by older communities shortly after arrival in the UK. Islamic educational institutions, too, generally transmit very distinctive Islamic traditions and to some extent appeal to populations with particular ethno-religious heritages. Islamic dispute resolution institutions certainly bear the imprint of particular Islamic traditions in the norms they follow, with some being Barelvi-oriented and others influenced by Deobandi and Salafi/Ahl i-Hadith[28] norms. Even so, they still, in Bano's words, 'aim to cater to the needs of all Muslims irrespective of ethnic, racial or national background'.[29] They emerged as part of an effort to develop community infrastructures, but reflect gradual changes within Islam in Britain and the diminishing – or refashioning – of ethnic and sectarian affiliations and norms of conduct.

In fact, change within British Islam has been fundamental to the emergence of Islamic dispute resolution institutions in the UK. While most mosques and educational institutions initially sought, consciously or unconsciously, to maintain particular Islamic traditions for Muslim migrants and their offspring, dispute resolution institutions emerged partly as a means of negotiating between Islamic traditions and the English legal system. (I speak of 'England' here and elsewhere in this chapter because laws in England and Wales are distinct from those in force elsewhere in Britain. I refer to Scottish law specifically where it is relevant.) Although, as we shall see, they do have a somewhat awkward relationship with English civil law, Islamic dispute resolution institutions did not emerge as a challenger to it or as part of an effort to undermine it. Indeed, what is particularly interesting about these institutions is that they do not simply operate according to the norms of the (mainly South Asian) legal traditions with which their founders were familiar. David Pearl and Werner Menski, in their work on Muslim law in the 1990s, popularized the Urdu term '*Angrezi Shariat*' ('English *Sharia*') as a way of highlighting how, in the last few decades, forms of Islamic law have emerged in Britain that have been distinguishable from the legal traditions in the regions from which most British Muslims originate. Legal practices have emerged that have 'built the requirements of English law into traditional legal structures'.[30] The very existence of Islamic dispute resolution institutions in England is, then, a testament to the adaptive tendencies of British Islam.

There is one particularly noteworthy reason why Islamic dispute resolution institutions were created. Within the classical Islamic tradition, the majority of legal schools give men the right to initiate divorce unilaterally without recourse to any external authority or institution.[31] All a man needs to do is declare *talaq* three times, usually in three consecutive months, and his marriage is ended. *Talaq* is one of a number of acts that, within the tradition of classical *fiqh*, has the quality of a legal judgement (*hukm*) even if no legal institution is involved.[32] (This differs from legal practice in many Muslim-majority countries today: in Pakistan, for example, a man pronouncing *talaq* has to register it in writing at the earliest opportunity.)[33] Within the same tradition, a woman seeking to obtain a divorce, by contrast, usually either has to ask for one from her husband (*khul'*) or, if her husband does not give his consent, appeal to some kind of formal authority for an annulment (*faskh*) or divorce (*tafriq*). Because no Islamic dispute resolution institutions were established in the UK, the argument goes, Muslim women were encountering serious difficulties. A woman might obtain a civil divorce, but because her husband had not agreed to a religious divorce her relatives and peers would still consider her to be married 'Islamically', making remarriage difficult. This situation has parallels in Jewish (particularly Orthodox or Haredi) contexts. In some traditional conceptions of Jewish law, women are not able to end a marriage without their husbands granting them a religious bill of divorce, known as a *get*.[34] Indeed, in this tradition the problem can be more acute because Jewish religious authorities (*dayans*), unlike their Islamic counterparts, will generally not grant a divorce when the husband does not consent to the marriage ending. Jewish courts (*beth dins*) regard their role as acting as witness to a couple's decision to divorce, rather than themselves dissolving marriages. Women who have been refused a *get* are often referred to as *agunot* (singular, *agunah*), literally meaning a person who is 'chained' to a marriage and is unable or unwilling to remarry and have children who might be deemed 'illegitimate'. In the UK, campaigns were launched in Jewish communities to deal with the problem in the 1990s,[35] and in 2002 the Divorce (Religious Marriages) Act was passed, giving civil judges the power to delay divorce proceedings between the two main stages (*decree nisi* and *decree absolute*) if there is an ongoing religious divorce. In January 2020 new laws against 'controlling behaviour' were applied to the problem too, with a Jewish husband being compelled to issue a divorce or risk jail.[36] To date however, although some legal scholars have suggested the 2002 Act could apply to Muslim marriages,[37] these measures have only been used in Jewish contexts, and what Pearl and Menski term 'limping marriages' remains a problem in Muslim contexts.

These already difficult situations can be further complicated when a couple has – by choice, neglect or deception – failed to register their marriage in civil law. The issue of marriage registration is a complex one and I shall return to it later in this chapter, but one can say with some confidence that the failure to register marriages is a serious problem in British Muslim contexts. Repeated studies have shown that, among those who contact Islamic dispute resolution institutions about an Islamic divorce, between half and two-thirds are not married according to civil law.[38] This seems to be reflected in the wider British Muslim population too: one survey of 923 married Muslim women across 14 British cities, carried out by the production company True Vision Aire and analysed by Rajnaara C. Akhtar, found that 60 per cent of Muslim women, and 80 per cent of those under 25, were not in legally recognized marriages.[39] When this is a matter of considered choice it may not be too concerning, but what is worrying is the number of Muslims who believe they are married according to civil law when they are not. In the same survey, 28 per cent of the Muslim women in religious-only marriages were not aware that a *nikah* (Islamic marriage) is not recognized in English law. Most concerning of all are cases of deception or broken promises, which seem common among women – and it is, due to the aforementioned Islamic marriage norms, normally women – who contact Islamic dispute resolution institutions. As Bano writes of her research with Muslim women who used an institution: 'In the majority of cases [of unregistered marriage] the women had in fact expected their religious marriages to be registered in accordance with civil law, but after the religious ceremony and consummation of the marriage their husbands had simply refused to complete the registration.'[40] In England civil marriages have to take place in a registered premises to be recognized in law, and the number of mosques registered also remains extremely low, not only compared to established religious groups but also to more recently settled ones. According to the Office for National Statistics (ONS), while 90 per cent of Catholic churches and 79 per cent of Sikh temples are registered, only 19 per cent of Britain's mosques are.[41] In True Vision Aire's survey, 31 per cent of respondents had married within a mosque and only a tiny 3.6 per cent of these involved a civil registration.[42] This is despite several campaigns for mosque and marriage registration by Muslim organizations, including one by the Muslim Institute and, more recently, another by the solicitor Aina Khan, whose favoured slogan on the issue is: 'If you register your car, you should be registering your marriage.'[43]

There are multiple factors behind these figures. Lack of knowledge among religious leaders and the general public plays a big part. Among the UK population, knowledge of laws relating to marriage is generally poor: 46 per cent of people in England and Wales think, wrongly, that cohabitation confers legal rights relating to custody and inheritance.[44] Muslims are no different in this regard: in focus groups conducted by Akhtar, many couples described registration using an individualistic language of 'personal choice', but, she comments, 'it was clear that knowledge about the reality of that "choice" in the form of legal repercussions was not evident in the majority of the participants'.[45] What distinguishes Muslims from the general public is that this generic problem is compounded by the fact that, as we saw in Chapter 3, as few as one in four imams has been based in the UK for more than ten years, while many marriages – especially among British Pakistani Muslims – are contracted transnationally.[46] This brings into play a wide range of jurisdictions, adding a layer of complexity. As Katharine Charsley and Anika Liversage point out, 'Although a *nikah* ... carried out in Pakistan is valid for immigration purposes, Islamic marriage conducted in secular Turkey holds no such legal status.'[47] Against this confusing backdrop, it becomes easier to see how a couple or an imam could be unsure about a relationship's legal standing.

Another contributory factor is the nature of marriage in the Islamic tradition. Many Muslim religious leaders in the UK are scathing about what they see as the unwillingness of mosques to register premises. As Abdul Kadir Barkatulah, formerly the senior imam at Finchley Mosque, north London, and an erstwhile scholar at the Islamic Sharia Council, laments: 'At the moment, what the mosques are doing, they are shutting the doors.'[48] But even such critics recognize that marriage in Islam differs from the Anglican norms in which British culture is steeped, with the process being more of a private matter. Usama Hasan, for example, led a network of British Muslim professionals, City Circle, in the early 2000s and was a part-time imam before joining the think tank Quilliam. (He is also the son and brother of leaders of the Islamic Sharia Council.) Although he stresses that the mosques for which he has worked have always been registered, he observes: 'I'll challenge anybody to show me that you need a holy man or an imam to conduct [an Islamic] marriage or divorce. ... You just need the couple and two witnesses and then that's it.'[49] The late Cassandra Balchin, who worked with the Muslim Women's Network and the activist network Women Living Under Muslim Laws before her death in 2012, was another campaigner for Islamic marriage reform and registration. She too, though, spoke of the benefits of the distinctive aspects of a *nikah* contract, lamenting that its status was only weakly recognized in England as a 'pre-nuptial agreement':

> [When I remarried] I found it very sad that because I'm here [in the UK] and it was more convenient, although I'm a Pakistani national as well ..., I didn't get a marriage contract and I'm very annoyed about that because I really wanted to put my conditions down. I actually like the fact that in Islam husband and wife can mutually agree to write certain things down. It sets the basis for marriage; it sets a clear basis on which to understand that human relationship. And most importantly if those conditions are broken the woman has the automatic right to seek divorce and keep all her financial rights, and I rather like that .... But there isn't room for that in the British system, and that's sad because that system

actually regards women as very autonomous. It says, you know, the woman is an equal party to the contract.[50]

A third contributory factor is that Muslims – especially younger Muslims – are opting for just an Islamic marriage because it allows them to enter into a physical relationship without judgement from peers and without being weighed down by civil recognition and the legal burdens that come with it. Research into this 'fledgling love' category of *nikah* is scarce, but cases were found in True Vision Aire's survey and Akhtar's qualitative research.[51] In these cases, Islamic marriage acts as a 'bridge' between cohabitation and civil marriage. Such unions are completely in keeping with the modern trend towards what Zygmunt Bauman calls 'liquid love', which eschews any fixed and durable bonds.[52] The question this raises, then, is, as Akhtar puts it, 'whether religious-only marriages display signs of isolation, or whether they in fact display signs of "integration"'.[53]

Risk, shame and coercion: The role of communal norms

Yet even if Muslim marriage trends seem, in certain respects, to be following contemporary British social trends, traditional conventions surrounding marriage remain significant, and without understanding these one cannot fully understand the problems that Islamic dispute resolution institutions were created to ameliorate or the context in which they operate. I observed in Chapter 2 that within the Muslim populations of the UK endogamous marriage is common, but said little regarding the norms and expectations that can shape the process of finding a marriage partner, especially among families originating from rural areas of Pakistan and Bangladesh.[54] In many South Asian contexts marriage is, as Roger Ballard puts it, 'a crucial component of [a] kinship system [that] is nevertheless set within, and to a large extent over-shadowed by, a much wider network of inter- and intra-generational ties of mutual reciprocity, largely ordered within the priority given to ties of patrilineal descent'.[55] Marriage can be a means of attaining increased prestige and gifts a way of maintaining social status. Interactions between extended families (in Urdu, *ghar*, literally meaning 'house') and wider kinship networks (*biraderis*) can be protracted, complex and consequential for all involved. Marriage between cousins is common and relatives – in particular, uncles and aunts – may expect 'first refusal' on a son or daughter.

In UK-based diasporic communities, such norms have been, as we saw in Chapter 2, profoundly disrupted, but there are still indications that among the British Pakistani population close kin transnational marriages remain common and perhaps in the majority.[56] These arrangements are a source of significant controversy, in part because of the health risks created. (A major longitudinal study of health in Bradford that compared health outcomes between white British and minority ethnic communities found that the risk of congenital abnormalities rises from 2.6 to 6.2 per cent in consanguineous unions.)[57] Nevertheless, they persist because, as well as being a way of enabling relatives to come to the UK from overseas, these unions can be viewed as a way of mitigating the risk of having one's offspring move to another, unfamiliar household.[58] Consequently, marriage negotiations, and the associated friction between families, still occur. As a young Pakistani put it in a research interview conducted by Yunas Samad and John Eade: Parents 'want their children … to stay within that family network so if they don't get married … then it can cause conflict between the brother and sister'.[59]

Honour (*izzat* in Urdu) can loom large in such negotiations. Withdrawal from an agreement to marry can lead to considerable 'dishonour' for a family. So, too, can a marriage to someone from the wrong status (*zat*) or from outside an extended kinship network. Although the general trend is towards giving children greater say in marriage, the pressure felt by families can, in some cases, cause parents to take drastic steps to undermine their children's choices. In Katherine Charsley's research in Bristol, for example, one Pakistani-heritage man's father had threatened to cut him off financially and did not speak to him until he abandoned his planned 'love marriage' and accepted a match with an extended family member.[60] Even in cases where parents' personal views are more flexible, there can still be a deep reluctance to go against social convention. As another of Charsley's participants remarked about his daughter's intentions to marry an Indian, rather than Pakistani, Muslim: 'Some people are brave, but I won't allow [this for] my children.'[61] For children, obviously, this can be a source of profound stress, but it is notable that children frequently sympathize with their parents' consternation when they break with social convention. One research participant from Bano's study, for example, a Pakistani woman who had chosen to marry a person from outside of her kinship network, described her parents' loss of face: 'I did understand where they were coming from because in Asian communities it's the norm to marry in your own *biraderi* and I knew that my parents were going to get a lot of stick from the community.'[62]

Of course, these conventions are fundamental to vexed debates about forced marriage and have bearing on broader conversations about control, especially control of the bodies and actions of young women. As we can see from the quotes above, pressure can be applied to both young men and women within the context of marriage negotiations. Nevertheless, the notion of family honour remains deeply intertwined with specifically *patriarchal* ideas and norms. Although activists – from both Muslim and secular backgrounds[63] – have sought over many years to contest or reclaim notions of 'honour' that have been transmitted to the UK from South Asia, the perception remains in some contexts that a family's '*izzat*' is something that needs to be maintained through disciplinary control of women, usually by male relatives. As one Bangladeshi elder observed in Samad and Eade's research: 'If a girl who's done something [i.e, had sexual relations outside marriage] she would then be taken to Bangladesh and married off. Such [a] step is necessary as it is a matter of maintaining *izzat*.'[64]

This kind of illegal coercion is something that Islamic dispute resolution institutions encounter with surprising – indeed, worrying – regularity. In Nurin Shah-Kazemi's early study of the Muslim Law (Shariah) Council, an institution in

Ealing which was set up by the late Zaki Badawi and is associated with the Muslim College (see Chapter 3), 28 of 308 marriages were identified as forced.[65] This is broadly consistent with Bano's smaller study of Muslim women, where the sample comprised 13 'arranged' marriages, 8 'own-choice' marriages and 4 'forced' marriages.[66] In Bowen's more recent work, 23 of 178 cases at the Islamic Sharia Council were classed as forced, while 40 involved domestic abuse.[67] Examples have also emerged of women visiting Islamic divorce services who are currently based in a women's refuge.[68] Most of these cases precede laws brought in to address such coercion, notably the Anti-social Behaviour, Crime and Policing Act 2014, which criminalized forced marriages. Still, there are plainly difficult questions that need to be asked about the way Islamic dispute resolution institutions address cases involving abuse.

These questions are difficult in part because the boundary between autonomously choosing one's partner, choosing with the assistance of others and being forced is often unclear. Coercion is not always explicit. Parents' or wider social expectations may influence children's choices. Where there is a disagreement, children may opt not to voice it because of material and emotional reliance on their parents and family networks. Those subjected to pressure may believe that kinship networks, while requiring personal sacrifices, also have benefits. As an example, consider the following excerpt from Bano's research, by a woman who had been forced into a marriage but who nonetheless observed that parental assistance remained important in her plans to remarry:

> Having an arranged marriage was the only option for me and I never thought about challenging my parents. Getting married the way I got married was like for … well, for keeping the family together; you're meant to be keeping the ties together. It's meant to be like this, you know, some sort of guarantee that if anything goes wrong, then you've got the family there to help sort things out.[69]

It is important to stress that these problems are not limited to Muslims. Close kin marriage is more common within South Asian Muslim families than in Hindu and Sikh marriages,[70] but abuse relating to transnational arranged marriage is found across religious traditions. Sundari Anitha et al. have highlighted the problem of 'transnational abandonment' in India, for example, where a Western husband arranges a marriage with an Indian wife, only to leave her stranded with few rights after the husband receives a dowry.[71] The majority of women affected in these cases are Hindu and Sikh. It is important to stress, too, that coercion, deception and other forms of abuse are by no means inherent to family involvement in choosing a partner. The sources I have been citing above all make it clear that religious and cultural inheritances are widely valued by all generations of South Asian Muslims and are seen as vital to personal flourishing. Nevertheless, in cases of deception, where a husband simply refuses to register a marriage with the civil authorities after a religious marriage has been contracted, such social norms relating to shame, honour and prestige can be transformed into weapons used to restrict the woman's ability to seek a remedy.

A response to the English legal system?

So far, I have looked at how classical Islamic legal traditions and South Asian cultural norms have facilitated the creation of British Islamic dispute resolution institutions, but have said little about Britain and its legal cultures, which is more than a little unfair; indeed, it risks pathologizing Muslims. It is, of course, valid to examine how ethno-religious cultural norms contribute to domestic violence and control, but Britain's own norms play a part too. Britain is a country that happily tolerates domestic abuse; each year, some 1.4 million women are abused in England and Wales alone, and even the most extreme cases barely register in the national psyche.[72] Laws passed in the UK have also contributed to the inability of ethnic minority women to escape abusive relationships, with changes to immigration regulations in the last twenty years having a particularly pernicious effect. During its thirteen years in power, New Labour extended the period during which couples must remain together in order to prove they have not entered into a 'sham marriage', creating pressure for women to remain in unhappy or abusive relationships.[73] Domestic violence applications were also specifically excluded from the appeal structure of the Immigration Act 2014, passed under the Liberal–Conservative coalition government.[74] Campaigning organizations such as Southall Black Sisters (which supported Anitha et al.'s research into transnational abandonment) have had some success in lobbying for domestic violence exemptions to such immigration and deportation regulations, notably securing the Domestic Violence Rule 2002, which makes it easier for women to leave an abusive relationship without fearing deportation.[75] Women with insecure immigration status only have limited recourse to such legal remedies, however. The situation has become particularly serious since the introduction of 'hostile environment' policies by the Conservatives after 2010. These compel public bodies to withhold services from irregular migrants, limiting women's access to medical and support services and making them wary of presenting at the charitable services that they can access. One of the tragic ironies of the moral panics about forced marriage and 'honour-based' violence among British Muslims is that, while leading to some positive change,[76] they have encouraged anti-immigrant sentiments and, through this, laws that facilitate abuse.

Another reason it is important to focus on the UK's legal cultures – and the English legal system in particular – is because a compelling argument can be made that Islamic dispute resolution institutions are a response to the peculiarities of English law. The Marriage Act of 1753, which sought to end unregulated 'clandestine' marriages, made the Anglican Church central to laws governing marriage in England.[77] Exemptions and rights were gradually extended to some religious minorities – notably Quakers and Jews – in one of the earliest examples of religious accommodation,[78] but religious marriage rights were extended to groups in a communalist manner from an Anglican starting point. A communalist approach to marriage law was also taken in British India. British rulers permitted marriage affairs in different religious communities to be governed by the traditions of those communities.[79] This approach allowed, or even encouraged, religious scholars to create alternative forums to adjudicate on marriage, and while Islamic scholars had limited success in setting up state-recognized courts in the early twentieth century, they did set up non-state Islamic councils which are known as *dar ul-qazas*. Part of the reason that Islamic dispute resolution institutions exist in the UK and not in France[80] is that those who set them up understood them to be consistent with past governance. British Islamic scholars endeavoured to replicate the non-state Islamic councils that were created in India, inspired by the communalist approach to personal law taken by colonial authorities.[81]

In England, the historical Anglican dominance of marriage law has bequeathed various legal peculiarities. Laws concerning marriage were gradually relaxed in England, with civil registration recognized in 1836 and regulations on premises being loosened in the 1990s so that marriages could be performed in hotels and stately homes as well as register offices and religious premises.[82] English law remains centred on premises rather than persons, however, meaning it contrasts not only with many countries outside the UK but with Scotland too, where marriage law has – famously – long been more accommodating. In addition to this, marriages conducted in Anglican churches have a different and more complicated set of preliminaries, with extensive rules dedicated to the reading of banns.[83] Marriages conducted outside of religious premises are also – in a way that seems out of step with the UK's generally moderate secularism – required to refrain from making all but incidental references to religion. Divorce law has its own set of idiosyncrasies too, in particular lengthy separation periods and the widely criticized need to prove 'fault' when a marriage breaks down. There is, in fact, a widely held view that the laws governing marriage and divorce in England and Wales are rigid, exclusionary (especially for groups such as humanists) and, in the words of the Law Commission in 2015, 'hopelessly out of date'.[84]

The exact way in which these complications affect Muslims' interactions with civil law is hard to determine, though it is reasonable to presume that these complex rules regarding premises, registration and fault in cases of divorce contribute to the confusions we have discussed so far. Certainly, Islamic dispute resolution institutions do seem to be a specifically *English* legal phenomenon, with (to the best of my knowledge, at least) no large dispute resolution institutions located in Scotland. The question this raises, then, is whether English laws need to change to adapt to present realities. There does appear to be the appetite for this. In 2018 the UK government asked the Law Commission to conduct a full review of laws relating to weddings in England and Wales with a view to proposing options for a simpler and fairer system that 'gives modern couples meaningful choice'.[85] One question to consider, then, is the extent to which Muslims' calls for change – of which there have been many, as we will see – can be factored into this public conversation about reforming English law.

Islamic dispute resolution institutions: The disease or the cure?

First, however, let's look in more detail at the work Islamic dispute resolution institutions do and the opinions that Islamic scholars and activists have about their work. We have seen that these institutions did not emerge in order to *impose* a normative order upon British Muslims who were living happily in the absence of Islamic law. Rather, they responded to an already existing set of cultural relations. Even so, one can ask about them: Do these institutions offer solutions to the problems British Muslims face, or do they in fact ultimately exacerbate them? The leaders of such institutions have tended to present themselves as people who provide a solution to the pre-existing problem of limping marriages. Indeed, those in charge of councils often describe themselves as interested mainly or even exclusively in the emancipation of vulnerable Muslim women. Consider, for example, the quotation below from Faizul Aqtab Siddiqi, principal of the Nuneaton-based Hijaz College (discussed in the previous chapter) and founder of the Muslim Arbitration Tribunal, which issues divorces and undertakes other forms of dispute resolution within the terms of the Arbitration Act (1996):

> It's argued that what *Shari'a* courts do is subjugate ... women. Nonsense! Absolute humbug! You know the reality is that some of these *Shari'a* councils were created to give women the right to walk away from marriages which they were stuck in for decades, so that they could walk away from them with certainty and a definitive cut from the past.[86]

This is an unusually forceful pronouncement, but one of many similar claims. The senior figures in the Islamic Sharia Council have described their work in the same terms.[87] Shahid Raza and the late Zaki Badawi, of the Ealing-based Muslim Law (Shariah) Council UK, have both cited this as their institution's main purpose, with the latter being quoted in both Menski's work and by another academic scholar, Ihsan Yilmaz.[88] It is an argument that has some force, especially when one considers the opposition that the councils faced from within Muslim communities when they were first set up. Islamic dispute resolution institutions are often described, especially by their critics, as one part of a communitarian system integrated into Muslim community infrastructures. They tend to be looked upon as a reactionary force that seeks to turn British Muslim populations into, in Chetan Bhatt's words, an 'ecological and self-governing culture ... steeped in tradition'.[89] This argument has some merit. It neglects, though, the level of opposition to the creation of Islamic dispute resolution institutions from within some Muslim community networks. Scholars working in such institutions have been accused of disrupting families and even reported cases of physical threats from ultra-conservative elements of the Muslim public. As Shahid Raza has said of the period just after the Muslim Law (Shariah) Council was set up, 'We would be walking down the street and people would say: "There are the people who want to attack families."'[90]

There is some evidence to show that, at times, Islamic dispute resolution institutions challenge patriarchal stereotypes in their proceedings, too. Julie Billaud recounts a case from her research of a woman who approached Birmingham Central Mosque's council requesting a divorce from her husband from whom she had been separated for two years and who had allegedly developed a 'violent attitude'.

The husband was disabled and so was represented by his son, who contended that his mother's request 'was motivated by her desire to lead the life of a "single woman", which would involve "loosening her modesty" and "abandoning her responsibilities as a mother"'. To this, the council, led by a female Islamic scholar, Amra Bone, responded not just by siding with the wife and granting the divorce but by stressing that, in Bone's words, 'Islam takes both parties as independent individuals' with reciprocal duties towards one another. As Billaud puts it, 'The young man, who was anxious about maintaining the honor and reputation of his family by controlling the modesty of his mother, [were] counterbalanced by [Bone's] arguments stressing the responsibility of the Council in avoiding greater harm'.[91] Such a judgement should not perhaps be entirely surprising from this council in particular: it was founded as a Muslim women's advice centre and only later did it begin to issue religious divorces.[92]

Siddiqi's quote, however, gives the impression that Islamic dispute resolution institutions function essentially as heroes on horseback, entering onto the scene and breaking down traditional norms in order to release vulnerable people in bondage. Such a portrayal unfortunately obscures several complicating factors. Principal among these is the fact that, while Islamic dispute resolution institutions were formed in response to Muslim women's needs, they do not, by and large, question established Islamic traditions, including the imbalance in access to divorce that puts British Muslim women in a difficult position in the first place. Indeed, they have often been hostile towards efforts to effect change. In 2008 the Muslim Institute, along with Balchin and Barkatullah, attempted to develop a *nikah* contract that equalized men's and women's right to divorce via a 'delegated right to divorce' (*talaq al tafwid*), something that is recognized in some form in various Muslim-majority jurisdictions, including Pakistan. This did not get far, however, in large part because they faced vigorous opposition from various Muslim organizations, including other leaders of the Islamic Sharia Council.[93]

This congratulatory portrayal is also silent about the processes those wanting a divorce must go through. In any context, divorce processes are complex and difficult, and Islamic dispute resolution institutions are no exception. There is usually discussion of grounds that touches on the behaviours of the parties. In practice, Islamic councils almost never refuse a divorce, whatever comments may be made by the Islamic scholars during the process. Even so, along the way forms of justification are sometimes made that raise questions about attitudes towards women and intrusion into people's personal lives. During his ethnographic research, for example, Bowen examined a case at the Islamic Sharia Council – an institution takes a more conservative line than the Birmingham council, despite following the same Hanafi school of law – in which a woman produced a doctor's certificate proving her virginity as evidence of non-consummation. Bowen also examined a case at the same institution in which one '*alim* (since dismissed following complaints) maintained that a wife's refusal to return to her Somali husband, who had been refused entry to the UK, constituted marital disobedience (*nushuz*) and grounds for the refusal of a divorce.[94] Such cases are hard to square with the depiction of councils as focused on women's rights.

There are also questions about legitimacy. Relevant to this is the *mahr* – typically translated as 'marriage gift' or 'dower'. A *mahr* is a gift given by a groom to a bride as part of a *nikah*. It can vary substantially both in form and value, from a hundred pounds worth of jewellery to tens of thousands of pounds (or an equivalent currency) in cash.[95] Often it is not paid in full at the time of marriage but is nevertheless usually negotiated in advance. If all goes well in a marriage a *mahr*, once given, is settled. However, in cases of divorce the fate of the *mahr* can be a source of fierce contestation and require discriminating judgement. Classical Islamic law generally stipulated that in cases of unilateral divorce by the husband (*talaq*) the wife retains her gifts and receives anything unpaid. The same occurs if a third party annuls a marriage (*faskh*) on grounds of impotence or some other consideration. In instances where the woman asks for a divorce in the form of a *khula*, however, she is required to return the *mahr*. This distinction, while simple enough in theory, often breaks down in real life. What, for example, should one do if the wife has been pushed to ask for a divorce by the husband's behaviour? Should the *mahr* still be repaid? Within the Hanafi school at least – which prevails in South Asia and thus in most Islamic dispute resolution institutions – the answer has usually been no, which then raises the question of how to decide what constitutes being 'pushed'.[96] There is an obvious incentive for husbands to try and recategorize a *talaq* as a *khula* in order to avoid his financial obligations, but what authority should decide if this is happening?

The research literature on Islamic dispute resolution institutions gives myriad cases of husbands being given short shrift when the *'ulama* believe them to be using classical Islamic principles strategically as a way of gaining financially or exiting a marriage quickly and easily. Even so, difficult questions about civil–religious interactions concerning the division of property and custody of children remain. In general, when a woman contacts a council to obtain a divorce the first thing the scholars do is send a notice to the husband of the woman's intentions to see if he will consent to the divorce. If he does not reply after being contacted several times over a series of months (which is common) the council will usually offer the woman a certificate that declares the marriage ended. During this process, however, the *'ulama* interview the parties and do their best to reconcile them through mediation, following advice contained in the Qur'an on marriage and divorce (4: 35). Records and first-hand accounts of these mediation sessions found in the literature include some troubling details.

Accounts of proceedings in Islamic dispute resolution institutions have found that discussions of custody and property – particularly pertaining to the *mahr* – may take place. For example, cases have been observed in which divorcing couples met for mediation sessions in order to work out whether unpaid *mahr* constitutes part of the financial settlement handed down by a civil court or whether it is a separate element that needs to be paid in addition.[97] In other cases, details negotiated within civil divorce courts concerning custody of children have been relitigated in *Shari'a* councils. One case file that Bano cites from the Muslim Law (Shariah) Council illustrates this well.[98] It referred to a young Muslim woman who was seeking an Islamic divorce at the same time as going through a civil divorce. The woman apparently had no desire to enter into mediation and, after speaking with her, the scholars concluded that reconciliation was unlikely to be successful. The husband initially refused her request for an Islamic divorce but, at some point during negotiations, his solicitor sent a letter to the council. This stated that if the woman would be willing to meet for mediation and allow the husband access to their children – which seems to have been denied by the civil courts, possibly due to violence and emotional abuse – then he would grant a swift Islamic divorce. Thus the council – although it defers to the authority of the state, as we will see below – nevertheless seemed to function in this instance as a setting in which the husband could challenge a civil judgement.

Bano's research is unusual because it is based on interviews with service users rather than archival research or observation of meetings in Islamic dispute resolution institutions. Her research is now over fifteen years old, so it is a little outdated; increased scrutiny of *Shari'a* councils recently has led to various internal reforms and improvements. Nevertheless, her participants give an indication of the problems that can arise in these settings. The interviewees' accounts of reconciliation sessions in Bano's study vary significantly. In some cases, the women viewed the mediation process as useful and constructive, but some of the accounts she presents are far more troubling, revealing some challenging intra-community inequalities. Consider these three quotations from different interviewees:

> They [the Islamic scholars] were right from the beginning on his side; they didn't even listen to what I was saying. I mean I do read books. I don't go into it that much but do know the basics, you know, what a husband has to do. I was really disappointed with the [imam] because he just wouldn't blame my ex-husband and I was blamed for everything.

> It was weird but it felt as though I was the one being told off and when I tried to put across what I thought was wrong … it's as though [the imam] didn't want to hear it.

> I told him that I left him because he was violent but he started saying things like, 'Oh, how violent was that because in Islam a man is allowed to beat his wife'! I mean, I was so shocked. He said it depends on whether he really hurt me! I was really shocked because I thought he was there to understand but he was trying to make me admit I had done wrong.[99]

Bowen's research, in which the *'alim*'s perspective is more prominent, is more sympathetic to those working for the councils, but he, too, writes of cases in which scholars asked mothers to offer oaths, in the presence of a solicitor, that they will allow fathers to see their children.[100] It is an overstatement to speak of Islamic law as a 'parallel jurisdiction' in the UK. Still, it is fair to ask why, given that these institutions do not have any legal authority to intervene, custody and property are discussed and whether they are a suitable setting for vulnerable and violently abused people to be negotiating divorce terms in.

Undermining civil law, or providing support?

Questions of jurisdiction bring us on to another crucial issue, namely how Islamic dispute resolution institutions perceive, and relate to, civil authority. Firstly, how do the largest institutions relate to civil law in their day-to-day work? And secondly, what do they and other interested parties see as the *ideal* relationship between civil and Islamic legal traditions?

We have seen already that the actual relationship between these two is far from perfect, but it is worth emphasizing that, barring a few complications, all the larger, semi-professional institutions are happy to accept the authority of civil law and indeed encourage registering Muslim marriages and divorces in civil law.[101] Of course, as these institutions tend to come into contact with couples only when they are looking to end a marriage, their ability to influence marriage registration is extremely limited, but non-registration remains a source of frustration for the scholars. As Shahid Raza, who took over running the Muslim Law (Shariah) Council after Badawi's death, observes:

> I would say that almost eighty percent of mosques and imams are still conducting Islamic marriages without conducting civil marriages first ....We have seen ... girls who are on some occasions vulnerable .... They go and marry according to *Shari'a* law, and maybe after three months the man walks away from the marriage. Then the girl comes here crying, cursing God, cursing Islam, cursing the Shariah Council and cursing Muslim custom. 'Who the hell are you?! You are not helping me; my husband has thrown me out. What are my rights? Where shall I go?' She has no rights. Nothing is protected according to the law of the country. We have been referred so many cases of that nature.[102]

What can we say, however, about the orientations of Islamic scholars towards civil law? On this there is more variation, and this gives an insight into not only how *'ulama* perceive their work but also how the problems above might be resolved. I want to sketch out three ideal-typical positions on this matter that allow us to enter more fully into a discussion about how the relationship between civil and religious spheres might be arranged to avoid conflicts and risks. I will provide examples as I go, but I want to emphasize from the outset that these three are, precisely, *ideal* types. Separating them out and presenting them as discrete options involves extracting them from a much more complicated reality in which they weave into one another in all manner of surprising ways. I also want to discourage the reader from thinking that these are the only options. Indeed, later in this chapter I will sketch out additional paths.

Formal pluralism

I shall use this phrase to refer to the argument that unofficial systems of Islamic law should be formally recognized in the English (or Scottish) legal system.

This argument gets frequent coverage in the UK media, although it is generally mooted only to be furiously dismissed as antithetical to British traditions or liberal freedoms. Among Islamic scholars, however, it does have a number of supporters. The now defunct Union of Muslim Organisations made such a call as far back as 1975 – with little effect – before large dispute resolution institutions had even been established.[103] A more recent prominent advocate is Ahmad Thomson, a barrister who runs a legal chambers that offers legal services oriented towards British Muslims.[104] Within the Islamic Sharia Council, in particular, formal pluralism remains popular. The late Sheikh Syed ad-Darsh (d. 1997), one of the council's founders, advocated legal recognition,[105] while Mohammed Abu Saeed, who has previously worked as chairman of the Islamic Sharia Council, is another long-time supporter, making the following proposal:

[If] Muslims ... persuade the British authority to recognise Muslim personal law as they did in British India ... it will be a historic step and [a move toward] a harmonious relationship between the host and guest communities.[106]

Such requests are usually limited to Islamic marriage and divorce, but sometimes domestic disputes are included in discussions. Faizul Aqtab Siddiqi has entered this territory, and his opinions on the matter, taken from a public debate on Islamic law, are worth quoting at length:

Where a woman has been beaten up by a man [often she] withdraws her statement – 'I'm sorry, I got the black eye because I fell down the stairs' – and [the police and courts] can't proceed ....What is the reality for that woman? She's actually taken a practical decision. She goes through with this issue of domestic violence – certain divorce, certain ostracisation from the community that she wants to belong to, and has a right to be with. So, she says, 'Well, at the end of the day it was only a black eye. I'll live with it' .... We would say, let the Muslim Arbitration Tribunal be charged with the issue of looking at the domestic violence of this woman. Now we know how we can apply a little bit of community pressure .... Now it's a matter of respect for the community. So the man, he turns up .... And you know, in a sense, there is not mediation but the man his knuckles are tapped a little bit – 'Don't you do that again!' – and you know some kind of social reprimand is given by the Muslim Arbitration Tribunal. The man is deeply embarrassed, but ... cajoling takes place that brings the woman back with the man again.[107]

Now, there is zero evidence that Islamic institutions are currently acting as an alternative to the Crown Prosecution Service, but this passage does demonstrate that some of their leaders wish to utilize the power of communal norms, employing shame, pride and loyalty to achieve a version of justice in cases of violent abuse. Here, the religious community acts as a *nomos* – that is, as an ordered social system providing individuals with a structure that determines the context and implications of their choices. Of course, Siddiqi depicts these sanctions as placing coercive pressure on the abusive man in the hypothetical case above. (Sometimes that is how it works in real life too: in 2015 the chief rabbi of the United Hebrew Congregations of the Commonwealth, Ephraim Mirvis, took the unusual step of denying Jewish burial rights to a man who was refusing his wife a *get*.)[108] In contexts where norms of shame and honour are applied to women more than to men, however, it is extremely hard to see how communal justice can lead to better outcomes for women overall. Indeed, because pressure would likely be put on women not to report to the police and instead use community-approved processes, the opposite effect is much more likely: women would be kept reliant on men for solutions, untimely reducing their autonomy.

Complementary law

The popular media's portrayal of Islamic dispute resolution institutions can give the impression that formal pluralism has across-the-board support among *'ulama*, and even within the British Muslim population at large. Indeed, academic scholars can give this impression too: 'Muslims do not only wish to be regulated by the principles of Islamic law when they are living in a non-Muslim state,' writes Yilmaz, 'they also seek to formalise such an arrangement within the state's own legal system.'[109] Such crude assumptions make it all the more important to emphasize that it is far from clear whether formal pluralism has majority, let alone universal, support across the leaders of *Shari'a* councils. Some of them prefer the situation as it is, supporting a system of Islamic law that operates alongside the civil system but not formal recognition of that system. This is the position taken by both Shahid Raza and, before his death, Zaki Badawi of the Muslim Law (Shariah) Council. Both individuals have argued that formal recognition of Islamic law risks ossifying a diverse and multivocal legal tradition,[110] while at the same time potentially limiting the rights of vulnerable people.[111] A similar attitude towards recognition appears to predominate at the Islamic Sharia Council in Birmingham Central Mosque too, with Amra Bone indicating that there is 'little appetite' for alterations to the present situation in that institution.[112] For these scholars, Islamic dispute resolution institutions are not an *alternative* to civil legal system, so there is no need for them to be treated as though they are.

What exactly, then, should the role of Islamic dispute resolution institutions be? The ideal role appears to be for Islamic law to *complement* English law, although what this means is not always clear. It can mean that the Islamic divorce service plays a role in supporting the state, acting as an intermediary between the civil system and British Muslims' religious and cultural traditions while deferring to the civil authorities on important matters. There is, however, another element in this complementary approach. In addition to mediating between the Muslim custom and English law, the Muslim Law (Shariah) Council regards itself as helping the Muslim communities of Britain to, in the words of Badawi, 'live up to' the *Shari'a*.[113] While it is not and does not want to be a legal regulator, then, its leaders do encourage Muslims to live in a certain way. It uses its position to encourage a certain manner of living. It might even be described as a moral guide that operates within a complex web of religio-cultural relations.

Overlapping consensus

The third position is covered even less often in debates about Islamic institutions for the simple reason that it undercuts the premise from which many of these debates start, namely, that Islamic law is an alternative, indeed a challenger, to Western legal systems. This position is that civil legal processes are in some sense *Islamically justified*. According to this position, when people perform a civil procedure they also, at the same time, perform an Islamic procedure: when a couple obtain a civil marriage or divorce certificate they are regarded as being immediately married or divorced 'Islamically'. Like formal pluralism, advocates see this position as a solution to the problem of having to marry and divorce twice. Usama Hasan, whom I referred to earlier, is a keen supporter of this stance. Muslims, he says, should see a civil marriage

> as *nikah* because all the essential elements are there, the consent of both parties, two witnesses minimum. They're equivalent, and … the same with divorce ….
> You've got to … make [Muslims] realise that British law actually works on the same principles as *Shari'a*, of justice and fairness, and you've got to include them and make them feel more integrated.[114]

Although, as I noted above, Hasan's father and sister work at the Islamic Sharia Council, he does not himself. The body with which he is presently affiliated, Quilliam, tends towards a centre-right liberalism and is opposed by large numbers of British Muslim activists, for reasons that we will explore in Chapter 5.[115] Overlapping consensus, however, is not a position that is supported only by liberal or modernist Muslims. For example, while it is true that the Islamic Sharia Council's senior scholars have advocated formal pluralism, it is also true that almost all of the same people support overlapping consensus in practice. Darsh, for instance, argued the following back in 1997:

> A civil marriage – if attended by the guardian of the girl and at least two male Muslim witnesses – amounts to a correct Islamic marriage. It is only the social aspect which leads to another ceremony in a mosque with an imam, although these things are not required Islamically.[116]

There are, of course, two notable caveats in this passage, both of which make the situation much more complex. Needless to say, no British registrar would ever attempt to dictate the faith or gender of the witnesses to a civil marriage or insist that the bride's father must be present. Serious consequences would rightly follow if they did. Darsh in this passage is certainly not going as far as Hasan does above. Even so, there is in his account still acceptance of what Bowen terms 'practical convergence' between the two legal spheres. In a more up-to-date example, Suhaib Hasan, Usama's father and currently one of the Islamic Sharia Council's most senior scholars, not only treats a civil marriage as equivalent to an Islamic marriage but also treats a husband's petition for a civil divorce as sufficient grounds to issue a divorce certificate to a wife.[117] Likewise, at the Islamic Sharia Council in Birmingham Central Mosque a civil divorce is seen as constituting its Islamic equivalent. As one of the *'ulama* based there, Talha Bokhari, comments, 'If he [the husband] agreed to the civil divorce in court or signed his agreement, then it is a *talaq* and they do not have to come here at all to be divorced.'[118] In the research literature on this subject, these Islamic scholars remain silent on the question of whether the same principle would apply if it was the woman who initiated the civil divorce without the husband's agreement. One presumes not. Still, in taking such tentative steps towards recognizing civil divorce and marriage the scholars also take steps towards removing the need for British Muslims to use Islamic institutions in the first place.

These 'practical convergences' provide important evidence for my overarching thesis, too. Islam in the UK has adapted so that in the largest Islamic dispute resolution institutions English civil marriages and divorces are typically recognized as carrying religious consequences, or even as religious acts. Bowen, whose research into such convergences is the most detailed available, has uncovered other instances of Islamic institutions reorienting themselves to adapt and respond to English legal norms.[119] For example, despite following and catering for different Islamic traditions, the *'ulama* at the Islamic Sharia Council (Deobandi/Ahl-i-Hadith) and the Muslim Law (Shariah) Council (Azhari/Barelvi) proceed in very similar ways, suggesting that English legal culture determines their process as much as religious tradition. At the former council, the *'ulama* have even developed formal, publicly available divorce procedures – including mandatory separation periods – that mimic the English civil process. Alongside such practical changes, there are also *'ulama* – notably Barkatullah – who argue for recognition of civil rulings concerning the division of property in divorce cases as *'urf*, a concept in Islamic law that allows for acknowledgement of local customary practice.[120] Often, as Bowen makes clear, such alterations mimicking the English system are made 'in hope of future, closer linkages' between civil and religious spheres, and potentially the formal recognition of the councils as legal authorities.[121] Nevertheless, what they make clear is that there is willingness among the *'ulama* for any recognition to be an adaptive process.

Legal accommodations, public justifications

This review of the spectrum of views brings us on to what is typically considered the million-dollar question in debates about Islamic law in the UK: What should the British state's response to Islamic dispute resolution institutions be? Arguments abound concerning the appropriate relationship between civil and Islamic legal traditions that range from, to borrow the legal theorist Maleiha Malik's categories, 'non-interference' on the one hand to 'outright prohibition' on the other.[122] The latter of these positions enjoys strong support within some secularist circles in the UK. For example, activists, academics and journalists led by the organization 'One Law for All' have called on the UK government to 'dismantle' all religious arbitration services, which they characterize as 'kangaroo courts' delivering 'discriminatory' 'second-rate justice'.[123] This argument is, however, easy to dismiss. With the category of '*Shari'a*' being so blurry and encompassing informal marriage counselling, it is hard to see how this blunt legal change could be implemented without undermining fundamental rights of association (say, of Muslim religious leaders to offer marriage guidance). Indeed, the argument for prohibition does not even succeed on its own terms. It emphasizes individual autonomy over rights of belief and association, but, because it offers no remedy to limping marriage, it presents a threat to the autonomy of Muslim women who are unable to leave a marriage. Flawed though Islamic dispute resolution institutions may be, outlawing them offers no solution.

Legal theorists consequently tend to favour a path that falls somewhere between these two, including, in Malik's categorization, 'mainstreaming', 'cultural voluntarism' and 'transformative accommodation'. The latter of these terms was coined by Ayelet Shachar, whose model of incorporation nuances formal pluralism by proposing a system of joint governance in which 'external protections' (recognition by the state) provide an incentive for religio-cultural groups to avoid 'internal restrictions' (limits to people's personal freedom).[124] This position has various merits: in England, as we have seen, even the faint prospect of some kind of recognition has already encouraged reform and adaptation within Islamic dispute resolution institutions. Malik and the political theorist Anne Phillips, however, have both found fault with the scope that transformative accommodation offers religious leaderships to mark the boundaries and terms of group membership.[125] While potentially being a useful guide in communalist legal systems operating in states such as India and Israel, in the UK a system of joint governance is unrealistic, in part simply because there is little demand for it. 'Mainstreaming', the most far-reaching of Malik's options, involves incorporating a norm of a minority legal order within the state legal system. The cases of overlapping consensus above all count, in Malik's reading, as examples of mainstreaming (as would, say, examples of the state taking on certain religious functions as part of a civil marriage or divorce process). This model promises to resolve confusions between religious and civil systems, but, as Malik observes, as a technique of accommodation it runs into difficulty when there are moral conflicts or when a religious group lacks the clout to influence democratic processes. Mainstreaming also struggles with the question of how, in a polity containing a variety of religious and non-religious traditions, a single civil legal system can 'mainstream' everyone.

This leaves 'cultural voluntarism', which is Malik's preferred approach. In this case, participation in the minority order remains voluntary and the state retains ultimate authority, with no joint governance. Judiciaries, however, retain some leeway to pick and choose, accommodating selected norms of a minority legal order based on certain set principles. This final model is closest to describing how things are in England at present, and real-world examples can help to illustrate how cultural voluntarism may function. We have seen that engagement with Islamic dispute resolution institutions in England is rarely completely a matter of free choice, but doing so remains, from the state's perspective, a form of voluntary association. A voluntarist model is also indirectly encouraged by English Islamic dispute resolution institutions' own willingness to recognize each other's judgements and proceedings as legitimate.[126] This enables what Douglas et al. call 'forum shopping' – that is, people selecting the dispute resolution institution that gives the best 'deal' when they are searching for a divorce certificate.[127] English courts themselves, furthermore, very occasionally give limited recognition to Islamic legal processes and religious norms, but on a case-by-case basis. In 2009, for example, in *Uddin* v. *Choudhry* the Court of Appeal recognized an Islamic marriage contract as, precisely, a binding agreement between two parties that was freely entered into, with deliberations centring on how the contract would have been understood by the parties.[128] Then in 2018, in the case of *Akhter* v. *Khan*, a judge decided that a Muslim husband's failure to register his marriage in the face of his wife's repeated requests meant that their *nikah* could be classified as a 'void' rather than an 'invalid' marriage. This meant the wife became entitled to the financial remedies available to divorcing couples.

The difficulty with cultural voluntarism, however, is that it appears to settle for a status quo that no one sees as satisfactory. Malik acknowledges that the weakness of cultural voluntarism is that it can create uncertainty, giving little clear direction to members of the public on what will and won't be accommodated. *Akhter* v. *Khan*, for example, did not set a precedent that a *nikah* could be treated as a civil marriage. The judgement rested on the background details of the case, and the judgement might have differed had those details differed. (Indeed, the 2018 judgement was overturned on appeal in 2020 by a judge who read the case differently.) None of the frameworks, then, offers a clear resolution.

Smaller proposed practical changes, even when they are made by level-headed individuals, also often throw up more problems than they solve. We saw in Chapter 2, for example, how in 2015 the Conservatives established a panel to carry out an independent review into the application of 'Shari'a law' in England and Wales, led by the Islamic studies scholar Mona Siddiqui. Although this report was (absurdly) commissioned as part of a government response to Islamist extremism, this panel nevertheless used the leeway it was given to produce a thoughtful response to the dilemmas Islamic normative orders can present in the UK. Along with various sensible measures, however, it recommended amending the Marriage Act 1949 and the Matrimonial Causes Act 1973 to ensure that the celebrant of any religious marriage would face penalties if they fail to ensure the marriage is civilly registered.[129] Such a move would, of course, resolve the issue of non-registration and the various problems linked to it, but it would also generate new problems that become clear if one looks beyond British Muslims. Some people in the UK – certain libertarians and followers of New Age traditions, for example – hold antinomian views that involve the rejection of state recognition of intimate relationships as a matter of principle. These people simply do not think it is any of the state's business validating their unions. Compelling celebrants to register religious marriages in law would create profound uncertainty about whether these individuals can publicly celebrate their relationships without being penalized. This change would also limit the options of those Muslim couples who freely choose to cohabit through a 'fledgling love' *nikah*.[130]

Perhaps, then, the framing of this discussion as a question of whether Islamic dispute resolution institutions can and should be recognized is itself part of the problem. The questions typically asked about Islamic law in the UK – 'How willing should the state be to recognize the Islamic tradition's legal norms?' 'Where, and how firmly, should the line be drawn when minority and civil legal norms diverge?' 'What can and should be done to incentivize or compel change in Muslim communities?' – are all vitally important. All, however, involve judgements *about*, but little contribution *from*, Muslim citizens. Most importantly, they deflect attention from the character of the state itself, meaning that it is unquestioned in debates about the place and future of Islamic law. Islamic affirmations of civil law *as it currently stands* are recognized as examples of 'mainstreaming', but vital questions about how Muslims might feed into conversations about substantive reform of the state are addressed nowhere.

We have already seen, though, that Muslims' orientations towards civil law in England do not just involve consent or rejection, but reasonable and sometimes compelling critiques of its character and effectiveness. One, for example, concerns the strictly non-religious character of civil marriage ceremonies: 'I think you should allow for a civil registration with hymns or Islamic songs, the recitation of the Qur'an,' Usama Hasan has remarked. 'If people are saying that religion is dividing everyone into the mosques and temples and things, I would say that this is one way of bringing them together.'[131] This view chimes with those of Akhtar's focus group participants, one of whom described her civil marriage ceremony in the following bleak terms: 'I thought, God, I am having to sit here and say these words when really, they have got nothing to do with my marriage.'[132] Changing this rule has increasing support beyond Muslim populations too, with academics and even some registrars highlighting how this norm drives a wedge between rights and rites.[133] Other complaints have focused, like Balchin above, on the weak recognition given to prenuptial agreements, which are viewed as limiting the inclusion of Islamic marriage contracts in civil law.[134] Still others have focused on the way marriage licences in England are anachronistically allocated to premises. These agreements and disagreements extend the discussion beyond legal *accommodation* and into the territory of *deliberation*, particularly the question of whether, and how, religious argumentation should ever influence secular legal systems. It is to the subject of public deliberation, then, that I now want to turn.

The limits of public reason

Bowen's research aside, discussions of Islamic law in the West do not touch on questions of public reasoning and deliberation, but it is a rich debate among liberal philosophers.[135] John Rawls's writing has been especially influential, and here I shall follow many others by setting out my arguments in relation to his work.[136] Rawls provides a detailed answer to the question of when an individual or a group in a diverse polity should rely on their fundamental beliefs when they seek to shape constitutional and legal arrangements. What I will suggest is that probing the flaws in Rawls's work can help us find a way through the impasse that has affected Muslims in the UK, and in England especially.

Rawls has a reputation among those who are only partly familiar with his texts as a 'secular liberal' who is hostile to religion. The historian Stephen Prothero has said of Rawls that he insists 'religion restrict itself to the individual heart, the pious home, and the religious congregation'.[137] Rawls has even been characterized as a 'secular fundamentalist'[138] who regards religion as 'presumptively irrational' and therefore in need of 'containment'.[139] This is undeserved and largely based on a misreading of Rawls's distinctive idiolect.[140] What can be said about him, however, is that he sought to limit when and where religious justifications are used in public. He can be classified as what Christopher J. Eberle calls a 'justificatory' liberal, who believes that public debates should be conducted in a language of 'public reasons' that 'all can accept as valid'.[141]

To get a sense of Rawls's position, it helps to explain some common misconceptions about his argument. These mostly stem from misunderstandings about what he meant by 'public'.[142] When Rawls argued that people should not employ religious justifications in public, he was not focusing on people sitting in a coffee shop (the 'background culture') but in offices of state: that is, legislators, judges and candidates for elected positions.[143] Nor did Rawls see 'public' as equivalent to 'secular'. Although his critics rarely acknowledge it,[144] Rawls consciously distinguished between 'public reasons' and 'secular reasons' in order to emphasize that he was not just interested in limiting religion. In his view, *all* 'comprehensive doctrines' should be restricted, religious and non-religious alike. Rawls considered it inappropriate for a politician to state baldly in a parliamentary debate that 'Abortion should be banned because a soul enters into a foetus at conception,' but he believed it equally wrong for his or her opponent to argue that 'Abortion should be legal because souls do not exist.' These philosophical differences will never be resolved, Rawls reasoned, so people should try to argue using terms and concepts that are uncontested.

Another confusion relates to *types* of religious (or to be precise, philosophically contested) speech. Rawls did not think politicians and other public officials should refrain from *all* forms of religious speech in public settings. He fully supported people's attempts to clarify their beliefs to others, or their attempts to show how their beliefs could lead to support of the liberal political status quo. He also supported people's efforts to explain the basis of conscientious objections when they made them. He would have no objection, then, to our scholars explaining why they view Islamic and civil law as equivalent. When Rawls referred to the norm of public reason, he was speaking, rather, about religious speech that *had the intention of winning support for a change in the law*. Even then, Rawls did not object to religious justifications being used as long as these are accompanied 'in due course' by public reasons based on values that all can accept (a principle Rawls termed the 'proviso').[145] There is a vast debate about what this rather ambiguously worded 'proviso' implies, as well as about what 'reasons that all can accept' means. But to leave these issues aside for a moment, we can sum up what Rawls believed using Eberle's wording: that a person invites moral judgement when he or she 'support[s] or oppose[s] a proposed law on the basis of religious convictions *alone*'.[146] This is particularly the case for public officials, but Rawls does stress that *ideally* citizens in a liberal state should act 'as if they were legislators' and work to this norm.[147] His position seems, then, to place a question over any cases of British Muslim activists seeking to effect legal change.

All of these arguments about public reason were made by Rawls with the overarching aim of facilitating what he termed a durable 'overlapping consensus' of 'reasonable comprehensive doctrines'. Rawls wanted every person, regardless of their ultimate beliefs, to be able to freely consent to the constitutional arrangements that govern them, and he reasoned that if, say, laws were set down on the basis that they represented 'God's will' most secular – as well as many religious – people would have trouble accepting them, endangering political stability. In Rawls's vocabulary, an overlapping consensus is distinct from a 'modus vivendi' in which people accept political arrangements because they simply go along with 'the balance of political and social forces'.[148] In an overlapping consensus, citizens wholeheartedly endorse the polity, supporting all its fundamental norms.

The question, however, is whether this argument about public reason contributes to such an overlapping consensus, or undermines it. To get at this, we need to ask: What arguments *can* one use when speaking only in the terms of public reason? By public reason, Rawls meant reasons that refer only to 'political values': to values that do not involve a claim upon contested doctrines or truths. This is consistent with Rawls's overall vision of a just state whose constitutional foundation is not any one religious or comprehensive doctrine but that is 'free-standing', philosophically speaking. Justice is 'political not metaphysical': the public, political domain is not one that is concerned with comprehensive philosophies.[149] Political values then, in Rawls's terms, are arguments that refer only to common-sense, evidenced data and terms taken from within a political culture itself (norms like the 'rule of law', for example). Rawls's conception of purely 'political' values, however, is beset by problems. Politicians have to make laws on topics that touch on weighty philosophical subjects, such as (in laws relating to abortion) the definition of human life itself. Staying on the philosophical surface, then, is not only not always easy but also not always *helpful*, with political debates potentially lapsing into euphemisms and vague generalizations.[150] Critics as diverse as the socialist Chantal Mouffe and the communitarian liberal Bhikhu Parekh have pointed to how, when he needs to, Rawls relies on Kantian philosophical concepts, in so doing undermining his claim that his theory of justice doesn't rest on a philosophical foundation.[151]

It is Rawls's other problem, however, that is of more relevance to our subject. Deriving one's justifications from the terms and norms that operate within one's political culture, as Rawls recommends,[152] makes some sense within the context of a strong constitutional tradition whose fundamental basis is agreed upon. We are able to reason using the terms handed down to us from the past, in much the same way as judges reason using the precedents handed down to them. But, as William Connolly remarks, 'What does a Rawlsian moralist appeal to when such a tradition is deeply conflictual, or weak, or active in some domains and absent in others?'[153] When a new moral tradition aligned with a distinctive normative order emerges in a society (as the Islamic tradition has in the UK in recent decades) what language should its affiliates use when they want to participate in public life to address conflicts and problems? On this, Rawls is not always completely clear. At one point in his second major work, *Political Liberalism*, he acknowledges that political values and comprehensive doctrines are 'somehow related' and that the former can flow directly from the latter.[154] This seems to suggest merely that it is good conduct to translate one's beliefs into a widely understood language when they form the basis of a political argument. In his final writing on public reason, however, Rawls very clearly argues that political values should be seen as completely independent of comprehensive doctrines and need not rely on any kind of philosophical grounding. Political values, he says, should be *complete*: they 'are not puppets manipulated from behind the scenes by comprehensive doctrines'.[155] Public and non-public reasons run, in David A. Reidy's words, on 'separate but parallel tracks'.[156]

What this second reading appears to imply is that people who follow any new moral tradition should just leave it to one side, working out the values in terms of which they are going to debate from their host political culture. Muslims who have migrated to the UK should leave their beliefs aside and instead speak in terms of political values derived from British political culture.According to Rawls's final writings, an Islamic scholar should be free to explain the details of their beliefs and how they can lend support to civil law *as it presently exists*. But these beliefs need to be stored separately from the public justifications that one uses to actually try to change things. Utilizing religious beliefs in an argument about effecting legal change invites moral judgement.

Whither Islamic law in Britain?

When writing about Islam in liberal states, a problem that one often encounters is the distance between ideals and reality. It is often simple enough to resolve conflicts between liberal theory and the Islamic tradition,[157] but liberal states frequently still act in illiberal ways towards their Muslim citizens and Islamic institutions. In this case, however, the problem is not simply one of failing to live up to the standards set out by liberal philosophers. I want to encourage readers to think of the tensions in Rawls's conception of public reason not as an abstract problem in one political theorist's philosophy but as emblematic of a *general* flaw in contemporary liberalism, one that cuts across liberal theory and practice and that British Muslims can illustrate in several ways. In the case of Islamic law in the UK, a Rawlsian imbalance leaves British Muslims stuck between two equally unfavourable positions. A majority of British policy and media elites, like Rawls, claim to favour a single cohesive political and legal system that includes diverse perspectives and stands opposed to a more rigid pluralism based on community self- or joint governance. In keeping with this, British Muslims who seek to adhere to a semi-autonomous system of norms are regarded as a threat to political cohesion and to the rights enshrined in civil legal systems. At the same time, though, those same elites require Muslims to refrain from drawing upon their moral tradition in public deliberations about the development of laws and policies. There is some deliberative space for Muslims to explain why they, as Muslims, *affirm* existing legal processes but much less space for critique and dissent justified in exactly the same terms. Another example of the same phenomenon, which I will look at in the next chapter, is what Khadijah Elshayyal calls the 'conditional inclusion' of Muslim organizations in state consultations, where contributions are allowed only from those who do not dispute basic policy assumptions.[158] In both cases, Islamically grounded argumentation is welcome nowhere and the only option for Muslims is to accept system without questioning it. The rules seem set up to deliver a form of liberalism modelled on the late, great football manager Brian Clough's method for managing dissenting players. ('If I had an argument with a player, we would sit down for twenty minutes, talk about it, and then decide I was right.') Of course, the question Rawls wrestles with is an important one: there *is* a need to work out how a multiplicity of incompatible philosophies can converse in a common deliberative language. This process cannot involve ruling out a philosophy's efforts to effect substantive political change, however.

Over the course of this chapter, what we have encountered is a complex network of Islamic dispute resolution institutions that have adapted to need and to social and legal context. Certainly, they are awkwardly placed in the English civil system, and some individuals that have worked within them hold deeply illiberal views. Because of this, considering steps that English courts and the UK government might take to limit their use and influence is reasonable. Treating the refusal of a religious divorce as a manifestation of controlling behaviour – in Muslim contexts as it has been in Jewish contexts – could be one sensible step in this direction, for example. What is important to recognize, however, is that these steps might not need to be taken in *opposition* to British Muslims or even to those working in Islamic dispute resolution institutions, who have themselves set in place processes whose aim is to limit the need for an Islamic divorce service. The UK's one-sided liberalism blinds public debate to this reality, leading to a situation where Islamic dispute resolution institutions are regarded as a problem to be solved or a threat, which makes resolving the dilemmas of Islamic law much harder. One can see this clearly in the UK government's rejection of the recommendations in Mona Siddiqui's review of *Shari'a* councils, for example. Alongside favouring changes to gradually reduce the need for Islamic dispute resolution institutions, Siddiqui's review proposed the state create a regulatory body 'to prevent discrimination in the immediate and medium term'.[159] While certainly not without risks, this step raises the possibility of, inter alia, allowing domestic violence support and advice services better access to individuals presenting at Islamic institutions. Yet rather than engaging, even critically, with this recommendation it was refused outright with the curt government response: 'Sharia law has no jurisdiction in the UK'.[160] Any kind of engagement with or contribution from *Shari'a* councils, even if it has the goal of transforming them from quasi-legal institutions into well-regulated mediation services, is viewed as legitimation of an alien and threatening system, or as a concession to an adversary. To take another case, Elham Manea – a fierce critic of Islamic dispute resolution institutions – has proposed that the English courts could provide Islamic divorces.[161] A more limited version of this same idea has been supported by Barkatullah, who favours civil courts offering a supplementary form that enables a divorcing couple to certify that they consider themselves divorced Islamically.[162] Again, these proposals raise questions: Manea's 'mainstreaming' in particular would involve the state taking on the awkward role of Islamic authority. What is pertinent here though is that, despite being favoured by a scholar consistently opposed to Islamic dispute resolution institutions, these ideas remain *unthinkable* in a public sphere that treats Islam as a pollutant rather than a tradition whose justifications can be involved in developing an overlapping consensus.

What makes this frustrating is that solutions to the problem of how to synthesize Islamic and civil spheres, rather than being found in a bold shift in how Islamic dispute resolution institutions are treated, are more likely to be found in smaller reforms of *both* English and Islamic laws and norms. What is worth emphasizing about the various legal frameworks Malik sets out is that almost all of them – mainstreaming, cultural voluntarism, non-interference and prohibition – can coexist in a single polity. A state will rightly want to prohibit certain norms and refrain from interfering in others. Limited accommodation of certain practices – as in the cases of *Uddin* v. *Choudhry* or *Akhter* v. *Khan* – does not rule out mainstreaming others. Even the principles of transformative accommodation can be utilized in a limited way: the state setting up an independent regulatory body, as Siddiqui proposes, might be seen as an example of this. There are multiple minor social and legal changes that one might contemplate: marriage registration campaigns, new systems to support the vulnerable, reforms to marriage preliminaries or alterations to how marriage contracts are treated in divorce cases. What matters ultimately, therefore, is the inclusivity of the deliberative process through which law and policy are negotiated. Islamic dispute resolution institutions are a response to a particular history and legal culture, and if that culture changes so might these institutions' role. The fundamental question is whether a multiplicity of voices and traditions can be adequately included in the negotiations that shape that legal culture. With a major review of English marriage law now underway as I write, it is pertinent to think about how the arguments of religious minorities might be involved in shaping laws. Finding the political will and vocabulary to engage meaningfully with Islamic law as a language and subject of debate is just a first step towards doing this.

Chapter 5

MUSLIMS AND THE STATE: NEITHER AGENTS NOR ENEMIES

Old problems, new settings

Fihi ma Fihi, the book of discourses authored by the thirteenth-century Muslim poet, mystic and scholar Jalal al-Din Rumi (d. 1273), opens with the following *hadith*:

> The Prophet, on whom be peace, said: 'The worst of scholars is he who visits princes, and the best of princes is he who visits scholars. Happy is the prince who stands at the poor man's door, and wretched is the poor man who stands at the door of the prince.'[1]

European and American writers often allege that, in contrast to the Christian traditions that have shaped the constitutional foundations of Western states, Islam knows no distinction between religion and politics; there is, they say, no Islamic equivalent to the Biblical injunction to 'Render unto Caesar the things that are Caesar's'.[2] Rumi's quotation, however, illustrates that the situation is not as simple as that. No one would doubt that spiritual and temporal authority have as tangled a history in the Islamic tradition as they do in the Christian. Yet, as Abdullahi An-Na'im has recently demonstrated, Islamic scholars – and if this *hadith* is sound,[3] possibly even the Prophet Muhammad himself – have repeatedly displayed an awareness of the need to carefully manage the interaction between religious knowledge and political power.[4]

There is, in fact, something especially appealing about the *hadith* Rumi quotes. Matthew 22 deals with whether communities of belief should submit to secular power, but this passage speaks to a wider constituency. Trade union representatives, academic scholars and spokespersons for ethnic and community associations: all will find it hard, when reading this narration, not to think about the fine line that they have to tread between influencing government and maintaining the ideological independence necessary to speak truth to power. For British Muslims, of course, it is especially relevant, and not just because they identify with the same tradition Rumi did. For Muslims in the UK, this fine line has been thinned down to the point where it is barely visible. The extraordinary level of public attention paid to British Muslims – and the legislative and policy changes that have followed from this attention – have generated opportunities and the need for Muslim voices to speak publicly on subjects as diverse as education regulation, foster caring, religious discrimination, family law and, of course, countering extremism. More often than not, however, opportunities for the leaders of Muslim organizations to engage with the state have been conditional – giving the impression that the situation is one of the 'scholar' going to visit the 'prince' rather than the other way round. This has, in turn, engendered an environment in which engaging with the state to win policy concessions or simply to bust the myths that public figures hold can mean, fairly or not, losing whatever credibility one has built up among the British Muslim public. This problem is then compounded by popular narratives which have circulated for many years about Muslim organizations representing only the interests of 'community elders', failing to be sufficiently self-critical or even aspiring to undermine liberal democratic institutions.

This chapter deals with the theme of Muslim–state relations, and in it I present a brief history of how Muslim organizations have engaged with the British state. Part of what I want to do here is explain how British governments have, especially since 2010, created such narrow conditions for engagement with the state. Alongside this, however, I also provide a more optimistic account that chimes with the two previous chapters about changes that have taken place within Muslim institutions. In what follows, I describe what I call, following the lead of Therese O'Toole and colleagues, the *maturation* of Muslim engagement with the British state.[5] I provide an overview of generational and philosophical transitions within Muslim organizations that have enabled them to operate and represent their constituencies' interests more responsively and effectively. These transitions, I suggest, provide the grounds to reject – or least qualify – the stereotypes of Muslim representative organizations as bodies that advance only the interests of conservative elders or that harbour anti-democratic tendencies. They also allow a picture of Muslim engagement to emerge that challenges the initial impression one can get of Muslim politics. In part because of the way the state has chosen its favoured partner organizations – anointing some while smearing others – the landscape of British Muslim representative bodies can seem fractious, with competing groups constantly at each other's throats. Yet if one looks behind the ill-tempered exterior of British Muslim public life, I want to show one can witness diverse and sophisticated interactions with different domains of British governance.

Of course, the very notion of 'Muslim representative organizations' is contentious. For many people, including various political theorists, all political representation outside of electoral representation is dubious, especially representation linked to social characteristics: politics, to borrow Anne Phillips's phrasing, should supposedly be about *ideas* rather than the *presence* of identity groups.[6] When Muslims organize *as Muslims* to pursue distinctive claims they are, therefore, widely seen as a disruptive influence. The theistic ideas and traditions on which Muslims draw are, as we saw in the previous chapter, often deemed out of place in public life. Even when Muslim mobilization has little to do with religion – which has often been the case in practice – they are viewed as trying to win unfair influence. In this chapter, therefore, I discuss theories of unelected representation while also drawing on the last chapter's argument about religion's place in public life. Drawing on my work with O'Toole and colleagues, as well as the work of the political theorist Michael Saward, I cautiously defend the political representation of identity groups. I make the case that in certain circumstances such representation is not just legitimate but necessary to the functioning of democratic politics. I also point to an increasingly diverse 'economy of representative claims making' emerging across various domains of governance and within the British Muslim public sphere.[7]

Community networks and the activist challenge

The phrase 'Muslim politics' can refer to a wide range of different (if overlapping) subjects. It can mean participation in elections and the voting patterns that Muslims follow[8] or the affiliation of Muslim organizations and personalities with specific parties, such as the now defunct Respect party.[9] It can also cover the impact of South Asian communal kinship networks (*biraderis*) on local governance (and indeed discrimination in public life that is rooted in generalizations about Muslims' political choices being due to '*biraderi* loyalty').[10] Here, though, I want to concentrate on Muslim pressure groups and split this into two types of association: representative organizations that typically act as umbrella bodies for mosques and other Muslim community institutions; and activist organizations typically aligned with a religio-political movement. In the UK, these two forms of organization have tended towards different types of activity: in Jonathan Birt's terms, the former have usually been more interested in 'lobbying', while the latter have preferred to go out 'marching'.[11] This has often translated into different relations with the state: the former are – in good times at least – the state's partners, the latter its antagonists. Largely because of these differences, in academic publications the two subjects are typically treated separately. While this split makes some sense, the line between the two has long been blurred and as one moves from the 1960s and 1970s to the present it breaks down. In the past, the members of Muslim activist groups have felt alienated from and criticized representative bodies in much the same way that young Muslims have felt alienated from and criticized the community infrastructures set up to serve them. The growth of Muslim activism in the 1980s and 1990s was in fact – as Sadek Hamid shows in his ground-breaking book *Sufis, Salafis and Islamists* – driven in part by the frustrations of second-generation Muslims at inward-looking religious institutions whose interest in political change was limited to, at most, local concerns.[12] As one moves towards the present, however, the boundary between these two domains does not just become more porous – with several 'poachers' becoming 'gamekeepers' in later life – but the British Muslim activist scene changes and matures, ultimately contributing to a remaking of Muslim politics.

Umbrella organizations

Examples of Muslims speaking to government as 'Muslim representatives' can be found across the twentieth century. One national-level British Muslim representative body, the Association of British Muslims (AOBM), even claims to trace a path back to 1889 and the pioneering British convert Abdullah Quilliam (although whether this path is unbroken remains an open question).[13] Such efforts became more common, however, from around the 1950s onwards. Until the 1990s, most Muslim lobbying was low-key and was typically organized around local mosque associations – groups such as the Federation of Muslim Organisations in Leicester (established 1984) and the Bradford Council for Mosques (established 1981), as well as their antecedents such as the Bradford Muslim Welfare Society (established 1961).[14] The low-profile nature of these associations' engagement with the state during this time was not, as is sometimes assumed, because Muslims kept their religion separate from their politics.[15] Rather, it was because new Muslim migrants' interest in the establishment of infrastructures and the transmission of traditions, which we covered in Chapter 2, translated into localized political concerns: the ability to buy premises for worship and expanding same-sex or confessional education. (The first calls for state-supported Muslim schools were made in the mid-1970s, around a quarter of a century before the first such school was established in 1998.)[16] These interactions did sometimes involve attempts to challenge prejudice, especially the way Islam was taught in state schools. Challenging prejudice was, however, more of a priority for anti-racist ethnic minority organizations where, even if Muslims were present in large numbers,[17] religious identity was not salient or even marginalized. Often, community organizing by Muslim representatives was couched in a conservative language, anathema to anti-racist groups, of 'protecting' younger Muslims from 'undesirable' social norms prevalent in British society.[18]

This localized lobbying work fed into the gradual formation of the first genuinely national Muslim umbrella bodies that brought together a collection of mosques and other community institutions from across the UK. The Union of Muslim Organisations of the UK and Ireland (UMO) was founded in 1970 and celebrated its 'silver jubilee' in 1995. The following decade then saw two significant umbrella bodies emerge: the Council of Mosques for the United Kingdom and Ireland (COM, founded 1984) and the Council of Imams and Mosques (COIM, founded 1985). As the almost simultaneous creation of these two groups hints, such umbrella bodies, while claiming a national reach and aspiring towards general representation, often in practice drew affiliates from specific Islamic traditions. The former was Deobandi-dominated, while the latter, which was set up by Zaki Badawi, attracted predominantly Barelvi organizations. Neither, ultimately, managed to make headway in shaping national politics.[19]

Activist networks

Muslim activism in Britain can also be traced back to the mid-twentieth century. In Chapter 2, I introduced a range of Islamist movement-inspired activist organizations founded in the 1960s or shortly after, from the UK Islamic Mission (UKIM, established 1963) and affiliated Islamic Youth Movement (latterly Young Muslims UK, YMUK) to the competing Dawat-ul-Islam and its own youth offshoot, the Young Muslims Organisation (YMO).[20] These groups, along with the pre-eminent British Muslim student body, the Federation of Student Islamic Societies (FOSIS, also established in 1963), all belonged to what I will term, after Hamid, the 'reformist Islamist' trend of Islamic activism, which took inspiration from the Muslim Brotherhood and Jamaat-i-Islami. This was one of four activist trends that emerged on the British scene between the 1960s and the 1990s. In the 1980s, a more confrontational 'separatist Islamism' emerged, exemplified by the UK branch of Hizb-ut-Tahrir, while 'Salafi revivalism', epitomized by the organization JIMAS, also garnered a broad following. These were then joined by the 'Traditional Islam' network, which, as we saw in Chapter 3, encompassed the Radical Middle Way as well as elements of the Muslim College and the Cambridge Muslim College. The Traditional Islam network affiliated with broadly Sufi (or 'neo-Sufi') traditions and found its feet later than the others, with formal alliances between the main personalities emerging only in the late 1990s.[21]

These four networks were marked by clear differences in the way they approached secular political life – or what Hamid terms *participation orientations*.[22] Salafi activism in the UK was, and remains today, in large part a conservative isolationist movement. While some of the followers of JIMAS took the decision to join conflicts overseas, notably the UK-supported Afghan war against the Soviets in the 1980s, the prevailing trend in UK Salafism has been to reject the spheres of politics and civil society entirely.[23] One of the points of contradistinction emphasized by Salafis against their Islamist rivals has been that their practices (or, in their terms, *manhaj*, or 'method') are grounded in a thorough knowledge of scriptural sources and Islamic scholarship. Like Salafis, Hizb-ut-Tahrir is anti-civil society, famously regarding democracy as *nizam-u-kufr* (a system of blasphemy) and participation in elections as *haram* (forbidden).[24] Unlike Salafis, however, it is highly politicized and focused on the goal of re-establishing a transnational caliphate. Its followers' attitude to Western society has been confrontational and frequently highly provocative, with offshoot groups, such as Al-Muhajiroun and its numerous successors, engaging in intentionally inflammatory demonstrations. The British 'reformist Islamist' groups influenced by Jamaat-i-Islami have, much like Hizb-ut-Tahrir, advocated utopian religio-political goals – with members seeing themselves as part of a transnational 'Islamic Movement' – but their strategy has been more integrationist. Affiliates of this trend have involved themselves in campaigns on concrete issues, and this, combined with the influence of modernist tendencies within Islamist thought, has meant that in more recent times many of these groups have broadened their horizons (as we will see). For their part, the followers of Traditional Islam share a preference for political engagement over confrontational protest but have often painted the Islam of both Salafis and Islamists as puritanical and stifling in contrast to the 'life-giving' classical Islamic tradition to which they themselves adhere.[25] Affiliates of Traditional Islam often make claims about 'Salafi burnout': the idea that the Salafi worldview is simply too austere for anyone to sincerely commit to for longer than a few years. Indeed, some of the representatives of this latter trend had been through this transition themselves. Abdul-Rehman Malik, formerly one of Radical Middle Way's most prominent spokespersons, describes his own affiliation with a 'Salafized' Islam, and his transition out of this, as follows:

> I was on that [Salafi Islam] for almost two years. I remember being very confident in the way I prayed again; I felt very confident in my worship. Worship became very externalised, although internal life was all but lost. I became a member of the Muslim Brotherhood for several years, and during that time my Salafism declined but my activism obviously grew …. [But] I grew out of [that worldview] – because of the severity of it, the austerity of it, the lack of mercy and compassion, and the cardboard two-dimensionality of the religion.[26]

Islamic activism in Britain was established by members of the same generation that set up the first Muslim community institutions. Khurram Murad (born 1932), the man credited as the spiritual father of YMUK and erstwhile leader of the Islamic Foundation (see Chapter 3), is marginally older than Pir Maroof Hussain Shah (born 1936), the individual who has done most to establish Barelvi institutions in the UK, especially in the north of England (see Chapter 2).[27] Islamic activist groups, however, attracted a thriving 'second generation' as the twentieth century wore on. Activist leaders, consciously reaching out to the young, concentrated on global political issues. These groups made English the lingua franca and pioneered events for Muslim women, with YMUK setting up the first national camp for Muslim women in 1987.[28] Politically radical Islamist movements are often portrayed as intent on repressing women – and for good reason. It is one of the paradoxes of British Islamic activism during the 1990s, however, that those espousing the ideal of a totalizing Islamic state were also more adept at involving both genders.[29]

This is not to suggest that Islamic activism was oriented towards progressive political objectives. Salafi groups and Hizb-ut-Tahrir, in particular, consistently advocated ultraconservative and anti-liberal ends as well as, in a small number of cases, violent means.[30] Various individuals formerly associated with Al-Muhajiroun have been convicted of acts of terrorism, including the 2013 murder of Fusilier Lee Rigby and the 2017 London Bridge attack. The political orientations of reformist Islamist groups such as YMUK have been more complex; Rachid Ghannouchi, the co-founder of the Ennahdha Party and the figure credited with helping to steer Tunisia to democracy in the wake of the Arab Spring, spoke at YMUK's events while he was exiled in Britain in the early 1990s.[31] These too, though, frequently claimed that a state grounded in a comprehensive code of Islamic law was the single available solution to humanity's problems. This emphasis often contributed to obliviousness to – if not acceptance of – crimes committed by *soi-disant* Islamic states overseas. While Western injustices were denounced, a blind eye was typically turned to crimes committed by the governments of Saudi Arabia or Iran, or by parties such as Jamaat-i-Islami.

These illiberal political commitments meant that British Islamic activists tended to remain at a distance from the anti-racist activism that emerged in the 1970s and 1980s. Islamic activism was, in common with much leftist activism, coloured by an anti-imperialist ethos but its insistence on specifically Islamic solutions meant it stood in opposition to an emerging discourse of black struggle. Growing out of ethnic minority trade union activism and street-level opposition to a strengthened far right, this discourse was based on the premise that African-Caribbean and Asian individuals in Britain form – and should see themselves as part of – a shared 'community of resistance' to racial and class exploitation.[32] Its supporters often took inspiration from socialist anti-imperialists, such as the executed Punjabi revolutionaries Bhagat Singh (d. 1931) and Udham Singh (aka Ram Mohammad Singh Azad, d. 1940), who consciously sought to transcend religious differences. Asian youth movements in Birmingham, Luton and elsewhere incorporated various religious backgrounds and motifs from Black Power movements as well as the anti-apartheid struggle.[33] For the most part during the 1970s and 1980s, these two forms of ethnic minority-led activism coexisted independently, but occasionally the differences between Islamic and secular anti-racist activists flared up into diasporic conflicts. Jamaat-i-Islami-influenced organizations have often conflicted with secular Bangladeshi organizations such as the UK branch of the Awami League and the Swadhinata Trust, for example, whose founders have campaigned for justice for those killed by Jamaat-i-Islami militias in the 1971 Bangladesh War of Independence. Conflict has been common especially in Tower Hamlets, where British Bangladeshis are most heavily concentrated and where the Trust and the Awami League's supporters have consistently opposed the influence of the Jamaat-i-Islami-influenced East London Mosque in local politics.[34] This conflict goes back decades but, like the tension between secular anti-racism and Islamic activism, it shapes local politics still today.

Islam goes public? The Rushdie affair and its consequences

These intersecting fault lines – between secularist and Islamic activist networks, and between Islamic activists and representative organizations – were dramatically reconfigured by the eruption of protests against Salman Rushdie's novel *The Satanic Verses* in Britain in the late 1980s.[35] The Rushdie affair is commonly seen as a turning point in British Muslim politics and a defining event in Muslim self-definition.[36] This is indisputable, but it is important to be clear in what sense the protests against *The Satanic Verses* marked a sea change. Jed Fazakarley has persuasively argued that the popular image of the Rushdie affair as *the* point of inception of a British Muslim political identity overstates the case, masking the debates among Muslims on these themes that stretch back to the mid-twentieth century and before.[37] Indeed, the portrayal of the protests in popular narratives as the 'Big Bang' moment in British Muslim political history has led to the Rushdie affair casting a distorting shadow over subsequent Muslim activism. The image of the affair – of books being burned, of threatened and actual instances of

violence against an author of fiction and his translators[38] – continues to influence
the thinking of many leftist and conservative commentators who were shocked
by the protests at the time.[39] Sometimes, these authors struggle to look at British
Muslim activism through any other lens and depict the groups and personalities
involved as the same now as they were then. Of course, a history of British Muslim
politics that ignores the Rushdie affair doesn't deserve the name, but what I want
to emphasize is that it is the unnoticed incremental changes within public British
Muslim organizations – rather than any single spectacular protest – that determine
the character of Muslim–state relations today.

One thing that was obviously distinctive about the protests against *The Satanic
Verses* was the sheer scale. British Muslims may have, in Fazakarley's words,
accorded 'considerable significance to their religion as an element of their social
and political identity essentially since they settled in Britain', but never before
had they mobilized in large numbers *as Muslims* as part of an appeal for national
political change.[40] This gave Muslims in Britain greater visibility, which in turn
brought about two widely recognized and decisive changes. The first of these
was that the protests, as Nasar Meer observes, 'interminably ruptured whatever
consensus, contested as it clearly was, of race relations and anti-racism that
existed' in Britain.[41] The Rushdie affair involved Muslims responding en masse
to a perceived attack on them as a *community of belief*. While it is impossible to
explain the protests without taking into account the marginal position of Muslims
in Britain, this mobilization could not be assimilated into a vocabulary of anti-
racism and political blackness and it exposed tensions in the secular anti-racist left
that had previously been masked. During the protests, some anti-racist activists
attempted to shift the focus away from the figure of Rushdie and towards Muslims'
social marginalization (with stickers reading, 'Fight racism, not Rushdie'), but these
efforts failed.[42] The intellectual basis of political blackness was also profoundly
challenged, notably by Tariq Modood.[43] Over a series of articles in the late 1980s
and early 1990s, Modood vigorously contested the idea that ethnic minorities'
solidarity and identity should depend on the majority's (hostile) attitudes towards
them and developed the argument that protest counted as an example of Muslims
marking out a distinctive sense of group pride.[44] These efforts then contributed
to a second decisive change, namely, in how Muslims were perceived by wider
British society. The visible emergence of 'Muslim consciousness', as Meer has more
recently termed it, sparked a shift – one that would become definitive following
11 September 2001 – in how journalists, politicians and scholars wrote about
Muslims: in religious, rather than ethnic, terms.

A third, less widely recognized way in which the Rushdie affair marked a
turning point was that it led to a blurring of the distinction between community
representation and activism, or between 'lobbying' and 'marching'. At full strength,
the protests against *The Satanic Verses* in Britain crossed Islamic traditions and
Muslim generations, but initially they were impelled predominantly by Islamist
activist networks. As Chetan Bhatt has observed, the reaction to the publication
of Rushdie's novel in 1988 was, to begin with, fairly muted.[45] Only after a Muslim
MP in the Indian opposition Janata Party started a campaign to ban the book did

objections start to emerge in the UK. The Islamic Foundation's then close links with Jamaat-i-Islami in South Asia (see Chapter 3) led to it becoming involved in an awareness raising campaign among British mosques a few months before Ayatollah Khomeini's infamous 1989 *fatwa* prompted greater media interest. The Islamic Foundation's awareness raising activity was highly successful, with both of the major mosque umbrella groups – the COM and the COIM – becoming involved in anti-Rushdie campaigning. Younger British-born activists, such as the members of YMUK, then began to get involved and used the protests as a means of drawing in new recruits.[46] As the mobilization gathered momentum, new Muslim organizations were established. Most uncompromising among these was the Muslim Parliament, which was linked with the older Muslim Institute and led by the same individuals. The Muslim Parliament's leaders considered *The Satanic Verses* tantamount to a 'declaration of war on Islam' and suggested that its publication was the consequence of an organized government attack. It advocated – in its 'Muslim Manifesto', authored by then leader Kalim Siddiqui – a campaign of civil disobedience and suggested Muslims should consider British laws illegitimate.[47] The Institute, if not the Parliament, is still in existence today, although it is important to stress that after Siddiqui died in 1996 it was taken over by Ghayasuddin Siddiqui (no relation), under whose guidance the organization has moderated its stance significantly. (The Muslim Institute was the main organization behind the liberalizing Muslim marriage contract, referred to in Chapter 4, and it has recently sought to build alliances between Muslim organizations and LGBT organizations.)[48]

Of greater lasting significance was the UK Action Committee on Islamic Affairs (UKACIA), which was convened in October 1988 by the Saudi diplomat Mughram al-Ghamdi, at the time director of the Central London Mosque in Regent's Park.[49] The UKACIA brought reformist Islamist activist organizations, including the Islamic Foundation and UKIM, together with community-focused organizations such as the COM and the pre-eminent UK-based Deobandi *dar al-ulum* located in Holcombe, Bury.[50] Representatives of local mosque umbrella bodies were also included, notably Sher Azam, leader of the Bradford Council of Mosques. (Bradford, of course, was where the infamous burning of Rushdie's novel took place.) This blurring of the divide between traditional community organizations and activist groups did not lead to a generational shift in leadership; all of the leaders of the groups in this alliance were born overseas, as indeed was the convenor of the UKACIA, Iqbal Sacranie, a businessman of Guajarati East African Asian heritage. This blurring did, however, lay some of the groundwork for more profound changes to come that were led by a British-born generation of Muslim activists.

New Labour, new governance?

What made the UKACIA of enduring significance was not its protests against Rushdie – none of the group's key demands were met – but rather its actions once the protests had died down. In March 1994, the then home secretary, Michael

Howard, hosted a widely reported meeting of Muslim activists and leaders of organizations, including Sacranie, during which the Conservative minister is reported to have argued that for Muslims to influence policymaking they would need to speak as one. As Maulana Shahid Raza, whom we met in Chapter 3 and who was present on that occasion, observes:

> When Michael Howard was Home Secretary we went to see him .... And there were fifteen Muslim representatives at the table and he came and he said, 'Look, I don't know who the leader is among you. I can speak with you and we can agree on something, but the next day my office might receive a call saying, "They are not the leaders; they are self-made representatives. We want to meet you. We are the real leaders." We can't keep meeting delegations of Muslims one after the other. We can't do that. We don't have ministers available for every Muslim who comes and demands a meeting. So you must sort this out.'[51]

This advice was seized on by the leadership of the UKACIA, which established a National Interim Committee on Muslim Affairs with the ambition of building a genuinely national, genuinely representative body for Muslims comparable to – and to some extent modelled on – the much older Board of Deputies of British Jews.[52] The organization that emerged out of this process was the Muslim Council of Britain (MCB), which was launched in 1997 a few months before the Conservatives were voted out of power in favour of a Tony Blair-led New Labour government. The MCB quickly built up a base of some 250 distinct affiliate organizations, which made it hard to dismiss out of hand as a significant voice of British Muslim institutions (if not, perhaps, the British Muslim population as a whole).[53] With Sacranie voted in as its first secretary general, the MCB was for many years the first port of call for British politicians seeking to consult on questions relating to British Muslims. Despite turbulence, even today it can fairly claim the title of, as Yahya Birt has said, the '*primus inter pares* among an increasingly large alphabet soup of representative bodies'.[54]

The timing of the MCB's foundation was fortuitous. It emerged on the scene just as the new prime minister sought to engender a new style of governance in the UK, promoting a model of 'active citizenship' in which partnerships between voluntary organizations and different branches of the state were central. New Labour tended to depict religious organizations (or 'faith communities') as repositories of 'social capital'[55] and accordingly encouraged local authorities to involve them in neighbourhood renewal.[56] It saw engagement with 'faith' as a way of bringing into the public domain socially excluded populations – British Muslims especially – whose 'master identity' appeared to be religious.[57] The early 1990s had already witnessed limited efforts to involve religious organizations in urban regeneration, notably via the creation of the Inner Cities Religious Council (of which Sacranie was a member).[58] Under New Labour, however, such initiatives expanded dramatically with the creation of bodies like the Faith Communities Consultative Council.[59] At the time, many academics viewed this shift as part of a general transition towards 'networked' forms of governance that aim to strengthen democracy by drawing an active civic community into partnerships with the state.[60] Within such literature, which dates back to the 1970s and 1980s, the transition towards networked governance is typically seen as part of the reworking of the boundaries between the state and civil society in response to neoliberal reforms of the public sector and the decentralization – indeed, the weakening – of the state.[61] The UK under New Labour came to be regarded as a context in which networked governance had become especially advanced, with the affirmative language of 'citizenship renewal' being employed enthusiastically across councils and numerous government departments.[62]

The MCB was well placed to fulfil the role of representative of British Muslim interests and it made several effective attempts to influence laws and policies between the new government's formation and 2005. This included lobbying successfully for strengthened religious discrimination legislation, legal accommodation for *halal* and *shechita* slaughter, state funding of a small number of Islamic schools and the introduction of a question about religious identity in the decennial national census.[63] These efforts usually involved joining forces with Christian or Jewish bodies and chimed with New Labour's broader aims.[64] Nevertheless, the MCB's ability to reach influential figures during this period was undoubted. Several senior ministers – including former home secretary Jack Straw, and former secretary of state for communities and local government John Denham – developed working relationships with the MCB's leadership.[65] Iqbal Sacranie's personal achievements were officially recognized with an OBE in 1999 and a knighthood in 2005, while Muhammad Abdul Bari, one of Sacranie's successors, was awarded an MBE in 2003.

Of course, this is not to claim that the MCB succeeded in its aim of developing a genuinely national and genuinely representative body. Its leadership reflected the makeup of the UKACIA, with its affiliates mostly being aligned with the Deobandi tradition and reformist Islamist (specifically Jamaat-i-Islami-influenced) movements.[66] Over the years, British Shia, Ahmadi and Barelvi groups have periodically complained of their marginalization and relative lack of influence in the organization, with these complaints becoming (for reasons we will explore shortly) vociferous in the wake of the attacks on London in July 2005. A more profound criticism was that the MCB has acted on behalf of its affiliate organizations at the expense of a broader population of non-organized Muslims, especially Muslim women and the young. The Traditional Islam-influenced magazine *Q-News* lampooned the MCB at one point as led by 'lassi Islamists' (a South Asian variant of 'champagne socialists'). '*Q-News*,' as Fozia Bora, one of the magazine's contributing editors, reflected in 2011, 'was jaded with all these institutions and made it clear that these organizations were not representative in any way.'[67] Abdul-Rehman Malik has been even more forceful in his criticism, referring to the UK state's approach as a strategy 'the Raj would have been proud of'.[68] Likewise, Cassandra Balchin, the late activist with the Muslim Women's Network whom we met in Chapter 4, opined in 2008 that New Labour usually paid attention only to 'the most conservative people imaginable' in its dealings with Muslims.[69]

This viewpoint has many supporters beyond Muslim organizations and populations too. Bhatt and the leadership of Women Against Fundamentalism, a leftist secularist organization that emerged out of the Rushdie affair, have contended that New Labour's model of faith engagement enhanced the position of reactionary religious elders and contributed to a situation in which 'wayward' community members, particularly South Asian women, could be disciplined and ostracized with impunity.[70] Liberal and conservative journalists and intellectuals, likewise, have made uncompromising claims both about the MCB specifically and about Labour's approach more generally, with many of these arguing that such problems are an inevitable consequence of giving privileged space to religious and ethnic minority identities in political life.[71]

These criticisms, in turn, fed into a critique of multicultural politics in general and New Labour-style 'faith engagement' in particular. This critique crossed all points on the political spectrum, but while those on the right tended to focus upon what they saw as the privileging of ethnic minority identities at the expense of national culture, those on the secular anti-racist left typically portrayed Labour's engagement with the MCB and similar bodies as an act of strategic containment. Even before the Rushdie affair, dedicated funding for ethnic and religious groups was viewed by those working for black unity as a threat to their ambitions. As Alana Lentin put it in a recent critique, 'policies aiming to take "ethnic minorities" under the state's wing, a step forward from seeing "immigrants" as temporary guest workers soon to return home, extinguished the fires of dissent lit by a generation coming to political consciousness in the 1980s'.[72] 'Leaders within Asian youth movements became co-opted', Timothy Peace adds, with 'some even going on to join the Labour party and start their political careers'.[73] Over time, this unease developed into full-throated leftist opposition to state-led multicultural policies, which were seen as, in Lentin's words again, 'a means of appeasing the autonomous anti-racist movement'.[74] Criticisms of the MCB followed similar lines, with Arun Kundnani, among others, suggesting that the New Labour government chose to interact with the MCB and other Muslim organizations not because of their grassroots support but 'on the basis of their effectiveness in containing dissent and serving strategic interests'.[75]

Do these criticisms have force? To some degree, they do. Or they did at least: in truth, one cannot properly evaluate these complaints without bringing this story up to date, so a full judgement needs to be reserved until later. One can, however, get a sense of the problems faced in the late 1990s by looking at where 'religion' fitted into the MCB's model of representation. Much like the Board of Deputies, the MCB cannot be easily classified as a 'religious organization'. Since its inception, it has sought to represent not 'Islam' but 'British citizens with an Islamic heritage'.[76] Its leadership consists of laypersons whose aim is not to articulate religious teachings but to represent 'community interests'. This differentiates the MCB from the corporatist models of Muslim representation in France and Germany, in which politicians have attempted to institutionalize Islam from above. (*Pace* Kundnani, the MCB's formation was, at least compared to France and Germany, bottom-up.)[77] This is also broadly consistent with the structure of many of the

UK's mosques, where the imam is subordinate to a governing committee. The model of community representation that the MCB follows is broadly in keeping with what Modood has said about the subject in his more recent defences of multiculturalism:

> As Peter Jones says, 'the recognition that is demanded is the recognition of a group of people rather than a system of belief ... e.g. what the majority is called upon to recognise is not Islam but Muslims – not a religious faith but those that subscribe to it'. Even 'subscribe' is probably too strong; or at least it doesn't mark where religion begins, for that is (in the present case) not those who subscribe to a faith but those who identify with the Muslim family of communities.[78]

What Modood is claiming here is, of course, right. One doesn't have to subscribe to the tenets of a religion to feel one belongs to a religious community. Muslims with no interest in religious scripture may still want to collectively organize around the issues of, say, protections for religious slaughter or anti-Muslim discrimination. Indeed, the MCB's lobbying against religious discrimination was actually supported by individuals, such as Abdul-Rehman Malik, who had been critical of the organization on most other matters.[79] More generally, Modood is trying to make the understandable case that Muslim organizations such as the MCB presently operate in civil society in much the same way as trade unions or other community associations. They speak not as an authoritative voice on religion but as the voice of a group of people. While they have an unclear relationship with the group they purport to represent, this could be said, too, for trade unions' claims about 'workers' – and this is not, outside of some right-wing circles, seen as a reason to disregard them as actors in civil society.

A difficulty in the case of the MCB, however, is that religious arguments have often been discernible, but have been articulated in the language of the wishes of 'the Muslim community'. For example, in 2007 the organization produced a report entitled *Towards Greater Understanding: Meeting the Needs of Muslim Pupils in State Schools*, which argued for various accommodations and exemptions for Muslim children. These accommodations included separate assemblies and worship for different religious groups and allowing Muslim children to limit their artistic production to 'calligraphy, textile art, ceramic glass, metal/woodwork [and] landscape drawing' rather than risk producing 'idolatrous' images of humans.[80] These arguments were based, ultimately, on an understanding of appropriate conduct that has its roots in a (conservative) reading of religious tradition.[81] *Towards Greater Understanding* certainly made many compelling points. In the UK, state support for Christian education is widespread and even secular schools in England and Wales are obliged – in theory at least – to include a daily act of collective worship of a 'mainly (or wholly) Christian character'.[82] This raises profound questions, picked up in the report, about the fairness of Muslim students being offered only Christian worship in state schools. At the same time, however, *Towards Greater Understanding* made stark presumptions about Muslim citizens' beliefs and criticized the idea of 'multicultural' exposure to a variety of worldviews.

It saw the transmission of Islamic tradition as one of the central functions of state education and justified this on the basis of assumptions about the wishes of the 'Muslim family of communities'. This should make clear the risks involved in state treating one Muslim voice as uncontested; indeed, this risk was recognized by competitor groups, such as British Muslims for Secular Democracy (BMSD), which responded by issuing its own, starkly contrasting, guidance.[83]

To say this is not necessarily to reject either the MCB as a lobbying organization or Modood's model of multiculturalism. As we will see, the MCB's representative claims have become more refined over time and Modood's conceptualization of multiculturalism is one that sees competition between claims – such as between the MCB and BMSD – as positive and productive. Nevertheless, this case does give an indication of how phrases such as 'British citizens with an Islamic heritage' can foster what Phillips calls a 'reified notion of cultural community' that 'exaggerates the unity and solidity' of minority populations.[84] It also highlights some of the problems that affected the landscape of Muslim–state relations in the early years of the New Labour government. Although the honeymoon period between the Blair government and the MCB was an improvement on what had gone before, at least giving some kind of conduit for the ventilation of Muslims' distinctive problems, it was too easily assumed by public figures that the MCB spoke for a constituency broader than its affiliates. All the concrete gains made by the MCB in this time can be justified as part of an effort to close what Khadijah Elshayyal has called the Muslim 'equality gap': the fact that Muslims did not (and, despite significant gains, do not) receive the same protections and recognition as comparable groups.[85] The premise that the organization advanced a conservative communitarian agenda is therefore questionable.[86] Even so, there is still some basis to the claim that the 1990s was an era of 'take me to your leader' politics.

The breakdown of the multicultural consensus?

Fierce as debates about Muslim representation were in this honeymoon period from 1997 to 2001, they were nothing compared to the vicious disputes that erupted in the new millennium. The previously close relationship between the MCB and Labour was strained following a series of public disagreements, beginning with British military involvement in Afghanistan in 2001 and Iraq in 2003. In the immediate aftermath of the attacks on New York in 2001, Blair's government had taken care to highlight the MCB's condemnation of the attackers and promised access to the prime minister as part of an effort to dissociate the Islamic tradition from violent Islamism in the public mind.[87] It soon became clear, however, that its access was dependent on the organization falling into line on action against the Taliban. Although the MCB's leadership initially equivocated, withdrawing support from the first anti-war march, it eventually publicly opposed the war under pressure from its affiliates. In the case of Iraq, the British Muslim public were even more overwhelmingly opposed and were galvanized by the massive popular protests.[88] Muslim organizations played a central role in the anti-war movement, notably the MCB-affiliated – and Muslim Brotherhood-inspired – Muslim Association of Britain (MAB).[89] Muslim voters turned away from the Labour party, preferring to side with the Liberal Democrats and the far-left Respect party.[90] This left the MCB with little option but to speak out against intervention, despite the damage this did to its relationship with Whitehall. The bridges between the MCB and government were further damaged by the MCB's tone-deaf decision to boycott Holocaust Memorial Day between 2005 and 2007.[91] Official links were then finally severed in March 2009 by Hazel Blears, at the time the secretary of state for communities and local government, after she and other unsympathetic ministers objected to a statement signed by the MCB's then deputy secretary general, Daud Abdullah, about the Israeli government's incursion into the Gaza strip during February of that year.

During the same period, public opinion turned against the patterns of multicultural participation New Labour had previously advocated. Commentators, both in academia and in the popular press, talked of the 'multicultural consensus being smashed' by events such as rioting by predominantly South Asian Youth in Oldham, Burnley and Bradford in 2001 and the attacks on London by four British-born Muslims in 2005.[92] The extent to which this shift in perceptions actually altered political practices is up for debate. Several scholars – myself included – have highlighted how patterns of multicultural engagement, especially at a local level, actually extended between 2000 and 2010.[93] Even so, while notices of the 'death of multiculturalism' may have been premature, there certainly was what Meer and Modood have termed a 'civic rebalancing' of national policy in Britain towards the goal of civic integration.[94] It became more risky, politically, for politicians to engage with Muslim community organizations, and collaborations with Muslim groups thus became less prominent.

The single most important change in this period occurred in 2006 in the immediate aftermath of the London bombings and in the lead-up to the expansion of Prevent in 2007. Ruth Kelly, then the secretary of state for communities and local government, announced an intention to 'rebalance' relations between the state and Muslim organizations. This meant government 'actively [seeking] to develop relationships with a wider network of Muslim organisations', especially those deemed to be 'taking a proactive leadership role in tackling extremism and defending our shared values'.[95] As well as further sidelining the MCB, this move led to the emergence – or the coming to prominence – of groups such as the British Muslim Forum, the Sufi Muslim Council, Progressive British Muslims and the aforementioned BMSD. The first two of these were aligned with Barelvi institutions and had been less critical of Labour policies concerning counterterrorism, while the others, as we have seen, set out to challenge the MCB's religious conservatism. Prevent, as we will see, also enabled the establishment of the Mosques and Imams National Advisory Board (MINAB) and the Quilliam Foundation (now 'Quilliam'), a 'counter-extremism think tank' set up by former Islamists. These all joined extant national-level organizations such as the reformist Islamist Islamic Society of Britain (ISB), transforming an already well-populated scene into an overcrowded and fractious marketplace.

During this period, the debate about Muslims and the state acquired not only a new intensity but also a new complexion, with the conversation becoming dominated by accusations and counter-accusations about associations with Islamist extremism. Where once critiques of multicultural policies focused on their alleged empowerment of religiously conservative elders, now they suggested that multiculturalism had offered an entry point into British public life for those who aspired to undermine liberal democracy. Broadsheets and tabloids alike – informed by a collection of centre-right think tanks and disillusioned leftist journalists – published a bewildering array of accusations that Muslim activist and representative organizations retained hidden sympathies for extremism.[96] The MCB has been the prime target for these accusations but they have been levelled at almost every politically active Muslim organization at one time or another. They are still made regularly today, the most recent case being the documentarian John Ware labelling MEND (Muslim Engagement and Development), a lobbying and social action group set up in 2014, an 'Islamist group'.[97] In most cases, such accusations fall to pieces under scrutiny. In 2014, for example, *Towards Greater Understanding* was resurrected and reimagined by the journalist Andrew Gilligan as 'a detailed blueprint for radical "Islamisation"'.[98] We have already seen that there were problems with the MCB's 2007 report, but describing it in these terms is absurd.[99] This was not the most egregious case of misrepresentation either. In 2007 Policy Exchange, a centre-right think tank whose trustees have included Conservative ministers, published a report by Denis MacEoin entitled *The Hijacking of British Islam*, which purported to reveal the extent to which extremist material was available in British Islamic bookshops.[100] When its findings were covered by the BBC news programme *Newsnight*, however, they found evidence that the receipts for these extremist materials had been forged.[101]

Often, it is very hard to see these claims as made in good faith. In November 2009, for example, the liberal journalist Nick Cohen denounced Inayat Bunglawala, at the time the MCB's media secretary, for an article he wrote supposedly defending Sheikh Yusuf al-Qaradawi, the hugely influential *'alim* based in Qatar. Why, Cohen asked, is Bunglawala entertained by MPs when he defends a cleric who supports the 'murder of apostates and homosexuals'?[102] Such noxious views can be attributed to Qaradawi, who was formed intellectually by the Egyptian Muslim Brotherhood before going on to lead the European Council for Fatwa and Research and International Union of Muslim Scholars. One does not need any sympathy for him or Bunglawala, though, to see something wrong with Cohen's claim. Bunglawala did not defend Qaradawi's arguments so much as criticize the decision to refuse him a visa to visit the UK for medical treatment.[103] (He made similar criticisms when the far-right anti-Islamic Dutch politician Geert Wilders was denied entry to the UK.)[104] Bunglawala has also argued that those who renounce Islam should be free to do so, encouraged the MCB (unsuccessfully) to include a gay Muslim support group as an affiliate organization and argued that the MCB ought to support protections against discrimination on grounds of sexual orientation.[105] These are not views that Bunglawala has kept closeted: they have all been published in the sister newspaper for which Cohen works as a columnist.

Given these cases – of which there are many, many more that I do not have the space to cover – it is tempting to dismiss all talk of 'Islamist infiltration' as the prejudiced 'slurs' of 'McCarthyite' policy think tanks that are engaged in a 'cold war against British Muslims'.[106] To do this is, though, to move too quickly. Sometimes, this is because the claims made about Muslim groups and individuals are harder to defend. Iqbal Sacranie, for example, has been repeatedly derided for stating during the protests against *The Satanic Verses* in 1989 that death was 'perhaps too easy' for Salman Rushdie.[107] Although Sacranie has expressed regret for this statement since, and although it actually formed part of a confused argument *against* capital punishment, far less incendiary comments have killed off much more significant political careers.[108] Some cases also raise complex and difficult questions about diasporic conflicts. Most difficult of all is that of Chowdhury Mueen-Uddin, who was a prominent figure in the MCB's early days and, among other things, has worked as director of Muslim Spiritual Care Provision in the NHS. Mueen-Uddin belongs to an older generation of Bangladeshi reformist Islamist activists and admits to supporting Jamaat-i-Islami as well as, before he moved to England, campaigning to keep Bangladesh and Pakistan united during the bloody 1971 war of independence. In Bangladesh, however, he has been accused of involvement in the war crimes carried out by Jamaat-backed militias. In 2013 he was tried in absentia and sentenced to death by the secularist Bangladeshi government, the Awami League, for the abduction and killing of eighteen intellectuals. Mueen-Uddin disputes this and denies any such involvement, professing willingness to stand trial in an independent forum outside of Bangladesh. With such a possibility being remote, however, his case remains as an open wound among diasporic factions.[109]

The other reason why it is unwise to ignore these claims as fabrications is that doing so means ignoring a revealing and important story. Reformist Islamism *does*, as we have already seen, provide an important foundation for early British Islamic political activism and participation. This is one reason why journalists can drop lines into broadcasts and media reports about the 'Islamist foundations' or 'Muslim Brotherhood influences' of prominent bodies like the MCB, the MAB, the Islamic Foundation or the ISB without risking legal proceedings. What is wrong about the claims made about Islamism and British Muslim activism is frequently not that facts are invented but that there is, wilfully or not, *a refusal to recognize religious change*. We saw already in Chapter 3 how the Islamic Foundation has markedly altered, evolving from reformist Islamist origins to develop Muslim chaplaincy training. Bunglawala, with many other members of the '1990s generation' of British Muslim activists, has a similar personal story. A member of YMUK during his younger years, Bunglawala was committed to utopian Islamism and accordingly to the idea that, in his words, 'secularism was akin to atheism and that only a truly Islamic state which enforced the *Shari'a* would provide the real answer to humanity's problems'.[110] He has since grown up and grown out of this perspective, but in such a way that retains the reformist Islamist ethos of participatory political engagement. Although he drew back from public engagement in the late 2010s to pursue less glamorous professional interests, Bunglawala can be regarded as an early example of the many British-born activists who, as they have moved into leadership positions, have taken steps to rework the public profile of British Islam and Muslims.

First, though, it is important to talk about the *effect* of these allegations. However tenuous claims about Muslim groups harbouring Islamist extremists may be, they have been employed to devastating effect by the political right, with an informal alliance of NGOs, politicians and media professionals gradually cementing an image of the British Muslim activist scene as threatening.[111] These claims fundamentally shaped Prevent, especially following the return to power of a Conservative-led government in 2010 under David Cameron. While both the Conservatives and Labour were split on the subject of engagement with Muslim organizations,[112] Cameron appeared to accept wholeheartedly the argument that many mainstream Muslim organizations harboured extremist factions, going so far as to claim in 2011 that Labour's engagement with Muslim organizations was 'like turning to a right-wing fascist party to fight a violent white supremacist movement'.[113] In 2008, he even named one Muslim group, the Cordoba Foundation, as a 'front' for the Muslim Brotherhood.[114] The popularity of such views among the UK's Great Offices of State meant that a distorting and constricting framework was imposed on Muslim–state relations, with conversations only taking place under extremely restrictive conditions. This has ensured that the evolution of Muslim activism has taken place largely out of public view.

Disciplinary governance? The divisive impact of Prevent

We saw in earlier chapters that Prevent impacted various government departments when it was expanded in 2007. Its effect was, however, most keenly felt within the Department for Communities and Local Government (CLG). The links between CLG and faith-based voluntary organizations, as well as between such organizations and local councils, were profoundly disrupted by a dramatic shift in policy goals and delivery. This expanded version of Prevent drew heavily upon Labour's pre-existing model of faith-led community regeneration, which until then had been directed by CLG and oriented towards the aim of building 'community cohesion'.[115] Prevent's expansion led to an injection of funding and consequently opened up possibilities for faith-based – especially Muslim – organizations, but rather than just being directed by CLG the Office for Security and Counter Terrorism (OSCT) also became involved and indeed came to dominate operations. As one senior civil servant based at OSCT commented in an interview with O'Toole et al.: 'We arrived in a rather security-like way with a very determined delivery plan, occasionally people were just run off the court. They didn't have as much money. They didn't, frankly, have as much drive. They didn't quite know what they were doing. And it was hard. So what happened was Prevent took over cohesion.'[116]

Funding associated with Prevent was distributed liberally across British Muslim organizations. At the same time as the MCB was being shown the door by government ministers, the 'Preventing Violent Extremism Community Leadership

Fund' was offered to groups such as (in 2007/2008) the Muslim Youth Helpline, Khayaal Theatre Company, the Muslim Youth Development Partnership, the Sufi Muslim Council, the Luqman Institute of Education and Development and the Fatima Women's Network.[117] Associated funding pots like the 'Community Leadership Fund' were made available to groups such as the BMF, BMSD, the Sufi Muslim Council (again) and MINAB. Other, larger grants were given to the Radical Middle Way and the Quilliam Foundation to cover the entirety of their running costs. Finally, money was targeted specifically at Muslim women's organisations such as the Muslim Women's Network, with the aim of 'enabling [women's] voices to be heard and empowering them to engage with Muslims at risk of being targeted by violent extremists'.[118]

Rather than being targeted at specific individuals who, for one reason or other, were deemed at risk of being recruited into a violent movement, these projects used community capacity building to try to refashion Muslim civil society and, through this, the British Muslim population. The funding facilitated the emergence of new and competing civil society partners, the aim seemingly being for these new or expanded organizations to win the loyalty of the wider British Muslim public.[119] This 'hearts and minds'[120] approach was, however, a dismal failure.[121] Non-Muslim community organizations felt that their voices were being neglected, while Muslim organizations felt Muslim communities were being unfairly targeted.[122] Work previously justified in terms of promoting civic engagement and integration was tainted by suddenly being reoriented towards the end of protecting people from extremism. Efforts to increase women's access to religious institutions, for example, now needed to be justified on the sexist basis that women have a 'naturally' caring role and are therefore well positioned to pacify their potentially violent husbands and sons.[123] Many councils felt that Prevent risked shattering carefully negotiated relationships and a number of them joined a wide range of Muslim organizations in refusing entirely to take Prevent money.[124] Conservative critics questioned whether such capacity-building interventions actually did anything to thwart violent movements.[125] Even those whose voices government sought to amplify were deeply uneasy about the strategy, as they found themselves accused – in the words of Tehmina Kazi, a former director of BMSD – of 'parroting the government's line', even when they were not actually in receipt of Prevent funding.[126] In the end, many in the Labour government conceded that its approach was flawed, with John Denham observing that 'there was no understood model of how Prevent was meant to work'.[127]

The most persistent and damaging criticism was that Prevent led to community groups being co-opted to 'spy' on British Muslims. Reports emerged of youth workers and councillors feeling coerced into providing information on individuals, and this alone was sufficient to weaken trust between Muslims groups and the state, undermining Prevent's own stated aims.[128] Government sources repeatedly stressed that this was a feeling only and not reflected in operations.[129] Since 2003, the government's CONTEST counterterrorism strategy has had four dimensions – 'Prevent', 'Pursue', 'Protect' and 'Prepare' – and in theory activities designed to identify and track violent extremists ('Pursue') are kept distinct from those designed to stop people becoming extremists in the first place ('Prevent'). Yet even if one accepts this argument, such distinctions were hard to see on the ground. What is and is not 'Prevent-funded' has rarely been clear even to those closely involved: one senior figure in a Muslim organization I interviewed in 2008 misled me – I think unintentionally – about whether his own organization's government funding counted as 'Prevent money' or not. Part of the reason for this is that Prevent seemed to permeate so deeply into all facets of the state, cutting across multiple government departments, including those tasked with capacity building and those interested in monitoring and 'unmaking' citizens.[130] Prevent thus became tied, in the public mind, to technically distinct surveillance projects such as 'Project Champion', a disastrous scheme led by the Association of Chief Police Officers (Terrorism and Allied Matters) involving the installation of 216 closed circuit television and automatic number plate recognition cameras in areas of Birmingham with a high Muslim population.[131] Ultimately, given civil servants from OSCT were engaging in community relations, it was unsurprising that voluntary workers in turn were perceived as in league with the security services.

When Labour were replaced by a Conservative–Liberal coalition government in May 2010 steps were already underway to revise Prevent, and a renewed strategy was – after considerable conflict between liberal and neoconservative wings of the new administration – published in 2011.[132] This model was strengthened in 2013 following the report of the Task Force on Tackling Radicalisation and Extremism (TERFOR), which was set up in the wake of the murder of Lee Rigby by Islamist extremists.[133] It was then given statutory grounding in 2015 by a new majority Conservative government through the Counter Terrorism and Security Act. The Conservative strategy made several significant changes to how Prevent operated, many of which were undoubtedly steps in the right direction. The 2011 report endeavoured to counter the criticism that Prevent unfairly targeted Muslim communities, emphasizing more obviously the threat posed by far-right extremism. It promised a clearer separation between counterterrorism and cohesion work and criticized the funding of community initiatives aimed at the British Muslim population as a whole. As the model progressed and was given legal footing, it also instituted an approach in which radicalization was conceptualized as vulnerability to exploitation, with the state's role therefore being one of 'safeguarding' citizens.

While, taken in isolation, these steps all represented improvements on previous iterations of Prevent, the strategy did not become more popular among scholars or activists in large part because they were undermined by other problems.[134] Instead of following a model of partnership working, the Conservative model tasked public institutions such as schools, hospitals, universities and prisons with delivering Prevent. Each of these and other public domains have been, since 2015, compelled to show they give 'due regard' to the risk of radicalization. What this has meant in practice is that masses of public sector employees are obliged to look out for possible signs of radicalization and to promote 'British values' as an antidote. The primary difficulty with this is that any prejudices these employees hold are carried into policy delivery. Scant Prevent training is offered and – in part because of an unwillingness to recognize anti-Muslim animus as a possible driver of extremism – the training that is offered does little to counter, and even reinforces, anti-Muslim stereotypes.[135] Unsurprisingly, therefore, while referrals to the government's 'deradicalization' programme 'Channel' are evenly split between Islamist and far-right extremism, 44 per cent of initial Prevent reports are for suspected Islamist extremism, compared with 18 per cent for far-right extremism.[136] Concerns about excessive scrutiny of Muslims have therefore not just remained but become more pressing. Additionally, even the best training works with the vague definition of extremism as 'opposition to fundamental British values' such as 'democracy' and 'tolerance' (see Chapter 3). This gives almost no help to non-expert individuals in actually assessing people's vulnerability to radicalization. Worse still, this definition reconnects counterterrorism policy with the theme of civic integration.

The Conservative government failed, then, to separate out cohesion and counterterrorism work, but they did weaken the former considerably in ways that are highly relevant to this chapter. Responsibility for Prevent was moved to the Home Office and practically all support offered to voluntary groups was – along with support for Blairite interfaith initiatives such as the Faith Communities Consultative Council – rapidly withdrawn. Prevent officers were appointed in local councils who reported directly to the Home Office, a move that caused considerable consternation within some local authorities.[137] What seemed clear was that government wanted direct control over Prevent's implementation, removing the ability of councils and the voluntary sector to bend Prevent to fit other, more community-focused, agendas.[138] Outside of Prevent, a few small state-funded integration projects did get the green light – notably the Church of England-led Near Neighbours programme – and in 2015 Cameron started to bring cohesion back into the frame as part of a new counter-extremism strategy, announcing funding for a 'Cohesive Communities Programme'.[139] The 'Building a Stronger Britain Together' programme (BSBT) that emerged out of this, however, was small compared to previous initiatives, with only £8.8 million being spread across over 250 projects between 2015 and 2019.[140] The details of, and rationale for, this distribution of funds also became extremely difficult to track, with freedom of information requests on the subject frequently being denied.[141] Only a few Muslim organizations were able to maintain any kind of partnership with the Conservative government: Quilliam, the Muslim women's and counter-extremism organization Inspire and the anti-Muslim hate crime monitoring group Tell MAMA became virtually the only associations capable of maintaining contact. Under Cameron's direction, Prevent followed the line that government would no longer work with 'non-violent extremists'. Yet as he, like so many others, believed that the majority of Muslim civil society organizations harboured extremist elements this meant that most were banished to the wilderness. Even when contact did occur, the terms of reference for partnership were limited. In 2018, for example, the Home Office set up a Commission for Countering Extremism (CCE) comprising various experts and led by former Inspire CEO Sara Khan. Yet despite involving figures such as David Anderson QC, the former independent reviewer of Terrorism Legislation, the successes and failures of Prevent and related counterterrorism policies were deemed outside the Commission's remit.[142] The function of the Commission was narrowed to considering 'public responses to extremism', without that discussion extending to terrorism and policies designed to address it. The promised separation of cohesion from Prevent, then, didn't decouple civic integration from terrorism, but it did work to limit civil society and expert critique of the shape of counterterrorism policies.

Given this history, it is easy to see why the predominant perception of Prevent among academic researchers is that it has functioned essentially as a disciplinary apparatus that quashes substantive critique of government policies by determining 'acceptable' and 'unacceptable' varieties of Muslim subjectivity and political positioning.[143] Within the Conservative model of Prevent, in particular, the conditions placed on engagement have been so stringent that only a very small number of 'approved voices' are given a platform. These voices are then characterized by centre-right and some liberal politicians and journalists as the few 'brave liberal Muslims' who are willing to speak out and fight back against the 'Islamists' who supposedly dominate representative and activist groups.[144] 'Liberalism', in these discourses, becomes less a philosophy of government and more a set of criteria against which Muslims can be judged and excluded.[145] Unfortunately, Muslim civil society organizations have themselves played along to this tune at times. Between several such groups – such as Tell MAMA and MEND, or the Muslim Women's Network and Inspire – vicious public disputes have erupted in which each characterizes the other in the most negative terms possible: as either a dangerous Islamist or a shill for the government. In reality, as Philip Lewis and Sadek Hamid observe, these arguments usually represent little more than 'a noisy public contestation for representational power, government patronage and access to resources'.[146] Substantive differences between British Muslim organizations are generally much smaller than they seem, but this jostling for influence has had the effect of lending credibility to individuals who claim that there is an ongoing battle for the very soul of British Islam.[147]

Certainly, between the groups above there are differences of substance and reasonable – and sometimes severe – criticisms can be made of them, but the leaders of most are committed and capable individuals, each inspiring in their own way. While none of these groups could be considered the single legitimate representative of Muslim Britain, all their aims are legitimate; none aspires to undermine liberal democracy and none is completely uncritical about the current state of it in the UK. The first report published by the CCE, *Challenging Hateful Extremism*, stands a useful illustration of this.[148] The writing of this report was far from trouble-free; research contributions by two Muslim scholars of British Islam, Sadek Hamid and Tahir Abbas, were rejected following a characteristically spurious 'exposé' by Andrew Gilligan.[149] Yet despite this and despite working within constricting terms of reference, Khan – who is typically characterized by critics of Prevent as little more than a public relations officer for the security services – made fundamental criticisms of Conservative strategy. Infuriating conservative critics,[150] her report pushed for a human rights-focused approach to combatting extremism and directly criticized the Conservative definition of extremism, labelling it as 'unhelpful'.[151] What this helps to show is that, while divisions between Muslim civil society organizations on political matters are real, they are magnified by the roles the state has forced them to play: in or out, liberal or Islamist, gamekeeper or poacher.

The Conservative reforms to Prevent, because they resulted in a large reduction in voluntary sector involvement, also appeared to weaken the Labour model of networked governance to the point where the phrase can no longer be accurately applied to the British state. Certainly, as far as Muslim participation in national governance is concerned, formal points of contact have decreased notably. Here, though, there is a richer story to be told. One of the weaknesses of analyses of Prevent that stress its disciplinary functions is that they tend only to take an interest in Muslim civil society organizations when the state does. This means that the autonomous emergence of Muslim activist networks and their agency in interactions with the state is, as O'Toole et al. have argued, usually bypassed.[152] Under-the-radar interactions with different arms of the state tend to go unacknowledged. To fill in these blanks we need to look at the more recent development of Muslim civil society organizations, including returning to the Muslim activist networks and representative organizations that I discussed earlier. Attending to these groups more closely not only allows us to discredit government and media narratives about the threat of 'non-violent extremism' but also complicates narratives of state discipline.

New Muslim publics

Let us again, then, review the 'activist trends' discussed earlier in this chapter, taking each in turn before broadening the picture out. Representatives of all four of these trends – whether separatist Islamist, reformist Islamist, Salafi or neo-Sufi – have had interactions with the state over the last twenty-five years. Analysing these interactions will allow us to see how British Muslim organizations have changed and the state's role in facilitating these changes. Of the four trends, it is unsurprisingly the one that is most politically accommodating – the 'Traditional Islam' network – that the British state has been most relaxed about interacting with. In part because of this, however, it has struggled recently against a backdrop of rising populism and authoritarianism in the UK and beyond. As we saw with the case of the Radical Middle Way in Chapter 3, this network's preference for participatory engagement meant that Western governments happily funded its work. Lately, however, as confrontational political leaders have emerged on the world stage, this has caused problems of credibility. In the UK in the 1990s and 2000s, the Traditional Islam network offered a route into the British Muslim public sphere for those who had struggled to find a voice, but it is a network that has always relied upon venerable *'ulama* overseas for its appeal and authority, and many of these have been, in Usaama al-Azami's words, 'severely compromised in the past decade'.[153] Hamza Yusuf – the founder of Zaytuna College in California and arguably the movement's most famous spokesperson, as well as one of the

Radical Middle Way's most prominent speakers – was widely criticized for attending Donald Trump's National Prayer Breakfast in Washington in February 2017.[154] Egypt's erstwhile Grand Mufti, Ali Gomaa – another Radical Middle Way speaker and an inspiration for many of the network's members – has aligned himself with Abdel Fattah al-Sisi, even going so far as to publicly celebrate the 2013 Rabaa massacre in which around a thousand civilians were killed. The network's 'theology of obedience', as Walaa Quisay and Thomas Parker term it, has become harder to justify as authoritarianism has advanced.[155] Today's emerging British Muslim scholars of Islam – al-Azami and Quisay are good examples – have accordingly become among the network's most penetrating critics. Its ideas are still prominent through a variety of publishers, internet sites, teaching hubs and religious leaders – not least Abdal-Hakim Murad's Cambridge Muslim College – but the network is now more fragmented and remote from public debates.[156]

Among Salafi and separatist Islamist organizations, alliances with government have been fewer, for reasons that should be obvious. There have, however, been some points of contact. During the years of New Labour, the Salafi organizations STREET (Strategy to Reach, Empower, Educate and Transform, Brixton), InnerCityGuidance (Birmingham) and IMPACT (Initiative for Muslim Progression and Advancement of Community Tolerance, West London) were supported to work with Muslims who may be vulnerable to violent extremism.[157] Conservative critics of Labour's model of Prevent have often seized upon these examples when making the case that the British centre-left has been dangerously tolerant of 'non-violent extremism'. Here as elsewhere, however, such criticisms underestimate the depth of the splits between Salafi groups on scriptural and political matters. The theory behind the Conservative critique is that these organizations differ from militant 'Salafi-jihadis' not in their ultimate ideals but only in the means considered acceptable: both supposedly want to see an end to democracy, but only the latter are willing to pursue this actively. However, in the case of STREET, at least, this criticism fails. STREET is aligned with Brixton mosque, a place which, although briefly attended by the so-called 'shoe bomber' Richard Reid, has long been dominated by a pietistic form of Salafism.[158] STREET's leader, Abdul Haqq Baker, firmly eschews both anti-democratic politics and isolation from civil society. STREET, like many similar civil society organizations, lost its financial backing amidst allegations of intolerance and illiberalism after the Conservative-led coalition government came to power.[159] What made this loss a particularly bitter pill for Baker to swallow was that he fell foul of a principle with which he actually agrees: that the UK government should only work with groups that subscribe to, in his own words, 'core values of Britishness and Western society'.[160]

One reason political divides within Salafi and separatist Islamist networks are so wide is that many of the members of these networks have shifted views as they have grown older, with some disavowing their former selves. As the leader of the militant Salafi organization JIMAS, Muhammad Manwar Ali (aka 'Abu Muntasir') inspired several individuals to travel overseas to Afghanistan and other conflict zones in the 1980s and 1990s. Ali very publicly renounced politicized varieties of Salafism in 2005, however, and subsequently JIMAS was transformed into a small

Muslim educational charity.[161] Ali himself has become involved in chaplaincy work and has advised local authorities on religious education. One of Ali's followers in the 1990s, Usama Hasan, whose views on Islamic marriage we came across in Chapter 4, followed a similar path. Having travelled to conflicts in Afghanistan as a young man, he began to adopt more 'modernist' positions from the mid-2000s, describing himself as a 'Wahhabi Sufi' in recognition of his Salafi background and more recent Sufi influences.[162] This change, however, brought him into conflict with elements of the north London mosque at which he worked as a part-time imam. Everything came to a head during an ugly dispute about human evolution that led to him receiving death threats, and he subsequently moved to work for Quilliam, becoming, like Ali, vocal in his opposition to extremism and broadly supportive of Prevent.

Quilliam is, in fact, in large part comprised of 'former extremists'. Its founders, Maajid Nawaz and Ed Husain, were prominent figures in Hizb ut-Tahrir in the UK, with the former even being imprisoned by the Egyptian government between 2001 and 2006 for Hizb ut-Tahrir-related activism. Like Hasan and Ali, Nawaz and Husain reversed their positions in the late 2000s, becoming among the most vocal supporters of Prevent. Quilliam was founded in part to disrupt what they perceived as, in Husain's words, the 'cosy' relationship between government and certain Muslim civil society organizations, the MCB in particular.[163] Nawaz and Husain did this not by claiming to represent a specific constituency but via a representational strategy that emphasized their supposedly unique insight into the struggles of the British Muslim population. They have always been quick to make accusations of extremist sympathies; they even submitted to Charles Farr, then the director general of OSCT, a secret (but subsequently leaked) analysis of Prevent in 2010 which sharply criticized CLG for engaging 'Islamist-dominated groups like ... the MCB'.[164] Quilliam's work continues in a similar vein today, although Husain left the organization to take up a post at the Council on Foreign Relations in New York during the early 2010s, while Nawaz has lately pursued a career as a talk radio controversialist.

Nawaz's current position as a presenter for the radio station LBC is a testament to how successfully the stories of former extremists have been marketed; they stand out among the case studies here because more than just a small network of activists and academic researchers are aware of them. Their narratives have a tendency, as Yahya Birt has remarked, to 'overshadow' all of the 'multifarious and untold human stories' of Muslim Britain. This is despite the fact – or perhaps because of it – that the authors of these stories are often remote from the institutional infrastructures of which they speak.[165] Nawaz, especially, is more likely to be seen in conversation with anti-Islamic writers such as Sam Harris than Muslim civil society networks. This disproportionate coverage makes it all the more important to give equal time to the fate of reformist Islamist organizations, because it is this strand of Islamic activism that has ultimately had a more profound influence. Here, too, one can find multiple examples of evolved and revised views. Whole organizations – such as the ISB – have transformed much as JIMAS did, but on a larger scale. The ISB was conceived in 1990 as a national English-speaking platform that would enable reformist Islamist organizations to work collaboratively.[166] It was influenced by Jamaat-i-Islami and accordingly was committed to the idea of a global 'Islamic movement'. Today it follows its original practices of recruiting and gathering members through large camps, residential training programmes and study circles, mostly aimed at middle-class Muslims. It has, however, shifted profoundly so that now, in the words of Dilwar Hussain, a former ISB president, it 'sees itself very much as an organisation for families, for a fairly progressive brand of Islam which is about synergising British identity, Muslim identity, families, fairly educated people'.[167] In 2014 the ISB even broke a glass ceiling when Sughra Ahmed – a former Islamic Foundation employee who is now based at Stanford University – was appointed the first female leader of national Muslim representative body.

The Cordoba Foundation is another important case, albeit one that is distinct in that its roots can be traced to the Middle East rather than South Asia. The Cordoba Foundation emerged out of the MAB, a body that derived general inspiration from the Muslim Brotherhood in Egypt.[168] Formally affiliated with the MCB, the MAB was focused on cultural and educational activity until the more politicized elements of its leadership – such as Anas Altikriti, whose father was associated with the Muslim Brotherhood in Iraq, and Osama Saeed, who subsequently became a Scottish National Party (SNP) activist – became involved in mobilizing opposition to the Iraq war in 2003.[169] Organizing the protests facilitated connections with the Metropolitan Police and eventually led to the MAB working with the Met to take over and transform Finsbury Park Mosque, which at the time was controlled by followers of Abu Hamza, the militant preacher who was arrested on charges of inciting violence in 2004 and extradited to the United States.[170] This prompted a division within the organization as well as disquiet among some international associates who could not accept a Muslim group partnering with secularists and socialists. Altikriti and other more politicized members thus moved on to form the Cordoba Foundation in the late 2000s.[171] The Cordoba Foundation bears the marks of this history, being interested in educational and interfaith activity as well as publishing commentaries on politics. Although certainly not beyond reproach – the Foundation's leadership was sympathetic toward Mohammed Morsi's Muslim Brotherhood-aligned government in Egypt, despite the Egyptian Brotherhood's continued vocal opposition to laws prohibiting rape within marriage[172] – Cameron's claim that the Cordoba Foundation is a 'front' for the Brotherhood is, today, little short of defamatory.

One can find numerous individual stories of reformist Islamist transformation too, alongside that of Bunglawala. Sarah Joseph, a convert to Islam, was, in Hamid's words, one of YMUK's 'brightest stars' in the 1990s. Having edited YMUK's newsletter, *Trends*, she moved on from utopian politics in the 2000s to become editor of the Muslim lifestyle magazine *emel*.[173] Similarly, Atif Imtiaz was an active member of YMUK and author of its 'manifesto' document *Striving for Revival*, which presented Islam as a totalizing ideological programme capable of addressing all of life's complexities and ambiguities. After completing a PhD in social psychology, however, he became academic director at Cambridge Muslim College (see Chapter 3) before moving into the Muslim charitable sector.[174] A third case is Tahmina Saleem, a keen member of YMUK who went on to co-found Inspire with Sara Khan.[175] Again and again, reformist Islamists have transitioned into positions in mainstream Muslim organizations. There is substantial truth, then, in the argument that not only has reformist Islamism adapted and developed upon its original political vision, but many of those initially attracted to it have shaped the British Islamic institutional landscape more widely.

Collectively, these shifts have contributed to the emergence of a more fragmented but more dynamic constellation of lobbying and activist organizations. They form one element of a story of the diversification of Muslim civil society representation. O'Toole and colleagues, in a major study of Muslim participation in UK governance between 1997 and 2010, mapped out how Muslim–state relations have become richer and more varied, with interactions cutting across several distinct but overlapping policy domains, from 'equalities' to interfaith and counterterrorism.[176] This, of course, was in part a consequence of Labour's model of consultative governance, but it is also a function of changes within the British Muslim population. One can now find multiple 'modes' of Muslim representation operating within the UK. More conventional 'delegate' forms of representation – in which grassroots support from community institutions is used to build credibility and influence – are increasingly supplemented by representation based upon a claim to specific expertise.[177] Such representation-through-expertise has become particularly important in enabling Muslim women to bypass male-dominated ethno-religious community infrastructures. In the wake of the 2005 London bombings, for example, a range of consultative forums were set up leading to the expansion of Prevent in 2007. Within these one could find numerous Muslim women 'whose official reason for inclusion was expertise developed in the private sector, in anti-discrimination or other public policy contexts, but whose identities as Muslims nonetheless were salient in those settings'.[178] The growing number of Muslim women in elite professional roles, then (see Chapter 2), seems to be reshaping British Muslim civil society, ensuring that Muslim organizations' claims always face healthy competition.

Evaluating representative claims

This idea of *competition* between representative claims invites us to look directly at what exactly 'good' Muslim representation looks like – if indeed such a thing can ever exist. Representation of identity groups is widely viewed as something that damages democracy, weakening the rights of marginal group members and encouraging a fragmented society. Often it is dismissed as faintly ridiculous, as with the political theorist James Roland Pennock's curt remark: 'No one would argue that morons should be represented by morons'.[179] Muslim identity is often viewed as particularly threatening. In early 2019, for example, the Tony Blair Institute for Global Change published an analysis of several British Muslim civil society organizations that suggested that if a group 'sees Muslim identity as a reference point for activism' then it overlaps with, and is on a continuum moving towards, anti-democratic Islamist groups.[180] In this and in many, many other cases, Muslim identity is understood as inherently dangerous, involving opposition to British society as well as, potentially, anti-democratic tendencies.

I hope the material presented across this book is sufficient to rebut any arguments about the dangerous and anti-democratic nature of Muslim identity, but the general criticisms concerning identity representation are harder to dismiss. From the Hindu right in India to white nationalists in the West, there is no contesting the point that many movements organized around ethnic or religious identity are a threat to people's rights and political stability. Even small community associations, when treated as privileged partners, have the potential to limit certain people's ability to speak out. At the same time, however, arguments against identity representation that are made without qualification rapidly collapse when they are subjected to scrutiny. Dismissing all political action organized around identity means dismissing the civil rights movement, lobbying for women's suffrage and campaigns to legalize same-sex intimacy, among many, many other just causes. The task, then, is less one of choosing to be for or against identity-based representation and more one of determining when identity claims are valid.

There are perhaps two types of legitimate Muslim (or identity-based) representative claim. In the last chapter, I described debates in liberal democracies as a process of translating distinctive moral languages into terms that can be widely understood. Languages are collectively sustained; we talk in terms that were handed down to us and can change those terms only through negotiation with others. Translating the moral language of Islam – or for that matter any comprehensive philosophy – into public discourse will thus always involve *groups* on some level. If we see this process of translation as healthy, as I argued we should, then we have to retain some kind of space for public action by communities of belief, both religious and non-religious. In addition to this, as the examples listed above illustrate, the case for a 'politics of presence' is strongest when an identity group is *excluded* for some reason.[181] A range of scholars, from Khadijah Elshayyal to Tariq Modood and Nasar Meer, have persuasively argued that the exclusion of Muslims provides a justification for Muslim mobilization and, in turn, identity representation.[182] As we saw earlier, Elshayyal describes this in terms of an 'equality gap' which can be understood in two overlapping senses: firstly, Muslims are discriminated against in various spheres of life and, before the equality acts of 2003–10, had limited legal protection against such discrimination; and secondly, they are misrepresented and misperceived. They may justly feel the need, then, to speak out not just to address exclusions but also as part of an effort to be understood on their own terms.

Saying all this doesn't, however, get us very far in determining what representation looks like when it is done well. Muslims may respond to an 'equality gap' but whose response should one listen to? What kinds of claims about the Islamic tradition should one acknowledge when talking about – to take previous examples – accommodation in schools or the integration of Islam in English family law? There is, of course, no one-size-fits-all answer to these questions, but the work of political philosopher Michael Saward offers a useful guide.[183] Saward's interest in representative claims-making begins from the faults of electoral representation, which may be the result of unfairness or just the inevitable limitations of political systems. His writing emphasizes the temporal, geographical and communication constraints within which elected representatives operate and to the many predetermined aspects of politics that elections cannot change, such as two-party systems, governmental structures, terms of parliament or constituency boundaries. These limitations, he argues, leave open the possibility for legitimate non-elective representative claims and help ensure that claims made by elected representatives are always open to challenge. Electoral representation is always partial and so it is always supplemented by a process of representative *construction*: citizens elect their representatives, but representatives also always, in a sense, bring into being their constituency. In day-to-day politics, elected and unelected political figures create an image of those they speak for ('hard-working families', 'traditional working-class voters' and so on). Representative constructions may resonate with an electorate or they may not, but the crucial point is that they are always unfinished: 'There is no representative claim without its being open to a counter-claim or a denial from part of the very audience that the claim invokes'.[184] In post-Brexit Britain, for example, a common complaint of ethnic minorities is that politicians' references to the 'traditional working class' tend to exclude them.

It follows from this that one way a political system can be evaluated is by looking at the extent to which claims made by elected or unelected representatives can be contested. Saward is highly sympathetic to unelected political actors, pointing out that they do things elected politicians can't or won't. They challenge and contest, traverse national and temporal boundaries, and, when a system is working well at least, have to work extremely hard to make their claims convincing precisely because 'the symbolic architecture of our political systems doesn't do that work for them'.[185] In practice, of course, things do not always work out as they should. Looking to the example of British Muslim civil society, a compelling case can be made that in the early years of its existence the MCB did not feel the need to reach out beyond its delegate base because it knew the government would have an open door regardless. On selected issues – religious discrimination legislation being chief among them – the MCB mobilized a broad spectrum of support, but right up until 2010 the organization, as Elshayyal observes, remained 'a long way from demonstrating a capacity for true inclusivity beyond the handful of groups to which it owed its patronage'.[186] The question becomes, then: What factors encourage claims-makers to fine-tune what they say? How do political systems facilitate dynamism in claims-making?

On this subject, Saward offers three criteria that can help evaluate the legitimacy of a claim by someone who is not elected:

1. 'Connecting' criteria: Is a claim part of a formal chain of delegation? Is it embedded in a larger democratic system? Is it locked into networks of accountability?
2. 'Confirming' criteria: Can a claim be tested? Are there signs of its validation from the subjects of the claim?

3. 'Untaintedness' criteria: Is the author of the claim free from conflicts of interest (e.g. arising from formal patronage by elected representatives) or other external pressures? Are claims free from political constraints?[187]

Of course, it isn't only the case that these criteria are difficult to apply but, as Saward readily acknowledges, they stand in tension with one another. It is almost impossible to be 'locked into networks of accountability' *and* 'free from political constraints' at the same time. These criteria only make sense, therefore, when they are seen as forces propelling an ongoing 'contest of discourses' in the absence of which representative claims-making ossifies into lethargic statements that fail to engage with the wishes of people represented.

Emerging from the past

Let's put these principles to the test. How closely does British Muslim activism reflect this landscape of competitive claims-making in which individuals and organizations must do work in order to make their representative claims convincing? Certainly, no one would claim that British Muslim civil society is perfect, but ultimately, over time, an increasingly sophisticated constellation of campaigning and representative organizations has established itself in the UK. Furthermore, even despite the unwillingness of the current British government to engage with Muslim organizations in a formal way, a wide range of points of meaningful contact with different arms of the British state remains.

To illustrate, I want to return again to the case of the MCB. What has become apparent to observers of the UK's largest Muslim representative body is that in its last ten years in the wilderness it has altered. The most vivid illustration of this was the appointment of the organization's first British-born secretary general, Harun Khan, in 2016. Although in itself a minor detail, Khan's appointment appears not to have been a cosmetic change but indicative of – even a driver of – internal changes in ethos and priorities. Not only is Khan the first British-born MCB leader but when he was appointed he was, at 46, also its youngest. Across the MCB's committee the average age of the office bearers has, according to one of its most senior representatives, gone down from over 50 years old to 37.[188] At the time of writing, 50 per cent of its office bearers are also women, as are the leads for the organization's three most important projects. This includes Samayya Afzal, the MCB's Bradford- and London-based community engagement manager. Afzal leads the organization's 'National Listening Exercise' – a project gathering evidence of Muslim views about counter-extremism policy – and is a driving force behind efforts to train Muslim women in mosque leadership, as well as a Muslim women's conference held in March 2019 and headlined by young poets, activists and academics. This event – which featured the talented activist-poet Suhaiymah Manzoor-Khan, the councillor Fadima Hassan and the academic Fatima Rajina, among other speakers – would have been unthinkable a decade ago, when Muslim women's voices were typically relegated by the MCB's leadership to separate 'sisters' circles' on the margins. That such an event is possible now is a testament not (only) to Khan's management but also to democratizing British Muslim initiatives that have been a constant source of pressure on the larger organizations, from the Inclusive Mosque Initiative, which was founded in 2012, to the more recently established Muslim Women's Council.

The development of mosque leadership training is consistent with what appears to be a general shift in the MCB's work to focus more on changing the character and public image of local Muslim institutions. Alongside this training, the MCB has organized a series of 'Our Mosques, Our Future' events looking at how religious institutions can better serve Muslim populations. Arguably its most successful venture is the establishment of an annual 'Visit My Mosque' day in which members of the public are invited to drop into *masjids* across the country. This initiative has expanded from 20 mosques in 2015 to include 80 in 2016, 150 in 2017 and 200 in 2018.[189] It is important to note, too, that this is potentially treacherous terrain for the organization to walk on given that the MCB remains reliant on mosques for much of its legitimacy and material support.

Its responses to political events and coverage of Muslims have also become more targeted, with less of the grandstanding that led to the Holocaust Memorial Day boycott and more focused efforts to correct misrepresentations. Most active on this has been Miqdaad Versi, the MCB's assistant secretary general. Versi is best known for his personal mission to correct inaccurate reporting of Muslims in the UK press: he was, as of April 2017, personally responsible for, he says, around '20–30 corrections of national newspapers that are solely accuracy-related, not just [complaints about] scaremongering'.[190] He has also led calls for an internal inquiry into Islamophobia within the Conservative party, in parallel to the procedures put in place to address antisemitism within Labour's left wing. When initially announced, this call seemed unlikely to get far. Indeed, at the time of writing the possibility of substantive change still appears remote.[191] As Conservative politicians and press outlets have continued to highlight antisemitism on the left, however, so the MCB's call had started to come to prominence, with the *Times, Observer, Guardian* and former chair of the Conservatives, Baroness Sayeeda Warsi, backing the call in 2018.[192] Versi and MCB, then, have managed to take an issue from a position of total obscurity and make it news.

Alongside these activities, the MCB has also, despite remaining out of favour with government, engaged with various public bodies without fanfare. As part of its media lobbying work its representatives have met with the Independent Press Standards Organisation (IPSO) multiple times. The organization consulted with David Anderson QC as part of his review into Prevent and met with representatives of Labour, the Liberal Democrats and, in a more limited sense, the Conservatives in relation to the 2015 Counter Terrorism and Security Act. While conceding that the MCB – and Muslim civil society more generally – has made little headway in influencing government policy since 2010, Versi believes this activity shaped the proposed amendments to the 2015 act. This is not work that the MCB keeps secret, but at the same time they do not promote it, primarily for reasons of capacity:[193] the MCB remains for the most part a volunteer-led organization, with even its senior figures, including Versi, working full-time in professions such as community work or management consultancy.

Such interactions are obscured by a scholarly debate focusing on the disciplinary aspects of UK government policy. Even now, when relations between Muslim civil society organizations are frosty at best, the agency of non-governmental organizations and the multifaceted nature of the state allow for exchanges, some of which, at least, have consequence. But the failure to recognize this lobbying, and the internal changes that have enabled it, keeps conversations about Muslim organizations stuck in the past. As recently as 2015 a government-initiated review into the Muslim Brotherhood by civil servants John Jenkins and Charles Farr, while acknowledging that substantive change has taken place within the ISB, rehearsed the claim that the Brotherhood played, and plays, an important role in shaping the MCB's activities and ethos.[194] Such claims, while always debatable, are now so outdated as to be ludicrous. Yet they remain the official rationale for rejecting the MCB even while comparable Jewish and Sikh groups are included.

One irony is that the recent changes within the MCB might not have happened had it not been placed at arm's length. Its National Listening Exercise on Prevent, in particular, represents a concerted effort to make it clear to its interlocutors that when it criticizes public policy in the area of counterterrorism its position is not – as the Muslim Brotherhood review and countless others have implied – due to the organization's sympathies with radical movements but a reflection of the Muslim population at large. It also uses polling data to show that more than half of Muslims feel it represents their views.[195] In Saward's terms, this is an exercise in doing the work necessary to be able to make an effective representative claim. The organization's independence helps with this, to a degree at least. The difficulty now, though, is that the state has sharpened the division between those who are 'in' and those who are 'out' – with the latter delegitimized and slandered – to the point that productive competition between representative claims-makers is extremely difficult. Over the last fifty years, the landscape of Muslim–state interaction in the UK has transformed. Periods of localized lobbying, of utopian activism and of a 'take me to your leader'-style politics have given way to a more sophisticated model of pragmatic engagement featuring a multiplicity of individuals and organizations. The social changes driving this are not reversible and will continue irrespective of the government of the day. The question now is whether the state is willing, or able, to bring itself up to date with British Islam.

Chapter 6

CONCLUSION

Breathing life into old traditions

In 1985 Robert Bellah and colleagues published *Habits of the Heart*, a book that, in America at least, had an uncommonly large impact for a piece of empirical sociology, making the front pages of a number of national journals and getting near the summit of various bestseller lists. The book, which was republished for a third time in 2008, sets itself an unusual task: to describe what the authors call the 'moral ecology' of the United States – that is, what Americans value, how they think they should live and what shape they think society should take. One of the things that makes it unusual is the way it links the lives of the people interviewed – therapists, activists, bankers – to the moral traditions by which they had been influenced: Protestant individualism, expressivism, utilitarianism and (small 'r') republicanism. Written in opposition to the free-market logic that was at the time emerging as orthodoxy across the political spectrum and to the idea of a purely managerial state, it ends with a provocative contention:

> We need to learn again from the cultural riches of the human species and to reappropriate and revitalise those riches so they can speak to our condition today .... This would not result in a neotraditionalism that would return us to the past. Rather, it might lead to a recovery of a genuine tradition, one that is always self-revising and in a state of development. It might help us find again the coherence we have almost lost.[1]

What concerned the authors of *Habits* was that the individuals they interviewed no longer seemed to be able to relate the narratives in terms of which they made sense of their lives to the new sociopolitical reality of the United States. Instead, they seemed to be retreating either into a narrow individualism or an aimless nostalgia for vanished community. The solution they proposed to what was fast becoming, in their view, a deep crisis in American public life was a conscious effort to revivify America's foundational moral traditions in order to revitalize public engagement and enable the country to renew itself. They suggested marshalling the power of tradition (defined, following Jaroslav Pelikan, as 'the living faith of the dead') while avoiding the temptation of traditionalism (or what Pelikan terms 'the dead faith of the living').[2]

Although successful, the book was widely criticized by both right and left, and while many of these criticisms were unfair,[3] some had force. The most glaring problem with the book is that it does not find a way of incorporating moral traditions that regard themselves as – or are viewed by others as – *outsiders* to American nationhood for whatever reason. The contemporary reader of *Habits* finds few lessons on how to understand and address, say, the conspiracy that Barack Obama is not a US-born citizen. Although it serves as a useful guide for understanding the social forces that led to the emergence of Donald Trump, it has very little to say about the US president's characterizations of black, Mexican, transgender or Muslim groups. The book's portrayal of nationhood, then, is too cosy, failing to engage with its darker side.

The flaw of that book, however, can provide this one with a useful concluding question. No one has yet written a *Habits of the Heart* for the UK. (It would be an interesting project to attempt.) But it is not controversial to claim that the crisis that Bellah et al. identified extends far beyond the United States and, on both sides of the Atlantic, has become deeper and more dangerous over the last thirty years. In Britain, the two main political parties no longer seem able to bridge the profound cultural and economic divides that have opened up across the country. The traditions by which they have long been guided no longer map onto large constituencies. From the 1980s through to the early 2010s, the UK witnessed what William Davies refers to as the 'disenchantment of politics by economics', with both parties allowing their political imaginations to be colonized by market logics.[4] Under Blair and Cameron in particular, the UK's political vocabulary was reduced to slogans – 'change', 'progress', 'forward' – emptied of clear meaning and direction. The political apathy this engendered strengthened a form of traditionalism that amounted to little more than a lament for a supposedly once proud but lost sense of English- or Britishness. This traditionalism, of course, found a winning cause in the 2016 referendum on the UK's EU membership, during which the Leave campaign broadcast a vision of a once proud country that could recover past glories if only it was allowed to flourish unencumbered by EU bureaucracy and migrants. Boris Johnson, the Vote Leave figurehead and (as I write) recently installed prime minister, appears intent on pursuing this vision relentlessly, overturning institutions and constitutional conventions as he does so. This has proven a winning strategy in the UK's no-longer-fit-for-purpose 'first past the post' electoral system, but as the isolated country is squeezed by larger trading partners it is, I suspect, likely to animate an ever more resentful variety of English nationalism.

Set against the backdrop of this deep crisis, breathing life into moral traditions that are seen as fundamental to the constitution of the British state and its political parties – the conservatism of Burke; the liberalism of Locke, Mill, Wollstonecraft and Fawcett; the social activism of Owen and Wesley – appears an impossibly tall order. How, then, should one begin to consider the demand that the Islamic tradition – a relative newcomer – bed itself into modern Britain, particularly given that many of those currently making that demand seem faintly suspicious of Islam, or even to believe that 'Britishness' can be roughly defined as that which is not Muslim? What might it take to develop, and what might be gained from developing, an Islamic tradition that the future writers of a UK-based *Habits of the Heart* might be able to count as among Britain's many and varied 'cultural riches'?

Building British Islam

As the start of this book, I said that I intended to develop three linked arguments: first, a qualified defence of liberal approaches to minority inclusion and to the incorporation of Muslim populations and institutions; second, a case against the pervasive view that liberal and Islamic traditions are incompatible; and third, an account disputing the notion that national identification inevitably results in coercive measures against minorities and the stifling of political dissent. I also said that these arguments would come together through an overarching narrative about the emergence of a distinctive British Islam. To make headway answering the question posed above, I'd like to return to these arguments, starting with the overarching narrative and working backwards.

The case for the emergence of a distinctive British Islam, in the sense outlined in the Introduction, is easy now to summarize. What is abundantly clear from the three preceding chapters is that, across different institutional contexts, there has been a gradual, but profound, remaking of British Islam's institutional landscape. A generation that came of age between the disturbances in Oldham, Burnley and Bradford in 2001 and the 7/7 attacks in 2005 is reworking British Islamic institutional infrastructures that previously were castigated for only expressing the perspectives of conservative, invariably male community elders. Islamic educational institutions, which were once mostly oriented towards maintaining and defending Islamic tradition in an unfamiliar environment, have responded to student and social need; reforms driven from the bottom up have facilitated a partial integration into the wider education sector and with secular educational institutions (Chapter 3). Islamic dispute resolution institutions have moulded their procedures around English law, creating space for deliberation about how the dissonance between English legal and Muslim norms night be resolved (Chapter 4). In the sphere of Muslim–state relations, countercultural Islamism has diminished as a force within mainstream representative bodies, with the energy of such organizations being redirected towards social reform and targeted lobbying. From the Islamic Society of Britain to the Islamic Foundation, from the East London Mosque to the Muslim Council of Britain (MCB), it is hard to point to an enduring Muslim activist or representative organization that *hasn't* shifted ethos significantly over the years (Chapter 5). Of course, there are counterexamples and anyone who wants to seek out an intolerant statement by a Muslim activist or religious leader will be able to find one. But overall, the dominant trend is unmistakable: it is towards the building of a rooted British Islam.

In addition to the material set out in preceding chapters, I would like to provide one more piece of evidence for this change. In October 2018, Asia Bibi, a Christian farm labourer held on death row after being convicted of allegedly insulting the

Prophet Muhammad in 2010, was acquitted by the Pakistani Supreme Court. This prompted a paroxysm of protest in several of Pakistan's largest cities, one that encompassed not just dedicated anti-blasphemy parties but members and leaders of Pakistan's Deobandi and Barelvi communities. In the UK, the case also sparked controversy after the government failed to make a public offer of asylum to Bibi, reportedly after an intervention from the then prime minister, Theresa May. Conservative journalists and some Christian solidarity campaigners perceived this as a capitulation to domestic and international Islamists by a government mindful, as one journalist put it, of the 'warrant for murder of a British novelist pumped out of mosques from Tehran to Bradford in 1989'.[5] The contrast between the British Muslim response to the Rushdie affair and to the Bibi protests could not, though, have been clearer. The Muslim Council of Britain (MCB), as we saw in Chapter 5, was formed partly in response to *The Satanic Verses*, with its founders – and the breadth of Muslim institutions – being heavily involved in protests against the book. The breadth of Muslim institutions – from the Muslim Council of Wales to Tell MAMA, British Muslims for Secular Democracy, the Association of British Muslims, She Speaks We Hear and New Horizons in British Islam – objected publicly in the Bibi case too, but this time *against the government's hard line*. The MCB, which draws its support from predominantly Deobandi affiliate bodies, spoke out against the 'nonsensical [and] divisive' reports that British Muslims were opposed to offering Bibi asylum. Miqdaad Versi, the MCB leader we met in Chapter 5, described her treatment as 'appalling'.[6]

Yet if this contrast was clear, it was given no recognition in a media ecosystem that seemed intent on closing its ears to what Muslim associations were actually saying. The same can be said for the general transition British Islamic institutions described in this book, which is given zero recognition within a public debate about Islam and its 'integration' that remains oriented around the image of an inward-looking older generation of Muslim migrants and their supposedly restless, alienated offspring. The British government continues to treat the MCB's spokespersons, for example, as personae non gratae on the basis of a dispute with ministers that took place in 2009 or, worse, on the basis of statements that were made by its founders over 30 years ago. I would go so far as to say that this refusal to acknowledge religious change is one of the ways in which Islamophobia manifests itself in British public discourse. Muslim organizations with conservative or reformist Islamist roots are never allowed to move beyond those roots; they face constant reminders, sometimes made in bad faith, that work to delegitimize their public actions and presence. Hopelessly out-of-date stereotypes abound of Deobandis as insular and 'anti-British' or of Islamic activist organizations as 'fronts for the Muslim Brotherhood'. As I noted in the Introduction, over the last ten years or so, there has been a move – exemplified by definitions of Islamophobia published by Runnymede in 2017 and the All Party Parliamentary Group on British Muslims in 2018[7] – towards conceptualizing Islamophobia as a form of racism. This is, in many ways, a positive change and it has been hard won by those who have painstakingly highlighted the ways Muslims are racialized and discriminated against. The conversation about Islamophobia, however, has barely even begun to address prejudices manifested in a refusal to acknowledge religious change. There is, then, a dire need for individuals concerned with equality and justice to argue more clearly – and more *politically* – for a revised and updated understanding of what British Islam looks like. Until this happens, it will remain impossible to speak meaningfully about the culture and contribution of Islamic Britain.

Whose liberalism? Which state?

It is more difficult to conclude my arguments about how Islam and liberalism fit together, primarily because across this book 'liberalism' has been hard to pin down, even despite my explanations in the Introduction. In titling this book *Islam and the Liberal State* I ipso facto credit Britain with being 'liberal'. But the obvious difficulty with this is that the UK has recently rejected, and is currently trying to extricate itself from, a political union regarded as fundamental to the post-war liberal international order. Since 2016, liberals in the UK have been forced into retreat and even in the pre-2016 'good times' the way Britain treated ethnic and religious minorities – and especially those with insecure migration status – often violated the most basic liberal principles. In Britain, the Home Office routinely places irregular migrants in detention centres indefinitely without any judge authorizing their incarceration.[8] Executive powers are regularly used to withdraw people's passports with barely any judicial or parliamentary oversight.[9] Recently, this practice has even extended to the home secretaries using executive orders to withdraw citizenship completely from individuals suspected of committing terrorism offences. For now, the UK's courts only permit this when the suspect is recognized as a citizen by another state, but this has created, in effect, a system of tiered citizenship in which the status of the UK's ethnic minorities – many of whom can claim citizenship overseas even if they have never left Britain – is conditional.[10] Any state that engages in such practices has a weak claim to be oriented around liberal ideals.

These illiberal tendencies have been apparent at various points in the preceding chapters and complicate this book's empirical claims. They can be seen in the proposals to regulate and 'vet' supplementary religious education and religious leaders (Chapter 3); in the incoherent official definition of extremism (Chapter 1); in the tactics the state uses to delegitimize dissenting Muslim groups (Chapter 5); and in the way state surveillance has been delegated to public and publicly funded institutions since 2015 (Chapter 5). This is a book about Muslim responses to and engagement with liberal institutions, but British institutions rarely follow liberal norms consistently. Indeed, liberal norms of governance are frequently suspended when Muslims are involved. The present Conservative government, for example, appears to see engagement with communal religious organizations as a necessary element of democratic participation and as a signal of an inclusive society, but while this has resulted in government maintaining close contact with Jewish, Sikh and Hindu groups, ministers refuse any engagement with broad-based Muslim civil society organizations.[11]

For some scholars, many working in the field of race and migration, examples like these reveal a story not of a government failing to follow the liberal principles it purports to uphold but one whose actions are consistent with what liberalism has always been: a civilizational project that has, from its origins, always involved the denigration of racialized and colonized subjects.[12] 'Liberalism', in such accounts, is not simply a set of normative ideals but a constellation of bureaucracies that are organized around certain epistemic norms, one of the most fundamental of these being an assumed hierarchy of human cultures. As an historical description of liberalism, these accounts, of course, have merit; recall that John Stuart Mill took it completely for granted that political liberty did not need to be extended to 'backward' societies 'where the race itself may be considered as in its nonage'.[13] As an argument about contemporary liberalism it has considerable force, too. Not only in Britain but also across the purportedly 'liberal' European Union[14] the need to preserve 'liberalism' in the face of 'backward' cultural traditions is one of the most common justifications for coercive 'integration' measures and restrictive migration and citizenship laws.[15] Colonialism may have formally ended and be rarely spoken of, but colonial history continues to influence the racial ordering of British citizenship (and its withdrawal).

This cannot, though, be the whole story, and indeed looking into this literature in a little more depth reveals a more interesting picture. Among the most insightful scholars who tend towards this perspective is Nisha Kapoor, whose analyses of deportation and citizenship withdrawal processes form part of a compelling critique of what she terms 'racial neoliberalism'[16] (by which she means, roughly, a governance regime in which the language of race and racism is 'muted', but which still functions to structurally disadvantage and exclude racialized minorities).[17] What is striking about Kapoor's writing is that, although it appears sceptical of liberal institutions' ability to challenge creeping authoritarianism, it is at its most forceful when it uncovers the truly *scandalous* means by which British Muslim citizens have been denied due process, from the extension of royal prerogative powers to the use of Kafkaesque 'closed proceedings' in which the accused is denied the right to review the evidence against them.[18] Although Kapoor's work does not present a 'liberal' critique, it nevertheless criticizes the erosion of liberal norms and in doing so implies that without liberal procedures, such as an independent judiciary and habeas corpus rights, justice cannot be served. Or, to put this another way, liberal proceduralism emerges in Kapoor's work as a normative ideal even if liberal politicians are not seen as especially well placed to defend that ideal.

Furthermore, although we have seen multiple examples of illiberal governmental practices, to base the conclusions of this book only on these cases would be to ignore half its contents. As Therese O'Toole and colleagues have argued in the case of Prevent, there are 'differences in practices, habits and perspectives across governance domains', especially as one begins to factor in the relationships and differences between national and municipal government.[19] While we have seen numerous examples of illiberal and disciplinary governance mechanisms, there have also been multiple cases of partnerships being enabled or created by the British state. Perhaps the clearest examples of these are the various 'soft measures' put in place by both Labour and Conservative governments to encourage connections between Islamic and secular higher education institutions that I reviewed in Chapter 3. These sit alongside several examples, found across both Chapters 3 and 5, of low-key and frequently locally negotiated varieties of multicultural inclusion, many of which facilitated the opening out of Muslim organizations. This suggests that there is more than one liberalism at work across the various domains of British governance.

This book offers a qualified defence of political liberalism. Leaving the qualifications to one side for a moment, what I want to stress is that this defence is not simply theoretical but involves an empirical claim too. Specifically, my claim is that *when British governance has followed norms consistent with political liberalism this has facilitated positive developments within British Islamic institutions*. One of the difficulties in making this claim is that scholars who tend to perceive liberalism as complicit in the exclusion and dehumanization of minorities also tend to see British governance in almost exclusively disciplinary terms. Even 'soft' measures are typically interpreted as disciplinary techniques – as attempts to subdue dissenting voices or to engineer more 'liberal' (i.e. uncritical) varieties of Islam. Of course, there is ample evidence to demonstrate that this perspective is valid; we need to look only at the many examples in Chapter 5 of governments trying to engineer change in British Muslim civil society or breaking off relations with Muslim groups rather than face even limited criticism. Even so, to see *all* such state intervention in this way is unhelpful. In the case of the state's attempts to build bridges between Islamic and secular educational institutions, for example, state intervention is entirely consistent with the wishes of those studying at *dar al-ulum*s. That is, there has been considerable *bottom-up* pressure to accredit seminary qualifications (Chapter 3) and to ignore this is to refuse the agency and aspirations of this part of the British Muslim population.

Autonomy and the governance of Muslim citizens

This argument has specific implications for Prevent and the debates surrounding it, and elaborating on these will help flesh out the points made above. One of the arguments I want to emphasize using the material in this book is that British Muslims have almost always been several steps ahead of the public debates about them. Discussions about the concept of 'British Islam' were taking place decades before New Labour picked up on the theme in 2007 (Chapter 1). Institutional responses to the disconnect between Islamic education and British society had been developed long before this domain became a focus of public policy (Chapter 3). Mosque and marriage registration campaigns had been developed years before the government review of '*Shari'a* councils' was announced in 2015 (Chapter 4). Certainly, British Muslims have not always been able to resolve their problems or even discuss them in an amicable way, as the continued difficulties surrounding the registration of Muslim marriages in England amply attest. What this does help to highlight, however, is how often British journalists and policymakers have – to use a fitting colonial metaphor – 'discovered' new territories that have already been mapped out by the people living in them.

Nowhere has this been clearer than in the case of Prevent. The initial expansion of Prevent under New Labour in the years following the 2005 attacks on London involved the security services suddenly discovering as relevant social issues previously left to other government departments, if not to Muslim populations to solve by themselves. Civic integration policies – and indeed policies concerned with everything from education and economic opportunity to gender equality – were re-envisaged as a means to the end of thwarting terrorism. Despite important changes to Prevent since, including recognition of the need to separate 'cohesion' and 'counterterrorism' work, policymakers have consistently viewed engagement with Islam and Muslims as valuable only to the extent that it supposedly helps to limit the risk of extremism. This has been a catastrophic mistake, for reasons both principled and pragmatic. As we saw in Chapter 5, it has distorted, rather than facilitated, the conversations on all the social issues listed above that have been ongoing within British Muslim civil society networks, with destructive divisions being engendered between those who do and don't work with government. With the possible exception of a limited number of targeted initiatives, there is very little evidence that such interventions functioned to reduce extremism, in part because, as I have sought to show across the last three chapters, mainstream institutionalized Islam in Britain has shifted away from anti-democratic crusading and towards integrationist political activism. There have been positive changes resulting from Prevent-related policy initiatives, such as those in the sphere of Islamic education, but these have usually had little, if anything, to do with preventing extremism. What I said earlier about political liberalism's impact on British Islam can then be reversed: when British governance has moved away from political liberalism to take a more interventionist approach to British Muslim civil society this has not only been, in many cases, morally wrong but ineffective too.

What this suggests is a need to completely decouple public policies concerning security and integration, with the separation between the two becoming much clearer than it is at present. In saying this, I am not claiming that violent extremism justified in Islamic terms is no longer a problem in Britain. Plainly, that is still true. I do not object in principle to governments trying to trace and convict those involved in, or encouraging, political violence (i.e. to 'Pursue' in the British policy jargon). I would even suggest, against prevailing scholarly opinion,[20] that the safeguarding elements of Prevent can potentially be justified if they can be appropriately implemented. In neither case is current law and policy fit for purpose (for reasons given above as well as in Chapters 3 and 5) but both tracing and safeguarding are the legitimate concern of government. Expanding Prevent beyond this, however, is *fundamentally* wrong. At a basic level, it misreads the relationship between Muslim community networks and extremism and, because of this, leads to British Muslims all being viewed through the prism of counterterrorism. This makes about as much sense as viewing the entire industry of professional football through the prism of fan violence; indeed, imagining a situation in which all public discussion of the English Premier League is oriented towards the goal of preventing football hooliganism gives a reasonable indication of the absurdities of recent debates about British Muslims. At an even more basic level, viewing Muslims through the prism of extremism involves, to quote a well-known liberal philosopher, treating people as a means and not as ends.[21] Maintaining citizens' security is a legitimate function of government, but the end of politics is still, ultimately, citizens' flourishing. One of the reasons the steps taken to build bridges between Islamic and secular education are justifiable – despite the language of 'security' being present – is that these measures are consistent with, and respond to, Muslim students' desire to develop. The lack of attention to these wishes, and the unwillingness to see such attention as inherently worthwhile, has damaged liberalism, and Muslims' engagement with it. Responding to such wishes is just one thing British politicians will need to do if they intend to fix this and bring public policy up to speed with Islamic Britain.

Islam, deliberation and change

With these arguments about British Muslims' autonomy and their flourishing in mind, I want to return now to the caveats in my defence of political liberalism. Among the most penetrating critiques of liberal politics is that it currently offers little more than an apology for the status quo. Certainly, this is the impression often given by the parties and movements that purport to occupy the liberal 'centre ground' today, where the rhetoric of 'change' often masks political inertia. From Clinton and Obama in the United States to the EU's spokespersons and even the leaders of the anti-Brexit movement in the UK, there is very little that liberal politics now appears to offer by way of far-reaching reform.[22] However appealing this absence of change might appear in comparison to resurgent ethnocentric nationalisms – especially to those whose lives are comfortable – this will never be sufficient in times of profound social, economic and ecological dislocation, when many people's lives are not comfortable at all. I hinted earlier in this chapter that radical critics of liberalism would do well – given that liberalism is now coming under sustained attack – to be more explicit about their support for liberal ideals, but this point can be reversed too: liberals are often too relaxed about the lack of opportunities available to people to comprehensively reform social and political structures.

It is not fair to say, either, that this problem is just one of distance between liberal theory and practice. Liberal theorists have mostly been concerned in recent decades with the question of how to manage and balance the different conceptions of the good that exist in a polity. This is, of course, not just a valid but an important concern, but the question of how traditions might be animated in order to drive substantive political change is spoken about rarely. The normative frameworks that liberal theorists advocate even, at times, indicate a need to subdue heartfelt calls for reform in the name of maintaining order. As I argued in Chapter 4, Rawls's influential conception of public reason leaves little space for people to draw upon traditions that are not a long embedded component of a constitutional culture as part of an argument for substantive change. Should they do so, they would act improperly and invite criticism. In this context, liberal theory and the cultural and political norms in liberal states seem to be aligned. Certainly, for Muslims in the UK, at least, attracting this kind of criticism is only too easy. In theory, Muslims in Britain are as welcome as anyone else to try and effect change on the basis of what they believe, but as soon as it becomes apparent that Islam is being used as a resource to motivate change conversations are rapidly closed down. We saw this in Chapter 4 in the way that Islamic legal traditions relating to marriage and divorce are treated as a problem to be dealt with, not a moral language to be drawn upon in a negotiation about the shape that family laws should take. The examples discussed in Chapter 5, too, suggest that part of the reason that the British state has been so selective in the Muslim civil society organizations it maintains formal contact with is that engagement with a broad range of Muslim organizations would mean the state being exposed to criticism, much of it justified.

It is particularly difficult to defend political liberalism against the charge that it limits the capacity for substantive political change. One of the reasons that political liberalism has won support over comprehensive varieties of liberalism is that the former eschews grand narratives of human perfection. Because it avoids such grand language, it is better suited to the task of finding common ground between different philosophies and less at risk of being co-opted into chauvinistic narratives of civilizational superiority. Avoiding this language, however, also means avoiding the terms that made liberalism appealing as a radical movement in the first place: the language of inalienable rights, of life-giving freedom and of self-realization. Political liberals prefer to emphasize the need for stability,[23] and while this is a noble goal one wonders if this very emphasis on 'stability' has been counterproductive, contributing to the political stagnation on which populist movements have recently capitalized. In this book, across Chapters 4 and 5 in particular, I argued against forms of political liberalism that recommend keeping public reasons and comprehensive philosophies separate. Part of my reason for this is that the separation has implications for equality: it gives public space to established moral and philosophical traditions that is denied to newer ones. At a more basic level, though, this separation has a constraining effect. It has, in William Connolly's words, 'muffled the public ventilation of diverse religious and irreligious perspectives needed to adjust public life to the multidimensional pluralism of today'.[24] Political liberalism has attempted to avoid conflict by removing contested terms from public life, but, in the end, this has bequeathed a liberalism that solves problems by ignoring them and that can only be defended as the least bad option available.

What this book consequently calls for is the articulation of an open liberalism, one that allows different philosophical traditions to enter into public conversations. Political liberalism, I want to suggest, will only have a long-term future if it can operate without constraining comprehensive philosophies or reducing them into familiar terms. Saying a little more about my argument concerning religious change can help elucidate this point. I have proposed that within British Islamic institutions – including many institutions aligned with or influenced by deeply conservative and Islamist movements – there has been a gradual reorientation and accommodation to liberal institutions. I would not want this to be read, however, as suggesting there has been a transition towards an endpoint involving the full acceptance of liberal norms of governance or economic principles. To say this would be to go too far and make a claim that the evidence does not support. Many British Muslims remain reluctant to find a way of accommodating heterodoxy within the Muslim *umma*, let alone more widely, and large numbers retain fundamental criticisms of the institutions governing them. Political liberalism has, in certain UK contexts, allowed the consolidation of changes that were already afoot within the British Muslim population, but it has not blunted the British Muslim population's critical edge, especially among the young, who are, as Khadijah Elshayyal has put it, 'taking their activism to new and more creative frontiers'.[25] This too should be regarded as, in general, a good thing. Blunting this and other philosophical traditions would mean liberalism losing its capacity for reform and, ultimately, for revitalization. Political liberalism should facilitate adaptation to established political norms, but it should also seek to facilitate diverse and penetrating criticisms that allow those norms to develop.

Islam in the liberal state

As well as outlining various arguments about liberalism and national identity, I also made the bold claim at the start of this book that, if done right, the incorporation of British Muslim minorities might facilitate democratic renewal. I hope what I meant by this will now be a little clearer. In saying this, I do not mean that the Islamic tradition contains the answers to all the questions that have bedevilled political philosophers in recent years (or centuries). Rather, my point is that considering the ways in which the Islamic tradition may legitimately contribute to public deliberations – and the ways in which this tradition has been unfairly excluded from these deliberations – can stimulate deeper questions about the limitations of contemporary liberalism. Specifically, it can prompt questions about liberalism's need to respond to the hopes people have about the shape that society and politics should take and to the fundamental beliefs that underpin these hopes. The same might be said about other philosophical traditions too, of course, but there is something to be said about how renewal and re-evaluation can be prompted by unacknowledged traditions in particular. One concrete illustration of this can be encountered in Chapter 4, where I sought to show that looking at the awkward way in which Islamic traditions of marriage and divorce fit into English civil law not only raises questions about British Islam but also allows one to see more clearly the limitations of the civil system.

In one of his less well-known essays, the philosopher Charles Taylor talks about this in more general terms, reflecting upon what one learns of oneself as one encounters another in an 'undistortive' way:

> Most of the great religions or secular world views are bound up with a depreciatory view of others in contrast to which they define themselves. Christianity relative

to Judaism as 'merely' a religion of law, or relative to Buddhism or Hinduism as religions unconcerned for the world – depreciatory stories abound. These stories provide some of the support system for faith everywhere. The contrasts are real; and so to come to understand the view against which one's own is defined, and hence to see its spiritual force, must bring about a profound change. The depreciatory story is no longer credible; this prop to faith is knocked away. Where the faith was nourished exclusively by the story, it will wither. But where not, it will be free to nourish itself on better food, on something like the intrinsic power of whatever the faith or vision points us toward. In this sense, understanding lets our own faith be too. It liberates ourselves along with the other.[26]

Taylor, who is himself Catholic, provides religious illustrations here; however, his point could apply equally to secular liberal traditions, which so often today bolster their authority and appeal by telling a 'depreciatory story' about the anti-intellectual nature of religion or about the Islamic tradition refusing the distinction between religion and politics. What happens when these stories are corrected – when this 'prop to faith is knocked away' – and when Islam and Muslims are spoken about in more realistic terms? Certainly, when liberalism can no longer be worn as a badge of identity and superiority one is forced to face hard questions about the tradition's ability to respond to political problems and social changes. That, indeed, may be part of the reason why liberalism has been mobilized against the Islamic tradition in recent years. The novelist James Baldwin once remarked, 'One of the reasons people cling to their hates so stubbornly is because they sense, once hate is gone, they will be forced to deal with pain.'[27] Clinging on to boastful claims about liberal societies' superiority, in much the same way, offers a means of avoiding facing up to challenges.

Yet at the same time, answers begin to emerge as well. The constant refrain about Muslims' lack of integration into liberal states forms part of a narrative not only about Muslims' failure but about the failures of liberal and multicultural governance too. If this narrative about Muslims' lack of integration does not have purchase, as I have tried to show in this book, then the associated claim about the inadequacy of liberal politics to meet the challenge of increasing cultural, moral and religious diversity is also placed into question. Seeing Muslim Britain as it actually is, rather than as the sinister force it is so often imagined to be, allows us to have more faith in liberal political formations (albeit not, perhaps, in the institutions and politicians currently governing 'liberal' states). As one starts to view the Islamic tradition as one of the UK's many and varied 'cultural riches' one also begins to perceive more clearly the liberal tradition's value.

NOTES

Preface and Acknowledgements

1 Take, for example, Robert Spencer, *Islam Unveiled: Disturbing Questions about the World's Fastest-Growing Faith* (San Francisco: Encounter Books, 2003).
2 Andrew F. March, *Islam and Liberal Citizenship: The Search for an Overlapping Consensus* (Oxford: Oxford University Press, 2009), 67.
3 Apologies to (I think) Rowan Williams for borrowing his turn of phrase.

Chapter 1: Introduction: Islam, Liberalism and the Nation State

1 Laura Clark and Laura Osborne, 'Revealed: Islamist Plot Dubbed "Trojan Horse" to Replace Teachers in Birmingham Schools with Radicals', *Mail Online*, 7 March 2014, http://www.dailymail.co.uk/news/article-2575759/Revealed-Islamist-plot-dubbed-Trojan-Horse-string-schools-Birmingham-self-styled-Jihad.html.
2 Andrew Norfolk, 'Christian Child Forced into Muslim Foster Care', *The Times*, 28 August 2017, sec. News, https://www.thetimes.co.uk/article/christian-child-forced-into-muslim-foster-care-by-tower-hamlets-council-3gcp6l8cs.
3 Ben Webster, 'Animals Dying in Pain Because of Muslim Ignorance over Stunning', *The Times*, 24 October 2016, http://www.thetimes.co.uk/article/more-animals-die-in-pain-because-scholars-are-ignorant-of-stunning-fsz83krtn.
4 The letter purporting to reveal the so-called 'Trojan Horse' plot was discredited and a professional misconduct case against teachers who were implicated collapsed (see *National College of Teaching and Learning [NCTL]* v. *Monzoor Hussain et al.*). The Independent Press Standards Organisation (IPSO) eventually forced the *Times* to acknowledge that its reporting of a fostering case in Tower Hamlets contained inaccuracies (see 20480-17 *Tower Hamlets Borough Council* v. *The Times*). The accusations of Muslims' 'ignorance' about slaughter techniques related to an academic study that actually demonstrated widespread *acceptance* of the practice of stunning animals before halal slaughter.
5 Erik Bleich, 'Where Do Muslims Stand on Ethno-Racial Hierarchies in Britain and France? Evidence from Public Opinion Surveys', *Patterns of Prejudice* 43, nos 3–4 (2009): 379–400.
6 Ingrid Storm, Maria Sobolewska and Robert Ford, 'Is Ethnic Prejudice Declining in Britain? Change in Social Distance Attitudes among Ethnic Majority and Minority Britons', *British Journal of Sociology* 68, no. 3 (2017): 410–34, https://doi.org/10.1111/1468-4446.12250.
7 These figures are based on searches of the LexisNexis database of UK newspapers. I am indebted to Carl Morris for alerting me to these patterns through his own searches of academic literature over the last 10 years (which reveal very similar results).

 8 For two rich accounts of this transition, see Nasar Meer, *Citizenship, Identity and the Politics of Multiculturalism: The Rise of Muslim Consciousness* (Basingstoke: Palgrave Macmillan, 2010); Khadijah Elshayyal, *Muslim Identity Politics: Islam, Activism and Equality in Britain* (London: I.B. Tauris, 2018). Further details can also be found in Chapter 5.

 9 On this asymmetry, see Anne Phillips, *Multiculturalism without Culture* (Princeton, NJ: Princeton University Press, 2007); Naaz Rashid, *Veiled Threats: Producing the Muslim Woman in Public Policy Discourses* (Bristol: Policy Press, 2016).

10 Apologies to Kwame Anthony Appiah for stealing his turn of phrase. See *The Ethics of Identity* (Princeton, NJ: Princeton University Press, 2005), 105.

11 Ruth Kelly, 'Time for a British Version of Islam …', *New Statesman*, 9 April 2007.

12 Department for Communities and Local Government, 'Preventing Violent Extremism: Winning Hearts and Minds' (Wetherby: Communities and Local Government Publications, 2007).

13 David Cameron, 'Speech to the Community Security Trust', *Conservatives*, 4 March 2008, http://www.conservatives.com/News/Speeches/2008/03/David_Cameron_Speech_to_the_Community_Security_Trust.aspx; David Cameron, 'PM's Speech at Munich Security Conference', Official Site of the British Prime Minister's Office, 2011, http://www.number10.gov.uk/news/pms-speech-at-munich-security-conference/.

14 HM Government, 'Prevent Strategy' (London: Stationery Office, 2011), enforced via the Counter-Terrorism and Security Act 2015.

15 Louise Casey, 'The Casey Review: A Review into Opportunity and Integration' (London: Department for Communities and Local Government, 12 May 2016), 168, https://www.gov.uk/government/publications/the-casey-review-a-review-into-opportunity-and-integration.

16 Across ethnic and religious minorities in Britain, commitment to minority identity does not reduce commitment to national identity. See Alita Nandi and Lucinda Platt, 'Patterns of Minority and Majority Identification in a Multicultural Society', *Ethnic and Racial Studies* 38, no. 15 (8 December 2015): 2615–34, https://doi.org/10.1080/01419870.2015.1077986. Qualitative and quantitative evidence also shows how British Muslims' strong religious identification does not conflict with, and often supports, their strong national identification: see Yasmin Hussain and Paul Bagguley, 'Citizenship, Ethnicity and Identity: British Pakistanis after the 2001 "Riots"', *Sociology* 39, no. 3 (2005): 407–25, https://doi.org/10.1177/0038038505052493; Saffron Karlsen and James Y. Nazroo, 'Ethnic and Religious Differences in the Attitudes of People towards Being "British"', *Sociological Review*, 1 June 2015, https://doi.org/10.1111/1467-954X.12313; Tania Saeed, *Islamophobia and Securitization: Religion, Ethnicity and the Female Voice*, 1st edn (New York: Palgrave Macmillan, 2016), 40.

17 Or in England, at least: along with the wider population, Muslims in Scotland appear to increasingly define themselves as Scottish. See Khadijah Elshayyal, 'Scottish Muslims in Numbers: Understanding Scotland's Muslims through the 2011 Census' (Edinburgh: The Alwaleed Centre for the Study of Islam in the Contemporary World, University of Edinburgh, 2016), 24, http://www.ed.ac.uk/files/atoms/files/scottish_muslims_in_numbers_web.pdf; Stefano Bonino, *Muslims in Scotland: The Making of Community in a Post-9/11 World* (Edinburgh: Edinburgh University Press, 2016), chap. 3.

18 Alita Nandi and Lucinda Platt, 'Britishness and Identity Assimilation among the UK's Minority and Majority Ethnic Groups', Understanding Society Working Paper Series (Essex: Understanding Society, 2013), 21–5; Nandi and Platt, 'Patterns of Minority

and Majority Identification in a Multicultural Society'; The Coexist Foundation, 'The Gallup Coexist Index 2009: A Global Study of Interfaith Relations' (London: Gallup, 2009), 19, http://www.muslimwestfacts.com/mwf/118249/Gallup-Coexist-Index-2009.aspx.

19 Consider, for example, Timothy Garton Ash, 'What Young British Muslims Say Can Be Shocking – Some of It Is Also True', *The Guardian*, 10 August 2006, https://www.theguardian.com/commentisfree/2006/aug/10/comment.race.

20 Yahya Birt, 'Good Imam, Bad Imam: Civic Religion and National Integration in Britain Post-9/11', *Muslim World* 96, no. 4 (2006): 687–705; M. Mamdani, 'Good Muslim, Bad Muslim: A Political Perspective on Culture and Terrorism', *American Anthropologist* 104, no. 3 (2002): 766–75.

21 See, for example, Stefano Bonino, 'The British State "Security Syndrome" and Muslim Diversity: Challenges for Liberal Democracy in the Age of Terror', *Contemporary Islam*, 4 April 2016, 1–25, https://doi.org/10.1007/s11562-016-0356-4; Jocelyne Cesari, 'The Securitisation of Islam in Europe', Research Paper (CEPS CHALLENGE Programme, EU Sixth Framework, 2009); Stuart Croft, *Securitizing Islam: Identity and the Search for Security* (New York: Cambridge University Press, 2012); Charlotte Heath-Kelly, 'Counter-Terrorism and the Counterfactual: Producing the "Radicalisation" Discourse and the UK PREVENT Strategy', *British Journal of Politics & International Relations* 15, no. 3 (2013): 394–415; Yasmin Hussain and Paul Bagguley, 'Securitized Citizens: Islamophobia, Racism and the 7/7 London Bombings', *Sociological Review* 60, no. 4 (1 November 2012): 715–34, https://doi.org/10.1111/j.1467-954X.2012.02130.x; Luca Mavelli, 'Between Normalisation and Exception: The Securitisation of Islam and the Construction of the Secular Subject', *Millennium: Journal of International Studies* 41, no. 2 (1 January 2013): 159–81; Derek McGhee, *Security, Citizenship and Human Rights: Shared Values in Uncertain Times* (Basingstoke: Palgrave Macmillan, 2010); Gabe Mythen, Sandra Walklate and Fatima Khan, "I'm a Muslim, but I'm Not a Terrorist': Victimization, Risky Identities and the Performance of Safety', *British Journal of Criminology* 49, no. 6 (2009): 736–54, https://doi.org/10.1093/bjc/azp032; Christina Pantazis and Simon Pemberton, 'Resisting the Advance of the Security State: The Impact of Frameworks of Resistance on the UK's Securitisation Agenda', *International Journal of Law, Crime and Justice* 41, no. 4 (2013): 358–74, https://doi.org/doi:10.1016/j.ijlcj.2013.07.009.

22 Bonino, *Muslims in Scotland*; Therese O'Toole et al., *Taking Part: Muslim Participation in Contemporary Governance* (Bristol: University of Bristol, 2013).

23 Khaled Abou El Fadl, *The Great Theft: Wrestling Islam from the Extremists* (San Francisco, CA: Harper, 2007).

24 Albert Hourani, *Arabic Thought in the Liberal Age* (London: Oxford University Press, 1962). For discussion of the distinctions and overlaps between Salafi and Wahhabi movements, see Chapter 2.

25 Philip Lewis, *Islamic Britain* (London: I.B. Tauris, 2002).

26 Jonathan Birt, 'Locating the British Imam: The Deobandi 'ulama between Contested Authority and Public Policy Post-9/11', in *European Muslims and the Secular State*, ed. Jocelyne Cesari and Seán McLoughlin (Aldershot: Ashgate, 2005), 183.

27 Ron Geaves, 'Muslims in Britain and Britishness in Islam: Historical and Religious Perspectives on British Muslim Past(s)' (BRAIS Annual Conference 2017, University of Chester, 17 April 2017); Sophie Gilliat-Ray, *Muslims in Britain: An Introduction* (Cambridge: Cambridge University Press, 2010), xiii.

28 For further discussion of this, see Thijl Sunier, 'Domesticating Islam: Exploring
    Academic Knowledge Production on Islam and Muslims in European Societies',
    Ethnic and Racial Studies 37, no. 6 (2014): 1138–55.
29 On this, see Tariq Modood, *Multiculturalism: A Civic Idea* (Cambridge: Polity, 2007).
30 Pnina Werbner, *Imagined Diasporas among Manchester Muslims* (Oxford: James
    Currey, 2002).
31 Anamik Saha, 'Negotiating the Third Space: British Asian Independent Record
    Labels and the Cultural Politics of Difference', *Popular Music and Society* 34, no. 4
    (2011): 437–54.
32 John Hutnyk, 'The Dialectic of "Here and There": Anthropology "at Home"', in
    A Postcolonial People: South Asians in Britain, ed. S. Sayyid, N. Ali and V. S. Kalra
    (London: C. Hurst, 2006), 74–90.
33 Nathal Dessing et al., eds, *Everyday Lived Islam in Europe*, new edn (Burlington,
    VT: Ashgate, 2013).
34 Examples include: Les Back, *The Art of Listening* (Oxford: Berg, 2007); Paul Gilroy,
    After Empire: Melancholia or Convivial Culture? (London: Routledge, 2004); Hannah
    Jones et al., 'Urban Multiculture and Everyday Encounters in Semi-Public, Franchised
    Cafe Spaces', *The Sociological Review* 63, no. 3 (1 August 2015): 644–61, https://doi.
    org/10.1111/1467-954X.12311; Michael Keith, *After the Cosmopolitan? Multicultural
    Cities and the Future of Racism* (Abingdon: Routledge, 2005).
35 For further discussion of the inclusion of religious groups in research into
    British multiculture, see: Stephen H. Jones, 'The "Metropolis of Dissent": Muslim
    Participation in Leicester and the "Failure" of Multiculturalism in Britain', *Ethnic
    and Racial Studies* 38, no. 11 (2 September 2015): 1969–85, https://doi.org/10.1
    080/01419870.2014.936891; Nasar Meer and Tariq Modood, 'The Multicultural
    State We're in: Muslims, "Multiculture" and the "Civic Re-Balancing" of
    British Multiculturalism', *Political Studies* 57, no. 3 (2009): 473–97, https://doi.
    org/10.1111/j.1467-9248.2008.00745.x.
36 Farah Elahi and Omar Khan, eds, *Islamophobia: Still a Challenge for Us All*
    (London: Runnymede, 2017); All-Party Parliamentary Group on British Muslims,
    'Islamophobia Defined: The Inquiry into a Working Definition of Islamophobia'
    (London: APPG on British Muslims, 2018).
37 Stephen H. Jones et al., ' "That's How Muslims Are Required to View the World": Race,
    Culture and Belief in Non-Muslims' Descriptions of Islam and Science', *Sociological
    Review*, 31 May 2018, https://doi.org/10.1177/0038026118778174.
38 Anthony Giddens, *Over to You, Mr Brown* (Cambridge: Polity, 2007), 145–62.
39 Clive D. Field, 'Young British Muslims since 9/11: A Composite Attitudinal Profile',
    Religion, State and Society 39, nos 2–3 (2011): 162.
40 On the isolation of the sociology of religion, see Jeffrey Guhin, 'Religion as Site
    Rather than Religion as Category: On the Sociology of Religion's Export Problem',
    Sociology of Religion 75, no. 4 (December 2014): 579–93; Rebecca Catto, 'Sociology
    of Religion in Great Britain: Interdisciplinarity and Gradual Diversification',
    Sociologies of Religion: National Traditions, 7 August 2015, 107–31, https://doi.
    org/10.1163/9789004297586_007.
41 See, for example, Edward W. Said, *Orientalism* (London: Vintage Books, 1979);
    Salman Sayyid, *A Fundamental Fear: Eurocentrism and the Emergence of Islamism*
    (London: Zed Books, 2003); Gil Anidjar, *The Jew, the Arab: A History of the Enemy*
    (Stanford, CA: Stanford University Press, 2003); Joseph A. Massad, *Islam in Liberalism*
    (Chicago, IL: University of Chicago Press, 2015).

42 Yahya Birt, 'Ministry of Justice Looks Set to Target Muslim Prison Chaplains', *Muslim News*, 26 February 2016, http://muslimnews.co.uk/newspaper/top-stories/ministry-of-justice-looks-set-to-target-muslim-prison-chaplains/.

43 David Wooding, 'Bash the Bishop', *The Sun*, 9 February 2008.

44 Of course, some secularists and liberals are as hostile and prejudiced towards the Islamic tradition as conservatives. See Aurelien Mondon and Aaron Winter, 'Articulations of Islamophobia: From the Extreme to the Mainstream?', *Ethnic and Racial Studies* 0, no. 0 (26 May 2017): 1–29, https://doi.org/10.1080/01419870.2017.1312008.

45 On this subject, see Philip Lewis and Sadek Hamid, *British Muslims: New Directions in Islamic Thought, Creativity and Activism* (Edinburgh: Edinburgh University Press, 2018).

46 Ron Geaves, *Islam in Victorian Britain: The Life and Times of Abdullah Quilliam* (Markfield: Kube, 2010).

47 I should, of course, add that these two areas of analysis are deeply intertwined and equally important.

48 'He who lets the world, or his own portion of it, choose his plan of life for him, has no need of any other faculty than the ape-like one of imitation. He who chooses his plan for himself, employs all his faculties'. John Stuart Mill, *On Liberty and Other Essays* (Oxford: Oxford University Press, 1991), 65–6.

49 John Rawls, *A Theory of Justice* (Cambridge, MA: Harvard University Press, 1971).

50 Ronald Dworkin, 'Liberalism', in *Public and Private Morality*, ed. Stuart Hampshire (Cambridge: Cambridge University Press, 1978), 113–43; Will Kymlicka, *Liberalism, Community and Culture* (Gloucestershire: Clarendon Press, 1991), 21. Kymlicka argues that, despite significant differences, this definition is accepted and supported not only by liberals but also by many of liberalism's 'communitarian' critics.

51 I use this term with reference to Iris Murdoch, *The Sovereignty of Good* (London: Routledge, 2001).

52 Maleiha Malik, 'Faith and the State of Jurisprudence', in *Faith in Law: Essays in Legal Theory*, ed. Sionaidh Douglas-Scott, Peter Oliver and Victor Tadros (London: Hart, 2000), 141.

53 Back, *The Art of Listening*.

54 See Jürgen Habermas, *The Structural Transformation of the Public Sphere* (Cambridge, MA: MIT Press, 1989); Nancy Fraser, 'Rethinking the Public Sphere: A Contribution to the Critique of Actually Existing Democracy', in *Habermas and the Public Sphere*, ed. Craig Calhoun (Cambridge, MA: MIT Press, 1992), 109–42.

55 John R. Bowen, *On British Islam: Religion, Law, and Everyday Practice in Sharia Councils* (Princeton, NJ: Princeton University Press, 2016), 7.

56 For a robust analysis and critique of this tendency, see Jonathan Chaplin, *Talking God: The Legitimacy of Religious Public Reasoning* (London: Theos, 2008).

57 See Massad, *Islam in Liberalism*; Anne Norton, *On the Muslim Question* (Princeton, NJ: Princeton University Press, 2013).

58 Cameron, 'PM's Speech at Munich Security Conference'.

59 Nisha Kapoor, *Deport, Deprive, Extradite: Twenty-First Century State Extremism* (London: Verso, 2018).

60 Andrew L. Whitehead, Landon Schnabel and Samuel L. Perry, 'Gun Control in the Crosshairs: Christian Nationalism and Opposition to Stricter Gun Laws', *Socius* 4 (1 January 2018), https://doi.org/10.1177/2378023118790189.

61 For excellent short summaries of political liberalism and its competitors, see Martha Nussbaum 'Rawls's Political Liberalism: A Reassessment', *Ratio Juris* 24, no. 1 (2011): 1–24; 'Perfectionist Liberalism and Political Liberalism', *Philosophy & Public Affairs* 39, no. 1 (1 January 2011): 3–45, https://doi.org/10.1111/j.1088-4963.2011.01200.x.

62 John Rawls, *Political Liberalism* (New York: Columbia University Press, 2005).

63 After Tariq Modood, 'Moderate Secularism and Multiculturalism', *Politics* 29, no. 1 (1 February 2009): 71–6, https://doi.org/10.1111/j.1467-9256.2008.01340.x.

64 Cameron, 'PM's Speech at Munich Security Conference'.

65 Modood, *Multiculturalism*; Iris Marion Young, *Inclusion and Democracy* (Oxford: Oxford University Press, 2002).

66 Jones, 'The "Metropolis of Dissent"'; Meer and Modood, 'The Multicultural State We're In'.

67 Tariq Modood, '2011 Paul Hanly Furfey Lecture: Is There a Crisis of Secularism in Western Europe?', *Sociology of Religion* 73, no. 2 (4 May 2012): 130–49.

68 Adam Dinham and Stephen H. Jones, 'Religion, Public Policy, and the Academy: Brokering Public Faith in a Context of Ambivalence?' *Journal of Contemporary Religion* 27, no. 2 (2012): 185–201.

69 O'Toole et al., 'Taking Part'.

70 Therese O'Toole and Ekaterina Braginskaia, 'Public Faith and Finance: Faith Responses to the Financial Crisis' (Birmingham: Barrow Cadbury Trust, July 2016), http://www.publicspirit.org.uk/assets/PubFaithFin-Report-Final.pdf.

Chapter 2: The Shifting Foundations of Islamic Britain

1 Matt Carr, 'You Are Now Entering Eurabia', *Race & Class* 48, no. 1 (2006): 2, https://doi.org/10.1177/0306396806066636.

2 Niall Ferguson, 'Eurabia?', *New York Times*, 4 April 2004, sec. Magazine, http://www.nytimes.com/2004/04/04/magazine/04WWLN.html.

3 Douglas Murray, *The Strange Death of Europe: Immigration, Identity, Islam* (London: Bloomsbury Continuum, 2018).

4 Pamela Duncan, 'Europeans Greatly Overestimate Muslim Population, Poll Shows', *The Guardian*, 13 December 2016, sec. Society, https://www.theguardian.com/society/datablog/2016/dec/13/europeans-massively-overestimate-muslim-population-poll-shows.

5 See Olivier Roy, *Globalised Islam: The Search for a New Ummah* (London: C. Hurst, 2004).

6 Karen Armstrong, *Muhammad: A Biography of the Prophet* (London: Phoenix, 2001); Sophie Gilliat-Ray, *Muslims in Britain: An Introduction* (Cambridge: Cambridge University Press, 2010); Brian Clegg, *The First Scientist: A Life of Roger Bacon* (London: Constable, 2003).

7 Toni Morrison, 'A Humanistic View' (Black Studies Center public dialogue, Portland State University, 30 May 1975), https://soundcloud.com/portland-state-library/portland-state-black-studies-1.

8 Philip Lewis, *Young, British and Muslim* (London: Continuum, 2007), 19.

9 Of these, 2,706,066 were based in England and Wales, approximately 77,000 in Scotland and 3,800 in Northern Ireland. Muslim Council of Britain, 'British Muslims

in Numbers: A Demographic, Socio-Economic and Health Profile of Muslims in Britain Drawing on the 2011 Census' (London: Muslim Council of Britain, 2015), 22.

10 Office for National Statistics, 'Muslim Population in the UK', Office for National Statistics, accessed 12 March 2019, https://www.ons.gov.uk/aboutus/transparencyandgovernance/freedomofinformationfoi/muslimpopulationintheuk?fbcl id=IwAR3Vti-dlX2R2qmNpDX2LptsdmFKWm5A6zJ5_raspkmjqyahs1gJZIQfDqw.

11 Pew Research Center, 'Europe's Growing Muslim Population' (Washington, DC: Pew Research Center, November 2017), 29, http://assets.pewresearch.org/wp-content/uploads/sites/11/2017/11/29103550/FULL-REPORT-FOR-WEB-POSTING.pdf.

12 Humayun Ansari, *The Infidel Within: Muslims in Britain since 1800* (London: C. Hurst, 2004), 26–7.

13 Quoted in Gilliat-Ray, *Muslims in Britain*, 16.

14 See the account of the Yemeni religious revivalist and community leader Abdullah Ali Al-Hakimi in Gilliat-Ray, *Muslims in Britain*, 34–9.

15 Ansari, *The Infidel Within*, 42–5, 97.

16 Ansari, *The Infidel Within*, 126–33.

17 While not a universal view, the majority view in medieval Islamic law was that apostasy is equivalent to treason and thus deserves capital punishment. See Mohammed Hashim Kamali, *Freedom of Expression in Islam* (Cambridge: Islamic Texts Society, 1997). This view is widely challenged and ignored today, but retains support among some conservative movements in Saudi Arabia, Sudan, Pakistan and other contexts.

18 Ansari, *The Infidel Within*, 125; see also Ron Geaves, *Islam in Victorian Britain: The Life and Times of Abdullah Quilliam* (Markfield: Kube, 2010).

19 Suhrawardy Abdullah al-Mamun al-, *The Sayings of Muhammad* (New York: Arno, 1980). This book – first published in 1938 – contains *hadiths* such as 'Every man who calls a Muslim infidel will have the epithet returned to him', 'Admonish your wives with kindness' and 'Make peace between one another: enmity and malice tear up heavenly rewards by the roots.'

20 There are of course exceptions, such as Yemen, where the British Empire did not withdraw until 1967. On Yemeni migrants, see Fred Halliday, *Arabs in Exile: Yemeni Migrants in Urban Britain* (London: I.B. Tauris, 1992).

21 Ansari, *The Infidel Within*, 152.

22 Ansari, *The Infidel Within*, 145–6.

23 Gilliat-Ray, *Muslims in Britain*, 46, 51.

24 Gurharpal Singh, 'A City of Surprises: Urban Multiculturalism and the "Leicester Model"', in *A Postcolonial People: South Asians in Britain*, ed. S. Sayyid, N. Ali and V. S. Kalra (London: C. Hurst, 2006), 291–304; Stephen H. Jones, 'The "Metropolis of Dissent": Muslim Participation in Leicester and the "Failure" of Multiculturalism in Britain', *Ethnic and Racial Studies* 38, no. 11 (2 September 2015): 1969–85, https://doi.org/10.1080/01419870.2014.936891.

25 Ceri Peach, 'Britain's Muslim Population: An Overview', in *Muslim Britain: Communities under Pressure*, ed. Tahir Abbas (London: Zed Books, 2005), 19.

26 Lewis, *Young, British and Muslim*, 19.

27 See Muhammad Anwar, *Myth of Return: Pakistanis in Britain* (London: Heinemann Educational Books, 1979); Marta Bolognani, 'The Myth of Return: Dismissal, Survival or Revival? A Bradford Example of Transnationalism as a Political Instrument', *Journal of Ethnic and Migration Studies* 33, no. 1 (1 January 2007): 59–76, https://doi.org/10.1080/13691830601043497.

28 See the case of the Imperial Typewriters strike in Seán McLoughlin, 'Discrepant Representations of Multi-Asian Leicester: Institutional Discourse and Everyday Life in the "Model" Multicultural City', in *Writing the City in British-Asian Diasporas*, ed. Sean McLoughlin et al. (London: Routledge, 2014).

29 Anshuman A. Mondal, *Young British Muslim Voices* (Oxford: Greenwood World, 2008), 4–5.

30 Seán McLoughlin, 'Mosques and the Public Space: Conflict and Cooperation in Bradford', *Journal of Ethnic and Migration Studies* 31, no. 6 (1 November 2005): 1045–66, https://doi.org/10.1080/13691830500282832.

31 Philip Lewis, *Islamic Britain* (London: I.B. Tauris, 2002), 56–8.

32 Halliday, *Arabs in Exile*.

33 Ansari, *The Infidel Within*, 343.

34 John R. Bowen, *On British Islam: Religion, Law, and Everyday Practice in Shari'a Councils* (Princeton, NJ: Princeton University Press, 2016), 26–9.

35 Barbara Metcalf, 'Madrasas and Minorities in Secular India', in *Schooling Islam: The Culture and Politics of Modern Muslim Education*, ed. Robert W. Hefner and Muhammad Qasim Zaman (Princeton, NJ: Princeton University Press, 2007), 94.

36 Chetan Bhatt, *Liberation and Purity: Race, New Religious Movements and the Ethics of Postmodernity* (London: Routledge, 1997), 118–19; Gilliat-Ray, *Muslims in Britain*, 92–8.

37 Ron Geaves, *Sectarian Influences within Islam in Britain: With Reference to the Concepts of 'Ummah' and 'Community'* (Leeds: University of Leeds, 1996), 95–7.

38 Lewis, *Islamic Britain*, 57.

39 Gilliat-Ray, *Muslims in Britain*, 95–6; Iram Asif, 'Hijaz College : Students of Islamic Religious Sciences in Contemporary British Society' (Master's, Lund University, 2006), http://www.lunduniversity.lu.se/lup/publication/1328980.

40 Bowen, *On British Islam*, 35.

41 Metcalf, 'Madrasas and Minorities in Secular India', 95.

42 Jonathan Birt, 'Locating the British Imam: The Deobandi 'ulama between Contested Authority and Public Policy Post-9/11', in *European Muslims and the Secular State*, ed. Jocelyne Cesari and Seán McLoughlin (Aldershot: Ashgate, 2005), 183; Lewis, *Islamic Britain*, 36–8.

43 It is important to emphasize that, while Deobandi scripturalism contrasts with Barelvi Sufi-inspired devotionalism, both follow the Hanafi legal school and draw on the same Sufi orders (which predate British rule).

44 Ansari, *The Infidel Within*, 347.

45 Muhammad Qasim Zaman, 'Tradition and Authority in Deobandi Madrasas of South Asia', in *Schooling Islam: The Culture and Politics of Modern Muslim Education*, ed. Robert W. Hefner and Muhammad Qasim Zaman (Princeton, NJ: Princeton University Press, 2007), 61–86.

46 Birt, 'Locating the British Imam'.

47 Imran Mogra, 'Tablighi Jama'at in the UK', in *Islamic Movements of Europe*, ed. Frank Peter and Rafael Ortega (London: I.B. Tauris, 2014), 187–90.

48 Indeed, Geaves suggests that 'the Barelwis can be seen as a conscious reaction to the Deobandi reformers'. Geaves, *Sectarian Influences within Islam in Britain*, 95.

49 Lewis, *Islamic Britain*, 40.

50 Lewis, *Islamic Britain*, 84.

51 Anya Hart Dyke, 'Mosques Made in Britain' (London: Quilliam Foundation, 2009), 30–1.

52 Inayat Bunglawala, 'Minab: Community Initiative, or Quango?', *The Guardian: Comment Is Free*, 15 May 2009, http://www.guardian.co.uk/commentisfree/belief/2009/may/15/minab-mosques-imams-islam.

53 Marta Bolognani and Paul Statham, 'The Changing Public Face of Muslim Associations in Britain: Coming Together for Common "Social" Goals?', *Ethnicities* 13, no. 2 (1 April 2013): 244, https://doi.org/10.1177/1468796812470892.

54 Ansari, *The Infidel Within*, 309–17; Khadijah Elshayyal, *Muslim Identity Politics: Islam, Activism and Equality in Britain* (London: I.B. Tauris, 2018), 57–61.

55 Richard Gale and Simon Naylor, 'Religion, Planning and the City: The Spatial Politics of Ethnic Minority Expression in British Cities and Towns', *Ethnicities* 2, no. 3 (2002): 387–409.

56 See Lewis, *Islamic Britain*, 81–9.

57 Ansari, *The Infidel Within*, 309–17.

58 Gale and Naylor, 'Religion, Planning and the City'; Simon Naylor and James R. Ryan, 'The Mosque in the Suburbs: Negotiating Religion and Ethnicity in South London', *Social & Cultural Geography* 3, no. 1 (2002): 39–59, https://doi.org/10.1080/14649360120114134.

59 Pnina Werbner, *Imagined Diasporas among Manchester Muslims* (Oxford: James Currey, 2002).

60 McLoughlin, 'Mosques and the Public Space'; Ansari, *The Infidel Within*, 278–82.

61 Hart Dyke, 'Mosques Made in Britain'.

62 Werbner, *Imagined Diasporas among Manchester Muslims*; Parveen Akhtar, *British Muslim Politics: Examining Pakistani Biraderi Networks* (Basingstoke: Palgrave Macmillan, 2013).

63 The demographer Ceri Peach describes Muslim marriage as a 'within ethnic group affair'. Peach, 'Britain's Muslim Population', 23.

64 Lewis, *Young, British and Muslim*, 21, 51–2; Akhtar, *British Muslim Politics*.

65 Ansari, *The Infidel Within*, 212–14.

66 Singh, 'A City of Surprises: Urban Multiculturalism and the "Leicester Model"'.

67 For example, see Steven Vertovec, 'Multicultural, Multi-Asian, Multi-Muslim Leicester: Dimensions of Social Complexity, Ethnic Organization and Local Government Interface', *Innovation: The European Journal of Social Sciences* 7, no. 3 (1994): 259–74.

68 See Ludi Simpson, 'Ageing, Ethnic Diversity and Myths of Migration', *Radical Statistics* 100 (2010): 28–45; Ludi Simpson and Nissa Finney, *'Sleepwalking to Segregation'? Challenging Myths about Race and Migration* (Bristol: Policy Press, 2012); Ludi Simpson, 'Statistics of Racial Segregation: Measures, Evidence and Policy', *Urban Studies* 41, no. 3 (2004): 661–81.

69 Ted Cantle, 'Community Cohesion: A Report of the Independent Review Team' (London: Home Office, 2001).

70 Steven Vertovec, 'Super-Diversity and Its Implications', *Ethnic and Racial Studies* 30, no. 6 (November 2007): 1024–54.

71 CoDE, 'How Has Ethnic Diversity Grown 1991-2001-2011?' (Manchester: CoDE/Joseph Rowntree Foundation, 2012), http://www.ethnicity.ac.uk/medialibrary/briefings/dynamicsofdiversity/how-has-ethnic-diversity-grown-1991-2001-2011.pdf; for a localized account see also Jones, 'The "Metropolis of Dissent"'.

72 See Suzanne M. Hall, 'Mooring "Super-Diversity" to a Brutal Migration Milieu', *Ethnic and Racial Studies* 40, no. 9 (2017): 1562–73, http://www.tandfonline.com/doi/abs/10.1080/01419870.2017.1300296.

73 England and Wales have a separate census to other areas of the UK so providing anything other than aggregate figures is difficult for the UK as a whole.

74 About 36.7 per cent of white Muslims classify themselves as white British, as opposed to 'other white'.

75 Stephen Jivraj, 'Muslims in England and Wales: Evidence from the 2011 Census', in *The New Muslims*, ed. Claire Alexander, Victoria Redclift and Ajmal Hussain (London: The Runnymede Trust, 2013), 16–19.

76 Stephen H. Jones and Dominic Baker, 'The Religious Life of a "Plural City"', Public Spirit, 19 September 2013, http://www.publicspirit.org.uk/the-religious-life-of-a-plural-city/.

77 I&DeA, 'Taking Forward Community Cohesion in Leicester' (Leicester: Improvement and Development Agency/Leicester City Council, 2002); John Clayton, 'Living the Multicultural City: Acceptance, Belonging and Young Identities in the City of Leicester, England', *Ethnic and Racial Studies* 35, no. 9 (2012): 1673–93.

78 Serena Hussain, 'Kurdish Muslim Identity: Religious Universalism or Ethno-Nationalism?' (unpublished paper, 2014).

79 With some important early exceptions, notably Halliday, *Arabs in Exile*.

80 On South Asian Shia Islam in Britain see Sufyan Abid Dogra, 'Living a Piety-Led Life beyond Muharram: Becoming or Being a South Asian Shia Muslim in the UK', *Contemporary Islam* 13, no. 3 (1 October 2019): 307–24, https://doi.org/10.1007/s11562-019-00437-8.

81 Innes Bowen, *Medina in Birmingham, Najaf in Brent: Inside British Islam* (London: C. Hurst, 2014), 146.

82 Bowen, *Medina in Birmingham, Najaf in Brent*; Emanuelle Degli Esposti, 'Fragmented Realities: The "Sectarianisation" of Space among Iraqi Shias in London', *Contemporary Islam* 13, no. 3 (1 October 2019): 259–85, https://doi.org/10.1007/s11562-018-0425-y; Oliver Scharbrodt, 'A Minority within a Minority? The Complexity and Multilocality of Transnational Twelver Shia Networks in Britain', *Contemporary Islam* 13, no. 3 (1 October 2019): 287–305, https://doi.org/10.1007/s11562-018-0431-0.

83 Brent Council, 'Brent Population by Ethnicity', Brent Open Data, 2019, https://app.powerbi.com/view?r=eyJrIjoiN2U0MzFi ZmMtNjdkZC00M2FmLTkxMWMtYjg0Zjc5ZDBjZTBhIiwidCI6IjIxODlc4N2F iLTM1N2YtNGQ3YS1hZjljLTU4NzBlM2QyZWI4MCIsImMiOjh9. These estimates are based on Greater London Authority housing data.

84 Bowen, *Medina in Birmingham, Najaf in Brent*, 162.

85 Scharbrodt, 'A Minority within a Minority?', 296.

86 Degli Esposti, 'Fragmented Realities'.

87 Anthony Heath and Yaojun Li, 'Review of the Relationship between Religion and Poverty: An Analysis for the Joseph Rowntree Foundation', CSI Working Paper (Oxford: Centre for Social Investigation, Nuffield College, January 2015), csi.nuff.ox.ac.uk/wp-content/uploads/2015/03/religion-and-poverty-working-paper.pdf.

88 Muslim Council of Britain, 'British Muslims in Numbers', 42, 46, 50.

89 These figures are based on the 2011 census data for England and Wales.

90 Nabil Khattab and Ron Johnston, 'Ethno-Religious Identities and Persisting Penalties in the UK Labor Market', *Social Science Journal* 52, no. 4 (December 2015): 490–502, https://doi.org/10.1016/j.soscij.2014.10.007; Nabil Khattab and Tariq Modood, 'Both Ethnic and Religious: Explaining Employment Penalties across 14 Ethno-Religious Groups in the United Kingdom', *Journal for the Scientific Study of Religion* 54, no. 3 (1 September 2015): 501–22, https://doi.org/10.1111/jssr.12220; Louis Reynolds and

Jonathan Birdwell, 'Rising to the Top' (London: Demos, 2015), http://www.demos.co.uk/wp-content/uploads/2015/10/Rising-to-the-Top-Report.pdf.

91 Pew Research Global Attitudes Project, 'Muslims in Europe: Economic Worries Top Concerns about Religious and Cultural Identity' (Washington, DC: Pew Research Center, 6 July 2006), http://www.pewglobal.org/2006/07/06/muslims-in-europe-economic-worries-top-concerns-about-religious-and-cultural-identity/.

92 Ben Clements, 'The Ethnic Minority British Election Study (EMBES) – Part II', *British Religion in Numbers* (blog), 7 March 2011, http://www.brin.ac.uk/news/2011/the-ethnic-minority-british-election-study-embes-part-ii/.

93 For a helpful short history of Muslims' involvement in Labour unions, see Timothy Peace, *European Social Movements and Muslim Activism: Another World but with Whom?* (Basingstoke: Palgrave Macmillan, 2015), 34–6.

94 Sunny Hundal, 'British Muslims Are Losing the War against ISIL', *Quartz*, 10 September 2015, http://qz.com/498409/british-muslims-are-losing-the-war-against-isil/; José Casanova, 'Immigration and the New Religious Pluralism: A European Union-United States Comparison', in *Secularism, Religion and Multicultural Citizenship*, ed. Geoffrey Brahm Levey and Tariq Modood (Cambridge: Cambridge University Press, 2009), 139–63.

95 I make this contrast with extreme caution because different wording is used in different national surveys. Nevertheless, 20–35 per cent of British Muslims respond positively to questions asking Muslims to express preference for a political system based primarily on Islamic law, compared with 10 per cent of US Muslims. See Dalia Mogahed and Fouad Pervez, 'American Muslim Poll: Participation, Priorities, and Facing Prejudice in the 2016 Elections' (Dearborn, MI: Institute for Social Policy and Understanding, 2016), 9, http://www.ispu.org/wp-content/uploads/2016/08/poll2016-1.pdf; Ridhi Kashyap and Valerie A. Lewis, 'British Muslim Youth and Religious Fundamentalism: A Quantitative Investigation', *Ethnic and Racial Studies* 36, no. 12 (26 April 2012): 2122, https://doi.org/10.1080/01419870.2012.672761.

96 Pew Research Center, 'Muslim Americans: No Signs of Growth in Alienation or Support for Extremism' (Washington, DC: Pew Forum on Religion & Public Life, 2011), 17, http://www.people-press.org/files/2011/08/muslim-american-report.pdf. Specifically, 14 per cent of US Muslims have a household income over $100,000 (compared with 16 per cent in the wider population) and 26 per cent have degrees (compared with 28 per cent).

97 Tariq Modood et al., *Ethnic Minorities in Britain: Diversity and Disadvantage – The Fourth National Survey of Ethnic Minorities*, 1st edn (London: Policy Studies Institute, 1997).

98 Nabil Khattab, 'Ethno-Religious Background as a Determinant of Educational and Occupational Attainment in Britain', *Sociology* 43, no. 2 (2009): 311.

99 Gilliat-Ray, *Muslims in Britain*, 126.

100 On the particularly severe penalties suffered by Muslim women in the Labour market see Sami Miaari, Nabil Khattab and Ron Johnston, 'Religion and Ethnicity at Work: A Study of British Muslim Women's Labour Market Performance', *Quality and Quantity*, 7 March 2018, https://doi.org/10.1007/s11135-018-0721-x.

101 Nabil Khattab, Ron Johnston and David Manley, 'Human Capital, Family Structure and Religiosity Shaping British Muslim Women's Labour Market Participation', *Journal of Ethnic and Migration Studies* 44, no. 9 (4 July 2018): 1541–59, https://doi.org/10.1080/1369183X.2017.1334541. This study is based not on the census but Labour Force Survey and Understanding Society data.

102 Gilliat-Ray, *Muslims in Britain*, 214; see also Fauzia Ahmad, 'Modern Traditions? British Muslim Women and Academic Achievement', *Gender and Education* 13, no. 2 (2001): 137–52.

103 Khattab, Johnston and Manley, 'Human Capital, Family Structure and Religiosity Shaping British Muslim Women's Labour Market Participation', 1549.

104 Roy, *Globalised Islam*, 139.

105 Fauzia Ahmad, 'The British Muslim Relationship Crisis' (The British Association of Islamic Studies Conference, London, 15 April 2015).

106 Very similar relationship problems have been observed by American sociologists. See Amy Poppinga, 'Religious/American Identity Negotiation of Young Muslims in the Pursuit of Marriage' (Annual Meeting of the Society for the Scientific Study of Religion, Atlanta, GA, 29 October 2016).

107 Fauzia Ahmad, 'Graduating towards Marriage? Attitudes towards Marriage and Relationships among University-Educated British Muslim Women', *Culture and Religion* 13, no. 3 (2012): 193–210, https://doi.org/10.1080/14755610.2012.674953.

108 Julie Billaud, 'Marriage "Sharia Style": Everyday Practices of Islamic Morality in England', *Contemporary Islam*, 8 November 2018, https://doi.org/10.1007/s11562-018-0430-1.

109 Yunas Samad and John Eade, *Community Perceptions of Forced Marriage* (London: Community Liaison Unit, Foreign and Commonwealth Office, 2002), 86; Richard Gale and Therese O'Toole, 'Young People and Faith Activism: British Muslim Youth, Glocalisation and the Umma', in *Faith in the Public Realm: Controversies Policies and Practices*, ed. Adam Dinham, Robert Furbey and Vivien Lowndes (Bristol: Policy Press, 2009), 149; see also Jessica Jacobson, *Islam in Transition: Religion and Identity among British Pakistani Youth* (London: Routledge, 1998); for a detailed analysis of this tendency, see Marta Bolognani and Jody Mellor, 'British Pakistani Women's Use of the "Religion versus Culture" Contrast: A Critical Analysis', *Culture and Religion* 13, no. 2 (1 June 2012): 211–26, https://doi.org/10.1080/14755610.2012.674952.

110 Ahmad, 'Graduating towards Marriage?'; for a complementary quantitative analysis, see Kaveri Qureshi, Katharine Charsley and Alison Shaw, 'Marital Instability among British Pakistanis: Transnationality, Conjugalities and Islam', *Ethnic and Racial Studies* 37, no. 2 (28 January 2014): 261–79, https://doi.org/10.1080/01419870.2012.720691.

111 Roy, *Globalised Islam*; Gale and O'Toole, 'Young People and Faith Activism'; Jacobson, *Islam in Transition*.

112 Lewis, *Young, British and Muslim*; Hart Dyke, 'Mosques Made in Britain'; Sadek Hamid, *Sufis, Salafis and Islamists: The Contested Ground of British Islamic Activism* (London: I.B. Tauris, 2015).

113 Fatima Zohra, 'London Divan: Spiced Spare Ribs' (London School of Economics, London, 24 April 2008), http://www.radicalmiddleway.co.uk/videos.php?id=22&art=22&vid=88.

114 Jasjit Singh, 'Keeping the Faith: Reflections on Religious Nurture among Young British Sikhs', *Journal of Beliefs & Values* 33, no. 3 (1 December 2012): 369–83, https://doi.org/10.1080/13617672.2012.732817.

115 For a superb overview of this debate see Kashyap and Lewis, 'British Muslim Youth and Religious Fundamentalism'.

116 Lucinda Platt, 'Is There Assimilation in Minority Groups' National, Ethnic and Religious Identity?', *Ethnic and Racial Studies* 37, no. 1 (2014): 46–70.

117 Kashyap and Lewis, 'British Muslim Youth and Religious Fundamentalism', 2131–3. This, notably, is despite young Muslims being *more* likely than older Muslims to agree that homosexuality is immoral.

118 Kashyap and Lewis, 'British Muslim Youth and Religious Fundamentalism'; Clive D. Field, 'Young British Muslims since 9/11: A Composite Attitudinal Profile', *Religion, State and Society* 39, nos 2–3 (2011): 159–75. In one survey Field cites, 37 per cent of young Muslims express a preference for 'Shari'a' over 'British law'.

119 Justin Gest, *Apart: Alienated and Engaged Muslims in the West* (New York: Columbia University Press, 2010); Field, 'Young British Muslims since 9/11'.

120 Hamid, *Sufis, Salafis and Islamists*; Lewis, *Young, British and Muslim*.

121 Anabel Inge, *The Making of a Salafi Muslim Woman: Paths to Conversion* (London: Oxford University Press, 2016), 9–11; see also Bowen, *Medina in Birmingham, Najaf in Brent*, 63.

122 See Talal Asad, *Formations of the Secular: Christianity, Islam, Modernity* (Stanford, CA: Stanford University Press, 2003), 199.

123 See Olivier Roy, *The Failure of Political Islam* (Cambridge, MA: Harvard University Press, 1996).

124 As Jocelyne Cesari puts it in her detailed overview of political Islam, Islamism 'cannot be read exclusively in light of the premodern Islamic tradition because it is the result of the Islamic tradition's dual processes of nationalization and reformation/westernization'. Jocelyne Cesari, *What Is Political Islam?* (Boulder, CO: Lynne Rienner, 2017), 2.

125 See, for example, Hamid, *Sufis, Salafis and Islamists*.

126 For further discussion of Tahtawi's interactions with Europe, see Khaled Abou El Fadl, *The Great Theft: Wrestling Islam from the Extremists* (San Francisco, CA: Harper, 2007), 176.

127 Albert Hourani, *Arabic Thought in the Liberal Age* (London: Oxford University Press, 1962), 103.

128 Rida was born in what is now Lebanon but moved to Cairo in his thirties. Hourani, *Arabic Thought in the Liberal Age*.

129 Oliver Scharbrodt, 'The Salafiyya and Sufism: Muḥammad 'Abduh and His Risālat al-Wāridāt (Treatise on Mystical Inspirations)', *Bulletin of the School of Oriental and African Studies, University of London* 70, no. 1 (2007): 90.

130 Quoted in Zaki Badawi, *The Reformers of Egypt* (London: Taylor & Francis, 1978), 113.

131 Gilliat-Ray, *Muslims in Britain*, 69. This aligns with a *hadith* stating that 'The best people are those of my generation, then those who come after them, then those who come after them' (Sahih al-Bukhari 6065, Sahih Muslim 2533).

132 Abou El Fadl, *The Great Theft*, 75–6.

133 Hourani, *Arabic Thought in the Liberal Age*, 170–83.

134 On Mawdudi's relationship to Salafism see Roy Jackson, *Mawlana Mawdudi and Political Islam: Authority and the Islamic State* (London: Routledge, 2010).

135 Ziad Munson, 'Islamic Mobilization: Social Movement Theory and the Egyptian Muslim Brotherhood', *Sociological Quarterly* 42, no. 4 (1 September 2001): 487–510, https://doi.org/10.1111/j.1533-8525.2001.tb01777.x.

136 Andrew F. March, *The Caliphate of Man: Popular Sovereignty in Modern Islamic Thought* (Cambridge, MA: Harvard University Press, 2019); Gilles Kepel, *Jihad: The Trail of Political Islam* (London: I.B. Tauris, 2009), 27.

137 Philip Lewis and Sadek Hamid, *British Muslims: New Directions in Islamic Thought, Creativity and Activism* (Edinburgh: Edinburgh University Press, 2018), 97.
138 Gilliat-Ray, *Muslims in Britain*, 70.
139 On the alliance between the Wahhabis, the Saudis and the British, see Abou El Fadl, *The Great Theft*, 45–94; Reza Aslan, *No God But God* (London: William Heinemann, 2005), 220–66.
140 Vicky Baker, 'Rape Victim Sentenced to 200 Lashes and Six Months in Jail', *The Guardian*, 16 November 2007, http://www.guardian.co.uk/world/2007/nov/17/ saudiarabia.international; Abou El Fadl, *The Great Theft*, 251.
141 Ziauddin Sardar, 'The Destruction of Mecca', *New York Times*, 30 September 2014, http://www.nytimes.com/2014/10/01/opinion/the-destruction-of-mecca.html.
142 Kepel, *Jihad*, 50–6.
143 Abou El Fadl, *The Great Theft*, 72–3.
144 Hourani, *Arabic Thought in the Liberal Age*, 231.
145 Abou El Fadl, *The Great Theft*, 79.
146 Jonathan Birt, 'Wahhabism in the United Kingdom: Manifestations and Reactions', in *Transnational Connections and the Arab Gulf*, ed. Madawi al-Rasheed (London: Routledge, 2005), 169.
147 Inge, *The Making of a Salafi Muslim Woman*.
148 Osama bin Laden was a member of a wealthy Saudi family while Al-Qaeda's current leader, Ayman al-Zawahiri, and its main intellectual inspiration, Sayyid Qutb, were members of the Muslim Brotherhood. See also Kepel, *Jihad*, 51.
149 Hamid, *Sufis, Salafis and Islamists*, 52–3.
150 Yahya Birt, 'Wahhabi Wrangles', *Yahya Birt* (blog), 2 November 2007, https:// yahyabirt1.wordpress.com/2007/11/02/wahhabi-wrangles/.
151 Abdal-Hakim Murad, 'Book Launch: A Muslim in Victorian America' (House of Lords, London, 22 November 2006), http://www.radicalmiddleway.co.uk/videos. php?id=1&art=11.
152 Hamid, *Sufis, Salafis and Islamists*; Ansari, *The Infidel Within*, 369–74.
153 This revealing name is taken from a specific *hadith*: 'My *ummah* will split into seventy-three sects, all of whom will be in Hell except one group.'
154 While Hizb in the UK has remained non-violent many members and leaders of these splinter movements, such as the Islam4UK spokesman Anjem Choudary, have been convicted of fomenting or participating in violence (see Chapter 5).
155 Geaves, *Sectarian Influences within Islam in Britain*.
156 Hamid, *Sufis, Salafis and Islamists*, 22.
157 Geaves, *Sectarian Influences within Islam in Britain*, 186; Kepel, *Jihad*, 35. There are exceptions to this, such as the AKP in Turkey, whose support base can be found in conservative rural areas.
158 Lewis, *Young, British and Muslim*, 138.
159 Hassan Saleemi, 'Islamic Activism in the UK: Then and Now' (Abrar House, London, 29 June 2007), http://www.thecitycircle.com/events_full_text2.php?id=453.
160 Kamali, *Freedom of Expression in Islam*, 160.
161 Roy, *Globalised Islam*, 40–54; Hamid, *Sufis, Salafis and Islamists*, 36.
162 Hamid, *Sufis, Salafis and Islamists*, 57.
163 Roy, *Globalised Islam*, 143–7.
164 Alan Travis, 'Cameron Backing Counter-Extremism Strategy Marks a Fundamental Shift', *The Guardian*, 29 June 2015, http://www.theguardian.com/politics/2015/jun/ 29/cameron-backing-theresa-may-counter-extremism-strategy-fundamental-shift.

165 I should note that the idea that UK university campuses act as recruiting grounds for Islamist extremists is fiercely contested. See Alison Scott-Baumann, '"Dual Use Research of Concern" and "Select Agents": How Researchers Can Use Free Speech to Avoid "Weaponising" Academia', *Journal of Muslims in Europe* 7, no. 2 (26 June 2018): 237–61, https://doi.org/10.1163/22117954-12341373.

166 See Field, 'Young British Muslims since 9/11'.

167 Lewis, *Young, British and Muslim*; Sadek Hamid, ed., *Young British Muslims: Between Rhetoric and Real Lives* (London: Routledge, 2016); Mondal, *Young British Muslim Voices*; Nahid A. Kabir, *Young British Muslims: Identity, Culture, Politics and the Media* (Edinburgh: Edinburgh University Press, 2012); Sughra Ahmed, 'Seen and Not Heard: Voices of Young British Muslims' (Leicester: Policy Research Centre, 2009).

168 Muslim Council of Britain, 'British Muslims in Numbers', 22.

169 Sophie Gilliat-Ray's *Muslims in Britain* took initial steps in this direction, which have since been built on in Lewis and Hamid, *British Muslims*.

Chapter 3: Islamic Education: Schooling for Naql-Heads?

1 See Majid Fakhry, *Averroes (Ibn Rushd): His Life, Works and Influence* (Oxford: OneWorld, 2001), 14.

2 Daniel Heller-Roazen, 'Philosophy before the Law: Averroës's Decisive Treatise', *Critical Inquiry* 32, no. 3 (2006): 414–42.

3 See, for example, Roger Scruton, *The West and the Rest: Globalisation and the Terrorist Threat* (London: Continuum, 2002), 22.

4 See Wael B. Hallaq, 'Was the Gate of Ijtihad Closed?', *International Journal of Middle East Studies* 16, no. 1 (1 March 1984): 3–41.

5 See Peter Mandaville, 'Globalization and the Politics of Religious Knowledge: Pluralising Authority in the Muslim World', *Theory, Culture and Society* 24, no. 2 (2007): 101–15; Gary R. Bunt, *Islam in the Digital Age: E-Jihad, Online Fatwas and Cyber Islamic Environments* (London: Pluto, 2003).

6 Francis Robinson, *The Ulama of Farangi Mahall and Islamic Culture in South Asia* (London: C. Hurst, 2001).

7 Ron Geaves, 'Drawing on the Past to Transform the Present: Contemporary Challenges for Training and Preparing British Imams', *Journal of Muslim Minority Affairs* 28, no. 1 (2008): 99–112.

8 See, inter alia, Department for Communities and Local Government, 'Preventing Violent Extremism: Winning Hearts and Minds' (Wetherby: Communities and Local Government, 2007); Paul Goodman, 'MINAB's Mosques May Not Be so Moderate', *Daily Telegraph*, 30 November 2007, http://www.telegraph.co.uk/comment/3644400/MINABs-mosques-may-not-be-so-moderate.html; Anya Hart Dyke, 'Mosques Made in Britain' (London: Quilliam Foundation, 2009); Cameron in Richard Vaughan, 'Ofsted Will Inspect Madrasas, Says Cameron', TES, 7 October 2015, https://www.tes.com/news/school-news/breaking-news/ofsted-will-inspect-madrasas-says-cameron; for a contrasting analysis, see Mohamed Mukadam and Alison Scott-Baumann, 'The Training and Development of Muslim Faith Leaders: Current Practice and Future Possibilities' (London: DCLG, October 2010).

9 Hamza Yusuf, 'Book Launch: A Muslim in Victorian America' (House of Lords, London, 22 November 2006), http://www.radicalmiddleway.co.uk/videos. php?id=1&art=11.

10 Kwame Anthony Appiah, *The Ethics of Identity* (Princeton, NJ: Princeton University Press, 2005).

11 I borrow this turn of phrase from Appiah.

12 Khadijah Elshayyal, *Muslim Identity Politics: Islam, Activism and Equality in Britain* (London: I.B. Tauris, 2018), 58; see also Humayun Ansari, *The Infidel Within: Muslims in Britain since 1800* (London: C. Hurst, 2004); Nasar Meer, *Citizenship, Identity and the Politics of Multiculturalism: The Rise of Muslim Consciousness* (Basingstoke: Palgrave Macmillan, 2010).

13 Overall, in 2015 there were 138 Islamic secondary schools registered with the Department for Education. See Alison Scott-Baumann and Sariya Cheruvallil-Contractor, *Islamic Education in Britain: New Pluralist Paradigms* (London: Bloomsbury, 2015), 42.

14 Mukadam and Scott-Baumann, 'The Training and Development of Muslim Faith Leaders', 73.

15 This is because of more relaxed registration requirements for post-16 education, as well as a tendency for private institutions of higher learning to be set up and then disappear over the course of just a few years. Mukadam and Scott-Bauman's survey does not name all the institutions discussed here, such as Hijaz College, the Institute of Ismaili Studies and the Institute for Leadership and Community Development.

16 Jonathan Birt and Philip Lewis, 'The Pattern of Islamic Reform in Britain: The Deobandis between Intra-Muslim Sectarianism and Engagement with Wider Society', in *Producing Islamic Knowledge: Transmission and Dissemination in Western Europe*, ed. Martin Van Bruinessen and Stefano Allievi (London: Routledge, 2007), 94–5.

17 This is an estimate given in Innes Bowen, *Medina in Birmingham, Najaf in Brent: Inside British Islam* (London: C. Hurst, 2014), 19. It is taken from an interview conducted in 2010, so is somewhat outdated.

18 Birt and Lewis, 'The Pattern of Islamic Reform in Britain', 97.

19 Ron Geaves, 'The Symbolic Construction of the Walls of Deoband', *Islam and Christian–Muslim Relations* 23, no. 3 (2012): 316.

20 Jonathan Birt, 'Locating the British Imam: The Deobandi 'ulama between Contested Authority and Public Policy Post-9/11', in *European Muslims and the Secular State*, ed. Jocelyne Cesari and Seán McLoughlin (Aldershot: Ashgate, 2005), 183–96; Philip Lewis, *Young, British and Muslim* (London: Continuum, 2007).

21 Birt and Lewis, 'The Pattern of Islamic Reform in Britain', 91–2; for detailed discussions of the modernity of the Deoband movement see also Barbara D. Metcalf, *Islamic Revival in British India: Deoband, 1860–1900* (Princeton, NJ: Princeton University Press, 1982); Brannon D. Ingram, *Revival from Below: The Deoband Movement and Global Islam* (Oakland: University of California Press, 2018).

22 Birt and Lewis, 'The Pattern of Islamic Reform in Britain', 97; for a full discussion of Thanawi's modern traditionalism, see Usamah Yasin Ansari, 'The Pious Self Is a Jewel in Itself: Agency and Tradition in the Production of "Shariatic Modernity"', *South Asia Research* 30, no. 3 (1 November 2010): 275–98, https://doi.org/10.1177/026272801003000304.

23 S. Irfan Habib and Dhruv Raina, 'Copernicus, Colombus, Colonialism and the Role of Science in Nineteenth Century India', *Social Scientist* 17, nos 3/4 (1989): 51–66, https://doi.org/10.2307/3517360.

24 Muhammad Qasim Zaman, 'Tradition and Authority in Deobandi Madrasas of South Asia', in *Schooling Islam: The Culture and Politics of Modern Muslim Education*, ed. Robert W. Hefner and Muhammad Qasim Zaman (Princeton, NJ: Princeton University Press, 2007), 72.

25 Bowen, *Medina in Birmingham, Najaf in Brent*, 13.

26 Sana Haroon, 'The Rise of Deobandi Islam in the North-West Frontier Province and Its Implications in Colonial India and Pakistan 1914–1996', *Journal of the Royal Asiatic Society* 18, no. 1 (2008): 47–70.

27 The status of Ahmadi Muslims, who see the founder of their tradition as a prophet, is a matter of fierce dispute in multiple Muslim-majority countries and has been a point of tension in Britain, especially following the jailing in 2016 of Tanveer Ahmed for the murder of Asad Shah, an Ahmadi Muslim shopkeeper based in Glasgow.

28 Haroon, 'The Rise of Deobandi Islam in the North-West Frontier Province and Its Implications in Colonial India and Pakistan 1914–1996'; Zaman, 'Tradition and Authority in Deobandi Madrasas of South Asia', 71–4.

29 Lewis, *Young, British and Muslim*, 100; see also Barbara Metcalf, 'Madrasas and Minorities in Secular India', in *Schooling Islam: The Culture and Politics of Modern Muslim Education*, ed. Robert W. Hefner and Muhammad Qasim Zaman (Princeton, NJ: Princeton University Press, 2007), 87–106.

30 Birt and Lewis, 'The Pattern of Islamic Reform in Britain', 93.

31 Bowen, *Medina in Birmingham, Najaf in Brent*, 31–2.

32 At one institution, Geaves negotiated access first with British students studying in India, who introduced him to a senior Deobandi scholar, who in turn convinced the institution's principal to allow him to stay longer than three days (which is the usual maximum allowed visit length for non-Muslims). See Geaves 'The "Death" Pangs of the Insider/Outsider Dichotomy in the Study of Religion' (Muslims in Britain Research Network, Cardiff University, 10 September 2014), http://sites.cardiff. ac.uk/islamukcentre/community-engagement/mbrn-islam-uk-centre-conference/ ron-geaves-keynote-lecture/.

33 Geaves, 'The Symbolic Construction of the Walls of Deoband', 323.

34 Marshall Sahlins, 'Goodby to Tristes Tropes: Ethnography in the Context of Modern World History', *Journal of Modern History* 65, no. 1 (1993): 3.

35 Appiah, *The Ethics of Identity*, 119.

36 Zaman, 'Tradition and Authority in Deobandi Madrasas of South Asia', 66; Muhammad Qasim Zaman, *The Ulama in Contemporary Islam: Custodians of Change* (Princeton, NJ: Princeton University Press, 2007), 68. I should note that there is some debate among historians based in India about whether Nizam al-Din ever composed a new syllabus, as is often claimed. I am grateful to Haroon Sidat for bringing this to my attention.

37 Birt and Lewis, 'The Pattern of Islamic Reform in Britain', 96; Iram Asif, 'Hijaz College : Students of Islamic Religious Sciences in Contemporary British Society' (Master's thesis, Lund University, 2006), http://www.lunduniversity.lu.se/lup/ publication/1328980.

38 Zaman, *The Ulama in Contemporary Islam*, 68.

39 Scott-Baumann and Cheruvallil-Contractor, *Islamic Education in Britain*, 42.

40 Birt and Lewis, 'The Pattern of Islamic Reform in Britain', 100.

41　Sophie Gilliat-Ray, 'Educating the 'ulama: Centres of Islamic Religious Training in Britain', *Islam and Christian-Muslim Relations* 17, no. 1 (2006): 66.

42　See Sophie Gilliat-Ray, 'Closed Worlds: (Not) Accessing Deobandi Dar Ul-Uloom in Britain', *Fieldwork in Religion* 1, no. 1 (2005): 7–33.

43　Birt and Lewis, 'The Pattern of Islamic Reform in Britain', 99; Bowen, *Medina in Birmingham, Najaf in Brent*, 17.

44　Hassan Rabbani, 'Training British Muslim Religious Leaders' (Abrar House, London, 27 November 2015), https://www.youtube.com/watch?v=DK5QQ_biMFU.

45　Abdur-Rahman Mangera, 'Training British Muslim Religious Leaders' (Abrar House, London, 27 November 2015), https://www.youtube.com/watch?v=DK5QQ_biMFU.

46　Safia Shahid, 'Training British Muslim Religious Leaders' (Abrar House, London, 27 November 2015), https://www.youtube.com/watch?v=DK5QQ_biMFU.

47　Geaves, 'Drawing on the Past to Transform the Present', 102–4; see also Lewis, *Young, British and Muslim*, 90.

48　For example, Hart Dyke, 'Mosques Made in Britain', 19–20.

49　Scott-Baumann and Cheruvallil-Contractor, *Islamic Education in Britain*.

50　Gilliat-Ray, 'Closed Worlds', 30, emphasis in original.

51　Christopher Hope, 'David Cameron: We Will "Drain the Swamp" Which Allows Muslim Extremists to Flourish', 3 June 2013, http://www.telegraph.co.uk/news/politics/10097006/David-Cameron-We-will-drain-the-swamp-which-allows-Muslim-extremists-to-flourish.html.

52　See Sue Reid 'Breeding Ground for Jihadis Where Even Ice Cream Lady Wears a Burka', *Mail Online*, 15 June 2015, http://www.dailymail.co.uk/news/article-3125530/The-breeding-ground-jihadis-ice-cream-lady-wears-burka-great-textile-town-Dewsbury-undergone-terrible-transformation.html.

53　In recognition of this difficulty, some British-born 'ulama have shifted away from Deobandi norms, such as references to revered elders, and adopted more charismatic preaching styles. Birt, 'Locating the British Imam', 185–6; see also Sadek Hamid, *Sufis, Salafis and Islamists: The Contested Ground of British Islamic Activism* (London: I.B. Tauris, 2015).

54　For a helpful review of literature on causes of radicalization that deals with the so-called 'conveyor belt thesis', see Francis, 'What Causes Radicalisation? Main Lines of Consensus in Recent Research', *Radicalisation Research*, 24 January 2012, http://www.radicalisationresearch.org/guides/francis-2012-causes-2/.

55　Olivier Roy, *Jihad and Death: The Global Appeal of Islamic State* (London: C. Hurst, 2017).

56　The Independent, 'David Cameron's Tory Conference Speech in Full', *The Independent*, 7 October 2015, http://www.independent.co.uk/news/uk/politics/tory-party-conference-2015-david-camerons-speech-in-full-a6684656.html.

57　Goodman, 'MINAB's Mosques May Not Be so Moderate'.

58　Therese O'Toole et al., 'Governing through Prevent? Regulation and Contested Practice in State–Muslim Engagement', *Sociology* 50, no. 1 (1 February 2016): 162, https://doi.org/10.1177/0038038514564437.

59　Three government departments were initially charged with delivering Prevent, each holding their own budget: the Home Office, particularly the Office for Security and Counter-Terrorism; the Department for Communities and Local Government; and the Foreign and Commonwealth Office. The practices of other areas of government, such as justice and education, were undoubtedly influenced too. After 2010, responsibility for Prevent was moved to the Home Office.

60 O'Toole et al., 'Governing through Prevent?', 162.

61 Quoted in Rob Paton, Haider Ali and Lee Taylor, 'Government Support for Faith-Based Organizations: The Case of a Development Programme for Faith Leaders', *Public Money & Management* 29, no. 6 (2009): 215.

62 Ataullah Siddiqui, *Islam at Universities in England: Meeting the Needs and Investing in the Future* (Leicester: Markfield Institute, 2007).

63 Interview with Siddiqui, 26 February 2015.

64 Higher Education Funding Council for England, 'Islamic Studies: Trends and Profiles' (London: HEFCE, 2008).

65 I should acknowledge that I have sat on the governing council for this association in my capacity as the Muslims in Britain Research Network's general secretary. For a brief history of the Association from the Islamic Studies Network see: Scott-Bauman and Cheruvallil Contractor *Islamic Education in Britain*.

66 Yasir Suleiman, 'Contextualising Islam in Britain: Exploratory Perspectives' (Cambridge: Centre of Islamic Studies, 2009).

67 Mukadam and Scott-Baumann, 'The Training and Development of Muslim Faith Leaders'.

68 Sariya Cheruvallil-Contractor and Alison Scott-Baumann, 'Collaborative Partnerships between Universities and Muslim Institutions: Dismantling the Roadblocks' (Derby: University of Derby, 2014), http://www.derby.ac.uk/media/derbyacuk/contentassets/documents/ehs/schoolofeducation/centreofsocietyreligionandbelief/Research-report.pdf; Ron Geaves, 'An Exploration of the Viability of Partnership between Dar Al-Ulum and Higher Education Institutions in North West England Focusing upon Pedagogy and Relevance' (Edinburgh: HEA, 30 July 2012), https://www.heacademy.ac.uk/sites/default/files/geaves_daralulums_final_report_isn.pdf; Amjad M. Hussain, 'Towards Solving the Crisis of Islam in Higher Education', *Journal of Beliefs & Values* 28, no. 3 (1 December 2007): 267–72, https://doi.org/10.1080/13617670701712455.

69 Quoted in Yvonne Yazbeck Haddad and Michael J. Balz, 'Taming the Imams: European Governments and Islamic Preachers since 9/11', *Islam and Christian–Muslim Relations* 19, no. 2 (2008): 222–3.

70 Sally Weale, 'Muslim Leaders Voice Concerns about Tory Crackdown on Madrasas', *The Guardian*, 7 October 2015, sec. World news, http://www.theguardian.com/world/2015/oct/07/muslim-leaders-voice-concerns-about-tory-crackdown-on-madrasas. The primary reason such policies have not been implemented is resistance from other faith groups who would have been affected (see below).

71 Andrew Gilligan, 'Imams Will Have to Register and Face Security Vetting under Home Office Plans', *The Telegraph*, 12 September 2015, http://www.telegraph.co.uk/news/uknews/terrorism-in-the-uk/11860993/Imams-will-have-to-register-and-face-security-vetting-under-Home-Office-plans.html.

72 HM Government, *Prevent Duty Guidance: For England and Wales* (London: Stationery Office, 2015), https://www.gov.uk/government/uploads/system/uploads/attachment_data/file/417943/Prevent_Duty_Guidance_England_Wales.pdf.

73 Haddad and Balz, 'Taming the Imams'; Charlotte Heath-Kelly, 'Counter-Terrorism and the Counterfactual: Producing the "Radicalisation" Discourse and the UK PREVENT Strategy', *British Journal of Politics & International Relations* 15, no. 3 (2013): 394–415; Arun Kundnani, *Spooked: How Not to Prevent Violent Extremism* (London: Institute of Race Relations, 2009); Luca Mavelli, 'Between Normalisation and Exception: The Securitisation of Islam and the Construction of the Secular

Subject', *Millennium: Journal of International Studies* 41, no. 2 (1 January 2013): 159–81; Christina Pantazis and Simon Pemberton, 'Resisting the Advance of the Security State: The Impact of Frameworks of Resistance on the UK'S Securitisation Agenda', *International Journal of Law, Crime and Justice* 41, no. 4 (2013): 358–74, https://doi.org/doi:10.1016/j.ijlcj.2013.07.009.

74 Derek McGhee, *The End of Multiculturalism? Terrorism, Integration and Human Rights* (Maidenhead: Open University Press, 2008).

75 On this theme, see also Stephen H. Jones, 'New Labour and the Re-Making of British Islam: The Case of the Radical Middle Way and the "Reclamation" of the Classical Islamic Tradition', *Religions* 4, no. 4 (4 November 2013): 550–66.

76 Interview, 25 February 2009.

77 See the similar comment in Sophie Gilliat-Ray, *Muslims in Britain: An Introduction* (Cambridge: Cambridge University Press, 2010), 163.

78 Lewis, *Young, British and Muslim*, 102–3.

79 Quoted in Peter Mandaville, 'Islamic Education in Britain: Approaches to Religious Knowledge in a Pluralistic Society', in *Schooling Islam: The Culture and Politics of Modern Muslim Education*, ed. Robert W. Hefner and Muhammad Qasim Zaman (Princeton, NJ: Princeton University Press, 2007), 234.

80 These are names of the four major traditional schools of Sunni Islamic law, or *madhhab*s.

81 Interview, 25 February 2009.

82 Mandaville, 'Islamic Education in Britain: Approaches to Religious Knowledge in a Pluralistic Society', 234.

83 In the 1980s, Badawi established the Council of Imams and Mosques, which had many Barelvi affiliates but few from the Deobandi tradition, whose members set up an alternative organization, the Council of Mosques. See Ansari, *The Infidel Within*, 361.

84 Mandaville, 'Islamic Education in Britain', 233–4.

85 The Muslim College, 'A Word from the Principal of The Muslim College', The Muslim College, n.d., http://muslimcollege.ac.uk/principal/. I have limited information on any changes made within the college under Benotman's leadership, but it is worth emphasizing that the staffing and course offering has remained broadly consistent.

86 Ron Geaves, *Sectarian Influences within Islam in Britain: With Reference to the Concepts of 'Ummah' and 'Community'* (Leeds: University of Leeds, 1996), 202.

87 Seán McLoughlin, 'The State, New Muslim Leaderships and Islam as a Resource for Public Engagement in Britain', in *European Muslims and the Secular State*, ed. Jocelyne Cesari and Seán McLoughlin (Aldershot: Ashgate, 2005), 62–5.

88 Chetan Bhatt, *Liberation and Purity: Race, New Religious Movements and the Ethics of Postmodernity* (London: Routledge, 1997), 117.

89 Stephen H. Jones, 'The "Metropolis of Dissent": Muslim Participation in Leicester and the "Failure" of Multiculturalism in Britain', *Ethnic and Racial Studies* 38, no. 11 (2 September 2015): 1969–85, https://doi.org/10.1080/01419870.2014.936891.

90 Hamid, *Sufis, Salafis and Islamists*, 80.

91 Gilliat-Ray, *Muslims in Britain*, 102.

92 Mandaville, 'Islamic Education in Britain', 235.

93 I base this comment on conversations with former staff at the Islamic Foundation as well as an account of recruitment processes in McLoughlin 'The State, New Muslim Leaderships and Islam as a Resource for Public Engagement in Britain', 62–5.

94 John Ware, 'A Question of Leadership', *Panorama* (BBC One, 21 August 2005), http://news.bbc.co.uk/1/hi/programmes/panorama/4171950.stm.

95   Hansard, 'House of Commons Daily Debates', United Kingdom Parliament, 25 May 2006, http://www.publications.parliament.uk/pa/cm200506/cmhansrd/vo060525/text/60525w0011.htm.

96   McLoughlin, 'The State, New Muslim Leaderships and Islam as a Resource for Public Engagement in Britain'.

97   See the contribution of former staff member Dilwar Hussain in House of Commons 'Preventing Violent Extremism: Sixth Report of Session 2009–10' (London: The Stationery Office, 2010).

98   One of the members of this group was Batool al-Toma, leader of the New Muslims Project at the Islamic Foundation. See Chris Allen and Surinder Guru, 'Between Political Fad and Political Empowerment: A Critical Evaluation of the National Muslim Women's Advisory Group (NMWAG) and Governmental Processes of Engaging Muslim Women', *Sociological Research Online* 17, no. 3 (2011): 17.

99   HM Government, 'Prevent Strategy' (London: Stationery Office, 2011).

100   This phrase literally refers to the 'roots of Islamic law', that is, the religious sources (Qur'an and *Sunnah*) and practise of reasoning by analogy (*qiyas*) to derive legal judgements.

101   Interview, 26 February 2015.

102   Interview, 27 August 2008.

103   Abdal-Hakim Murad, ed., *Muslim Songs of the British Isles: Arranged for Schools* (London: Quilliam Press, 2005).

104   Abdal-Hakim Murad, 'British and Muslim?', Masud, 1997, http://www.masud.co.uk/ISLAM/ahm/british.htm.

105   Atif Imtiaz, 'Contextualising Islam in the United Kingdom: A Matter of Confidence?' (Muslim Leadership in Britain, UCLAN, 1 April 2015).

106   Mukadam and Scott-Baumann, 'The Training and Development of Muslim Faith Leaders', 73.

107   Interview, 13 March 2018.

108   Scott-Baumann and Cheruvallil-Contractor, *Islamic Education in Britain*, 47.

109   Cambridge Muslim College, 'BA Programme Validated', *Unity: Newsletter of the Cambridge Muslim College*, October 2017.

110   Kirstine Sinclair, 'An Islamic University in the West and the Question of Modern Authenticity', *Numen* 66, no. 4 (18 June 2019): 403–21, https://doi.org/10.1163/15685276-12341546.

111   Kecia Ali, *Sexual Ethics and Islam: Feminist Reflections on Qur'an, Hadith and Jurisprudence* (Oxford: Oneworld, 2006), 197.

112   Alison Scott-Baumann et al., 'Towards Contextualized Islamic Leadership: Paraguiding and the Universities and Muslim Seminaries Project (UMSEP)', *Religions* 10, no. 12 (December 2019): 12, https://doi.org/10.3390/rel10120662.

113   For further detail on these, see Philip Lewis and Sadek Hamid, *British Muslims: New Directions in Islamic Thought, Creativity and Activism* (Edinburgh: Edinburgh University Press, 2018).

114   Giulia Liberatore, 'Guidance as "Women's Work": A New Generation of Female Islamic Authorities in Britain', *Religions* 10, no. 11 (November 2019): 5, https://doi.org/10.3390/rel10110601.

115   Liberatore, 'Guidance as "Women's Work"', 5.

116   Scott-Baumann and Cheruvallil-Contractor, *Islamic Education in Britain*, 40–1.

117   Rushanara Ali, 'Launch of Maslaha' (Young Foundation, London, 22 May 2009).

118 Jones, 'New Labour and the Re-Making of British Islam'.

119 See, for example, Gilliat-Ray, *Muslims in Britain*, 236–8.

120 Jones, 'New Labour and the Re-Making of British Islam'.

121 Scott-Baumann and Cheruvallil-Contractor, *Islamic Education in Britain*, 117.

122 Hansard, 'Memorandum from Radical Middle Way (PVE 73)', February 2010, http://www.publications.parliament.uk/pa/cm200910/cmselect/cmcomloc/memo/previoex/m7302.htm.

123 Interview, 26 August 2008.

124 See https://www.facebook.com/RadicalMiddleWay/.

125 See Stephen H. Jones, 'Religious Literacy in Higher Education', in *Religious Literacy in Policy and Practice*, ed. Adam Dinham and Matthew Francis (Bristol: Policy Press, 2015), 185–204.

126 Robert Wuthnow, 'Can Faith Be More than a Sideshow in the Contemporary Academy?', in *The American University in a Postsecular Age*, ed. Douglas Jacobsen and Rhonda H. Jacobsen (Oxford: Oxford University Press, 2008), 31–44.

127 For data on the decline in humanities applicants, see Universities UK, 'Patterns and Trends 2016' (London: Universities UK, 2017), 15, http://public.tableau.com/views/PatternsAndTrends2016/Patterns2016?:embed=y&:showVizHome=no&:host_url=https%3A%2F%2Fpublic.tableau.com%2F&:tabs=yes&:toolbar=yes&:animate_transition=yes&:display_static_image=no&:display_spinner=yes&:display_overlay=yes&:display_count=yes&:loadOrderID=0.

128 British Future and Universities UK, 'International Students and the UK Immigration Debate' (London: Universities UK, 2014), https://www.universitiesuk.ac.uk/policy-and-analysis/reports/Pages/international-students-uk-immigration-debate.aspx.

129 At the time of writing, only students based at institutions that are listed on both the official UK Visas and Immigration Sponsor list and the list of HEFCE's 'recognized bodies' can work while studying.

130 Interview, 26 February 2015.

131 David Matthews, 'University of Wales Pulls in Its Tentacles', *Times Higher Education*, 4 October 2011, https://www.timeshighereducation.co.uk/news/university-of-wales-pulls-in-its-tentacles/417649.article.

132 All UK universities are independent organizations, but in the past a clear distinction could be made between 'private' institutions and those supported by public funds.

133 Religious tests were only fully abolished in Oxford and Cambridge in 1871: see Sophie Gilliat-Ray, *Religion in Higher Education: The Politics of the Multi-Faith Campus* (Aldershot: Ashgate, 2000).

134 Jones, 'Religious Literacy in Higher Education', 191; for detailed consideration of the sharp decline in theology and religion see The British Academy, 'Theology and Religious Studies Provision in UK Higher Education' (London: British Academy, May 2019), https://www.thebritishacademy.ac.uk/publications/theology-religious-studies-provision-uk-higher-education.

135 Tristram Hughes et al., 'Privately Funded Providers of Higher Education in the UK' (London: Department for Business Innovation and Skills, 2013).

136 These comments are based largely on conversations with the director and records made at the event, 'British Values and the Place of Religion in Schools', held at the ICLD on 25 November 2014.

137 See John Clarke, 'So Many Strategies, So Little Time … Making Universities Modern', *International Journal of Higher Education in the Social Sciences* 3, no. 3 (2010): 91–116.

138 This regulatory process, formerly administered by HEFCE and overseen by the Department for Business, Innovation and Skills (BIS), is in flux as I write due to HEFCE being restructured into the Office for Students and responsibility for higher education being passed from BIS (now BEIS) to the Department for Education.

139 Ofsted, 'Darul Uloom Al Arabiya Al Islamiya: Inspection Report' (Manchester: Ofsted, 23 November 2016), para. 2 [2] [a], https://reports.ofsted.gov. uk/inspection-reports/find-inspection-report/provider/ELS/105372.

140 For full details about this campaign, see http://keepmosquesindependent.org/.

141 Stephen L. Carter, *The Culture of Disbelief* (New York: Basic Books, 1993), 36–7.

142 Amy Gutmann, *Democratic Education*, rev. edn (Princeton, NJ: Princeton University Press, 1999).

143 John Rawls, *Political Liberalism* (New York: Columbia University Press, 2005), 471.

144 On political liberalism, see Rawls, *Political Liberalism*; Martha C. Nussbaum, 'Perfectionist Liberalism and Political Liberalism', *Philosophy & Public Affairs* 39, no. 1 (1 January 2011): 3–45, https://doi.org/10.1111/j.1088-4963.2011.01200.x; Stephen Macedo, 'Liberal Civic Education and Religious Fundamentalism: The Case of God vs. John Rawls?', *Ethics* 105, no. 3 (1995): 468–96.

145 'Gutmann's stronger position is also justified primarily in terms of social reproduction, but her account involves greater emphasis on nurturing individuals' deliberative capacities. See Amy Gutmann, *Democratic Education*, 44-5.'

146 Les Back, *The Art of Listening* (Oxford: Berg, 2007).

147 Joel Busher et al., 'What the Prevent Duty Means for Schools and Colleges in England: An Analysis of Educationalists' Experiences' (Coventry: Coventry University, 2017), https://pure.coventry.ac.uk/ws/portalfiles/portal/11090509; O'Toole et al., 'Governing through Prevent?'

148 For a full account, see Nisha Kapoor and Kasia Narkowicz, 'Unmaking Citizens: Passport Removals, Pre-Emptive Policing and the Reimagining of Colonial Governmentalities', *Ethnic and Racial Studies* 42, no. 16 (2017): 45–62, https://doi.org /10.1080/01419870.2017.1411965.

149 See, for example, Department for Innovation, Universities and Skills, 'Promoting Good Campus Relations, Fostering Shared Values and Preventing Violent Extremism in Universities and Higher Education Colleges' (London: Department for Business Innovation and Skills, 2007).

150 See 'Two Concepts of Liberty', in Isaiah Berlin, *The Proper Study of Mankind* (New York: Farrar, Strauss and Giroux, 1997), 191–243.

151 Appiah, *The Ethics of Identity*.

152 The Amish Supreme Court case was successful and led to children being removed from school, the Protestant Circuit Court case was not. See Macedo 'Liberal Civic Education and Religious Fundamentalism'.

153 Appiah, *The Ethics of Identity*, 156.

154 Cheruvallil-Contractor and Scott-Baumann, 'Collaborative Partnerships between Universities and Muslim Institutions'.

155 Scott-Baumann and Cheruvallil-Contractor, *Islamic Education in Britain*, 33.

156 Warwick University, 'Postgraduate Award in Islamic Education', Warwick University, n.d., https://warwick.ac.uk/fac/soc/ces/prospective/postgraduate/taught/islamicpga/.

157 Al Mahdi Institute, 'AMI Signs Agreement with University of Birmingham for Masters in Islamic Studies', *Al-Mahdi Institute* (blog), 21 August 2018, https://www. almahdi.edu/ami-signs-agreement-with-university-of-birmingham-for-masters-in-islamic-studies/.

158 Mukadam and Scott-Baumann, 'The Training and Development of Muslim Faith Leaders', 47.

159 For further similar examples and proposals, see Scott-Baumann and Cheruvallil-Contractor, *Islamic Education in Britain*, 170.

160 Antony Bushfield, 'Government to Ditch Plans for Ofsted Inspections at Sunday Schools', Premier, 10 July 2016, https://www.premier.org.uk/News/UK/Government-to-ditch-plans-for-Ofsted-inspections-at-Sunday-schools.

161 Mathew Guest et al., *Christianity and the University Experience: Understanding Student Faith* (London: Bloomsbury, 2013).

162 The University of Birmingham has historic links to the Selly Oak network of theological colleges and retains associations with a nearby Quaker institution.

163 Olivier Roy, *Holy Ignorance: When Religion and Culture Part Ways* (London: C. Hurst, 2010).

164 Olivier Roy, *Globalised Islam: The Search for a New Ummah* (London: C. Hurst, 2004).

165 Jones, 'Religious Literacy in Higher Education'.

166 See HM Government, 'Prevent Strategy': I discuss this argument further in Chapter 5.

167 Scott-Baumann and Cheruvallil-Contractor in *Islamic Education in Britain* develop this argument in greater length with reference to Contact Theory.

168 Scott-Baumann and Cheruvallil-Contractor, 169.

169 See the quotations in Appiah, *The Ethics of Identity*, 200.

170 On ethnic and religious minority attainment see Universities UK, 'Black, Asian and Minority Ethnic Student Attainment at UK Universities: #closingthegap' (London: Universities UK, 2 May 2019), https://www.universitiesuk.ac.uk/policy-and-analysis/reports/Pages/bame-student-attainment-uk-universities-closing-the-gap.aspx; Gurnam Singh, 'Black and Minority Ethnic (BME) Students' Participation in Higher Education: Improving Retention and Success' (York: HEA, 2011).

171 Gilliat-Ray, *Religion in Higher Education*, 79.

172 James A. Beckford and Ilona C.M. Cairns, 'Muslim Prison Chaplains in Canada and Britain', *Sociological Review* 63, no. 1 (1 February 2015): 36–56, https://doi.org/10.1111/1467-954X.12224.

173 Birt and Lewis, 'The Pattern of Islamic Reform in Britain', 97.

174 Sophie Gilliat-Ray, Mansur Ali and Stephen Pattison, *Understanding Muslim Chaplaincy* (Farnham: Ashgate, 2013).

175 Gilliat-Ray, Ali and Pattison, *Understanding Muslim Chaplaincy*.

176 Interview, 26 February 2015.

177 Haroon Sidat, 'Between Tradition and Transition: An Islamic Seminary, or Dar al-Uloom in Modern Britain', *Religions* 9, no. 10 (15 October 2018): 314, https://doi.org/10.3390/rel9100314.

178 Geaves, 'An Exploration of the Viability of Partnership between Dar Al-Ulum and Higher Education Institutions in North West England Focusing upon Pedagogy and Relevance'.

179 Ron Geaves, 'On Higher Education and Dar Al-Ulums in Britain' (Muslims in Britain Research Network, Leeds, 11 January 2012).

180 Geaves, 'An Exploration of the Viability of Partnership between Dar Al-Ulum and Higher Education Institutions in North West England Focusing upon Pedagogy and Relevance', 9–10.

181 Sophie Gilliat-Ray, 'From "Closed Worlds" to "Open Doors": (Now) Accessing Deobandi Darul Uloom in Britain', *Fieldwork in Religion* 13, no. 2 (2018): 137, https://doi.org/doi.org/10.1558/firn.35029.
182 Manuel Castells, *The Power of Identity* (Oxford: Blackwell, 2004).
183 Gilliat-Ray, 'From "Closed Worlds" to "Open Doors"', 135.
184 Geaves, 'On Higher Education and Dar Al-Ulums in Britain'.
185 Ofsted, 'Darul Uloom Al Arabiya Al Islamiya'.
186 Mangera, 'Training British Muslim Religious Leaders'.
187 Gilliat-Ray, 'From "Closed Worlds" to "Open Doors"', 133; see also Haroon Sidat, 'Shedding Light on the Modalities of Authority in a Dar Al-Uloom, or Religious Seminary, in Britain', *Religions* 10, no. 12 (December 2019): 653, https://doi.org/10.3390/rel10120653.

Chapter 4: What Is the Future for Muslim Personal Law in Britain?

1 Michel Foucault, 'The Order of Discourse', in *Untying the Text: A Post-Structuralist Reader*, ed. Robert Young (London: Routledge, 1981), 67.
2 Alex Marshall, 'How ISIS Got Its Anthem', *The Guardian*, 9 November 2014, http://www.theguardian.com/music/2014/nov/09/nasheed-how-isis-got-its-anthem.
3 For further discussion and empirical substantiation of this, see Stephen H. Jones et al., '"That's How Muslims Are Required to View the World": Race, Culture and Belief in Non-Muslims' Descriptions of Islam and Science', *Sociological Review*, 31 May 2018, https://doi.org/10.1177/0038026118778174.
4 Khaled Abou El Fadl, *The Great Theft: Wrestling Islam from the Extremists* (San Francisco, CA: Harper, 2007), 34.
5 See Wael B. Hallaq, 'Was Al-Shafi'i the Master Architect of Islamic Jurisprudence?', *International Journal of Middle East Studies* 25, no. 4 (1993): 587–605.
6 For excellent discussions of this, see Philip Lewis and Sadek Hamid, *British Muslims: New Directions in Islamic Thought, Creativity and Activism* (Edinburgh: Edinburgh University Press, 2018), 96–104; Abou El Fadl, *The Great Theft*, 30–8.
7 This example survey question is taken from Munira Mirza, Abi Senthilkumaran and Zein Ja'far, 'Living Apart Together: British Muslims and the Paradox of Multiculturalism' (London: Policy Exchange, 2007), 46, http://www.policyexchange.org.uk/images/libimages/246.pdf.
8 Yahya Michot, 'Muslims under Non-Muslim Rule: A Classical Fatwa' (Abrar House, London, 18 July 2008).
9 Charles Moore, 'Archbishop, You Can't Just Have a Bit of Sharia – It's All or Nothing', *Daily Telegraph*, 9 February 2008. This article was one of many scathing op-eds written after the then Archbishop of Canterbury, Rowan Williams, delivered a lecture on Islamic law's place in English civil law.
10 On the latter, see Jessica Carlisle, *Muslim Divorce in the Middle East: Contesting Gender in the Contemporary Courts* (Cham, Switzerland: Palgrave Macmillan, 2019).
11 Samia Bano, 'Complexity, Difference and "Muslim Personal Law": Rethinking the Relationship between Shariah Councils and South Asian Muslim Women in Britain' (PhD diss., Warwick: University of Warwick, 2004), 70–1.

12 See, for example, Denis MacEoin, *Sharia Law or 'One Law for All'?* (London: Civitas, 2009); Sally Bowman, 'Should Sharia Councils Be Banned?', *Inside Out East Midlands* (Leicester: BBC One East Midlands, 2 November 2015), http://www.bbc.co.uk/programmes/b06n5s5q.

13 Senay Boztas, 'Sharia Courts in Britain Lock Women into "Marital Captivity", Study Says', *The Independent*, 4 December 2015, http://www.independent.co.uk/news/uk/home-news/sharia-courts-in-britain-lock-women-into-marital-captivity-study-says-a6761141.html; for the full study, see Machteld Zee, *Choosing Sharia* (The Hague: Eleven International Publishing, 2016).

14 Julie Billaud, 'Ethics and Affects in British Shariah Councils: "A Simple Way of Getting to Paradise"', in *Islam and Public Controversy in Europe*, ed. Nilüfer Göle (Burlington: Ashgate, 2014), 159–72; John R. Bowen, *On British Islam: Religion, Law, and Everyday Practice in Shari'a Councils* (Princeton, NJ: Princeton University Press, 2016); Rajnaara C. Akhtar, 'British Muslims and Transformative Processes of the Islamic Legal Traditions: Negotiating Law, Culture and Religion with Specific Reference to Islamic Family Law and Faith Based Alternative Dispute Resolution' (PhD diss., Warwick: University of Warwick, 2013), http://webcat.warwick.ac.uk/record=b2689316~S1; Elham Manea, *Women and Sharia Law: The Impact of Legal Pluralism in the UK* (London: I.B. Tauris, 2016); Nurin Shah-Kazemi, *Untying the Knot: Muslim Women, Divorce and the Sharia* (London: Nuffield Foundation, 2001).

15 Gillian Douglas et al., 'Social Cohesion and Civil Law: Marriage, Divorce and Religious Courts' (Cardiff: Cardiff University, 2011), http://www.law.cf.ac.uk/clr/Social%20Cohesion%20and%20Civil%20Law%20Full%20Report.pdf.

16 Douglas et al., 'Social Cohesion and Civil Law', 28. Douglas et al. derive this figure from a Civitas report and it is quoted by the authors with a degree of scepticism.

17 Prakash Shah, 'The Relationship between the Courts, Society and Civil Law: A Response' (Britain's Religious Courts: Marriage, Divorce and Civil Law, Cardiff University, 18 May 2011).

18 See the comparisons with Christian and Jewish divorce services in Douglas et al., 'Social Cohesion and Civil Law'.

19 Bowen, *On British Islam*, 61.

20 Billaud, 'Ethics and Affects in British Shariah Councils'.

21 Bano, 'Complexity, Difference and "Muslim Personal Law"', 306–10.

22 Bowen, *On British Islam*, 56.

23 This figure is from Douglas et al., 'Social Cohesion and Civil Law', 35–6.

24 David Pearl and Werner Menski, *Muslim Family Law*, 3rd edn (London: Sweet & Maxwell, 1998), 79.

25 The exact figure varies between one hundred and twenty thousand and one hundred and fifty thousand. Office for National Statistics, 'Divorce in the UK', Text, Office for National Statistics, 22 September 2014, http://www.ons.gov.uk/ons/about-ons/business-transparency/freedom-of-information/what-can-i-request/previous-foi-requests/population/the-number-of-people-divorced-in-the-uk-in-the-last-decade-/index.html.

26 Kaveri Qureshi, Katharine Charsley and Alison Shaw, 'Marital Instability among British Pakistanis: Transnationality, Conjugalities and Islam', *Ethnic and Racial Studies* 37, no. 2 (28 January 2014): 261–79, https://doi.org/10.1080/01419870.2012.720691.

27 Bano, 'Complexity, Difference and "Muslim Personal Law"', 122.

28 Ahl i-Hadith (literally, 'the people of *hadith*') is a South Asian Islamic movement that seeks to return to the scriptural sources of Islam and bears some comparison to

Salafi groups. Its presence in the UK is limited but it has some representatives in legal institutions.

29 Bano, 'Complexity, Difference and "Muslim Personal Law"', 122.

30 Pearl and Menski, *Muslim Family Law*, 74–7; see also Werner F. Menski, 'Angrezi Shariat: Glocalised Plural Arrangements by Migrants in Britain', *Law Vision*, no. 10 (2008): 10–12.

31 For an overview of the variants of talaq and the conditions that make it valid, as well as other forms of divorce available to women, see Judith E. Tucker, *Women, Family and Gender in Islamic Law* (Cambridge: Cambridge University Press, 2008), 86–100.

32 John R. Bowen, 'How Could English Courts Recognize Shariah?', *University of St. Thomas Law Journal* 7, no. 3 (19 September 2011): 414, http://ir.stthomas.edu/ustlj/vol7/iss3/3.

33 This stipulation, which was brought in as part of the Muslim Family Laws Ordinance 1961, has been partially eroded since the Zina Ordinance 1979, which introduced into the Pakistani legal system the possibility of abuse. See Abdullahi Ahmed An-Na'im, ed., *Islamic Family Law in a Changing World: A Global Resource Book* (London: Zed Books, 2002), 234.

34 See Ayelet Shachar, *Multicultural Jurisdictions: Cultural Differences and Women's Rights* (Cambridge: Cambridge University Press, 2001), 57–60.

35 See www.agunot-campaign.org.uk.

36 Jewish News, 'Legal First as Jail Threat Makes Man Grant "Get"', *Jewish News*, 15 January 2020, https://jewishnews.timesofisrael.com/chained-wife-wins-private-prosecution-to-force-ex-husband-to-grant-get/. I am grateful to Ralph Grillo and to the Pluri-Legal network for alerting me to this case.

37 Rajnaara C. Akhtar, 'Plural Approaches to Faith-Based Dispute Resolution by Britain's Muslim Communities', *Child and Family Law Quarterly* 31, no. 3 (2019): 189–209.

38 Douglas et al., 'Social Cohesion and Civil Law', 39; Richard Jones and Welhengama Gnanapala, *Ethnic Minorities in English Law* (Stoke-on-Trent: Trentham, 2000), 104; Ihsan Yilmaz, *Muslim Laws, Politics and Society in Modern Nation States* (Aldershot: Ashgate, 2005), 72; Samia Bano, 'Muslim Family Justice and Human Rights: The Experience of British Muslim Women', *Journal of Comparative Law* 2, no. 2 (2007): 15.

39 Rajnaara C. Akhtar, 'The Truth about Muslim Marriages' (Channel 4, 21 November 2017), https://assemble.me/uploads/websites/39/files/5a140876945ed.pdf.

40 Bano, 'Muslim Family Justice and Human Rights', 15.

41 Chris Nelson, 'Is the UK Turning a Blind Eye to Muslim Polygamy?', *Newsnight* (London: BBC2, 23 July 2009), http://news.bbc.co.uk/1/hi/programmes/newsnight/8164961.stm.

42 Akhtar, 'The Truth about Muslim Marriages'.

43 Aina Khan, 'Nikkah: To Register or Not to Register?' (Abrar House, London, 2 October 2015), http://www.thecitycircle.com/events/33-events/past-events/866-nikkah-to-register-or-not-to-register; https://www.youtube.com/watch?v=uJesuFkCUsE.

44 Miranda Phillips, 'Common Law Marriage: A Peculiarly Persistent Myth', NatCen Social Research, 22 January 2019, http://www.natcen.ac.uk/blog/common-law-marriage-a-peculiarly-persistent-myth. Under the Family Law (Scotland) Act 2006, cohabitants based in Scotland who separate have greater, but still limited, rights.

45 Rajnaara C. Akhtar, 'Modern Traditions in Muslim Marriage Practices, Exploring English Narratives', *Oxford Journal of Law and Religion*, 16 August 2018, 12, https://doi.org/10.1093/ojlr/rwy030.

46 Katharine Charsley, 'Risk, Trust, Gender and Transnational Cousin Marriage among British Pakistanis', *Ethnic and Racial Studies* 30, no. 6 (2007): 1117–31, https://doi.org/10.1080/01419870701599549.

47 Katharine Charsley and Anika Liversage, 'Transforming Polygamy: Migration, Transnationalism and Multiple Marriages among Muslim Minorities', *Global Networks* 13, no. 1 (2013): 66, https://doi.org/10.1111/j.1471-0374.2012.00369.x.

48 Abdul K. Barkatullah, 'Launch of the Muslim Marriage Contract' (Abrar House, London, 8 August 2008).

49 Usama Hasan, 'Launch of the Muslim Marriage Contract' (Abrar House, London, 9 November 2008).

50 Cassandra Balchin, 'Kingdom of God: The Archbishop, the Shari'a and the Law of the Land' (Abrar House, London, 18 February 2008), http://www.thecitycircle.com/blog2.php?cann_id=532&vid=1502083.

51 Akhtar, 'Modern Traditions in Muslim Marriage Practices, Exploring English Narratives', 19–20.

52 Zygmunt Bauman, *Liquid Love: On the Frailty of Human Bonds* (Cambridge: Polity, 2003).

53 Akhtar, 'Modern Traditions in Muslim Marriage Practices, Exploring English Narratives', 3.

54 I draw extensively in this section on the following publications: Charsley, 'Risk, Trust, Gender and Transnational Cousin Marriage among British Pakistanis'; Qureshi, Charsley and Shaw, 'Marital Instability among British Pakistanis'; Alison Shaw, 'Kinship, Cultural Preference and Immigration: Consanguineous Marriage among British Pakistanis', *Journal of the Royal Anthropological Institute* 7, no. 2 (1 June 2001): 315–34, https://doi.org/10.1111/1467-9655.00065; Yunas Samad and John Eade, 'Community Perceptions of Forced Marriage' (London: Community Liaison Unit, Foreign and Commonwealth Office, 2002); Bano, 'Complexity, Difference and "Muslim Personal Law"'; Roger Ballard, 'Inside and Outside: Contrasting Perspectives on the Dynamics of Kinship and Marriage in Contemporary South Asian Transnational Networks', in *The Family in Question: Immigrant and Ethnic Minorities in Multicultural Europe*, 1st edn, ed. Ralph Grillo (Amsterdam: Amsterdam University Press, 2014), 37–70.

55 Ballard, 'Inside and Outside', 49–50.

56 Shaw, 'Kinship, Cultural Preference and Immigration'; Neil Small et al., 'Endogamy, Consanguinity and the Health Implications of Changing Marital Choices in the UK Pakistani Community', *Journal of Biosocial Science* 49, no. 4 (July 2017): 435–46, https://doi.org/10.1017/S0021932016000419.

57 Small et al., 'Endogamy, Consanguinity and the Health Implications of Changing Marital Choices in the UK Pakistani Community'. The wider project from which this publication emerges, 'Born in Bradford', offers an excellent example of how to work with communities on these and other sensitive health issues. See https://borninbradford.nhs.uk/.

58 Charsley, 'Risk, Trust, Gender and Transnational Cousin Marriage among British Pakistanis'.

59 Samad and Eade, 'Community Perceptions of Forced Marriage', 39.

60 Charsley, 'Risk, Trust, Gender and Transnational Cousin Marriage among British Pakistanis', 1122.

61 Charsley, 'Risk, Trust, Gender and Transnational Cousin Marriage among British Pakistanis', 1122.

62 Bano, 'Complexity, Difference and "Muslim Personal Law"', 108.

63 See Bano, 'Complexity, Difference and "Muslim Personal Law"', 100–2; Fauzia Ahmad, 'Graduating towards Marriage? Attitudes towards Marriage and Relationships among University-Educated British Muslim Women', *Culture and Religion* 13, no. 3 (2012): 193–210, https://doi.org/10.1080/14755610.2012.674953; Gita Sahgal and Nira Yuval-Davis, eds, *Refusing Holy Orders: Women and Fundamentalism in Britain* (London: Virago, 1992).

64 Samad and Eade, 'Community Perceptions of Forced Marriage', 76.

65 Shah-Kazemi, *Untying the Knot: Muslim Women, Divorce and the Sharia*, 22.

66 Bano, 'Complexity, Difference and "Muslim Personal Law"', 98.

67 Bowen, *On British Islam*, 69.

68 Billaud, 'Ethics and Affects in British Shariah Councils', 161.

69 Bano, 'Complexity, Difference and "Muslim Personal Law"', 103.

70 Ballard, 'Inside and Outside'.

71 Sundari Anitha, Anupama Roy and Harshita Yalamarty, *Disposable Women: Abuse, Violence and Abandonment in Transnational Marriages: Issues for Policy and Practice in the UK and India* (Lincoln: University of Lincoln, 2016).

72 Alan Travis, '1.4 Million Women Suffered Domestic Abuse Last Year, ONS Figures Show', *The Guardian*, 12 February 2015, sec. Society, http://www.theguardian.com/society/2015/feb/12/14-million-women-suffered-domestic-abuse-last-year-ons-figures-show.

73 Nira Yuval-Davis, Floya Anthias and Eleonore Kofman, 'Secure Borders and Safe Haven and the Gendered Politics of Belonging: Beyond Social Cohesion', *Ethnic and Racial Studies* 28, no. 3 (2005): 519–20.

74 Anitha, Roy and Yalamarty, 'Disposable Women', 33.

75 Anitha, Roy and Yalamarty, 'Disposable Women', 5.

76 For example, the Forced Marriage (Civil Protection) Act 2007, which introduced Forced Marriage Protection Orders.

77 Rebecca Probert and Liam D'arcy Brown, 'The Impact of the Clandestine Marriages Act: Three Case-Studies in Conformity', *Continuity and Change* 23, no. 2 (August 2008): 309–30, https://doi.org/10.1017/S0268416008006759.

78 Ihsan Yilmaz, 'Law as Chameleon: The Question of Incorporation of Muslim Personal Law into the English Law', *Journal of Muslim Minority Affairs* 21, no. 2 (October 2001): 297–308.

79 Bowen, *On British Islam*, 52–3.

80 See Bowen, 'How Could English Courts Recognize Shariah?'

81 Bowen, *On British Islam*, 53, 62.

82 For a full overview of relevant legislation see Law Commission, 'Getting Married: A Scoping Paper' (London: Law Commission, 2015), 36–7, http://www.lawcom.gov.uk/wp-content/uploads/2015/12/Getting_Married_scoping_paper.pdf.

83 Law Commission, 'Getting Married: A Scoping Paper', 35–41.

84 John Bingham, 'British Marriage Laws Are "Hopelessly Out of Date", Government Told', 16 December 2015, http://www.telegraph.co.uk/news/religion/12055060/British-marriage-laws-are-hopelessly-out-of-date-government-told.html.

85 Law Commission, 'Government Asks Law Commission to Conduct a Full Review of Weddings Law', 8 November 2018, https://www.lawcom.gov.uk/government-asks-law-commission-to-conduct-a-full-review-of-weddings-law/.

86 Faizal A. Siddiqi, 'Kingdom of God: The Archbishop, the Shari'a and the Law of the Land' (Abrar House, London, 18 February 2008), http://www.thecitycircle.com/blog2.php?cann_id=532.

87   Pearl and Menski, *Muslim Family Law*, 303.
88   Zaki Badawi, 'Muslim Justice in a Secular State', in *God's Law versus State Law* (London: Grey Seal, 1995), 73–80; Yilmaz, 'Law as Chameleon', 303.
89   Chetan Bhatt, 'The Fetish of the Margins: Religious Absolutism, Anti-Racism and Postcolonial Silence', *New Formations* 59 (2006): 103.
90   Quoted in Bowen, *On British Islam*, 62–3.
91   Billaud, 'Ethics and Affects in British Shariah Councils', 164.
92   Bowen, *On British Islam*, 124.
93   Islamic Shari'a Council, 'ISC Standing on the Muslim Marriage Contract' (Islamic Shari'a Council, 2008), http://www.islamic-sharia.org/news/isc-standing-on-the-marriage-contract.html.
94   Bowen, *On British Islam*, 96 and 104–8.
95   For an overview and example cases, see Bowen, 'How Could English Courts Recognize Shariah?'; for a wide-ranging discussion encompassing a range of European states, see Rubya Mehdi and Jørgen S. Nielsen, eds, *Embedding Mahr in the European Legal System* (Copenhagen: DJØF, 2011).
96   Bowen, *On British Islam*, 49–50.
97   Bowen, *On British Islam*, 80.
98   Bano, 'Complexity, Difference and "Muslim Personal Law"', 173–4.
99   Bano, 'Complexity, Difference and "Muslim Personal Law"', 248. The scholar's position in this third quote seems to be based on perhaps the most controversial verse in the Qur'an (4:34), which appears to permit husbands to hit their wives if they are being 'disobedient' (*nushuz*). One of the most common interpretations of this verse is that it authorizes a single light strike, but not repeated abuse or grievous violence. Some of the scholars based in Islamic dispute resolution institutions read the verse in a different way, suggesting the verse can only be read as endorsement to lightly push one's wife away. See Bowen, *On British Islam*, 160–1.
100 Bowen, 'How Could English Courts Recognize Shariah?', 420; Billaud, 'Ethics and Affects in British Shariah Councils', 167.
101 See Bowen, *On British Islam*; Douglas et al., 'Social Cohesion and Civil Law'; Billaud, 'Ethics and Affects in British Shariah Councils'.
102 Interview, 25 February 2009.
103 Humayun Ansari, *The Infidel Within: Muslims in Britain since 1800* (London: C. Hurst, 2004), 229–30.
104 Ahmad Thomson, 'The Relationship between the Courts, Society and Civil Law: A Response' (Britain's Religious Courts: Marriage, Divorce and Civil Law, Cardiff University, 18 May 2011), http://www.wynnechambers.co.uk/pdf/Britains_Religious_Courts_Society_&_Civil_Law.pdf.
105 Samia Bano, 'Muslim South Asian Women and Customary Law in Britain', *Journal of South Pacific Law* 4 (2000), http://www.paclii.org/journals/fJSPL/vol04/6.shtml.
106 Saeed quoted in Bano, 'Complexity, Difference and "Muslim Personal Law"', 193.
107 Siddiqi, 'Kingdom of God: The Archbishop, the Shari'a and the Law of the Land'.
108 Simon Rocker, 'Men Who Refuse a Get May Lose Burial Rights', *Jewish Chronicle*, 12 November 2015, http://www.thejc.com/news/uk-news/149144/men-who-refuse-a-get-may-lose-burial-rights.
109 Yilmaz, 'Law as Chameleon', 299.
110 Zaki Badawi, 'True Submission? An Interview with Zaki Badawi', *Third Way*, 23 April 1996, http://www.thirdway.org.uk/past/showpage.asp?page=3923.
111 Bano, 'Complexity, Difference and "Muslim Personal Law"', 193–4.

112 Amra Bone, 'The Relationship between the Courts, Society and Civil Law: A Response' (Britain's Religious Courts: Marriage, Divorce and Civil Law, Cardiff University, 18 May 2011).

113 Bano, 'Complexity, Difference and "Muslim Personal Law"', 194.

114 Interview, 11 September 2008.

115 Hasan affiliated with militant Salafi groups in his youth but separated from these and the mosque at which he had previously worked, Masjid al-Tawhid, following an ugly factional dispute in which personal animus and theological divisions became blurred. He joined Quilliam following his expulsion from the mosque's board of trustees (see Chapter 5 for further details).

116 Syed M. Darsh, *Questions and Answers about Islam* (London: TaHa, 1997).

117 Bowen, *On British Islam*, 92 and 215.

118 Bokhari quoted in Bowen, *On British Islam*, 92.

119 For some examples, see Bowen, *On British Islam*, 75–6, 82, 85.

120 Barkatullah, 'Launch of the Muslim Marriage Contract'.

121 Bowen, *On British Islam*, 82.

122 Maleiha Malik, 'Minority Legal Orders in the UK: Minorities, Pluralism and the Law' (London: British Academy Policy Centre, 2012), http://www.britac.ac.uk/policy/ Minority-legal-orders.cfm.

123 Maryam Namazie, '395 Signatories Call to Dismantle Parallel Legal Systems', *One Law for All* (blog), 9 October 2015, http://www.onelawforall.org.uk/sharia-courts/.

124 Shachar, *Multicultural Jurisdictions*.

125 Anne Phillips, *Multiculturalism without Culture* (Princeton, NJ: Princeton University Press, 2007), 150–7.

126 Bowen, *On British Islam*, 61–4.

127 Douglas et al., 'Social Cohesion and Civil Law', 43.

128 On this case, see Bowen, 'How Could English Courts Recognize Shariah?'; Malik, 'Minority Legal Orders in the UK', 45. Malik actually interprets this judgement as an example of 'mainstreaming', but the one-off nature of the accommodation means it fits better, in my view, into the category of cultural voluntarism.

129 Mona Siddiqui et al., 'The Independent Review into the Application of Sharia Law in England and Wales' (London: Counter Extremism Unit, 2018), https://www.gov.uk/ government/publications/applying-sharia-law-in-england-and-wales-independent- review.

130 For a thorough critique of this proposal, which echoes the wider arguments of this chapter, see Russell Sandberg, 'Criminalising Imams Will Not Solve the Problem of Unregistered Marriages', *Family Law* (blog), 15 January 2019, https://www.familylaw. co.uk/news_and_comment/criminalising-imams-will-not-solve-the-problem-of- unregistered-marriages.

131 Interview, 11 September 2008.

132 Akhtar, 'Modern Traditions in Muslim Marriage Practices, Exploring English Narratives', 17.

133 Stephanie Pywell and Rebecca Probert, 'Neither Sacred nor Profane: The Permitted Content of Civil Marriage Ceremonies', *Child and Family Law Quarterly* 30 (December 2018): 415–36.

134 It is important to note that since Balchin made that comment prenuptial agreements have been given greater recognition in English law. Following the case of *Radmacher v. Granatino* in 2010 prenuptial agreements are now considered legally binding unless they are deemed to be unfair by a court (especially to children).

135 See Bowen, *On British Islam*, 225–8.
136 In particular, John Rawls, *Political Liberalism* (New York: Columbia University Press, 2005).
137 Stephen Prothero, *Religious Literacy: What Every American Needs to Know – and Doesn't* (New York: Harper, 2008), 29.
138 Paul F. Campos, 'Secular Fundamentalism', *Columbia Law Review* 94, no. 6 (1994): 1814–27.
139 T. S. Shah quoted in Robert Furbey, 'Controversies of "Public Faith"', in *Faith in the Public Realm: Controversies Policies and Practices*, ed. Adam Dinham, Robert Furbey and Vivien Lowndes (Bristol: Policy Press, 2009), 32.
140 For a rebuttal see Martha Nussbaum, 'Rawls's Political Liberalism: A Reassessment', *Ratio Juris* 24, no. 1 (2011): 1–24; Stephen de Wijze, 'Shamanistic Incantations? Rawls, Reasonableness and Secular Fundamentalism', *Politics and Ethics Review* 3, no. 1 (2007): 109–28.
141 Christopher Eberle, *Religious Conviction in Liberal Politics* (New York: Cambridge University Press, 2002). Eberle uses this phrase in a more expansive way than the person who coined it, Gerald F. Gaus.
142 They also stem from the fact that Rawls developed his position on public reason over an extended period and revised it significantly in 'The Idea of Public Reason Revisited'. The version of *Political Liberalism* I cite here includes 'The Idea ...' as an additional chapter.
143 Rawls, *Political Liberalism*, 443–4.
144 For an example of an (otherwise astute) author who sees no significant difference between 'public' and 'secular' reasons, see Jonathan Chaplin, *Talking God: The Legitimacy of Religious Public Reasoning* (London: Theos, 2008).
145 Rawls, *Political Liberalism*, 462.
146 Eberle, *Religious Conviction in Liberal Politics*, 9, my emphasis.
147 Rawls, *Political Liberalism*, 444.
148 Rawls, *Political Liberalism*, xxxviii, see also xl–xli; 144–50.
149 John Rawls, 'Justice as Fairness: Political Not Metaphysical', *Philosophy and Public Affairs* 14, no. 3 (1985): 223–51.
150 Bader thus describes political values as 'under-determined'. Veit Bader, 'Secularism, Public Reason, or Moderately Agnostic Democracy?', in *Secularism, Religion and Multicultural Citizenship* (Cambridge: Cambridge University Press, 2009), 126.
151 See Bhikhu Parekh, *Rethinking Multiculturalism: Cultural Diversity and Political Theory* (London: Palgrave Macmillan, 2000); Chantal Mouffe, 'Deliberative Democracy or Agonistic Pluralism', *Reihe Politikwissenschaft: Political Science Series*, no. 72 (December 2000), http://www.ihs.ac.at/publications/pol/pw_72.pdf.
152 Rawls, *Political Liberalism*, 453.
153 William Connolly, *Why I Am Not a Secularist* (London: University of Minnesota Press, 1999), 64.
154 Rawls, *Political Liberalism*, xix.
155 Rawls, *Political Liberalism*, 454.
156 David A. Reidy, 'Rawls's Wide View of Public Reason: Not Wide Enough', *Res Publica* 6, no. 1 (1 January 2000): 51.
157 Andrew F. March, *Islam and Liberal Citizenship: The Search for an Overlapping Consensus* (Oxford: Oxford University Press, 2009).
158 Khadijah Elshayyal, *Muslim Identity Politics: Islam, Activism and Equality in Britain* (London: I.B. Tauris, 2018).

159 Siddiqui et al., 'The Independent Review into the Application of Sharia Law in England and Wales', 6.
160 Harriet Sherwood, 'Register Islamic Marriages under Civil Law, Sharia Review Says', *The Guardian*, 1 February 2018, sec. Law, https://www.theguardian.com/law/2018/feb/01/sharia-councils-review-islamic-marriages-uk-law.
161 Hannah Summers, 'UK Courts Should Be Able to Issue Islamic Divorces, Sharia Expert Says', *The Guardian*, 4 September 2016, sec. Law, https://www.theguardian.com/law/2016/sep/04/uk-courts-should-be-able-to-issue-islamic-divorces-sharia-expert-says.
162 Bowen, *On British Islam*, 217.

Chapter 5: Muslims and the State: Neither Agents Nor Enemies

1 A. J. Arberry, *Discourses of Rumi* (London: John Murray, 1961), 13.
2 See, for example, Roger Scruton, *The West and the Rest: Globalisation and the Terrorist Threat* (London: Continuum, 2002), 4.
3 Not every *hadith* is considered authentic (*sahih*), with some having a more reliable 'chain of transmission' (*isnad*) than others. According to Arberry, Rumi is quoting al-Ghazali's (1058–1111) magnum opus the *Ihya*, arguably the greatest work of Sunni Muslim spirituality. I am unable to comment on its provenance beyond that.
4 Abdullahi Ahmed An-Na'im, *Islam and the Secular State: Negotiating the Future of the Shari'a* (Cambridge, MA: Harvard University Press, 2008). One can also point to several concepts in Islamic jurisprudence that illustrate the sophistication of classical Islamic political thought: *maqasid* (objectives/rights), *maslaha* (common good), *shura* (consultation) and the distinction between *ibadat* (worship) and *mu'amalat* (public affairs).
5 Therese O'Toole et al., 'Taking Part: Muslim Participation in Contemporary Governance' (Bristol: University of Bristol, 2013).
6 Anne Phillips, *The Politics of Presence* (Oxford: Oxford University Press, 1995).
7 I borrow this phrase from Michael Saward, 'Authorisation and Authenticity: Representation and the Unelected', *Journal of Political Philosophy* 17, no. 1 (1 March 2009): 3.
8 See Parveen Akhtar, 'British Muslim Political Participation: After Bradford', *The Political Quarterly* 83, no. 4 (1 October 2012): 762–6, https://doi.org/10.1111/j.1467-923X.2012.02352.x; David Sanders et al., 'The Democratic Engagement of Britain's Ethnic Minorities', *Ethnic and Racial Studies* 37, no. 1 (2014): 120–39; Manlio Cinalli and Marco Giugni, 'Electoral Participation of Muslims in Europe: Assessing the Impact of Institutional and Discursive Opportunities', *Journal of Ethnic and Migration Studies* 42, no. 2 (26 January 2016): 309–24, https://doi.org/10.1080/1369183X.2015.1102043.
9 Timothy Peace, 'Muslims and Electoral Politics in Britain: The Case of the Respect Party', in *Muslim Political Participation in Europe*, ed. Jørgen S. Nielsen (Edinburgh: Edinburgh University Press, 2013), 299–321.
10 Parveen Akhtar, *British Muslim Politics: Examining Pakistani Biraderi Networks* (Basingstoke: Palgrave Macmillan, 2013); Kingsley Purdam, 'Democracy in Practice: Muslims and the Labour Party at the Local Level', *Politics* 21, no. 3 (1 September 2001): 147–57, https://doi.org/10.1111/1467-9256.00146.

11 Jonathan Birt, 'Lobbying and Marching: British Muslims and the State', in *Muslim Britain: Communities under Pressure*, ed. Tahir Abbas (London: Zed Books, 2005), 92–106.

12 Sadek Hamid, *Sufis, Salafis and Islamists: The Contested Ground of British Islamic Activism* (London: I.B. Tauris, 2015).

13 See http://aobm.org/. On Quilliam see Ron Geaves, *Islam in Victorian Britain: The Life and Times of Abdullah Quilliam* (Markfield: Kube, 2010).

14 On these associations, see respectively: Stephen H. Jones, 'The "Metropolis of Dissent": Muslim Participation in Leicester and the "Failure" of Multiculturalism in Britain', *Ethnic and Racial Studies* 38, no. 11 (2 September 2015): 1969–85, https://doi.org/10.1080/01419870.2014.936891; Marta Bolognani and Paul Statham, 'The Changing Public Face of Muslim Associations in Britain: Coming Together for Common "Social" Goals?', *Ethnicities* 13, no. 2 (1 April 2013): 229–49, https://doi.org/10.1177/1468796812470892; Philip Lewis, *Islamic Britain* (London: I.B. Tauris, 2002), 58.

15 For a detailed critique of this assumption, see Jed Fazakarley, *Muslim Communities in England 1962–90: Multiculturalism and Political Identity* (Cham, Switzerland: Palgrave Macmillan, 2017).

16 Fazakarley, *Muslim Communities in England 1962–90*, 80.

17 See the account of Asian Youth Movements in Timothy Peace, *European Social Movements and Muslim Activism: Another World but with Whom?* (Basingstoke: Palgrave Macmillan, 2015), 37–9.

18 Humayun Ansari, *The Infidel Within: Muslims in Britain since 1800* (London: C. Hurst, 2004), 309–17.

19 Ansari, *The Infidel Within*, 361.

20 Ansari, *The Infidel Within*, 349; Hamid, *Sufis, Salafis and Islamists*, 6.

21 Hamid, *Sufis, Salafis and Islamists*, 80. The term 'neo-Sufi' is occasionally used to describe Sufi-influenced movements in the West that are not aligned with traditional Sufi orders (such as the Chishti, Naqshabandi and Qadiri orders).

22 Hamid, *Sufis, Salafis and Islamists*, 13; see also Khadijah Elshayyal, *Muslim Identity Politics: Islam, Activism and Equality in Britain* (London: I.B. Tauris, 2018), 64–74.

23 Anabel Inge, *The Making of a Salafi Muslim Woman: Paths to Conversion* (London: Oxford University Press, 2016).

24 Azzam Tamimi, 'Islam and Democracy from Tahtawi to Ghannouchi', *Theory, Culture & Society* 24, no. 2 (1 March 2007): 52.

25 Stephen H. Jones, 'New Labour and the Re-Making of British Islam: The Case of the Radical Middle Way and the "Reclamation" of the Classical Islamic Tradition', *Religions* 4, no. 4 (4 November 2013): 550–66.

26 Interview, 26 August 2008.

27 On these two individuals see, respectively, Hamid, *Sufis, Salafis and Islamists*, 22; Lewis, *Islamic Britain*, 58.

28 Hamid, *Sufis, Salafis and Islamists*, 23.

29 Philip Lewis, *Young, British and Muslim* (London: Continuum, 2007).

30 On violent Islamist movements in the UK, including Salafi and Hizb offshoots, see Philip Lewis and Sadek Hamid, *British Muslims: New Directions in Islamic Thought, Creativity and Activism* (Edinburgh: Edinburgh University Press, 2018), 134–54.

31 Hamid, *Sufis, Salafis and Islamists*, 26; on Ghannouchi's understanding of democracy see Tamimi, 'Islam and Democracy from Tahtawi to Ghannouchi'.

32 See A. Sivanandan, *Communities of Resistance: Writings on Black Struggles for Socialism* (London: Verso, 1990).

33 Peace, *European Social Movements and Muslim Activism*, 38.

34 Daniel Nilsson DeHanas, *London Youth, Religion, and Politics: Engagement and Activism from Brixton to Brick Lane* (Oxford: Oxford University Press, 2016); J. Eade and D. Garbin, 'Competing Visions of Identity and Space: Bangladeshi Muslims in Britain', *Contemporary South Asia* 15, no. 2 (2006): 181–93.

35 I do not have space to discuss *The Satanic Verses* itself here, but I would highlight the superb analyses of the book and of the response to Muslims' protests in the last two chapters of Talal Asad, *Genealogies of Religion: Discipline and Reasons of Power in Christianity and Islam* (London: John Hopkins University Press, 1993).

36 See, for example, the diverse accounts of Anthony McRoy, *From Rushdie to 7/7: The Radicalisation of Islam in Britain* (London: Social Affairs Unit, 2006); Kenan Malik, *From Fatwa to Jihad: The Rushdie Affair and Its Legacy* (London: Atlantic Books, 2009); Akhtar, *British Muslim Politics*.

37 Fazakarley, *Muslim Communities in England 1962–90*, 9.

38 For a short overview of these episodes, see Grace Davie, *Religion in Modern Europe: A Memory Mutates* (Oxford: Oxford University Press, 2000), 126–9.

39 For example, Malik, *From Fatwa to Jihad: The Rushdie Affair and Its Legacy*; Nick Cohen, *What's Left? How the Left Lost Its Way* (London: Fourth Estate, 2007).

40 Fazakarley, *Muslim Communities in England 1962–90*, 9.

41 Nasar Meer, *Citizenship, Identity and the Politics of Multiculturalism: The Rise of Muslim Consciousness* (Basingstoke: Palgrave Macmillan, 2010), 75.

42 Tariq Modood, 'Muslims, Race and Equality in Britain: Some Post-Rushdie Affair Reflections', *Third Text* 4, no. 11 (1 June 1990): 127–34, https://doi.org/10.1080/09528829008576269; Meer, *Citizenship, Identity and the Politics of Multiculturalism*, 75.

43 See, inter alia, Tariq Modood, 'Political Blackness and British Asians', *Sociology* 28, no. 4 (1 November 1994): 859–76.

44 Some of Modood's essays on the Rushdie affair are collected in Tariq Modood, *Still Not Easy Being British: Struggles for a Multicultural Citizenship* (London: Trentham, 2010).

45 Chetan Bhatt, *Liberation and Purity: Race, New Religious Movements and the Ethics of Postmodernity* (London: Routledge, 1997), 112–25.

46 Hamid, *Sufis, Salafis and Islamists*.

47 Kalim Siddiqui, 'The Muslim Manifesto: A Strategy for Survival' (The Muslim Parliament, n.d.), http://www.muslimparliament.org.uk/MuslimManifesto.pdf.

48 I am grateful to Shanon Shah for his insights into the Institute's work on LGBT issues.

49 David Herbert, *Religion and Civil Society: Rethinking Public Religion in the Contemporary World* (Aldershot: Ashgate, 2003), 186–7.

50 Bhatt, *Liberation and Purity*, 120.

51 Interview, 25 February 2009. For further accounts of this episode, see Ansari, *The Infidel Within*, 364; Seán McLoughlin, 'The State, New Muslim Leaderships and Islam as a Resource for Public Engagement in Britain', in *European Muslims and the Secular State*, ed. Jocelyne Cesari and Seán McLoughlin (Aldershot: Ashgate, 2005), 60; Birt, 'Lobbying and Marching', 99.

52 Elshayyal, *Muslim Identity Politics*, 91. The Board of Deputies was established in 1760. See https://www.bod.org.uk/.

53 Konrad Pedziwiatr, 'Creating New Discursive Arenas and Influencing the Policies of the State: The Case of the Muslim Council of Britain', *Social Compass* 54, no. 2 (2007): 267–80. At the time this article was published, the MCB listed some four hundred affiliates but this number included regional branches of other organizations listed. The umbrella group currently claims to have 'over 500' member organizations.

54 Yahya Birt, 'The Next Ten Years: An Open Letter to the MCB', *Musings on the Britannic Crescent* (blog), 27 June 2008, http://www.yahyabirt.com/?p=146.

55 After Robert D. Putnam, *Bowling Alone: The Collapse and Revival of American Community* (New York: Simon & Schuster, 2001).

56 See, among many similar reports, Department of Communities and Local Government, 'Face to Face and Side by Side: A Framework for Partnership in Our Multi Faith Society' (London: HMSO, July 2008).

57 See Adam Dinham, *Faiths, Public Policy and Civil Society: Problems, Policies, Controversies* (Basingstoke: Palgrave Macmillan, 2009); Adam Dinham and Vivien Lowndes, 'Religion, Resources and Representation: Three Narratives of Faith Engagement in British Urban Governance', *Urban Affairs Review* 43, no. 6 (2008): 817–45; Rachael Chapman and Vivien Lowndes, 'Faith in Governance? The Potential and Pitfalls of Involving Faith Groups in Urban Governance', *Planning, Practice & Research* 23, no. 1 (2008): 57–75.

58 Inner Cities Religious Council, 'Review of the Inner Cities Religious Council: A Report of the Review Team' (London: HMSO, 1998).

59 Department of Communities and Local Government, 'Face to Face and Side by Side', 39–40.

60 For an overview of this shift, see Janet Newman, *Remaking Governance: Peoples, Politics and the Public Sphere* (Bristol: Policy Press, 2005); for a discussion of the UK case, see R. A. W. Rhodes, 'The New Governance: Governing without Government', *Political Studies* 44, no. 3 (1996): 652–67; for a study of British Muslims and governance, see O'Toole et al., 'Taking Part'.

61 See Mark Bevir, 'Governance and Governmentality after Neoliberalism', *Policy & Politics* 39, no. 4 (2011): 457–71.

62 Mike Geddes, 'Neoliberalism and Local Governance: Cross-National Perspectives and Speculations', *Policy Studies* 26, nos. 3/4 (2005): 361.

63 Stephen H. Jones et al., 'A "System of Self-Appointed Leaders"? Examining Modes of Muslim Representation in Governance in Britain', *British Journal of Politics and International Relations* 17, no. 2 (2015): 210, https://doi.org/10.1111/1467-856X.12051; for a detailed account of campaigning around the census, see Jamil Sherif, 'A Census Chronicle: Reflections on the Campaign for a Religion Question in the 2001 Census for England and Wales', *Journal of Beliefs & Values* 32, no. 1 (2011): 1–18, https://doi.org/10.1080/13617672.2011.549306.

64 For example, one of New Labour's projects between 1997 and 2010 was to expand and consolidate legislation outlawing discrimination on the basis of personal characteristics, notably via the Equality Act 2010.

65 I base these comments on interviews with Denham and Straw conducted by my colleagues for the 'Muslim Participation in Contemporary Governance' project. See also O'Toole et al., 'Taking Part'; Jones et al., 'A "System of Self-Appointed Leaders"?'

66 McLoughlin, 'The State, New Muslim Leaderships and Islam as a Resource for Public Engagement in Britain'.

67 Interview with Bora, 6 March 2012, quoted in Jones, 'New Labour and the Re-Making of British Islam', 558.

68 Abdul-Rehman Malik, 'Take Me to Your Leader: Post-Secular Society and the Islam Industry', *Eurozine*, 23 April 2007, http://www.eurozine.com/articles/2007-04-23-armalik-en.html.

69 Interview, 11 November 2008.

70 Chetan Bhatt, 'The Fetish of the Margins: Religious Absolutism, Anti-Racism and Postcolonial Silence', *New Formations* 59 (2006): 98–115; Gita Sahgal and Nira Yuval-Davis, eds, *Refusing Holy Orders: Women and Fundamentalism in Britain* (London: Virago, 1992).

71 Sunny Hundal, 'This System of Self-Appointed Leaders Can Hurt Those It Should Be Protecting', *The Guardian*, 20 November 2006, sec. Comment is Free, http://www.theguardian.com/commentisfree/2006/nov/20/thissystemofselfappointedl; Malik, *From Fatwa to Jihad: The Rushdie Affair and Its Legacy*.

72 Alana Lentin, 'Post-Race, Post Politics: The Paradoxical Rise of Culture after Multiculturalism', *Ethnic and Racial Studies* 37, no. 8 (3 July 2014): 1277–8, https://doi.org/10.1080/01419870.2012.664278.

73 Peace, *European Social Movements and Muslim Activism*, 39.

74 Lentin, 'Post-Race, Post Politics'; see also Paul Gilroy, *There Ain't No Black in the Union Jack: The Cultural Politics of Race and Nation* (London: Routledge, 2002); Gita Sahgal, 'Two Cheers for Multiculturalism', in *Warning Signs of Fundamentalisms*, ed. Ayesha Imam, Jenny Morgan and Nira Yuval-Davis (London: WLUML, 2004), 51–60; Sukhwant Dhaliwal and Nira Yuval-Davis, eds, *Women against Fundamentalism: Stories of Dissent and Solidarity* (London: Lawrence & Wishart, 2014).

75 Arun Kundnani, *The End of Tolerance: Racism in 21st Century Britain* (London: Pluto Press, 2007), 181.

76 MCB quoted in McLoughlin, 'The State, New Muslim Leaderships and Islam as a Resource for Public Engagement in Britain', 60.

77 See Tariq Modood, '2011 Paul Hanly Furfey Lecture: Is There a Crisis of Secularism in Western Europe?', *Sociology of Religion* 73, no. 2 (4 May 2012): 130–49; José Casanova, 'Immigration and the New Religious Pluralism: A European Union-United States Comparison', in *Secularism, Religion and Multicultural Citizenship*, ed. Geoffrey Brahm Levey and Tariq Modood (Cambridge: Cambridge University Press, 2009), 139–63.

78 Tariq Modood, *Multiculturalism: A Civic Idea* (Cambridge: Polity, 2007), 136; quoting Peter Jones, 'Equality, Recognition and Difference', *Critical Review of International Social and Political Philosophy* 9, no. 1 (2006): 29.

79 Malik, 'Take Me to Your Leader: Post-Secular Society and the Islam Industry'.

80 Muslim Council of Britain, *Towards Greater Understanding: Meeting the Needs of Muslim Pupils in State Schools* (London: MCB, 2007), 44, 53.

81 It is worth noting that, while aniconism is dominant in the Islamic tradition, there are established and widely practiced Islamic artistic traditions, notably miniature paintings, that involve depicting humans.

82 John Holmwood and Therese O'Toole, *Countering Extremism in British Schools: The Truth about the Birmingham Trojan Horse Affair* (Bristol: Policy Press, 2018), 89–97.

83 British Muslims for Secular Democracy, 'Advice for Schools: Brief Guidance for Handling Muslim Parental Concern' (London: BMSD, 2010), http://www.bmsd.org.uk/pdfs/schools.pdf.

84 Anne Phillips, *Multiculturalism without Culture* (Princeton, NJ: Princeton University Press, 2007), 8.

85 Elshayyal, *Muslim Identity Politics*.
86 The introduction of state-funded Islamic schools is one arguable exception to this. It is a development I have reservations about myself, but it is hard to argue against such schools being set up when Christian state schools are so common.
87 Birt, 'Lobbying and Marching', 94.
88 See Ron Geaves, 'Negotiating British Citizenship and Muslim Identity', in *Muslim Britain: Communities under Pressure*, ed. Tahir Abbas (London: Zed Books, 2005), 66–77.
89 Richard Phillips, 'Standing Together: The Muslim Association of Britain and the Anti-War Movement', *Race & Class* 50, no. 2 (1 October 2008): 101–13, https://doi.org/10.1177/0306396808096396; on the relationship between the MAB and other elements of the Stop the War Coalition, see Peace, *European Social Movements and Muslim Activism*.
90 On the local impact of the Iraq war on election outcomes, see Jones, 'The "Metropolis of Dissent"'; on Respect, see Peace, 'Muslims and Electoral Politics in Britain: The Case of the Respect Party'.
91 This decision was purportedly the result of the MCB's frustration at the absence of public recognition of Palestinians' sovereignty and human rights, but, by conflating anti-Semitism and the Holocaust with the contemporary politics of Israel, it did little more than make the MCB appear prejudiced towards Jews.
92 Jeffrey C. Alexander, 'Struggling over the Mode of Incorporation: Backlash against Multiculturalism in Europe', *Ethnic and Racial Studies* 36, no. 4 (2013): 531–56; Christian Joppke, 'The Retreat of Multiculturalism in the Liberal State: Theory and Policy', *British Journal of Sociology* 55, no. 2 (2004): 237–57; Gilles Kepel, 'Europe's Answer to Londonistan', *OpenDemocracy*, 24 August 2005, http://www.opendemocracy.net/conflict-terrorism/londonistan_2775.jsp.
93 Jones, 'The "Metropolis of Dissent"'.
94 Nasar Meer and Tariq Modood, 'The Multicultural State We're in: Muslims, "Multiculture" and the "Civic Re-balancing" of British Multiculturalism', *Political Studies* 57, no. 3 (2009): 473–97; Modood, '2011 Paul Hanly Furfey Lecture: Is There a Crisis of Secularism in Western Europe?'
95 Ruth Kelly, 'Britain: Our Values, Our Responsibilities', British Embassy Berlin, 10 October 2006, http://ukingermany.fco.gov.uk/en/news/?view=Speech&id=4615992.
96 See, inter alia, Martin Bright, 'When Progressives Treat with Reactionaries: The British State's Flirtation with Radical Islamism'. (London: Policy Exchange, 2006); Shiraz Maher and Martyn Frampton, 'Choosing Our Friends Wisely: Criteria for Engagement with Muslim Groups' (London: Policy Exchange, 2009); Bhatt, 'The Fetish of the Margins'.
97 John Ware, 'The Puzzle of Baroness Warsi's Links with Islamist Group', *Jewish Chronicle*, 26 April 2018, https://www.thejc.com/news/news-features/puzzle-of-baroness-sayeeda-warsi-s-links-with-islamist-group-1.463152.
98 Andrew Gilligan, 'Guide to School Islamisation, by "Ringleader" of Trojan Horse Plot', *The Telegraph*, 26 April 2014, http://www.telegraph.co.uk/education/educationnews/10790441/Guide-to-school-Islamisation-by-ringleader-of-Trojan-Horse-plot.html.
99 This claim was made as part of a wider set of allegations that formed part of the so-called 'Trojan horse scandal'. In 2014, the co-author of this report, Tahir Alam, who previously chaired the MCB's education committee, was alleged to have acted as the ringleader in a plot to 'Islamize' state schools in Birmingham. At the time

of writing, he remains barred from all teaching roles in the UK, despite various procedural irregularities and the cases against his fellow teachers collapsing in 2017. For a detailed analysis of the case, see Holmwood and O'Toole, *Countering Extremism in British Schools*.

100 Denis MacEoin, *The Hijacking of British Islam: How Extremist Literature Is Subverting Mosques in the UK* (London: Policy Exchange, 2007).

101 Newsnight, 'Talk about Newsnight: Policy Exchange Dispute – Update', BBC, 29 May 2008, https://www.bbc.co.uk/blogs/newsnight/2008/05/policy_exchange_dispute_update.html.

102 Nick Cohen, 'Where Are All These Militant Atheists Ruining Britain?', *The Observer*, 22 November 2009, http://www.guardian.co.uk/commentisfree/2009/nov/22/islam-bnp-atheism-nick-cohen.

103 Inayat Bunglawala, 'So Much for Free Speech', *The Guardian*, 7 February 2008, sec. Opinion, http://www.theguardian.com/commentisfree/2008/feb/07/somuchforfreespeech.

104 Inayat Bunglawala, 'Geert Wilders, the "Pre-Criminal"', *The Guardian*, 15 October 2009, sec. Opinion, http://www.theguardian.com/commentisfree/libertycentral/2009/oct/15/home-office-geert-wilders.

105 Inayat Bunglawala, 'There Really Is No Compulsion in Religion', *The Guardian: Comment Is Free*, 21 July 2009, http://www.guardian.co.uk/commentisfree/belief/2009/jul/21/apostasy-islam-quran-sharia; Inayat Bunglawala, 'Gay Muslims Need Support', *The Guardian: Comment Is Free*, 5 October 2009, http://www.guardian.co.uk/commentisfree/belief/2009/oct/05/gay-muslims-support.

106 Quotes taken, respectively, from Paul Thomas, *Responding to the Threat of Violent Extremism: Failing to Prevent* (London: Bloomsbury Academic, 2012), 70; Vikram Dodd, 'List Sent to Terror Chief Aligns Peaceful Muslim Groups with Terrorist Ideology', *The Guardian*, 4 August 2010, sec. UK news, https://www.theguardian.com/uk/2010/aug/04/quilliam-foundation-list-alleged-extremism; Tom Mills, Tom Griffin and David Miller, 'The Cold War on British Muslims: An Examination of Policy Exchange and the Centre for Social Cohesion' (Glasgow: Spinwatch, 2011).

107 Les Back, *The Art of Listening* (Oxford: Berg, 2007), 140.

108 Sacranie's point was that Rushdie should face punishment in the afterlife rather than his life being threatened now.

109 BBC, 'Chowdhury Mueen-Uddin Says Bangladesh War Crime Trial Was "Corrupt"', BBC News, 4 November 2013, http://www.bbc.co.uk/news/world-asia-24813078.

110 Quoted in Hamid, *Sufis, Salafis and Islamists*, 119–20.

111 For an analysis of the means and motives of organizations seeking to shift the public view of Muslim groups, see Narzanin Massoumi, Tom Mills and David Miller, eds, *What Is Islamophobia? Racism, Social Movements and the State* (London: Pluto Press, 2017).

112 Therese O'Toole, Stephen H. Jones and Daniel Nilsson DeHanas, 'The New Prevent: Will It Work? Can It Work?', *Arches Quarterly* 5, no. 9 (2012): 56–62.

113 David Cameron, 'PM's Speech at Munich Security Conference', Official Site of the British Prime Minister's Office, 2011, http://www.number10.gov.uk/news/pms-speech-at-munich-security-conference/.

114 David Cameron, 'Speech to the Community Security Trust', Conservatives, 4 March 2008, http://www.conservatives.com/News/Speeches/2008/03/David_Cameron_Speech_to_the_Community_Security_Trust.aspx.

115 'Community cohesion' was a policy agenda focused on cross-cultural interaction that emerged in response to disturbances in several northern towns in 2001. See Ted Cantle, 'Community Cohesion: A Report of the Independent Review Team' (London: Home Office, 2001).

116 Quoted in Therese O'Toole et al., 'Governing through Prevent? Regulation and Contested Practice in State–Muslim Engagement', *Sociology* 50, no. 1 (1 February 2016): 168, https://doi.org/10.1177/0038038514564437.

117 Hansard, 'House of Commons Daily Debates', United Kingdom Parliament, 26 February 2009, http://www.publications.parliament.uk/pa/cm200809/cmhansrd/cm090226/text/90226w0033.htm.

118 Hansard, 'House of Commons Daily Debates', United Kingdom Parliament, 15 March 2011, http://www.publications.parliament.uk/pa/cm201011/cmhansrd/cm110315/halltext/110315h0001.htm#11031559000001.

119 See O'Toole et al., 'Governing through Prevent?', 162.

120 Department for Communities and Local Government, 'Preventing Violent Extremism: Winning Hearts and Minds' (Wetherby: Communities and Local Government Publications, 2007).

121 See Paul Thomas, 'Failed and Friendless: The UK's "Preventing Violent Extremism" Programme', *British Journal of Politics & International Relations* 12, no. 3 (2010): 442–58.

122 Yahya Birt, 'Promoting Virulent Envy? Reconsidering the UK's Terrorist Prevention Strategy', *Royal United Services Institute Journal* 154, no. 4 (2009): 52–8. This perception was reinforced by the fact that the 2006 Prevent 'pathfinder' fund was offered only to areas with a certain percentage of Muslim population: see Arun Kundnani, *Spooked: How Not to Prevent Violent Extremism* (London: Institute of Race Relations, 2009), 13–14.

123 Katherine E. Brown, 'The Promise and Perils of Women's Participation in UK Mosques: The Impact of Securitisation Agendas on Identity, Gender and Community', *British Journal of Politics and International Relations* 10, no. 3 (2008): 472–91; Naaz Rashid, *Veiled Threats: Producing the Muslim Woman in Public Policy Discourses* (Bristol: Policy Press, 2016).

124 O'Toole et al., 'Governing through Prevent?'; Charles Husband and Yunis Alam, *Social Cohesion and Counter-Terrorism: A Policy Contradiction?* (Bristol: Policy Press, 2011).

125 Tax Payers' Alliance, 'Foreign Office Prevent Grants' (Tax Payers' Alliance, 2009), http://www.taxpayersalliance.com/fcoprevent.pdf.

126 Tehmina Kazi, 'How Prevent Undermined Cohesion', *The Guardian: Comment Is Free*, 16 July 2010, http://www.guardian.co.uk/commentisfree/belief/2010/jul/16/prevent-cohesion-communities-islam.

127 John Denham quoted in O'Toole et al., 'Governing through Prevent?', 168.

128 Kundnani, *Spooked*.

129 See House of Commons Communities and Local Government Committee, 'Preventing Violent Extremism: Sixth Report of Session 2009–10' (London: The Stationery Office, 2010), 3; HM Government, 'Prevent Strategy' (London: The Stationery Office, 2011), 31.

130 On this latter phenomenon, see Nisha Kapoor and Kasia Narkowicz, 'Unmaking Citizens: Passport Removals, Pre-Emptive Policing and the Reimagining of Colonial Governmentalities', *Ethnic and Racial Studies* 42, no. 16 (2017): 45–62, https://doi.org/10.1080/01419870.2017.1411965.

131 Project Champion was implemented with very little oversight and consultation and was ultimately thwarted by a public campaign led by civil liberties campaigners and local residents. See Arshad Isakjee and Chris Allen, ' "A Catastrophic Lack of Inquisitiveness": A Critical Study of the Impact and Narrative of the Project Champion Surveillance Project in Birmingham', *Ethnicities*, 9 July 2013, 1468796813492488.

132 HM Government, 'Prevent Strategy'; on the internal conflicts over Prevent see O'Toole, Jones and DeHanas, 'The New Prevent'.

133 HM Government, 'Tackling Extremism in the UK: Report from the Prime Minister's Task Force on Radicalisation and Extremism' (London: Cabinet Office, 2013), https://www.gov.uk/government/uploads/system/uploads/attachment_data/file/263181/ETF_FINAL.pdf.

134 For insightful critiques of this new approach, see Charlotte Heath-Kelly, 'The Geography of Pre-Criminal Space: Epidemiological Imaginations of Radicalisation Risk in the UK Prevent Strategy, 2007–2017', *Critical Studies on Terrorism* 10, no. 2 (4 May 2017): 297–319, https://doi.org/10.1080/17539153.2017.132 7141; Katy Sian, 'Born Radicals? Prevent, Positivism, and "Race-Thinking"', *Palgrave Communications* 3, no. 1 (27 October 2017), https://doi.org/10.1057/s41599-017-0009-0.

135 For examples of reinforcement, see Sian, 'Born Radicals?' 4.

136 Helen Warrell, 'Inside Prevent, the UK's Controversial Anti-Terrorism Programme', *Financial Times*, 24 January 2019, https://www.ft.com/content/a82e18b4-1ea3-11e9-b126-46fc3ad87c65.

137 In Leicester, for example, the Labour mayor refused to host a Prevent officer: see O'Toole et al., 'Governing through Prevent?', 170–1.

138 O'Toole et al., 'Governing through Prevent?'

139 HM Government, 'Counter-Extremism Strategy' (London: Home Office, 2015), https://www.gov.uk/government/uploads/system/uploads/attachment_data/file/470088/51859_Cm9148_Accessible.pdf.

140 Ipsos Mori, 'Building a Stronger Britain Together (BSBT) Progress Report 2019: Interim Evaluation Findings' (London: Home Office, 2019).

141 Maria W. Norris, 'The Secretive World of Counter-Terrorism Funding', *Public Spirit* (blog), 2017, http://www.publicspirit.org.uk/the-secretive-world-of-counter-extremism-funding/.

142 Home Office, 'Charter for the Commission for Countering Extremism', Gov.uk, 2018, https://www.gov.uk/government/publications/charter-for-the-commission-for-countering-extremism/charter-for-the-commission-for-countering-extremism.

143 See Chapter 1 for a full list of relevant literature.

144 See, for example, Nick Cohen, 'How Brave Muslims Are Being Silenced', *The Guardian*, 3 October 2015, sec. Opinion, http://www.theguardian.com/commentisfree/2015/oct/04/how-brave-muslims-are-being-silenced.

145 A similar situation can be found in certain policy contexts too. The implementation of Prevent post-2010 involved civil society partners being made to sign declarations confirming their commitment to liberal principles before entering into a partnership with local governments.

146 Lewis and Hamid, *British Muslims*, 165.

147 See Sara Khan and Tony McMahon, *The Battle for British Islam: Reclaiming Muslim Identity from Extremism* (London: Saqi Books, 2016).

148 Commission for Countering Extremism, 'Challenging Hateful Extremism' (London: Commission for Countering Extremism, October 2019), https://www.gov. uk/government/publications/challenging-hateful-extremism.

149 This centred on the claim that both Hamid and Abbas had shared antisemitic content via social media, although the two authors' criticisms of Prevent also likely played a role. For a full account of the episode, see Sadek Hamid, 'The Perils of Engaging CVE Policy Making: A British Case Study', *Maydan* (blog), 4 December 2019, https:// themaydan.com/2019/12/the-perils-of-engaging-cve-policy-making-a-british-case-study/.

150 Martin Parsons, 'What Is the Point of the Commission for Countering Extremism?', Conservative Home, 10 October 2019, https://www.conservativehome.com/ platform/2019/10/martin-parsons-what-is-the-point-of-the-commission-for-countering-extremism.html.

151 Commission for Countering Extremism, 'Challenging Hateful Extremism', 79.

152 O'Toole et al., 'Governing through Prevent?'; Therese O'Toole, Daniel Nilsson DeHanas and Tariq Modood, 'Balancing Tolerance, Security and Muslim Engagement in the United Kingdom: The Impact of the "Prevent" Agenda', *Critical Studies on Terrorism* 5, no. 3 (1 December 2012): 373–89, https://doi.org/10.1080/17 539153.2012.725570; Jones, 'New Labour and the Re-Making of British Islam'.

153 Usaama al-Azami, 'How Have the Arab Revolutions Affected Western Muslims?', *Centre for the Study of Islam in the UK* (blog), 4 February 2020, http://sites.cardiff. ac.uk/islamukcentre/2020/02/04/usaama-al-azami-how-have-the-arab-revolutions-affected-western-muslims/.

154 Yahya Birt, 'Blowin' in the Wind: Trumpism and Traditional Islam in America', *Medium* (blog), 14 February 2017, https://medium.com/@yahyabirt/https-medium-com-yahyabirt-blowin-in-the-wind-trumpism-and-traditional-islam-in-america-40ba056486d8.

155 Walaa Quisay and Thomas Parker, 'On the Theology of Obedience: An Analysis of Shaykh Bin Bayyah and Shaykh Hamza Yusuf's Political Thought', *Maydan* (blog), 8 January 2019, https://www.themaydan.com/2019/01/theology-obedience-analysis-shaykh-bin-bayyah-shaykh-hamza-yusufs-political-thought/.

156 Hamid, *Sufis, Salafis and Islamists*, 130–2.

157 Inge, *The Making of a Salafi Muslim Woman*, 32.

158 Inge, *The Making of a Salafi Muslim Woman*, 36.

159 Dominic Casciani, 'Preventing Violent Extremism: A Failed Policy?', 7 June 2011, sec. UK, https://www.bbc.com/news/uk-13686586.

160 Haqq-Baker quoted in O'Toole, Jones and DeHanas, 'The New Prevent', 60.

161 Hamid, *Sufis, Salafis and Islamists*, 125–6.

162 Interview with Hasan, 11 September 2008.

163 Quoted in Jones et al., 'A "System of Self-Appointed Leaders"?', 217.

164 Quilliam Foundation, 'Preventing Terrorism: Where Next for Britain?', Strategic Briefing Paper (secret) (London: Quilliam Foundation, 2010), 27, http://www.scribd. com/doc/34834977/Secret-Quilliam-Memo-to-government.

165 Yahya Birt, 'This Dance between "Extremists" and "Formers" Is Past Its Sell-By Date: A Review of ITV's "Jihad" Documentary', *Yahya Birt* (blog), 16 June 2015, https://yahyabirt1.wordpress.com/2015/06/16/this-dance-between-extremists-and-formers-is-past-its-sell-by-date-a-review-of-itvs-jihad-documentary/.

166 Hamid, *Sufis, Salafis and Islamists*, 27.

167 Interview with Hussain, 18 May 2012.

168 See Sophie Gilliat-Ray, *Muslims in Britain: An Introduction* (Cambridge: Cambridge University Press, 2010), 75–6.

169 Phillips, 'Standing Together'.

170 Innes Bowen, *Medina in Birmingham, Najaf in Brent: Inside British Islam* (London: C. Hurst, 2014), 108–9.

171 Phillips, 'Standing Together', 108.

172 For an insight into Altikriti's views on the Muslim Brotherhood today, see Anas Altikriti, 'Jubilant Crowds May Yet Come to Regret End of Brotherhood Government', *Huffington Post UK*, 5 July 2013, http://www.huffingtonpost.co.uk/anas-altikriti/egypt-morsi-coup_b_3550723.html; for a recent Brotherhood statement on women's rights see Muslim Brotherhood, 'Muslim Brotherhood Statement Denouncing UN Women Declaration for Violating Sharia Principles', Ikhwanweb, 14 March 2013, http://www.ikhwanweb.com/article.php?id=30731.

173 Hamid, *Sufis, Salafis and Islamists*, 118.

174 Hamid, *Sufis, Salafis and Islamists*, 24. Imtiaz currently works for the Muslim Charities Forum.

175 John R. Bowen, *On British Islam: Religion, Law, and Everyday Practice in Shari'a Councils* (Princeton, NJ: Princeton University Press, 2016), 38–9.

176 O'Toole et al., 'Taking Part'.

177 Jones et al., 'A "System of Self-Appointed Leaders"?'; Jan Dobbernack, 'Making a Presence: Images of Polity and Constituency in British Muslim Representative Politics', *Ethnicities* 19, no. 2 (1 April 2019): 292–310, https://doi.org/10.1177/1468796817728095.

178 Jones et al., 'A "System of Self-Appointed Leaders"?', 217.

179 James Roland Pennock, *Democratic Political Theory* (Princeton: Princeton University Press, 1979), 314; see also the summary of criticisms in Jane Mansbridge, 'Should Blacks Represent Blacks and Women Represent Women? A Contingent "Yes"', *Journal of Politics* 61, no. 3 (1999): 314.

180 Tony Blair Institute for Global Change, 'Narratives of Division: The Spectrum of Islamist Worldviews in the UK' (Tony Blair Institute for Global Change, January 2019), 9, https://institute.global/news/narratives-division-islamist-worldviews.

181 Phillips, *The Politics of Presence*; Iris Marion Young, *Inclusion and Democracy* (Oxford: Oxford University Press, 2002).

182 Elshayyal, *Muslim Identity Politics*; Modood, *Multiculturalism*; Meer, *Citizenship, Identity and the Politics of Multiculturalism*.

183 Saward, 'Authorisation and Authenticity'; see also Michael Saward, *The Representative Claim* (Oxford: Oxford University Press, 2010).

184 Michael Saward, 'The Representative Claim', *Contemporary Political Theory* 5, no. 3 (2006): 304.

185 Saward, 'Authorisation and Authenticity'.

186 Elshayyal, *Muslim Identity Politics*, 170.

187 Adapted from Saward, 'Authorisation and Authenticity'.

188 Interview with Miqdaad Versi, MCB assistant secretary general, 4 April 2017.

189 Stephen H. Jones and Sadek Hamid, 'United Kingdom', in *Yearbook of Muslims in Europe*, ed. Oliver Scharbrodt et al., vol. 10 (Leiden: Brill, 2018), 713.

190 Interview with Versi, 4 April 2017. See also Catrin Nye, 'The Man Correcting Stories about Muslims', *BBC News*, 19 January 2017, sec. UK, https://www.bbc.com/news/uk-38655760.

191 During the campaign that led to Boris Johnson being elected Conservative leader, all the candidates pledged to hold an independent inquiry into Islamophobia in the party, but this was watered down immediately after Johnson became prime minister, with Sajid Javid, who initiated the pledge, being effectively forced from his role as chancellor in early 2020. One of the main obstacles to such an inquiry is the history of obviously Islamophobic claims by senior Conservative ministers. For example, former defence secretary Michael Fallon was successfully sued for falsely claiming Suliman Gani, a London-based imam, was a supporter of ISIS as part of an effort to derail Sadiq Khan's campaign to be London mayor. David Cameron made similar claims, but did not face legal action because he made them under the protection of parliamentary privilege. See Heather Stewart, 'Michael Fallon Pays Damages to Imam at Centre of Sadiq Khan Storm', *The Guardian*, 23 June 2016, sec. Politics, https://www.theguardian.com/politics/2016/jun/23/michael-fallon-damages-imam-suliman-gani-sadiq-khan.

192 Peter Walker and Nicola Slawson, 'Conservatives under Fire for Failing to Tackle Party's Islamophobia', *The Guardian*, 31 May 2018, sec. Politics, https://www.theguardian.com/politics/2018/may/31/muslim-council-calls-for-inquiry-into-conservative-party-islamophobia.

193 Interview with Versi, 4 April 2017.

194 House of Commons, 'Muslim Brotherhood Review: Main Findings' (London: Prime Minister's Office, 17 December 2015), https://www.gov.uk/government/publications/muslim-brotherhood-review-main-findings.

195 ICM Unlimited, 'C4/Juniper Survey of Muslims 2015' (London: ICM Unlimited, 2015).

Chapter 6: Conclusion

1 Robert N. Bellah et al., *Habits of the Heart: Individualism and Commitment in American Life* (London: University of California Press, 2008), 283.

2 Pelikan quoted in Bellah et al., *Habits of the Heart*, 140.

3 These criticisms are summarized, and countered, in Robert N. Bellah, 'Reading and Misreading Habits of the Heart', *Sociology of Religion* 68, no. 2 (2007): 189–93.

4 William Davies, *The Limits of Neoliberalism: Authority, Sovereignty and the Logic of Competition* (Thousand Oaks, CA: SAGE, 2014), 4.

5 Tom Grein, 'The Deeper Consternation of the Asia Bibi Scandal', *The Spectator*, 5 January 2019, https://www.spectator.co.uk/2019/01/the-deeper-consternation-of-the-asia-bibi-scandal/.

6 Quoted in Stephen H. Jones and Khadijah Elshayyal, 'United Kingdom', in *Yearbook of Muslims in Europe*, ed. Oliver Scharbrodt et al., vol. 11 (Leiden: Brill, 2019), 661.

7 Farah Elahi and Omar Khan, eds, *Islamophobia: Still a Challenge for Us All* (London: Runnymede, 2017); All-Party Parliamentary Group on British Muslims, 'Islamophobia Defined: The Inquiry into a Working Definition of Islamophobia' (London: APPG on British Muslims, 2018).

8 Stephanie J. Silverman and Melanie Griffiths, 'Immigration Detention in the UK' (Oxford: Migration Observatory, COMPAS, University of Oxford, 2019), https://migrationobservatory.ox.ac.uk/resources/briefings/immigration-detention-in-the-uk/.

9 Nisha Kapoor and Kasia Narkowicz, 'Unmaking Citizens: Passport Removals, Pre-Emptive Policing and the Reimagining of Colonial Governmentalities', *Ethnic and Racial Studies* 42, no. 16 (2017): 45–63, https://doi.org/10.1080/01419870.2017.1411965.

10 See the case of Shamima Begum in Khadijah Elshayyal and Stephen H. Jones, 'United Kingdom', in *Yearbook of Muslims in Europe*, ed. Egdunas Racius et al., vol. 12 (Leiden: Brill, forthcoming).

11 Khadijah Elshayyal, 'Securitisation, Fundamental British Values and the Neutralisation of Dissent within Muslim Discourses in the UK', *Maydan* (blog), 26 February 2020, https://themaydan.com/2020/02/securitisation-fundamental-british-values-and-the-neutralisation-of-dissent-within-muslim-discourses-in-the-uk/.

12 See, inter alia, Luke de Noronha, 'Deportation, Racism and Multi-Status Britain: Immigration Control and the Production of Race in the Present', *Ethnic and Racial Studies* 42, no. 14 (26 October 2019): 2413–30, https://doi.org/10.1080/0141 9870.2019.1585559; Alana Lentin, 'Post-Race, Post Politics: The Paradoxical Rise of Culture after Multiculturalism', *Ethnic and Racial Studies* 37, no. 8 (3 July 2014): 1268–85, https://doi.org/10.1080/01419870.2012.664278; Nadine El-Enany, *Bordering Britain: Law, Race and Empire* (Manchester: Manchester University Press, 2020).

13 John Stuart Mill, *On Liberty and Other Essays* (Oxford: Oxford University Press, 1991), 14.

14 Elspeth Guild, Kees Groenendijk and Sergio Carrera, *Illiberal Liberal States: Immigration, Citizenship and Integration in the EU* (Farnham: Ashgate, 2009).

15 Aurelien Mondon and Aaron Winter, 'Articulations of Islamophobia: From the Extreme to the Mainstream?', *Ethnic and Racial Studies* 40, no. 13 (2017): 2151–79, https://doi.org/10.1080/01419870.2017.1312008.

16 After David Theo Goldberg, *The Threat of Race: Reflections on Racial Neoliberalism* (Malden, MA: Wiley-VCH, 2008).

17 Nisha Kapoor, 'The Advancement of Racial Neoliberalism in Britain', *Ethnic and Racial Studies* 36, no. 6 (1 June 2013): 1028–46.

18 Kapoor and Narkowicz, 'Unmaking Citizens'.

19 Therese O'Toole et al., 'Governing through Prevent? Regulation and Contested Practice in State–Muslim Engagement', *Sociology* 50, no. 1 (1 February 2016): 160–77, https://doi.org/10.1177/0038038514564437.

20 Many commentators on recent Prevent policy appear (on my reading at least) to reject the safeguarding approach entirely. See Charlotte Heath-Kelly, 'The Geography of Pre-Criminal Space: Epidemiological Imaginations of Radicalisation Risk in the UK Prevent Strategy, 2007–2017', *Critical Studies on Terrorism* 10, no. 2 (4 May 2017): 297–319, https://doi.org/10.1080/17539153.2017.1327141; Katy Sian, 'Born Radicals? Prevent, Positivism, and "Race-Thinking"', *Palgrave Communications* 3, no. 1 (27 October 2017), https://doi.org/10.1057/s41599-017-0009-0.

21 Immanuel Kant, *Groundwork of the Metaphysics of Morals*, ed. Mary Gregor and Jens Timmerman, rev. edn (Cambridge: Cambridge University Press, 2012).

22 See Zygmunt Bauman, *In Search of Politics* (Cambridge: Polity, 1999).

23 Stability is a concern in recent theories of both political and comprehensive liberalism. Advocates of comprehensive liberalism argue that inculcating a liberal worldview will lead to widespread support for liberal political structures. The question of how to maintain stability in a pluralistic context is, however, the starting point for theories of political liberalism. On this debate, see Martha C. Nussbaum, 'Perfectionist

Liberalism and Political Liberalism', *Philosophy & Public Affairs* 39, no. 1 (1 January 2011): 3–45, https://doi.org/10.1111/j.1088-4963.2011.01200.x.

24 William Connolly, *Why I Am Not a Secularist* (London: University of Minnesota Press, 1999), 4.

25 Elshayyal, 'Securitisation, Fundamental British Values and the Neutralisation of Dissent within Muslim Discourses in the UK'.

26 Charles Taylor, *Philosophical Arguments* (Cambridge, MA: Harvard University Press, 1997), 164.

27 James Baldwin, *James Baldwin: Collected Essays* (New York: Penguin Random House USA, 1998), 75.

BIBLIOGRAPHY

Abdullah al-Mamun al-, Suhrawardy. *The Sayings of Muhammad*. New York: Arno, 1980.

Abou El Fadl, Khaled. *The Great Theft: Wrestling Islam from the Extremists*. San Francisco, CA: Harper, 2007.

Ahmad, Fauzia. 'Graduating towards Marriage? Attitudes towards Marriage and Relationships among University-Educated British Muslim Women'. *Culture and Religion* 13, no. 3 (2012): 193–210. https://doi.org/10.1080/14755610.2012.674953.

Ahmad, Fauzia. 'Modern Traditions? British Muslim Women and Academic Achievement'. *Gender and Education* 13, no. 2 (2001): 137–52.

Ahmad, Fauzia. 'The British Muslim Relationship Crisis'. Presented at the British Association of Islamic Studies Conference, London, 15 April 2015.

Ahmed, Sughra. *Seen and Not Heard: Voices of Young British Muslims*. Leicester: Policy Research Centre, 2009.

Akhtar, Parveen. 'British Muslim Political Participation: After Bradford'. *Political Quarterly* 83, no. 4 (1 October 2012): 762–66. https://doi.org/10.1111/j.1467-923X.2012.02352.x.

Akhtar, Parveen. *British Muslim Politics: Examining Pakistani Biraderi Networks*. Basingstoke: Palgrave Macmillan, 2013.

Akhtar, Rajnaara C. 'British Muslims and Transformative Processes of the Islamic Legal Traditions: Negotiating Law, Culture and Religion with Specific Reference to Islamic Family Law and Faith Based Alternative Dispute Resolution'. PhD diss., Warwick: University of Warwick, 2013. http://webcat.warwick.ac.uk/record=b2689316~S1.

Akhtar, Rajnaara C. 'Modern Traditions in Muslim Marriage Practices, Exploring English Narratives'. *Oxford Journal of Law and Religion*, 16 August 2018. https://doi.org/10.1093/ojlr/rwy030.

Akhtar, Rajnaara C. 'Plural Approaches to Faith-Based Dispute Resolution by Britain's Muslim Communities'. *Child and Family Law Quarterly* 31, no. 3 (2019): 189–209.

Akhtar, Rajnaara C. 'The Truth about Muslim Marriages'. Channel 4, 21 November 2017. https://assemble.me/uploads/websites/39/files/5a140876945ed.pdf.

Al Mahdi Institute. 'AMI Signs Agreement with University of Birmingham for Masters in Islamic Studies'. *Al-Mahdi Institute* (blog), 21 August 2018. https://www.almahdi.edu/ami-signs-agreement-with-university-of-birmingham-for-masters-in-islamic-studies/.

Alexander, Jeffrey C. 'Struggling over the Mode of Incorporation: Backlash against Multiculturalism in Europe'. *Ethnic and Racial Studies* 36, no. 4 (2013): 531–56.

Ali, Kecia. *Sexual Ethics and Islam: Feminist Reflections on Qur'an, Hadith and Jurisprudence*. Oxford: Oneworld, 2006.

Ali, Rushanara. 'Launch of Maslaha'. Presented at the Young Foundation, London, 22 May 2009.

Allen, Chris, and Surinder Guru. 'Between Political Fad and Political Empowerment: A Critical Evaluation of the National Muslim Women's Advisory Group (NMWAG) and Governmental Processes of Engaging Muslim Women'. *Sociological Research Online* 17, no. 3 (2011): 17.

All-Party Parliamentary Group on British Muslims. 'Islamophobia Defined: The Inquiry into a Working Definition of Islamophobia'. London: APPG on British Muslims, 2018.

Altikriti, Anas. 'Jubilant Crowds May Yet Come to Regret End of Brotherhood Government'. *Huffington Post UK*, 5 July 2013. http://www.huffingtonpost.co.uk/anas-altikriti/egypt-morsi-coup_b_3550723.html.

Anidjar, Gil. *The Jew, the Arab: A History of the Enemy*. Stanford, CA: Stanford University Press, 2003.

Anitha, Sundari, Anupama Roy and Harshita Yalamarty. *Disposable Women: Abuse, Violence and Abandonment in Transnational Marriages: Issues for Policy and Practice in the UK and India*. Lincoln: University of Lincoln, 2016.

An-Na'im, Abdullahi Ahmed. *Islam and the Secular State: Negotiating the Future of the Shari'a*. Cambridge, MA: Harvard University Press, 2008.

An-Na'im, Abdullahi Ahmed, ed. *Islamic Family Law in a Changing World: A Global Resource Book*. London: Zed Books, 2002.

Ansari, Humayun. *The Infidel Within: Muslims in Britain since 1800*. London: C. Hurst, 2004.

Ansari, Usamah Yasin. 'The Pious Self Is a Jewel in Itself: Agency and Tradition in the Production of "Shariatic Modernity"'. *South Asia Research* 30, no. 3 (1 November 2010): 275–98. https://doi.org/10.1177/026272801003000304.

Anwar, Muhammad. *Myth of Return: Pakistanis in Britain*. London: Heinemann Educational Books, 1979.

Appiah, Kwame Anthony. *The Ethics of Identity*. Princeton, NJ: Princeton University Press, 2005.

Arberry, A. J. *Discourses of Rumi*. London: John Murray, 1961.

Armstrong, Karen. *Muhammad: A Biography of the Prophet*. London: Phoenix, 2001.

Asad, Talal. *Formations of the Secular: Christianity, Islam, Modernity*. Stanford, CA: Stanford University Press, 2003.

Asad, Talal. *Genealogies of Religion: Discipline and Reasons of Power in Christianity and Islam*. London: John Hopkins University Press, 1993.

Ash, Timothy Garton. 'What Young British Muslims Say Can Be Shocking – Some of It Is Also True'. *The Guardian*, 10 August 2006. https://www.theguardian.com/commentisfree/2006/aug/10/comment.race.

Asif, Iram. 'Hijaz College : Students of Islamic Religious Sciences in Contemporary British Society'. Master's thesis, Lund University, 2006. http://www.lunduniversity.lu.se/lup/publication/1328980.

Aslan, Reza. *No God but God*. London: William Heinemann, 2005.

Azami, Usaama al-. 'How Have the Arab Revolutions Affected Western Muslims?' *Centre for the Study of Islam in the UK* (blog), 4 February 2020. http://sites.cardiff.ac.uk/islamukcentre/2020/02/04/usaama-al-azami-how-have-the-arab-revolutions-affected-western-muslims/.

Back, Les. *The Art of Listening*. Oxford: Berg, 2007.

Badawi, Zaki. 'Muslim Justice in a Secular State'. In *God's Law versus State Law*, 73–80. London: Grey Seal, 1995.

Badawi, Zaki. *The Reformers of Egypt*. London: Taylor & Francis, 1978.

Badawi, Zaki. 'True Submission? An Interview with Zaki Badawi'. *Third Way*, 23 April 1996. http://www.thirdway.org.uk/past/showpage.asp?page=3923.

Bader, Veit. 'Secularism, Public Reason, or Moderately Agnostic Democracy?' In *Secularism, Religion and Multicultural Citizenship*, 110–35. Cambridge: Cambridge University Press, 2009.

Baker, Vicky. 'Rape Victim Sentenced to 200 Lashes and Six Months in Jail'. *The Guardian*, 16 November 2007. http://www.guardian.co.uk/world/2007/nov/17/saudiarabia. international.

Balchin, Cassandra. 'Kingdom of God: The Archbishop, the Shari'a and the Law of the Land'. Presented at the Abrar House, London, 18 February 2008. http://www. thecitycircle.com/blog2.php?cann_id=532&vid=1502083.

Baldwin, James. *James Baldwin: Collected Essays*. New York: Penguin Random House USA, 1998.

Ballard, Roger. 'Inside and Outside: Contrasting Perspectives on the Dynamics of Kinship and Marriage in Contemporary South Asian Transnational Networks'. In *The Family in Question: Immigrant and Ethnic Minorities in Multicultural Europe*, edited by Ralph Grillo, 1st edn, 37–70. Amsterdam: Amsterdam University Press, 2014.

Bano, Samia. 'Complexity, Difference and "Muslim Personal Law": Rethinking the Relationship between Shariah Councils and South Asian Muslim Women in Britain'. PhD diss., Warwick: University of Warwick, 2004.

Bano, Samia. 'Muslim Family Justice and Human Rights: The Experience of British Muslim Women'. *Journal of Comparative Law* 2, no. 2 (2007): 1–29.

Bano, Samia. 'Muslim South Asian Women and Customary Law in Britain'. *Journal of South Pacific Law* 4 (2000). http://www.paclii.org/journals/fJSPL/vol04/6.shtml.

Barkatulah, Abdul K. 'Launch of the Muslim Marriage Contract'. Presented at the Abrar House, London, 8 August 2008.

Bauman, Zygmunt. *In Search of Politics*. Cambridge: Polity, 1999.

Bauman, Zygmunt. *Liquid Love: On the Frailty of Human Bonds*. Cambridge: Polity, 2003.

BBC. 'Chowdhury Mueen-Uddin Says Bangladesh War Crime Trial Was "Corrupt"'. BBC News, 4 November 2013. http://www.bbc.co.uk/news/world-asia-24813078.

Beckford, James A., and Ilona C. M. Cairns. 'Muslim Prison Chaplains in Canada and Britain'. *Sociological Review* 63, no. 1 (1 February 2015): 36–56. https://doi. org/10.1111/1467-954X.12224.

Bellah, Robert N. 'Reading and Misreading Habits of the Heart'. *Sociology of Religion* 68, no. 2 (2007): 189–93.

Bellah, Robert N., Richard Madsen, William M. Sullivan, Ann Swidler and Steven M. Tipton. *Habits of the Heart: Individualism and Commitment in American Life*. London: University of California Press, 2008.

Berlin, Isaiah. *The Proper Study of Mankind*. New York: Farrar, Strauss and Giroux, 1997.

Bevir, Mark. 'Governance and Governmentality after Neoliberalism'. *Policy & Politics* 39, no. 4 (2011): 457–71.

Bhatt, Chetan. *Liberation and Purity: Race, New Religious Movements and the Ethics of Postmodernity*. London: Routledge, 1997.

Bhatt, Chetan. 'The Fetish of the Margins: Religious Absolutism, Anti-Racism and Postcolonial Silence'. *New Formations* 59 (2006): 98–115.

Billaud, Julie. 'Ethics and Affects in British Shariah Councils: "A Simple Way of Getting to Paradise"'. In *Islam and Public Controversy in Europe*, edited by Nilüfer Göle, 159–72. Burlington: Ashgate, 2014.

Billaud, Julie. 'Marriage "Sharia Style": Everyday Practices of Islamic Morality in England'. *Contemporary Islam*, 8 November 2018. https://doi.org/10.1007/s11562-018-0430-1.

Bingham, John. 'British Marriage Laws Are "hopelessly out of Date", Government Told', 16 December 2015. http://www.telegraph.co.uk/news/religion/12055060/British-marriage-laws-are-hopelessly-out-of-date-government-told.html.

Birt, Jonathan. 'Lobbying and Marching: British Muslims and the State'. In *Muslim Britain: Communities under Pressure*, edited by Tahir Abbas, 92–106. London: Zed Books, 2005.

Birt, Jonathan. 'Locating the British Imam: The Deobandi 'ulama between Contested Authority and Public Policy Post-9/11'. In *European Muslims and the Secular State*, edited by Jocelyne Cesari and Seán McLoughlin, 183–96. Aldershot: Ashgate, 2005.

Birt, Jonathan. 'Wahhabism in the United Kingdom: Manifestations and Reactions'. In *Transnational Connections and the Arab Gulf*, edited by Madawi al-Rasheed, 168–84. London: Routledge, 2005.

Birt, Jonathan, and Philip Lewis. 'The Pattern of Islamic Reform in Britain: The Deobandis between Intra-Muslim Sectarianism and Engagement with Wider Society'. In *Producing Islamic Knowledge: Transmission and Dissemination in Western Europe*, edited by Martin Van Bruinessen and Stefano Allievi, 91–120. London: Routledge, 2007.

Birt, Yahya. 'Blowin' in the Wind: Trumpism and Traditional Islam in America'. *Medium* (blog), 14 February 2017. https://medium.com/@yahyabirt/https-medium-com-yahyabirt-blowin-in-the-wind-trumpism-and-traditional-islam-in-america-40ba056486d8.

Birt, Yahya. 'Good Imam, Bad Imam: Civic Religion and National Integration in Britain Post-9/11'. *Muslim World* 96, no. 4 (2006): 687–705.

Birt, Yahya. 'Ministry of Justice Looks Set to Target Muslim Prison Chaplains'. *Muslim News*, 26 February 2016. http://muslimnews.co.uk/newspaper/top-stories/ministry-of-justice-looks-set-to-target-muslim-prison-chaplains/.

Birt, Yahya. 'Promoting Virulent Envy? Reconsidering the UK's Terrorist Prevention Strategy'. *Royal United Services Institute Journal* 154, no. 4 (2009): 52–8.

Birt, Yahya. 'The next Ten Years: An Open Letter to the MCB'. *Musings on the Britannic Crescent* (blog), 27 June 2008. http://www.yahyabirt.com/?p=146.

Birt, Yahya. 'This Dance between "Extremists" and "Formers" Is past Its Sell-By Date: A Review of ITV's "Jihad" Documentary'. *Yahya Birt* (blog), 16 June 2015. https://yahyabirt1.wordpress.com/2015/06/16/this-dance-between-extremists-and-formers-is-past-its-sell-by-date-a-review-of-itvs-jihad-documentary/.

Birt, Yahya. 'Wahhabi Wrangles'. *Yahya Birt* (blog), 2 November 2007. https://yahyabirt1.wordpress.com/2007/11/02/wahhabi-wrangles/.

Bleich, Erik. 'Where Do Muslims Stand on Ethno-Racial Hierarchies in Britain and France? Evidence from Public Opinion Surveys'. *Patterns of Prejudice* 43, nos 3–4 (2009): 379–400.

Bolognani, Marta. 'The Myth of Return: Dismissal, Survival or Revival? A Bradford Example of Transnationalism as a Political Instrument'. *Journal of Ethnic and Migration Studies* 33, no. 1 (1 January 2007): 59–76. https://doi.org/10.1080/13691830601043497.

Bolognani, Marta, and Jody Mellor. 'British Pakistani Women's Use of the "Religion versus Culture" Contrast: A Critical Analysis'. *Culture and Religion* 13, no. 2 (1 June 2012): 211–26. https://doi.org/10.1080/14755610.2012.674952.

Bolognani, Marta, and Paul Statham. 'The Changing Public Face of Muslim Associations in Britain: Coming Together for Common "Social" Goals?' *Ethnicities* 13, no. 2 (1 April 2013): 229–49. https://doi.org/10.1177/1468796812470892.

Bone, Amra. 'The Relationship between the Courts, Society and Civil Law: A Response'. Presented at the Britain's Religious Courts: Marriage, Divorce and Civil Law, Cardiff University, 18 May 2011.

Bonino, Stefano. *Muslims in Scotland: The Making of Community in a Post-9/11 World*. Edinburgh: Edinburgh University Press, 2016.

Bonino, Stefano. 'The British State "Security Syndrome" and Muslim Diversity: Challenges for Liberal Democracy in the Age of Terror'. *Contemporary Islam*, 4 April 2016, 1–25. https://doi.org/10.1007/s11562-016-0356-4.

Bowen, Innes. *Medina in Birmingham, Najaf in Brent: Inside British Islam*. London: C. Hurst, 2014.

Bowen, John R. 'How Could English Courts Recognize Shariah?' *University of St. Thomas Law Journal* 7, no. 3 (19 September 2011). http://ir.stthomas.edu/ustlj/vol7/iss3/3.

Bowen, John R. *On British Islam: Religion, Law, and Everyday Practice in Sharia Councils*. Princeton, NJ: Princeton University Press, 2016.

Bowman, Sally. 'Should Sharia Councils Be Banned?' *Inside Out East Midlands*. Leicester: BBC One East Midlands, 2 November 2015. http://www.bbc.co.uk/programmes/b06n5s5q.

Boztas, Senay. 'Sharia Courts in Britain Lock Women into "Marital Captivity", Study Says'. *The Independent*, 4 December 2015. http://www.independent.co.uk/news/uk/home-news/sharia-courts-in-britain-lock-women-into-marital-captivity-study-says-a6761141.html.

Brent Council. 'Brent Population by Ethnicity'. Brent Open Data, 2019. https://app.powerbi.com/view?r=eyJrIjoiN2U0MzFiZmMtNjdkZC00M2FmLTkxMWMtYjg0Zjc5ZDBjZTBhIiwidCI6IjIxODc4N2FiLTM1N2YtNGQ3YS1hZjljLTU4NzBlM2QyZW4I4MCIsImMiOjh9.

Bright, Martin. 'When Progressives Treat with Reactionaries: The British State's Flirtation with Radical Islamism'. London: Policy Exchange, 2006.

British Future, and Universities UK. 'International Students and the UK Immigration Debate'. London: Universities UK, 2014. https://www.universitiesuk.ac.uk/policy-and-analysis/reports/Pages/international-students-uk-immigration-debate.aspx.

British Muslims for Secular Democracy. 'Advice for Schools: Brief Guidance for Handling Muslim Parental Concern'. London: BMSD, 2010. http://www.bmsd.org.uk/pdfs/schools.pdf.

Brown, Katherine E. 'The Promise and Perils of Women's Participation in UK Mosques: The Impact of Securitisation Agendas on Identity, Gender and Community'. *British Journal of Politics and International Relations* 10, no. 3 (2008): 472–91.

Bunglawala, Inayat. 'Gay Muslims Need Support'. *The Guardian: Comment Is Free*, 5 October 2009. http://www.guardian.co.uk/commentisfree/belief/2009/oct/05/gay-muslims-support.

Bunglawala, Inayat. 'Geert Wilders, the "Pre-Criminal"'. *The Guardian*, 15 October 2009, sec. Opinion. http://www.theguardian.com/commentisfree/libertycentral/2009/oct/15/home-office-geert-wilders.

Bunglawala, Inayat. 'Minab: Community Initiative, or Quango?' *The Guardian: Comment Is Free*, 15 May 2009. http://www.guardian.co.uk/commentisfree/belief/2009/may/15/minab-mosques-imams-islam.

Bunglawala, Inayat. 'So Much for Free Speech'. *The Guardian*, 7 February 2008, sec. Opinion. http://www.theguardian.com/commentisfree/2008/feb/07/somuchforfreespeech.

Bunglawala, Inayat. 'There Really Is No Compulsion in Religion'. *The Guardian: Comment Is Free*, 21 July 2009. http://www.guardian.co.uk/commentisfree/belief/2009/jul/21/apostasy-islam-quran-sharia.

Bunt, Gary R. *Islam in the Digital Age: E-Jihad, Online Fatwas and Cyber Islamic Environments*. London: Pluto, 2003.

Busher, Joel, Tufyal Choudhury, Paul Thomas and Gareth Harris. 'What the Prevent Duty Means for Schools and Colleges in England: An Analysis of Educationalists' Experiences'. Coventry: Coventry University, 2017. https://pure.coventry.ac.uk/ws/portalfiles/portal/11090509.

Bushfield, Antony. 'Government to Ditch Plans for Ofsted Inspections at Sunday Schools'. Premier, 10 July 2016. https://www.premier.org.uk/News/UK/Government-to-ditch-plans-for-Ofsted-inspections-at-Sunday-schools.

Cambridge Muslim College. 'BA Programme Validated'. *Unity: Newsletter of the Cambridge Muslim College*, October 2017.

Cameron, David. 'PM's Speech at Munich Security Conference'. Official Site of the British Prime Minister's Office, 2011. http://www.number10.gov.uk/news/pms-speech-at-munich-security-conference/.

Cameron, David. 'Speech to the Community Security Trust'. Conservatives, 4 March 2008. http://www.conservatives.com/News/Speeches/2008/03/David_Cameron_Speech_to_the_Community_Security_Trust.aspx.

Campos, Paul F. 'Secular Fundamentalism'. *Columbia Law Review* 94, no. 6 (1994): 1814–27.

Cantle, Ted. 'Community Cohesion: A Report of the Independent Review Team'. London: Home Office, 2001.

Carlisle, Jessica. *Muslim Divorce in the Middle East: Contesting Gender in the Contemporary Courts*. Cham, Switzerland: Palgrave Macmillan, 2019.

Carr, Matt. 'You Are Now Entering Eurabia'. *Race & Class* 48, no. 1 (2006): 1–22. https://doi.org/10.1177/0306396806066636.

Carter, Stephen L. *The Culture of Disbelief*. New York: Basic Books, 1993.

Casanova, José. 'Immigration and the New Religious Pluralism: A European Union-United States Comparison'. In *Secularism, Religion and Multicultural Citizenship*, edited by Geoffrey Brahm Levey and Tariq Modood, 139–63. Cambridge: Cambridge University Press, 2009.

Casciani, Dominic. 'Preventing Violent Extremism: A Failed Policy?', 7 June 2011, sec. UK. https://www.bbc.com/news/uk-13686586.

Casey, Louise. 'The Casey Review: A Review into Opportunity and Integration'. London: Department for Communities and Local Government, 12 May 2016. https://www.gov.uk/government/publications/the-casey-review-a-review-into-opportunity-and-integration.

Castells, Manuel. *The Power of Identity*. Oxford: Blackwell, 2004.

Catto, Rebecca. 'Sociology of Religion in Great Britain: Interdisciplinarity and Gradual Diversification'. *Sociologies of Religion: National Traditions*, 7 August 2015, 107–31. https://doi.org/10.1163/9789004297586_007.

Cesari, Jocelyne. 'The Securitisation of Islam in Europe'. Research Paper. CEPS CHALLENGE Programme, EU Sixth Framework, 2009.

Cesari, Jocelyne. *What Is Political Islam?* 1st edn. Boulder: Lynne Rienner, 2017.

Chaplin, Jonathan. *Talking God: The Legitimacy of Religious Public Reasoning*. London: Theos, 2008.

Chapman, Rachael, and Vivien Lowndes. 'Faith in Governance? The Potential and Pitfalls of Involving Faith Groups in Urban Governance'. *Planning, Practice & Research* 23, no. 1 (2008): 57–75.

Charsley, Katharine. 'Risk, Trust, Gender and Transnational Cousin Marriage among British Pakistanis'. *Ethnic and Racial Studies* 30, no. 6 (2007): 1117–31. https://doi.org/10.1080/01419870701599549.

Charsley, Katharine, and Anika Liversage. 'Transforming Polygamy: Migration, Transnationalism and Multiple Marriages among Muslim Minorities'. *Global Networks* 13, no. 1 (2013): 60–78. https://doi.org/10.1111/j.1471-0374.2012.00369.x.

Cheruvallil-Contractor, Sariya, and Alison Scott-Baumann. 'Collaborative Partnerships between Universities and Muslim Institutions: Dismantling the Roadblocks'. Derby: University of Derby, 2014. http://www.derby.ac.uk/media/derbyacuk/contentassets/documents/ehs/schoolofeducation/centreofsocietyreligionandbelief/Research-report.pdf.

Cinalli, Manlio, and Marco Giugni. 'Electoral Participation of Muslims in Europe: Assessing the Impact of Institutional and Discursive Opportunities'. *Journal of Ethnic and Migration Studies* 42, no. 2 (26 January 2016): 309–24. https://doi.org/10.1080/1369183X.2015.1102043.

Clark, Laura, and Laura Osborne. 'Revealed: Islamist Plot Dubbed "Trojan Horse" to Replace Teachers in Birmingham Schools with Radicals'. *Mail Online*, 7 March 2014. http://www.dailymail.co.uk/news/article-2575759/Revealed-Islamist-plot-dubbed-Trojan-Horse-string-schools-Birmingham-self-styled-Jihad.html.

Clarke, John. 'So Many Strategies, So Little Time … Making Universities Modern'. *International Journal of Higher Education in the Social Sciences* 3, no. 3 (2010): 91–116.

Clayton, John. 'Living the Multicultural City: Acceptance, Belonging and Young Identities in the City of Leicester, England'. *Ethnic and Racial Studies* 35, no. 9 (2012): 1673-1693.

Clegg, Brian. *The First Scientist: A Life of Roger Bacon*. London: Constable, 2003.

Clements, Ben. 'The Ethnic Minority British Election Study (EMBES) – Part II'. *British Religion in Numbers* (blog), 7 March 2011. http://www.brin.ac.uk/news/2011/the-ethnic-minority-british-election-study-embes-part-ii/.

CoDE. 'How Has Ethnic Diversity Grown 1991–2001–2011?' Manchester: CoDE/Joseph Rowntree Foundation, 2012. http://www.ethnicity.ac.uk/medialibrary/briefings/dynamicsofdiversity/how-has-ethnic-diversity-grown-1991-2001-2011.pdf.

Cohen, Nick. 'How Brave Muslims Are Being Silenced'. *The Guardian*, 3 October 2015, sec. Opinion. http://www.theguardian.com/commentisfree/2015/oct/04/how-brave-muslims-are-being-silenced.

Cohen, Nick. *What's Left? How the Left Lost Its Way*. London: Fourth Estate, 2007.

Cohen, Nick. 'Where Are All These Militant Atheists Ruining Britain?' *The Observer*, 22 November 2009. http://www.guardian.co.uk/commentisfree/2009/nov/22/islam-bnp-atheism-nick-cohen.

Commission for Countering Extremism. 'Challenging Hateful Extremism'. London: Commission for Countering Extremism, October 2019. https://www.gov.uk/government/publications/challenging-hateful-extremism.

Connolly, William. *Why I Am Not a Secularist*. London: University of Minnesota Press, 1999.

Croft, Stuart. *Securitizing Islam: Identity and the Search for Security*. New York: Cambridge University Press, 2012.

Darsh, Syed M. *Questions and Answers about Islam*. London: TaHa, 1997.

Davie, Grace. *Religion in Modern Europe: A Memory Mutates*. Oxford: Oxford University Press, 2000.

Davies, William. *The Limits of Neoliberalism: Authority, Sovereignty and the Logic of Competition*. Thousand Oaks, CA: SAGE, 2014.

Degli Esposti, Emanuelle. 'Fragmented Realities: The "Sectarianisation" of Space among Iraqi Shias in London'. *Contemporary Islam* 13, no. 3 (1 October 2019): 259–85. https://doi.org/10.1007/s11562-018-0425-y.

DeHanas, Daniel Nilsson. *London Youth, Religion, and Politics: Engagement and Activism from Brixton to Brick Lane*. Oxford: Oxford University Press, 2016.

Department for Communities and Local Government. 'Preventing Violent Extremism: Winning Hearts and Minds'. Wetherby: Communities and Local Government Publications, 2007.

Department for Innovation, Universities and Skills. 'Promoting Good Campus Relations, Fostering Shared Values and Preventing Violent Extremism in Universities and Higher Education Colleges'. London: Department for Business Innovation and Skills, 2007.

Department of Communities and Local Government. 'Face to Face and Side by Side: A Framework for Partnership in Our Multi Faith Society'. London: HMSO, July 2008.

Dessing, Nathal, Nadia Jeldtoft, Jørgen Nielsen and Linda Woodhead, eds. *Everyday Lived Islam in Europe*, new edn. Burlington, VT: Ashgate, 2013.

Dhaliwal, Sukhwant, and Nira Yuval-Davis, eds. *Women against Fundamentalism: Stories of Dissent and Solidarity*. London: Lawrence & Wishart, 2014.

Dinham, Adam. *Faiths, Public Policy and Civil Society: Problems, Policies, Controversies*. Basingstoke: Palgrave Macmillan, 2009.

Dinham, Adam, and Stephen H. Jones. 'Religion, Public Policy, and the Academy: Brokering Public Faith in a Context of Ambivalence?' *Journal of Contemporary Religion* 27, no. 2 (2012): 185–201.

Dinham, Adam, and Vivien Lowndes. 'Religion, Resources and Representation: Three Narratives of Faith Engagement in British Urban Governance'. *Urban Affairs Review* 43, no. 6 (2008): 817–45.

Dobbernack, Jan. 'Making a Presence: Images of Polity and Constituency in British Muslim Representative Politics'. *Ethnicities* 19, no. 2 (1 April 2019): 292–310. https://doi.org/10.1177/1468796817728095.

Dodd, Vikram. 'List Sent to Terror Chief Aligns Peaceful Muslim Groups with Terrorist Ideology'. *The Guardian*, 4 August 2010, sec. UK news. https://www.theguardian.com/uk/2010/aug/04/quilliam-foundation-list-alleged-extremism.

Dogra, Sufyan Abid. 'Living a Piety-Led Life beyond Muharram: Becoming or Being a South Asian Shia Muslim in the UK'. *Contemporary Islam* 13, no. 3 (1 October 2019): 307–24. https://doi.org/10.1007/s11562-019-00437-8.

Douglas, Gillian, Norman Doe, Sophie Gilliat-Ray, Russell Sandberg and Asma Khan. 'Social Cohesion and Civil Law: Marriage, Divorce and Religious Courts'. Cardiff: Cardiff University, 2011. http://www.law.cf.ac.uk/clr/Social%20Cohesion%20and%20Civil%20Law%20Full%20Report.pdf.

Duncan, Pamela. 'Europeans Greatly Overestimate Muslim Population, Poll Shows'. *The Guardian*, 13 December 2016, sec. Society. https://www.theguardian.com/society/datablog/2016/dec/13/europeans-massively-overestimate-muslim-population-poll-shows.

Dworkin, Ronald. 'Liberalism'. In *Public and Private Morality*, edited by Stuart Hampshire, 113–43. Cambridge: Cambridge University Press, 1978.

Eade, J., and D. Garbin. 'Competing Visions of Identity and Space: Bangladeshi Muslims in Britain'. *Contemporary South Asia* 15, no. 2 (2006): 181–93.

Eberle, Christopher. *Religious Conviction in Liberal Politics*. New York: Cambridge University Press, 2002.

Elahi, Farah, and Omar Khan, eds. *Islamophobia: Still a Challenge for Us All*. London: Runnymede, 2017.

El-Enany, Nadine. *Bordering Britain: Law, Race and Empire*. Manchester: Manchester University Press, 2020.

Elshayyal, Khadijah. *Muslim Identity Politics: Islam, Activism and Equality in Britain*. London: I.B. Tauris, 2018.

Elshayyal, Khadijah. 'Scottish Muslims in Numbers: Understanding Scotland's Muslims through the 2011 Census'. Edinburgh: The Alwaleed Centre for the Study of Islam in the Contemporary World, University of Edinburgh, 2016. http://www.ed.ac.uk/files/atoms/files/scottish_muslims_in_numbers_web.pdf.

Elshayyal, Khadijah. 'Securitisation, Fundamental British Values and the Neutralisation of Dissent within Muslim Discourses in the UK'. *Maydan* (blog), 26 February 2020. https://themaydan.com/2020/02/securitisation-fundamental-british-values-and-the-neutralisation-of-dissent-within-muslim-discourses-in-the-uk/.

Elshayyal, Khadijah, and Stephen H. Jones. 'United Kingdom'. In *Yearbook of Muslims in Europe*, edited by Egdunas Racius, Samim Akgönül, Ahmet Alibai and Jørgen S. Nielsen, vol. 12. Leiden: Brill, forthcoming.

Fakhry, Majid. *Averroes (Ibn Rushd): His Life, Works and Influence*. Oxford: OneWorld, 2001.

Fazakarley, Jed. *Muslim Communities in England 1962–90: Multiculturalism and Political Identity*, 1st edn. Cham, Switzerland: Palgrave Macmillan, 2017.

Ferguson, Niall. 'Eurabia?' *New York Times*, 4 April 2004, sec. Magazine. http://www.nytimes.com/2004/04/04/magazine/04WWLN.html.

Field, Clive D. 'Young British Muslims since 9/11: A Composite Attitudinal Profile'. *Religion, State and Society* 39, nos 2–3 (2011): 159–75.

Foucault, Michel. 'The Order of Discourse'. In *Untying the Text: A Post-Structuralist Reader*, edited by Robert Young, 48–78. London: Routledge, 1981.

Francis, Matthew. 'What Causes Radicalisation? Main Lines of Consensus in Recent Research'. Radicalisation Research, 24 January 2012. http://www.radicalisationresearch.org/guides/francis-2012-causes-2/.

Fraser, Nancy. 'Rethinking the Public Sphere: A Contribution to the Critique of Actually Existing Democracy'. In *Habermas and the Public Sphere*, edited by Craig Calhoun, 109–42. Cambridge, MA: MIT Press, 1992.

Furbey, Robert. 'Controversies of "Public Faith"'. In *Faith in the Public Realm: Controversies Policies and Practices*, edited by Adam Dinham, Robert Furbey and Vivien Lowndes, 21–40. Bristol: Policy Press, 2009.

Gale, Richard, and Simon Naylor. 'Religion, Planning and the City: The Spatial Politics of Ethnic Minority Expression in British Cities and Towns'. *Ethnicities* 2, no. 3 (2002): 387–409.

Gale, Richard, and Therese O'Toole. 'Young People and Faith Activism: British Muslim Youth, Glocalisation and the Umma'. In *Faith in the Public Realm: Controversies Policies and Practices*, edited by Adam Dinham, Robert Furbey and Vivien Lowndes, 143–62. Bristol: Policy Press, 2009.

Geaves, Ron. 'An Exploration of the Viability of Partnership between Dar Al-Ulum and Higher Education Institutions in North West England Focusing upon Pedagogy and Relevance'. Edinburgh: HEA, 30 July 2012. https://www.heacademy.ac.uk/sites/default/files/geaves_daralulums_final_report_isn.pdf.

Geaves, Ron. 'Drawing on the Past to Transform the Present: Contemporary Challenges for Training and Preparing British Imams'. *Journal of Muslim Minority Affairs* 28, no. 1 (2008): 99–112.

Geaves, Ron. *Islam in Victorian Britain: The Life and Times of Abdullah Quilliam*. Markfield: Kube, 2010.

Geaves, Ron. 'Muslims in Britain and Britishness in Islam: Historical and Religious Perspectives on British Muslim Past(s)'. Presented at the BRAIS Annual Conference 2017, University of Chester, 17 April 2017.

Geaves, Ron. 'Negotiating British Citizenship and Muslim Identity'. In *Muslim Britain: Communities under Pressure*, edited by Tahir Abbas, 66–77. London: Zed Books, 2005.

Geaves, Ron. 'On Higher Education and Dar Al-Ulums in Britain'. Presented at the Muslims in Britain Research Network, Leeds, 11 January 2012.

Geaves, Ron. *Sectarian Influences within Islam in Britain: With Reference to the Concepts of 'Ummah' and 'Community'*. Leeds: University of Leeds, 1996.

Geaves, Ron. 'The "Death" Pangs of the Insider/Outsider Dichotomy in the Study of Religion'. Presented at the Muslims in Britain Research Network, Cardiff University, 10 September 2014. http://sites.cardiff.ac.uk/islamukcentre/community-engagement/mbrn-islam-uk-centre-conference/ron-geaves-keynote-lecture/.

Geaves, Ron. 'The Symbolic Construction of the Walls of Deoband'. *Islam and Christian–Muslim Relations* 23, no. 3 (2012): 315–28.

Geddes, Mike. 'Neoliberalism and Local Governance: Cross-National Perspectives and Speculations'. *Policy Studies* 26, nos 3/4 (2005): 359–77.

Gest, Justin. *Apart: Alienated and Engaged Muslims in the West*. New York: Columbia University Press, 2010.

Giddens, Anthony. *Over to You, Mr Brown*. Cambridge: Polity, 2007.

Gilliat-Ray, Sophie. 'Closed Worlds: (Not) Accessing Deobandi Dar Ul-Uloom in Britain'. *Fieldwork in Religion* 1, no. 1 (2005): 7–33.

Gilliat-Ray, Sophie. 'Educating the 'ulama: Centres of Islamic Religious Training in Britain'. *Islam and Christian-Muslim Relations* 17, no. 1 (2006): 55–76.

Gilliat-Ray, Sophie. 'From "Closed Worlds" to "Open Doors": (Now) Accessing Deobandi Darul Uloom in Britain'. *Fieldwork in Religion* 13, no. 2 (2018): 127–50. https://doi.org/doi.org/10.1558/firn.35029.

Gilliat-Ray, Sophie. *Muslims in Britain: An Introduction*. Cambridge: Cambridge University Press, 2010.

Gilliat-Ray, Sophie. *Religion in Higher Education: The Politics of the Multi-Faith Campus*. Aldershot: Ashgate, 2000.

Gilliat-Ray, Sophie, Mansur Ali and Stephen Pattison. *Understanding Muslim Chaplaincy*. Farnham: Ashgate, 2013.

Gilligan, Andrew. 'Guide to School Islamisation, by "ringleader" of Trojan Horse Plot'. *The Telegraph*, 26 April 2014. http://www.telegraph.co.uk/education/educationnews/10790441/Guide-to-school-Islamisation-by-ringleader-of-Trojan-Horse-plot.html.

Gilligan, Andrew. 'Imams Will Have to Register and Face Security Vetting under Home Office Plans'. *The Telegraph*, 12 September 2015. http://www.telegraph.co.uk/news/uknews/terrorism-in-the-uk/11860993/Imams-will-have-to-register-and-face-security-vetting-under-Home-Office-plans.html.

Gilroy, Paul. *After Empire: Melancholia or Convivial Culture?* London: Routledge, 2004.

Gilroy, Paul. *There Ain't No Black in the Union Jack: The Cultural Politics of Race and Nation*. London: Routledge, 2002.

Goldberg, David Theo. *The Threat of Race: Reflections on Racial Neoliberalism*. Malden, MA: Wiley-VCH, 2008.

Goodman, Paul. 'MINAB's Mosques May Not Be so Moderate'. *Daily Telegraph*, 30 November 2007. http://www.telegraph.co.uk/comment/3644400/MINABs-mosques-may-not-be-so-moderate.html.

Grein, Tom. 'The Deeper Consternation of the Asia Bibi Scandal'. *The Spectator*, 5 January 2019. https://www.spectator.co.uk/2019/01/the-deeper-consternation-of-the-asia-bibi-scandal/.

Guest, Mathew, Kristin Aune, Sonya Sharma and Rob Warner. *Christianity and the University Experience: Understanding Student Faith*. London: Bloomsbury, 2013.

Guhin, Jeffrey. 'Religion as Site Rather Than Religion as Category: On the Sociology of Religion's Export Problem'. *Sociology of Religion* 75, no. 4 (December 2014): 579–93.

Guild, Elspeth, Kees Groenendijk and Sergio Carrera. *Illiberal Liberal States: Immigration, Citizenship and Integration in the EU*. Farnham: Ashgate, 2009.

Gutmann, Amy. *Democratic Education*. Revised edn. Princeton, NJ: Princeton University Press, 1999.

Habermas, Jürgen. *The Structural Transformation of the Public Sphere*. Cambridge, MA: MIT Press, 1989.

Habib, S. Irfan, and Dhruv Raina. 'Copernicus, Colombus, Colonialism and the Role of Science in Nineteenth Century India'. *Social Scientist* 17, nos 3/4 (1989): 51–66. https://doi.org/10.2307/3517360.

Haddad, Yvonne Yazbeck, and Michael J. Balz. 'Taming the Imams: European Governments and Islamic Preachers since 9/11'. *Islam and Christian–Muslim Relations* 19, no. 2 (2008): 215–35.

Hall, Suzanne M. 'Mooring "Super-Diversity" to a Brutal Migration Milieu'. *Ethnic and Racial Studies* 40, no. 9 (2017): 1562-73. http://www.tandfonline.com/doi/abs/10.1080/01419870.2017.1300296.

Hallaq, Wael B. 'Was Al-Shafi'i the Master Architect of Islamic Jurisprudence?' *International Journal of Middle East Studies* 25, no. 4 (1993): 587–605.

Hallaq, Wael B. 'Was the Gate of Ijtihad Closed?' *International Journal of Middle East Studies* 16, no. 1 (1 March 1984): 3–41.

Halliday, Fred. *Arabs in Exile: Yemeni Migrants in Urban Britain*. London: I.B. Tauris, 1992.

Hamid, Sadek. *Sufis, Salafis and Islamists: The Contested Ground of British Islamic Activism*. London: I.B. Tauris, 2015.

Hamid, Sadek. 'The Perils of Engaging CVE Policy Making: A British Case Study'. *Maydan* (blog), 4 December 2019. https://themaydan.com/2019/12/the-perils-of-engaging-cve-policy-making-a-british-case-study/.

Hamid, Sadek, ed. *Young British Muslims: Between Rhetoric and Real Lives*. London: Routledge, 2016.

Hansard. 'House of Commons Daily Debates'. United Kingdom Parliament, 25 May 2006. http://www.publications.parliament.uk/pa/cm200506/cmhansrd/vo060525/text/60525w0011.htm.

Hansard. 'House of Commons Daily Debates'. United Kingdom Parliament, 26 February 2009. http://www.publications.parliament.uk/pa/cm200809/cmhansrd/cm090226/text/90226w0033.htm.

Hansard. 'House of Commons Daily Debates'. United Kingdom Parliament, 15 March
    2011. http://www.publications.parliament.uk/pa/cm201011/cmhansrd/cm110315/
    halltext/110315h0001.htm#11031559000001.
Hansard. 'Memorandum from Radical Middle Way (PVE 73)', February 2010. http://
    www.publications.parliament.uk/pa/cm200910/cmselect/cmcomloc/memo/previoex/
    m7302.htm.
Haroon, Sana. 'The Rise of Deobandi Islam in the North-West Frontier Province and Its
    Implications in Colonial India and Pakistan 1914–1996'. *Journal of the Royal Asiatic
    Society* 18, no. 1 (2008): 47–70.
Hart Dyke, Anya. 'Mosques Made in Britain'. London: Quilliam Foundation, 2009.
Hasan, Usama. 'Launch of the Muslim Marriage Contract'. Presented at the Abrar House,
    London, 9 November 2008.
Heath, Anthony, and Yaojun Li. 'Review of the Relationship between Religion and
    Poverty: An Analysis for the Joseph Rowntree Foundation'. CSI Working Paper.
    Oxford: Centre for Social Investigation, Nuffield College, January 2015. csi.nuff.ox.ac.
    uk/wp-content/uploads/2015/03/religion-and-poverty-working-paper.pdf.
Heath-Kelly, Charlotte. 'Counter-Terrorism and the Counterfactual: Producing the
    'Radicalisation' Discourse and the UK PREVENT Strategy'. *British Journal of Politics &
    International Relations* 15, no. 3 (2013): 394–415.
Heath-Kelly, Charlotte. 'The Geography of Pre-Criminal Space: Epidemiological
    Imaginations of Radicalisation Risk in the UK Prevent Strategy, 2007–2017'. *Critical
    Studies on Terrorism* 10, no. 2 (4 May 2017): 297–319. https://doi.org/10.1080/1753915
    3.2017.1327141.
Heller-Roazen, Daniel. 'Philosophy before the Law: Averroës's Decisive Treatise'. *Critical
    Inquiry* 32, no. 3 (2006): 414–42.
Herbert, David. *Religion and Civil Society: Rethinking Public Religion in the Contemporary
    World*. Aldershot: Ashgate, 2003.
Higher Education Funding Council for England. 'Islamic Studies: Trends and Profiles'.
    London: HEFCE, 2008.
HM Government. 'Counter-Extremism Strategy'. London: Home Office, 2015.
    https://www.gov.uk/government/uploads/system/uploads/attachment_data/
    file/470088/51859_Cm9148_Accessible.pdf.
HM Government. *Prevent Duty Guidance: For England and Wales*. London: Stationery
    Office, 2015. https://www.gov.uk/government/uploads/system/uploads/attachment_
    data/file/417943/Prevent_Duty_Guidance_England_Wales.pdf.
HM Government. 'Prevent Strategy'. London: Stationery Office, 2011.
HM Government. 'Tackling Extremism in the UK: Report from the Prime Minister's
    Task Force on Radicalisation and Extremism'. London: Cabinet Office, 2013. https://
    www.gov.uk/government/uploads/system/uploads/attachment_data/file/263181/
    ETF_FINAL.pdf.
Holmwood, John, and Therese O'Toole. *Countering Extremism in British Schools: The
    Truth about the Birmingham Trojan Horse Affair*. Policy Press, 2018.
Home Office. 'Charter for the Commission for Countering Extremism'. Gov.uk, 2018.
    https://www.gov.uk/government/publications/charter-for-the-commission-for-
    countering-extremism/charter-for-the-commission-for-countering-
    extremism.
Hope, Christopher. 'David Cameron: We Will "Drain the Swamp" Which Allows
    Muslim Extremists to Flourish', 3 June 2013. http://www.telegraph.co.uk/news /

politics/10097006/David-Cameron-We-will-drain-the-swamp-which-allows-Muslim-extremists-to-flourish.html.

Hourani, Albert. *Arabic Thought in the Liberal Age*. London: Oxford University Press, 1962.

House of Commons. 'Muslim Brotherhood Review: Main Findings'. London: Prime Minister's Office, 17 December 2015. https://www.gov.uk/government/publications/muslim-brotherhood-review-main-findings.

House of Commons Communities and Local Government Committee. 'Preventing Violent Extremism: Sixth Report of Session 2009–10'. London: Stationery Office, 2010.

Hughes, Tristram, Aaron Porter, Stephen H. Jones and Jonathan Sheen. 'Privately Funded Providers of Higher Education in the UK'. London: Department for Business Innovation and Skills, 2013.

Hundal, Sunny. 'British Muslims Are Losing the War against ISIL'. *Quartz*, 10 September 2015. http://qz.com/498409/british-muslims-are-losing-the-war-against-isil/.

Hundal, Sunny. 'This System of Self-Appointed Leaders Can Hurt Those It Should Be Protecting'. *The Guardian*, 20 November 2006, sec. Comment is Free. http://www.theguardian.com/commentisfree/2006/nov/20/thissystemofselfappointedl.

Husband, Charles, and Yunis Alam. *Social Cohesion and Counter-Terrorism: A Policy Contradiction?* Bristol: Policy Press, 2011.

Hussain, Amjad M. 'Towards Solving the Crisis of Islam in Higher Education'. *Journal of Beliefs & Values* 28, no. 3 (1 December 2007): 267–72. https://doi.org/10.1080/13617670701712455.

Hussain, Serena. 'Kurdish Muslim Identity: Religious Universalism or Ethno-Nationalism?' Unpublished paper, 2014.

Hussain, Yasmin, and Paul Bagguley. 'Citizenship, Ethnicity and Identity: British Pakistanis after the 2001 "Riots"'. *Sociology* 39, no. 3 (2005): 407–25. https://doi.org/10.1177/0038038505052493.

Hussain, Yasmin, and Paul Bagguley. 'Securitized Citizens: Islamophobia, Racism and the 7/7 London Bombings'. *Sociological Review* 60, no. 4 (1 November 2012): 715–34. https://doi.org/10.1111/j.1467-954X.2012.02130.x.

Hutnyk, John. 'The Dialectic of "Here and There": Anthropology "at Home"'. In *A Postcolonial People: South Asians in Britain*, edited by S. Sayyid, N. Ali and V. S. Kalra, 74–90. London: C. Hurst, 2006.

ICM Unlimited. 'C4/Juniper Survey of Muslims 2015'. London: ICM Unlimited, 2015.

I&DeA. 'Taking Forward Community Cohesion in Leicester'. Leicester: Improvement and Development Agency/Leicester City Council, 2002.

Imtiaz, Atif. 'Contextualising Islam in the United Kingdom: A Matter of Confidence?' Presented at the Muslim Leadership in Britain, UCLAN, 1 April 2015.

Inge, Anabel. *The Making of a Salafi Muslim Woman: Paths to Conversion*. London: Oxford University Press, 2016.

Ingram, Brannon D. *Revival From Below: The Deoband Movement and Global Islam*. Oakland: University of California Press, 2018.

Inner Cities Religious Council. 'Review of the Inner Cities Religious Council: A Report of the Review Team'. London: HMSO, 1998.

Ipsos Mori. 'Building a Stronger Britain Together (BSBT) Progress Report 2019: Interim Evaluation Findings'. London: Home Office, 2019.

Isakjee, Arshad, and Chris Allen. '"A Catastrophic Lack of Inquisitiveness": A Critical Study of the Impact and Narrative of the Project Champion Surveillance Project in Birmingham'. *Ethnicities*, 9 July 2013, 1468796813492488.

Islamic Shari'a Council. 'ISC Standing on the Muslim Marriage Contract'. Islamic Shari'a Council, 2008. http://www.islamic-sharia.org/news/isc-standing-on-the-marriage-contract.html.

Jackson, Roy. *Mawlana Mawdudi and Political Islam: Authority and the Islamic State*. Routledge, 2010.

Jacobson, Jessica. *Islam in Transition: Religion and Identity among British Pakistani Youth*. London: Routledge, 1998.

Jewish News. 'Legal First as Jail Threat Makes Man Grant "Get"'. *Jewish News*, 15 January 2020. https://jewishnews.timesofisrael.com/chained-wife-wins-private-prosecution-to-force-ex-husband-to-grant-get/.

Jivraj, Stephen. 'Muslims in England and Wales: Evidence from the 2011 Census'. In *The New Muslims*, edited by Claire Alexander, Victoria Redclift, and Ajmal Hussain, 16–19. London: The Runnymede Trust, 2013.

Jones, Hannah, Sarah Neal, Giles Mohan, Kieran Connell, Allan Cochrane and Katy Bennett. 'Urban Multiculture and Everyday Encounters in Semi-Public, Franchised Cafe Spaces'. *Sociological Review* 63, no. 3 (1 August 2015): 644–61. https://doi.org/10.1111/1467-954X.12311.

Jones, Peter. 'Equality, Recognition and Difference'. *Critical Review of International Social and Political Philosophy* 9, no. 1 (2006): 23–36.

Jones, Richard, and Welhengama Gnanapala. *Ethnic Minorities in English Law*. Stoke-on-Trent: Trentham, 2000.

Jones, Stephen H. 'New Labour and the Re-Making of British Islam: The Case of the Radical Middle Way and the "Reclamation" of the Classical Islamic Tradition'. *Religions* 4, no. 4 (4 November 2013): 550–66.

Jones, Stephen H. 'Religious Literacy in Higher Education'. In *Religious Literacy in Policy and Practice*, edited by Adam Dinham and Matthew Francis, 185–204. Bristol: Policy Press, 2015.

Jones, Stephen H. 'The "Metropolis of Dissent": Muslim Participation in Leicester and the "Failure" of Multiculturalism in Britain'. *Ethnic and Racial Studies* 38, no. 11 (2 September 2015): 1969–85. https://doi.org/10.1080/01419870.2014.936891.

Jones, Stephen H., and Dominic Baker. 'The Religious Life of a "Plural City"'. Public Spirit, 19 September 2013. http://www.publicspirit.org.uk/the-religious-life-of-a-plural-city/.

Jones, Stephen H., and Khadijah Elshayyal. 'United Kingdom'. In *Yearbook of Muslims in Europe*, edited by Oliver Scharbrodt, Samim Akgönül, Ahmet Alibai, Jørgen S. Nielsen, and Egdunas Racius, vol. 11: 656–74. Leiden: Brill, 2019.

Jones, Stephen H., and Sadek Hamid. 'United Kingdom'. In *Yearbook of Muslims in Europe*, edited by Oliver Scharbrodt, Samim Akgönül, Ahmet Alibai, Jørgen S. Nielsen and Egdunas Racius, vol. 10: 703–21. Leiden: Brill, 2018.

Jones, Stephen H., Rebecca Catto, Tom Kaden and Fern Elsdon-Baker. ' "That's How Muslims Are Required to View the World": Race, Culture and Belief in Non-Muslims' Descriptions of Islam and Science'. *Sociological Review*, 31 May 2018. https://doi.org/10.1177/0038026118778174.

Jones, Stephen H., Therese O'Toole, Daniel Nilsson DeHanas, Tariq Modood and Nasar Meer. 'A "System of Self-Appointed Leaders"? Examining Modes of Muslim Representation in Governance in Britain'. *British Journal of Politics and International Relations* 17, no. 2 (2015): 207–23. https://doi.org/10.1111/1467-856X.12051.

Joppke, Christian. 'The Retreat of Multiculturalism in the Liberal State: Theory and Policy'. *British Journal of Sociology* 55, no. 2 (2004): 237–57.

Kabir, Nahid A. *Young British Muslims: Identity, Culture, Politics and the Media.* Edinburgh: Edinburgh University Press, 2012.

Kamali, Mohammed Hashim. *Freedom of Expression in Islam.* Cambridge: Islamic Texts Society, 1997.

Kant, Immanuel. *Groundwork of the Metaphysics of Morals.* Edited by Mary Gregor and Jens Timmerman. Revised edn. Cambridge: Cambridge University Press, 2012.

Kapoor, Nisha. *Deport, Deprive, Extradite: Twenty-First Century State Extremism.* London: Verso, 2018.

Kapoor, Nisha. 'The Advancement of Racial Neoliberalism in Britain'. *Ethnic and Racial Studies* 36, no. 6 (1 June 2013): 1028–46.

Kapoor, Nisha, and Kasia Narkowicz. 'Unmaking Citizens: Passport Removals, Pre-Emptive Policing and the Reimagining of Colonial Governmentalities'. *Ethnic and Racial Studies* 42, no. 16 (2017): 45–62. https://doi.org/10.1080/01419870.2017.1411965.

Karlsen, Saffron, and James Y. Nazroo. 'Ethnic and Religious Differences in the Attitudes of People towards Being "British"'. *Sociological Review*, 1 June 2015, n/a-n/a. https://doi.org/10.1111/1467-954X.12313.

Kashyap, Ridhi, and Valerie A. Lewis. 'British Muslim Youth and Religious Fundamentalism: A Quantitative Investigation'. *Ethnic and Racial Studies* 36, no. 12 (26 April 2012): 2117–40. https://doi.org/10.1080/01419870.2012.672761.

Kazi, Tehmina. 'How Prevent Undermined Cohesion'. *The Guardian*, 16 July 2010, sec. Comment is Free. http://www.guardian.co.uk/commentisfree/belief/2010/jul/16/prevent-cohesion-communities-islam.

Keith, Michael. *After the Cosmopolitan? Multicultural Cities and the Future of Racism.* Abingdon: Routledge, 2005.

Kelly, Ruth. 'Britain: Our Values, Our Responsibilities'. British Embassy Berlin, 10 October 2006. http://ukingermany.fco.gov.uk/en/news/?view=Speech&id=4615992.

Kelly, Ruth. 'Time for a British Version of Islam …' *New Statesman*, 9 April 2007.

Kepel, Gilles. 'Europe's Answer to Londonistan'. *OpenDemocracy*, 24 August 2005. http://www.opendemocracy.net/conflict-terrorism/londonistan_2775.jsp.

Kepel, Gilles. *Jihad: The Trail of Political Islam.* London: I.B. Tauris, 2009.

Khan, Aina. 'Nikkah: To Register or Not to Register?' Presented at the Abrar House, London, 2 October 2015. http://www.thecitycircle.com/events/33-events/past-events/866-nikkah-to-register-or-not-to-register https://www.youtube.com/watch?v=uJesuFkCUsE.

Khan, Sara, and Tony McMahon. *The Battle for British Islam: Reclaiming Muslim Identity from Extremism.* London: Saqi Books, 2016.

Khattab, Nabil. 'Ethno-Religious Background as a Determinant of Educational and Occupational Attainment in Britain'. *Sociology* 43, no. 2 (2009): 304–22.

Khattab, Nabil, and Ron Johnston. 'Ethno-Religious Identities and Persisting Penalties in the UK Labor Market'. *Social Science Journal* 52, no. 4 (December 2015): 490–502. https://doi.org/10.1016/j.soscij.2014.10.007.

Khattab, Nabil, Ron Johnston, and David Manley. 'Human Capital, Family Structure and Religiosity Shaping British Muslim Women's Labour Market Participation'. *Journal of Ethnic and Migration Studies* 44, no. 9 (4 July 2018): 1541–59. https://doi.org/10.1080/1369183X.2017.1334541.

Khattab, Nabil, and Tariq Modood. 'Both Ethnic and Religious: Explaining Employment Penalties across 14 Ethno-Religious Groups in the United Kingdom'. *Journal for*

the Scientific Study of Religion 54, no. 3 (1 September 2015): 501–22. https://doi.
     org/10.1111/jssr.12220.
Kundnani, Arun. *Spooked: How Not to Prevent Violent Extremism*. London: Institute of
     Race Relations, 2009.
Kundnani, Arun. *The End of Tolerance: Racism in 21st Century Britain*. London: Pluto
     Press, 2007.
Kymlicka, Will. *Liberalism, Community and Culture*. Gloucestershire: Clarendon
     Press, 1991.
Law Commission. 'Getting Married: A Scoping Paper'. London: Law Commission, 2015.
     http://www.lawcom.gov.uk/wp-content/uploads/2015/12/Getting_Married_scoping_
     paper.pdf.
Law Commission. 'Government Asks Law Commission to Conduct a Full Review
     of Weddings Law', 8 November 2018. https://www.lawcom.gov.uk/
     government-asks-law-commission-to-conduct-a-full-review-of-weddings-law/.
Lentin, Alana. 'Post-Race, Post Politics: The Paradoxical Rise of Culture after
     Multiculturalism'. *Ethnic and Racial Studies* 37, no. 8 (3 July 2014): 1268–85. https://
     doi.org/10.1080/01419870.2012.664278.
Lewis, Philip. *Islamic Britain*. London: I.B. Tauris, 2002.
Lewis, Philip. *Young, British and Muslim*. London: Continuum, 2007.
Lewis, Philip, and Sadek Hamid. *British Muslims: New Directions in Islamic Thought,
     Creativity and Activism*. Edinburgh: Edinburgh University Press, 2018.
Liberatore, Giulia. 'Guidance as "Women's Work": A New Generation of Female Islamic
     Authorities in Britain'. *Religions* 10, no. 11 (November 2019): 601. https://doi.
     org/10.3390/rel10110601.
Macedo, Stephen. 'Liberal Civic Education and Religious Fundamentalism: The Case of
     God vs. John Rawls?' *Ethics* 105, no. 3 (1995): 468–96.
MacEoin, Denis. *Sharia Law or 'One Law for All'?* London: Civitas, 2009.
MacEoin, Denis. *The Hijacking of British Islam: How Extremist Literature Is Subverting
     Mosques in the UK*. London: Policy Exchange, 2007.
Maher, Shiraz, and Martyn Frampton. 'Choosing Our Friends Wisely: Criteria for
     Engagement with Muslim Groups'. London: Policy Exchange, 2009.
Malik, Abdul-Rehman. 'Take Me to Your Leader: Post-Secular Society and the Islam
     Industry'. *Eurozine*, 23 April 2007. http://www.eurozine.com/articles/2007-04-23-
     armalik-en.html.
Malik, Kenan. *From Fatwa to Jihad: The Rushdie Affair and Its Legacy*. London: Atlantic
     Books, 2009.
Malik, Maleiha. 'Faith and the State of Jurisprudence'. In *Faith in Law: Essays in Legal
     Theory*, edited by Sionaidh Douglas-Scott, Peter Oliver and Victor Tadros, 129–49.
     London: Hart, 2000.
Malik, Maleiha. 'Minority Legal Orders in the UK: Minorities, Pluralism and the Law'.
     London: British Academy Policy Centre, 2012. http://www.britac.ac.uk/policy/
     Minority-legal-orders.cfm.
Mamdani, M. 'Good Muslim, Bad Muslim: A Political Perspective on Culture and
     Terrorism'. *American Anthropologist* 104, no. 3 (2002): 766–75.
Mandaville, Peter. 'Globalization and the Politics of Religious Knowledge: Pluralising
     Authority in the Muslim World'. *Theory, Culture and Society* 24, no. 2 (2007): 101–15.
Mandaville, Peter. 'Islamic Education in Britain: Approaches to Religious Knowledge in
     a Pluralistic Society'. In *Schooling Islam: The Culture and Politics of Modern Muslim*

Education, edited by Robert W. Hefner and Muhammad Qasim Zaman, 224–41. Princeton, NJ: Princeton University Press, 2007.

Manea, Elham. *Women and Sharia Law: The Impact of Legal Pluralism in the UK*. London: I.B. Tauris, 2016.

Mangera, Abdur-Rahman. 'Training British Muslim Religious Leaders'. Presented at the Abrar House, London, 27 November 2015. https://www.youtube.com/watch?v=DK5QQ_biMFU.

Mansbridge, Jane. 'Should Blacks Represent Blacks and Women Represent Women? A Contingent "Yes"'. *Journal of Politics* 61, no. 3 (1999): 628–57.

March, Andrew F. *Islam and Liberal Citizenship: The Search for an Overlapping Consensus*. Oxford: Oxford University Press, 2009.

March, Andrew F. *The Caliphate of Man: Popular Sovereignty in Modern Islamic Thought*. Cambridge, MA: Harvard University Press, 2019.

Marshall, Alex. 'How Isis Got Its Anthem'. *The Guardian*, 9 November 2014. http://www.theguardian.com/music/2014/nov/09/nasheed-how-isis-got-its-anthem.

Massad, Joseph A. *Islam in Liberalism*. Chicago, IL: University of Chicago Press, 2015.

Massoumi, Narzanin, Tom Mills and David Miller, eds. *What Is Islamophobia? Racism, Social Movements and the State*. London: Pluto Press, 2017.

Matthews, David. 'University of Wales Pulls in Its Tentacles'. *Times Higher Education*, 4 October 2011. https://www.timeshighereducation.co.uk/news/university-of-wales-pulls-in-its-tentacles/417649.article.

Mavelli, Luca. 'Between Normalisation and Exception: The Securitisation of Islam and the Construction of the Secular Subject'. *Millennium: Journal of International Studies* 41, no. 2 (1 January 2013): 159–81.

McGhee, Derek. *Security, Citizenship and Human Rights: Shared Values in Uncertain Times*. Basingstoke: Palgrave Macmillan, 2010.

McGhee, Derek. *The End of Multiculturalism? Terrorism, Integration and Human Rights*. Maidenhead: Open University Press, 2008.

McLoughlin, Seán. 'Discrepant Representations of Multi-Asian Leicester: Institutional Discourse and Everyday Life in the "Model" Multicultural City'. In *Writing the City in British-Asian Diasporas*, edited by Sean McLoughlin, William Gould, Ananya Jahanara Kabir and Emma Tomalin. London: Routledge, 2014.

McLoughlin, Seán. 'Mosques and the Public Space: Conflict and Cooperation in Bradford'. *Journal of Ethnic and Migration Studies* 31, no. 6 (1 November 2005): 1045–66. https://doi.org/10.1080/13691830500282832.

McLoughlin, Seán. 'The State, New Muslim Leaderships and Islam as a Resource for Public Engagement in Britain'. In *European Muslims and the Secular State*, edited by Jocelyne Cesari and Seán McLoughlin, 55–70. Aldershot: Ashgate, 2005.

McRoy, Anthony. *From Rushdie to 7/7: The Radicalisation of Islam in Britain*. London: Social Affairs Unit, 2006.

Meer, Nasar. *Citizenship, Identity and the Politics of Multiculturalism: The Rise of Muslim Consciousness*. Basingstoke: Palgrave Macmillan, 2010.

Meer, Nasar, and Tariq Modood. 'The Multicultural State We're In: Muslims, "Multiculture" and the "Civic Re-Balancing" of British Multiculturalism'. *Political Studies* 57, no. 3 (2009): 473–97. https://doi.org/10.1111/j.1467-9248.2008.00745.x.

Mehdi, Rubya, and Jørgen S. Nielsen, eds. *Embedding Mahr in the European Legal System*. Copenhagen: DJØF, 2011.

Menski, Werner F. 'Angrezi Shariat: Glocalised Plural Arrangements by Migrants in Britain'. *Law Vision*, no. 10 (2008): 10–12.

Metcalf, Barbara D. 'Madrasas and Minorities in Secular India'. In *Schooling Islam: The Culture and Politics of Modern Muslim Education*, edited by Robert W. Hefner and Muhammad Qasim Zaman, 87–106. Princeton, NJ: Princeton University Press, 2007.

Metcalf, Barbara D. *Islamic Revival in British India: Deoband, 1860–1900*. Princeton, NJ: Princeton University Press, 1982.

Miaari, Sami, Nabil Khattab and Ron Johnston. 'Religion and Ethnicity at Work: A Study of British Muslim Women's Labour Market Performance'. *Quality and Quantity*, 7 March 2018. https://doi.org/10.1007/s11135-018-0721-x.

Michot, Yahya. 'Muslims under Non-Muslim Rule: A Classical Fatwa'. Presented at the Abrar House, London, 18 July 2008.

Mill, John Stuart. *On Liberty and Other Essays*. Oxford: Oxford University Press, 1991.

Mills, Tom, Tom Griffin and David Miller. 'The Cold War on British Muslims: An Examination of Policy Exchange and the Centre for Social Cohesion'. Glasgow: Spinwatch, 2011.

Mirza, Munira, Abi Senthilkumaran and Zein Ja'far. 'Living Apart Together: British Muslims and the Paradox of Multiculturalism'. London: Policy Exchange, 2007. http://www.policyexchange.org.uk/images/libimages/246.pdf.

Modood, Tariq. '2011 Paul Hanly Furfey Lecture: Is There a Crisis of Secularism in Western Europe?' *Sociology of Religion* 73, no. 2 (4 May 2012): 130–49.

Modood, Tariq. 'Moderate Secularism and Multiculturalism'. *Politics* 29, no. 1 (1 February 2009): 71–6. https://doi.org/10.1111/j.1467-9256.2008.01340.x.

Modood, Tariq. *Multiculturalism: A Civic Idea*. Cambridge: Polity, 2007.

Modood, Tariq. 'Muslims, Race and Equality in Britain: Some Post-Rushdie Affair Reflections'. *Third Text* 4, no. 11 (1 June 1990): 127–34. https://doi.org/10.1080/09528829008576269.

Modood, Tariq. 'Political Blackness and British Asians'. *Sociology* 28, no. 4 (1 November 1994): 859–76.

Modood, Tariq. *Still Not Easy Being British: Struggles for a Multicultural Citizenship*. London: Trentham Books, 2010.

Modood, Tariq, Richard Berthoud, Jane Lakey, James Nazroo, Patten Smith, Satnam Virdee and Sharon Beishon. *Ethnic Minorities in Britain: Diversity and Disadvantage – The Fourth National Survey of Ethnic Minorities*, 1st edn. London: Policy Studies Institute, 1997.

Mogahed, Dalia, and Fouad Pervez. 'American Muslim Poll: Participation, Priorities, and Facing Prejudice in the 2016 Elections'. Dearborn, MI: Institute for Social Policy and Understanding, 2016. http://www.ispu.org/wp-content/uploads/2016/08/poll2016-1.pdf.

Mogra, Imran. 'Tablighi Jama'at in the UK'. In *Islamic Movements of Europe*, edited by Frank Peter and Rafael Ortega, 187–90. London: I.B. Tauris, 2014.

Mondal, Anshuman A. *Young British Muslim Voices*. Oxford: Greenwood World, 2008.

Mondon, Aurelien, and Aaron Winter. 'Articulations of Islamophobia: From the Extreme to the Mainstream?' *Ethnic and Racial Studies* 40, no. 13 (2017): 2151–79. https://doi.org/10.1080/01419870.2017.1312008.

Moore, Charles. 'Archbishop, You Can't Just Have a Bit of Sharia – It's All or Nothing'. *Daily Telegraph*, 9 February 2008.

Morrison, Toni. 'A Humanistic View'. Presented at the Black Studies Center public dialogue, Portland State University, 30 May 1975. https://soundcloud.com/portland-state-library/portland-state-black-studies-1.

Mouffe, Chantal. 'Deliberative Democracy or Agonistic Pluralism'. *Reihe Politikwissenschaft: Political Science Series*, no. 72 (December 2000). http://www.ihs. ac.at/publications/pol/pw_72.pdf.

Mukadam, Mohamed, and Alison Scott-Baumann. 'The Training and Development of Muslim Faith Leaders: Current Practice and Future Possibilities'. London: DCLG, October 2010.

Munson, Ziad. 'Islamic Mobilization: Social Movement Theory and the Egyptian Muslim Brotherhood'. *Sociological Quarterly* 42, no. 4 (1 September 2001): 487–510. https://doi. org/10.1111/j.1533–8525.2001.tb01777.x.

Murad, Abdal-Hakim. 'Book Launch: A Muslim in Victorian America'. Presented at the House of Lords, London, 22 November 2006. http://www.radicalmiddleway.co.uk/ videos.php?id=1&art=11.

Murad, Abdal-Hakim. 'British and Muslim?' Masud, 1997. http://www.masud.co.uk/ ISLAM/ahm/british.htm.

Murad, Abdal-Hakim, ed. *Muslim Songs of the British Isles: Arranged for Schools.* London: Quilliam Press, 2005.

Murdoch, Iris. *The Sovereignty of Good.* London: Routledge, 2001.

Murray, Douglas. *The Strange Death of Europe: Immigration, Identity, Islam.* London: Bloomsbury Continuum, 2018.

Muslim Brotherhood. 'Muslim Brotherhood Statement Denouncing UN Women Declaration for Violating Sharia Principles'. Ikhwanweb, 14 March 2013. http://www. ikhwanweb.com/article.php?id=30731.

Muslim Council of Britain. 'British Muslims in Numbers: A Demographic, Socio-Economic and Health Profile of Muslims in Britain Drawing on the 2011 Census'. London: Muslim Council of Britain, 2015.

Muslim Council of Britain. *Towards Greater Understanding: Meeting the Needs of Muslim Pupils in State Schools.* London: MCB, 2007.

Mythen, Gabe, Sandra Walklate and Fatima Khan. '"I'm a Muslim, but I'm Not a Terrorist": Victimization, Risky Identities and the Performance of Safety'. *British Journal of Criminology* 49, no. 6 (2009): 736–54. https://doi.org/10.1093/bjc/azp032.

Namazie, Maryam. '395 Signatories Call to Dismantle Parallel Legal Systems'. *One Law for All* (blog), 9 October 2015. http://www.onelawforall.org.uk/sharia-courts/.

Nandi, Alita, and Lucinda Platt. 'Britishness and Identity Assimilation among the UK's Minority and Majority Ethnic Groups'. Understanding Society Working Paper Series. Essex: Understanding Society, 2013.

Nandi, Alita, and Lucinda Platt. 'Patterns of Minority and Majority Identification in a Multicultural Society'. *Ethnic and Racial Studies* 38, no. 15 (8 December 2015): 2615–34. https://doi.org/10.1080/01419870.2015.1077986.

Naylor, Simon, and James R. Ryan. 'The Mosque in the Suburbs: Negotiating Religion and Ethnicity in South London'. *Social & Cultural Geography* 3, no. 1 (2002): 39–59. https:// doi.org/10.1080/14649360120114134.

Nelson, Chris. 'Is the UK Turning a Blind Eye to Muslim Polygamy?' *Newsnight.* London: BBC2, 23 July 2009. http://news.bbc.co.uk/1/hi/programmes/ newsnight/8164961.stm.

Newman, Janet. *Remaking Governance: Peoples, Politics and the Public Sphere.* Bristol: Policy Press, 2005.

Newsnight. 'Talk about Newsnight: Policy Exchange Dispute – Update'. BBC, 29 May 2008. https://www.bbc.co.uk/blogs/newsnight/2008/05/policy_exchange_dispute_ update.html.

Norfolk, Andrew. 'Christian Child Forced into Muslim Foster Care'. *The Times*, 28 August 2017, sec. News. https://www.thetimes.co.uk/article/christian-child-forced-into-muslim-foster-care-by-tower-hamlets-council-3gcp6l8cs.

Noronha, Luke de. 'Deportation, Racism and Multi-Status Britain: Immigration Control and the Production of Race in the Present'. *Ethnic and Racial Studies* 42, no. 14 (26 October 2019): 2413–30. https://doi.org/10.1080/01419870.2019.1585559.

Norris, Maria W. 'The Secretive World of Counter-Terrorism Funding'. *Public Spirit* (blog), 2017. http://www.publicspirit.org.uk/the-secretive-world-of-counter-extremism-funding/.

Norton, Anne. *On the Muslim Question*. Princeton, NJ: Princeton University Press, 2013.

Nussbaum, Martha C. 'Rawls's Political Liberalism: A Reassessment'. *Ratio Juris* 24, no. 1 (2011): 1–24.

Nussbaum, Martha C. 'Perfectionist Liberalism and Political Liberalism'. *Philosophy & Public Affairs* 39, no. 1 (1 January 2011): 3–45. https://doi.org/10.1111/j.1088-4963.2011.01200.x.

Nye, Catrin. 'The Man Correcting Stories about Muslims'. *BBC News*, 19 January 2017, sec. UK. https://www.bbc.com/news/uk-38655760.

Office for National Statistics. 'Divorce in the UK'. Text. Office for National Statistics, 22 September 2014. http://www.ons.gov.uk/ons/about-ons/business-transparency/freedom-of-information/what-can-i-request/previous-foi-requests/population/the-number-of-people-divorced-in-the-uk-in-the-last-decade-/index.html.

Office for National Statistics. 'Muslim Population in the UK'. Office for National Statistics. Accessed 12 March 2019. https://www.ons.gov.uk/aboutus/transparencyandgovernance/freedomofinformationfoi/muslimpopulationintheuk?fbclid=IwAR3Vti-dlX2R2qmNpDX2LptsdmFKWm5A6zJ5_raspkmjqyahs1gJZIQfDqw.

Ofsted. 'Darul Uloom Al Arabiya Al Islamiya: Inspection Report'. Manchester: Ofsted, 23 November 2016. https://reports.ofsted.gov.uk/inspection-reports/find-inspection-report/provider/ELS/105372.

O'Toole, Therese, and Ekaterina Braginskaia. 'Public Faith and Finance: Faith Responses to the Financial Crisis'. Birmingham: Barrow Cadbury Trust, July 2016. http://www.publicspirit.org.uk/assets/PubFaithFin-Report-Final.pdf.

O'Toole, Therese, Daniel Nilsson DeHanas and Tariq Modood. 'Balancing Tolerance, Security and Muslim Engagement in the United Kingdom: The Impact of the "Prevent" Agenda'. *Critical Studies on Terrorism* 5, no. 3 (1 December 2012): 373–89. https://doi.org/10.1080/17539153.2012.725570.

O'Toole, Therese, Daniel Nilsson DeHanas, Tariq Modood, Nasar Meer and Stephen H. Jones. 'Taking Part: Muslim Participation in Contemporary Governance'. Bristol: University of Bristol, 2013.

O'Toole, Therese, Stephen H. Jones and Daniel Nilsson DeHanas. 'The New Prevent: Will It Work? Can It Work?' *Arches Quarterly* 5, no. 9 (2012): 56–62.

O'Toole, Therese, Nasar Meer, Daniel Nilsson DeHanas, Stephen H. Jones and Tariq Modood. 'Governing through Prevent? Regulation and Contested Practice in State–Muslim Engagement'. *Sociology* 50, no. 1 (1 February 2016): 160–77. https://doi.org/10.1177/0038038514564437.

Pantazis, Christina, and Simon Pemberton. 'Resisting the Advance of the Security State: The Impact of Frameworks of Resistance on the UK'S Securitisation Agenda'. *International Journal of Law, Crime and Justice* 41, no. 4 (2013): 358–74. https://doi.org/doi:10.1016/j.ijlcj.2013.07.009.

Parekh, Bhikhu. *Rethinking Multiculturalism: Cultural Diversity and Political Theory.* London: Palgrave Macmillan, 2000.

Parsons, Martin. 'What Is the Point of the Commission for Countering Extremism?' Conservative Home, 10 October 2019. https://www.conservativehome.com/platform/2019/10/martin-parsons-what-is-the-point-of-the-commission-for-countering-extremism.html.

Paton, Rob, Haider Ali and Lee Taylor. 'Government Support for Faith-Based Organizations: The Case of a Development Programme for Faith Leaders'. *Public Money & Management* 29, no. 6 (2009): 363–70.

Peace, Timothy. 'Muslims and Electoral Politics in Britain: The Case of the Respect Party'. In *Muslim Political Participation in Europe*, edited by Jørgen S. Nielsen, 299–321. Edinburgh: Edinburgh University Press, 2013.

Peace, Timothy. *European Social Movements and Muslim Activism: Another World but with Whom?* Basingstoke: Palgrave MacMillan, 2015.

Peach, Ceri. 'Britain's Muslim Population: An Overview'. In *Muslim Britain: Communities under Pressure*, edited by Tahir Abbas, 18–30. London: Zed Books, 2005.

Pearl, David, and Werner Menski. *Muslim Family Law*, 3rd edn. London: Sweet & Maxwell, 1998.

Pedziwiatr, Konrad. 'Creating New Discursive Arenas and Influencing the Policies of the State: The Case of the Muslim Council of Britain'. *Social Compass* 54, no. 2 (2007): 267–80.

Pennock, James Roland. *Democratic Political Theory.* Princeton, NJ: Princeton University Press, 1979.

Pew Research Center. 'Muslim Americans: No Signs of Growth in Alienation or Support for Extremism'. Washington, DC: Pew Forum on Religion & Public Life, 2011. http://www.people-press.org/files/2011/08/muslim-american-report.pdf.

Pew Research Centre. 'Europe's Growing Muslim Population'. Washington, DC: Pew Research Centre, November 2017. http://assets.pewresearch.org/wp-content/uploads/sites/11/2017/11/29103550/FULL-REPORT-FOR-WEB-POSTING.pdf.

Pew Research Global Attitudes Project. 'Muslims in Europe: Economic Worries Top Concerns about Religious and Cultural Identity'. Washington, DC: Pew Research Centre, 6 July 2006. http://www.pewglobal.org/2006/07/06/muslims-in-europe-economic-worries-top-concerns-about-religious-and-cultural-identity/.

Phillips, Anne. *Multiculturalism without Culture.* Princeton, NJ: Princeton University Press, 2007.

Phillips, Anne. *The Politics of Presence.* Oxford: Oxford University Press, 1995.

Phillips, Miranda. 'Common Law Marriage: A Peculiarly Persistent Myth'. NatCen Social Research, 22 January 2019. http://www.natcen.ac.uk/blog/common-law-marriage-a-peculiarly-persistent-myth.

Phillips, Richard. 'Standing Together: The Muslim Association of Britain and the Anti-War Movement'. *Race & Class* 50, no. 2 (1 October 2008): 101–13. https://doi.org/10.1177/0306396808096396.

Platt, Lucinda. 'Is There Assimilation in Minority Groups' National, Ethnic and Religious Identity?' *Ethnic and Racial Studies* 37, no. 1 (2014): 46–70.

Poppinga, Amy. 'Religious/American Identity Negotiation of Young Muslims in the Pursuit of Marriage'. Presented at the Annual Meeting of the Society for the Scientific Study of Religion, Atlanta, GA, 29 October 2016.

Probert, Rebecca, and Liam D'arcy Brown. 'The Impact of the Clandestine Marriages Act: Three Case-Studies in Conformity'. *Continuity and Change* 23, no. 2 (August 2008): 309–30. https://doi.org/10.1017/S0268416008006759.

Prothero, Stephen. *Religious Literacy: What Every American Needs to Know – and Doesn't*. New York: Harper, 2008.

Purdam, Kingsley. 'Democracy in Practice: Muslims and the Labour Party at the Local Level'. *Politics* 21, no. 3 (1 September 2001): 147–57. https://doi.org/10.1111/1467-9256.00146.

Putnam, Robert D. *Bowling Alone: The Collapse and Revival of American Community*. New York: Simon & Schuster, 2001.

Pywell, Stephanie, and Rebecca Probert. 'Neither Sacred nor Profane: The Permitted Content of Civil Marriage Ceremonies'. *Child and Family Law Quarterly* 30 (December 2018): 415–36.

Quilliam Foundation. 'Preventing Terrorism: Where Next for Britain?' Strategic Briefing Paper (secret). London: Quilliam Foundation, 2010. http://www.scribd.com/doc/34834977/Secret-Quilliam-Memo-to-government.

Quisay, Walaa, and Thomas Parker. 'On the Theology of Obedience: An Analysis of Shaykh Bin Bayyah and Shaykh Hamza Yusuf's Political Thought'. *Maydan* (blog), 8 January 2019. https://www.themaydan.com/2019/01/theology-obedience-analysis-shaykh-bin-bayyah-shaykh-hamza-yusufs-political-thought/.

Qureshi, Kaveri, Katharine Charsley and Alison Shaw. 'Marital Instability among British Pakistanis: Transnationality, Conjugalities and Islam'. *Ethnic and Racial Studies* 37, no. 2 (28 January 2014): 261–79. https://doi.org/10.1080/01419870.2012.720691.

Rabbani, Hassan. 'Training British Muslim Religious Leaders'. Presented at the Abrar House, London, 27 November 2015. https://www.youtube.com/watch?v=DK5QQ_biMFU.

Rashid, Naaz. *Veiled Threats: Producing the Muslim Woman in Public Policy Discourses*. Bristol: Policy Press, 2016.

Rawls, John. *A Theory of Justice*. Cambridge, MA: Harvard University Press, 1971.

Rawls, John. 'Justice as Fairness: Political Not Metaphysical'. *Philosophy and Public Affairs* 14, no. 3 (1985): 223–51.

Rawls, John. *Political Liberalism*. New York: Columbia University Press, 2005.

Reid, Sue. 'Breeding Ground for Jihadis Where Even Ice Cream Lady Wears a Burka'. *Mail Online*, 15 June 2015. http://www.dailymail.co.uk/news/article-3125530/The-breeding-ground-jihadis-ice-cream-lady-wears-burka-great-textile-town-Dewsbury-undergone-terrible-transformation.html.

Reidy, David A. 'Rawls's Wide View of Public Reason: Not Wide Enough'. *Res Publica* 6, no. 1 (1 January 2000): 49–72.

Reynolds, Louis, and Jonathan Birdwell. 'Rising to the Top'. London: Demos, 2015. http://www.demos.co.uk/wp-content/uploads/2015/10/Rising-to-the-Top-Report.pdf.

Rhodes, R. A. W. 'The New Governance: Governing without Government'. *Political Studies* 44, no. 3 (1996): 652–67.

Robinson, Francis. *The Ulama of Farangi Mahall and Islamic Culture in South Asia*. London: C. Hurst, 2001.

Rocker, Simon. 'Men Who Refuse a Get May Lose Burial Rights'. *Jewish Chronicle*, 12 November 2015. http://www.thejc.com/news/uk-news/149144/men-who-refuse-a-get-may-lose-burial-rights.

Roy, Olivier. *Globalised Islam: The Search for a New Ummah*. London: C. Hurst, 2004.

Roy, Olivier. *Holy Ignorance: When Religion and Culture Part Ways*. London: C. Hurst, 2010.

Roy, Olivier. *Jihad and Death: The Global Appeal of Islamic State*. London: C. Hurst, 2017.

Roy, Olivier. *The Failure of Political Islam*. Cambridge, MA: Harvard University Press, 1996.

Saeed, Tania. *Islamophobia and Securitization: Religion, Ethnicity and the Female Voice*, 1st edn. New York: Palgrave Macmillan, 2016.

Saha, Anamik. ' "Negotiating the Third Space: British Asian Independent Record Labels and the Cultural Politics of Difference" '. *Popular Music and Society* 34, no. 4 (2011): 437–54.

Sahgal, Gita. 'Two Cheers for Multiculturalism'. In *Warning Signs of Fundamentalisms*, edited by Ayesha Imam, Jenny Morgan and Nira Yuval-Davis, 51–60. London: WLUML, 2004.

Sahgal, Gita, and Nira Yuval-Davis, eds. *Refusing Holy Orders: Women and Fundamentalism in Britain*. London: Virago, 1992.

Sahlins, Marshall. 'Goodby to Tristes Tropes: Ethnography in the Context of Modern World History'. *Journal of Modern History* 65, no. 1 (1993): 1–25.

Said, Edward W. *Orientalism*. London: Vintage Books, 1979.

Saleemi, Hassan. 'Islamic Activism in the UK: Then and Now'. Presented at the Abrar House, London, 29 June 2007. http://www.thecitycircle.com/events_full_text2. php?id=453.

Samad, Yunas, and John Eade. 'Community Perceptions of Forced Marriage'. London: Community Liaison Unit, Foreign and Commonwealth Office, 2002.

Sandberg, Russell. 'Criminalising Imams Will Not Solve the Problem of Unregistered Marriages'. *Family Law* (blog), 15 January 2019. https://www.familylaw.co.uk/news_ and_comment/criminalising-imams-will-not-solve-the-problem-of- unregistered-marriages.

Sanders, David, Stephen D. Fisher, Anthony Heath and Maria Sobolewska. 'The Democratic Engagement of Britain's Ethnic Minorities'. *Ethnic and Racial Studies* 37, no. 1 (2014): 120–39.

Sardar, Ziauddin. 'The Destruction of Mecca'. *New York Times*, 30 September 2014. http:// www.nytimes.com/2014/10/01/opinion/the-destruction-of-mecca.html.

Saward, Michael. 'Authorisation and Authenticity: Representation and the Unelected'. *Journal of Political Philosophy* 17, no. 1 (1 March 2009): 1–22.

Saward, Michael. 'The Representative Claim'. *Contemporary Political Theory* 5, no. 3 (2006): 297–318.

Saward, Michael. *The Representative Claim*. Oxford: Oxford University Press, 2010.

Sayyid, Salman. *A Fundamental Fear: Eurocentrism and the Emergence of Islamism*. London: Zed Books, 2003.

Scharbrodt, Oliver. 'A Minority within a Minority? The Complexity and Multilocality of Transnational Twelver Shia Networks in Britain'. *Contemporary Islam* 13, no. 3 (1 October 2019): 287–305. https://doi.org/10.1007/s11562-018-0431-0.

Scharbrodt, Oliver. 'The Salafiyya and Sufism: Muḥammad 'Abduh and His Risālat al-Wāridāt (Treatise on Mystical Inspirations)'. *Bulletin of the School of Oriental and African Studies, University of London* 70, no. 1 (2007): 89–115.

Scott-Baumann, Alison. ' "Dual Use Research of Concern" and "Select Agents": How Researchers Can Use Free Speech to Avoid "Weaponising" Academia'. *Journal of Muslims in Europe* 7, no. 2 (26 June 2018): 237–61. https://doi. org/10.1163/22117954-12341373.

Scott-Baumann, Alison, and Sariya Cheruvallil-Contractor. *Islamic Education in Britain: New Pluralist Paradigms*. London: Bloomsbury Academic, 2015.

Scott-Baumann, Alison, Alyaa Ebbiary, Shams Ad Duha Mohammad, Safiyya Dhorat, Shahanaz Begum, Hasan Pandor and Julia Stolyar. 'Towards Contextualized Islamic Leadership: Paraguiding and the Universities and Muslim Seminaries Project (UMSEP)'. *Religions* 10, no. 12 (December 2019): 662. https://doi.org/10.3390/rel10120662.

Scruton, Roger. *The West and the Rest: Globalisation and the Terrorist Threat*. London: Continuum, 2002.

Shachar, Ayelet. *Multicultural Jurisdictions: Cultural Differences and Women's Rights*. Cambridge: Cambridge University Press, 2001.

Shah, Prakash. 'The Relationship between the Courts, Society and Civil Law: A Response'. Presented at the Britain's Religious Courts: Marriage, Divorce and Civil Law, Cardiff University, 18 May 2011.

Shahid, Safia. 'Training British Muslim Religious Leaders'. Presented at the Abrar House, London, 27 November 2015. https://www.youtube.com/watch?v=DK5QQ_biMFU.

Shah-Kazemi, Nurin. *Untying the Knot: Muslim Women, Divorce and the Sharia*. London: Nuffield Foundation, 2001.

Shaw, Alison. 'Kinship, Cultural Preference and Immigration: Consanguineous Marriage among British Pakistanis'. *Journal of the Royal Anthropological Institute* 7, no. 2 (1 June 2001): 315–34. https://doi.org/10.1111/1467–9655.00065.

Sherif, Jamil. 'A Census Chronicle: Reflections on the Campaign for a Religion Question in the 2001 Census for England and Wales'. *Journal of Beliefs & Values* 32, no. 1 (2011): 1–18. https://doi.org/10.1080/13617672.2011.549306.

Sherwood, Harriet. 'Register Islamic Marriages under Civil Law, Sharia Review Says'. *The Guardian*, 1 February 2018, sec. Law. https://www.theguardian.com/law/2018/feb/01/sharia-councils-review-islamic-marriages-uk-law.

Sian, Katy. 'Born Radicals? Prevent, Positivism, and "Race-Thinking"'. *Palgrave Communications* 3, no. 1 (27 October 2017). https://doi.org/10.1057/s41599-017-0009-0.

Sidat, Haroon. 'Between Tradition and Transition: An Islamic Seminary, or Dar al-Uloom in Modern Britain'. *Religions* 9, no. 10 (15 October 2018): 314. https://doi.org/10.3390/rel9100314.

Sidat, Haroon. 'Shedding Light on the Modalities of Authority in a Dar Al-Uloom, or Religious Seminary, in Britain'. *Religions* 10, no. 12 (December 2019): 653. https://doi.org/10.3390/rel10120653.

Siddiqi, Faizal A. 'Kingdom of God: The Archbishop, the Shari'a and the Law of the Land'. Presented at the Abrar House, London, 18 February 2008. http://www.thecitycircle.com/blog2.php?cann_id=532.

Siddiqui, Ataullah. *Islam at Universities in England: Meeting the Needs and Investing in the Future*. Leicester: The Markfield Institute, 2007.

Siddiqui, Kalim. 'The Muslim Manifesto: A Strategy for Survival'. The Muslim Parliament, n.d. http://www.muslimparliament.org.uk/MuslimManifesto.pdf.

Siddiqui, Mona, Anne-Marie Hutchinson, Sam Momtaz and Mark Hedley. 'The Independent Review into the Application of Sharia Law in England and Wales'. London: Counter Extremism Unit, 2018. https://www.gov.uk/government/publications/applying-sharia-law-in-england-and-wales-independent-review.

Silverman, Stephanie J., and Melanie Griffiths. 'Immigration Detention in the UK'. Oxford: Migration Observatory, COMPAS, University of Oxford, 2019. https://migrationobservatory.ox.ac.uk/resources/briefings/immigration-detention-in-the-uk/.

Simpson, Ludi. 'Ageing, Ethnic Diversity and Myths of Migration'. *Radical Statistics* 100 (2010): 28–45.

Simpson, Ludi. 'Statistics of Racial Segregation: Measures, Evidence and Policy'. *Urban Studies* 41, no. 3 (2004): 661–81.

Simpson, Ludi, and Nissa Finney. *'Sleepwalking to Segregation'? Challenging Myths about Race and Migration*. Bristol: Policy Press, 2012.

Sinclair, Kirstine. 'An Islamic University in the West and the Question of Modern Authenticity'. *Numen* 66, no. 4 (18 June 2019): 403–21. https://doi.org/10.1163/15685276-12341546.

Singh, Gurharpal. 'A City of Surprises: Urban Multiculturalism and the "Leicester Model"'. In *A Postcolonial People: South Asians in Britain*, edited by S. Sayyid, N. Ali and V. S. Kalra, 291–304. London: C. Hurst, 2006.

Singh, Gurnam. 'Black and Minority Ethnic (BME) Students' Participation in Higher Education: Improving Retention and Success'. York: HEA, 2011.

Singh, Jasjit. 'Keeping the Faith: Reflections on Religious Nurture among Young British Sikhs'. *Journal of Beliefs & Values* 33, no. 3 (1 December 2012): 369–83. https://doi.org/10.1080/13617672.2012.732817.

Sivanandan, A. *Communities of Resistance: Writings on Black Struggles for Socialism*. London: Verso, 1990.

Small, Neil, Alan H. Bittles, Emily S. Petherick and John Wright. 'Endogamy, Consanguinity and the Health Implications of Changing Marital Choices in the UK Pakistani Community'. *Journal of Biosocial Science* 49, no. 4 (July 2017): 435–46. https://doi.org/10.1017/S0021932016000419.

Spencer, Robert. *Islam Unveiled: Disturbing Questions about the World's Fastest-Growing Faith*. San Francisco, CA: Encounter Books, 2003.

Stewart, Heather. 'Michael Fallon Pays Damages to Imam at Centre of Sadiq Khan Storm'. *The Guardian*, 23 June 2016, sec. Politics. https://www.theguardian.com/politics/2016/jun/23/michael-fallon-damages-imam-suliman-gani-sadiq-khan.

Storm, Ingrid, Maria Sobolewska, and Robert Ford. 'Is Ethnic Prejudice Declining in Britain? Change in Social Distance Attitudes among Ethnic Majority and Minority Britons'. *British Journal of Sociology* 68, no. 3 (2017): 410–34. https://doi.org/10.1111/1468-4446.12250.

Suleiman, Yasir. 'Contextualising Islam in Britain: Exploratory Perspectives'. Cambridge: Centre of Islamic Studies, 2009.

Summers, Hannah. 'UK Courts Should Be Able to Issue Islamic Divorces, Sharia Expert Says'. *The Guardian*, 4 September 2016, sec. Law. https://www.theguardian.com/law/2016/sep/04/uk-courts-should-be-able-to-issue-islamic-divorces-sharia-expert-says.

Sunier, Thijl. 'Domesticating Islam: Exploring Academic Knowledge Production on Islam and Muslims in European Societies'. *Ethnic and Racial Studies* 37, no. 6 (2014): 1138–55.

Tamimi, Azzam. 'Islam and Democracy from Tahtawi to Ghannouchi'. *Theory, Culture & Society* 24, no. 2 (1 March 2007): 39–58.

Tax Payers' Alliance. 'Foreign Office Prevent Grants'. Tax Payers' Alliance, 2009. http://www.taxpayersalliance.com/fcoprevent.pdf.

Taylor, Charles. *Philosophical Arguments*. Cambridge, MA: Harvard University Press, 1997.

The British Academy. 'Theology and Religious Studies Provision in UK Higher Education'. London: British Academy, May 2019. https://www.thebritishacademy.ac.uk/publications/theology-religious-studies-provision-uk-higher-education.

The Coexist Foundation. 'The Gallup Coexist Index 2009: A Global Study of Interfaith Relations'. London: Gallup, 2009. http://www.muslimwestfacts.com/mwf/118249/Gallup-Coexist-Index-2009.aspx.

The Independent. 'David Cameron's Tory Conference Speech in Full'. *The Independent*, 7 October 2015. http://www.independent.co.uk/news/uk/politics/tory-party-conference-2015-david-camerons-speech-in-full-a6684656.html.

The Muslim College. 'A Word from the Principal of the Muslim College'. Muslim College, n.d. http://muslimcollege.ac.uk/principal/.

Thomas, Paul. 'Failed and Friendless: The UK's 'Preventing Violent Extremism' Programme'. *British Journal of Politics & International Relations* 12, no. 3 (2010): 442–58.

Thomas, Paul. *Responding to the Threat of Violent Extremism: Failing to Prevent*. London: Bloomsbury Academic, 2012.

Thomson, Ahmad. 'The Relationship between the Courts, Society and Civil Law: A Response'. Presented at the Britain's Religious Courts: Marriage, Divorce and Civil Law, Cardiff University, 18 May 2011. http://www.wynnechambers.co.uk/pdf/Britains_Religious_Courts_Society_&_Civil_Law.pdf.

Tony Blair Institute for Global Change. 'Narratives of Division: The Spectrum of Islamist Worldviews in the UK'. Tony Blair Institute for Global Change, January 2019. https://institute.global/news/narratives-division-islamist-worldviews.

Travis, Alan. '1.4 Million Women Suffered Domestic Abuse Last Year, ONS Figures Show'. *The Guardian*, 12 February 2015, sec. Society. http://www.theguardian.com/society/2015/feb/12/14-million-women-suffered-domestic-abuse-last-year-ons-figures-show.

Travis, Alan. 'Cameron Backing Counter-Extremism Strategy Marks a Fundamental Shift'. *The Guardian*, 29 June 2015. http://www.theguardian.com/politics/2015/jun/29/cameron-backing-theresa-may-counter-extremism-strategy-fundamental-shift.

Tucker, Judith E. *Women, Family and Gender in Islamic Law*. Cambridge: Cambridge University Press, 2008.

Universities UK. 'Black, Asian and Minority Ethnic Student Attainment at UK Universities: #closingthegap'. London: Universities UK, 2 May 2019. https://www.universitiesuk.ac.uk/policy-and-analysis/reports/Pages/bame-student-attainment-uk-universities-closing-the-gap.aspx.

Universities UK. 'Patterns and Trends 2016'. London: Universities UK, 2017. http://public.tableau.com/views/PatternsAndTrends2016/Patterns2016?:embed=y&:showVizHome=no&:host_url=https%3A%2F%2Fpublic.tableau.com%2F&:tabs=yes&:toolbar=yes&:animate_transition=yes&:display_static_image=no&:display_spinner=yes&:display_overlay=yes&:display_count=yes&:loadOrderID=0.

Vaughan, Richard. 'Ofsted Will Inspect Madrasas, Says Cameron'. TES, 7 October 2015. https://www.tes.com/news/school-news/breaking-news/ofsted-will-inspect-madrasas-says-cameron.

Vertovec, Steven. 'Multicultural, Multi-Asian, Multi-Muslim Leicester: Dimensions of Social Complexity, Ethnic Organization and Local Government Interface'. *Innovation: The European Journal of Social Sciences* 7, no. 3 (1994): 259–74.

Vertovec, Steven. 'Super-Diversity and Its Implications'. *Ethnic and Racial Studies* 30, no. 6 (November 2007): 1024–54.

Walker, Peter, and Nicola Slawson. 'Conservatives under Fire for Failing to Tackle Party's Islamophobia'. *The Guardian*, 31 May 2018, sec. Politics. https://www.theguardian.com/politics/2018/may/31/muslim-council-calls-for-inquiry-into-conservative-party-islamophobia.

Ware, John. 'A Question of Leadership'. *Panorama*. BBC One, 21 August 2005. http://news.bbc.co.uk/1/hi/programmes/panorama/4171950.stm.

Ware, John. 'The Puzzle of Baroness Warsi's Links with Islamist Group'. *Jewish Chronicle*, 26 April 2018. https://www.thejc.com/news/news-features/puzzle-of-baroness-sayeeda-warsi-s-links-with-islamist-group-1.463152.

Warrell, Helen. 'Inside Prevent, the UK's Controversial Anti-Terrorism Programme'. *Financial Times*, 24 January 2019. https://www.ft.com/content/a82e18b4-1ea3-11e9-b126-46fc3ad87c65.

Warwick University. 'Postgraduate Award in Islamic Education'. Warwick University, n.d. https://warwick.ac.uk/fac/soc/ces/prospective/postgraduate/taught/islamicpga/.

Weale, Sally. 'Muslim Leaders Voice Concerns about Tory Crackdown on Madrasas'. *The Guardian*, 7 October 2015, sec. World news. http://www.theguardian.com/world/2015/oct/07/muslim-leaders-voice-concerns-about-tory-crackdown-on-madrasas.

Webster, Ben. 'Animals Dying in Pain Because of Muslim Ignorance over Stunning'. *The Times*, 24 October 2016. http://www.thetimes.co.uk/article/more-animals-die-in-pain-because-scholars-are-ignorant-of-stunning-fsz83krtn.

Werbner, Pnina. *Imagined Diasporas among Manchester Muslims*. Oxford: James Currey, 2002.

Whitehead, Andrew L., Landon Schnabel and Samuel L. Perry. 'Gun Control in the Crosshairs: Christian Nationalism and Opposition to Stricter Gun Laws'. *Socius* 4 (1 January 2018): 2378023118790189. https://doi.org/10.1177/2378023118790189.

Wijze, Stephen de. 'Shamanistic Incantations? Rawls, Reasonableness and Secular Fundamentalism'. *Politics and Ethics Review* 3, no. 1 (2007): 109–28.

Wooding, David. 'Bash the Bishop'. *The Sun*, 9 February 2008.

Wuthnow, Robert. 'Can Faith Be More than a Sideshow in the Contemporary Academy?' In *The American University in a Postsecular Age*, edited by Douglas Jacobsen and Rhonda H. Jacobsen, 31–44. Oxford: Oxford University Press, 2008.

Yilmaz, Ihsan. 'Law as Chameleon: The Question of Incorporation of Muslim Personal Law into the English Law'. *Journal of Muslim Minority Affairs* 21, no. 2 (October 2001): 297–308.

Yilmaz, Ihsan. *Muslim Laws, Politics and Society in Modern Nation States*. Aldershot: Ashgate, 2005.

Young, Iris Marion. *Inclusion and Democracy*. Oxford: Oxford University Press, 2002.

Yusuf, Hamza. 'Book Launch: A Muslim in Victorian America'. Presented at the House of Lords, London, 22 November 2006. http://www.radicalmiddleway.co.uk/videos.php?id=1&art=11.

Yuval-Davis, Nira, Floya Anthias, and Eleonore Kofman. 'Secure Borders and Safe Haven and the Gendered Politics of Belonging: Beyond Social Cohesion'. *Ethnic and Racial Studies* 28, no. 3 (2005): 513–35.

Zaman, Muhammad Qasim. *The Ulama in Contemporary Islam: Custodians of Change*. Princeton: Princeton University Press, 2007.

Zaman, Muhammad Qasim. 'Tradition and Authority in Deobandi Madrasas of South Asia'. In *Schooling Islam: The Culture and Politics of Modern Muslim Education*, edited by Robert W. Hefner and Muhammad Qasim Zaman, 61–86. Princeton, NJ: Princeton University Press, 2007.

Zee, Machteld. *Choosing Sharia*. The Hague: Eleven International, 2016.

Zohra, Fatima. 'London Divan: Spiced Spare Ribs'. Presented at the London School of Economics, London, 24 April 2008. http://www.radicalmiddleway.co.uk/videos.php?id=22&art=22&vid=88.

INDEX